IRISH STEAM
LOCOMOTIVE REGISTER

1st Edition

J W P Rowledge

ISBN 0-947773-33-9

Typeset by StreetWise, 18 North Terrace, Birstall, Batley WF17 9EU (0924) 444412

CONTENTS

NOTES

The public railways and tramways are grouped together within the larger twentieth century companies and national undertakings as shown in the contents list. Thus a locomotive new to the Great Southern Railways first appears in that company's list, but those of a constituent of the GSR will have their initial building details, numbering, etc., shown against the first owner, changes made by the GSR being given in the GSR list. This avoids laborious searching of the lists of no less than 17 railways which contributed locomotives to the GSR at the 1925 amalgamation should a list of locomotives in the years 1925 to 1944 be required.

In the case of contractors and industrial locomotives it has proved simpler to list them by builder, showing successive owners in Ireland. No attempt has been made to show users outside Ireland, before or afterwards, except where necessary for identification.

The tabular matter contains the following data:-

No. & Name.	First number and/or name, or new number of a locomotive taken into stock from another railway or user.
Type	Wheel arrangement.
Class	Official classification used by the railway company,
Date & Builder	Year of building and builder (for builders progressive numbers see the Analysis of Locomotives by Builder section), or previous owner and number of locomotives acquired by amalgamations, etc.
Renumbered	Change of number and year of alteration.
Rebuilt	Only major changes, such as altered wheel arrangement, superheating, substitution by a Belaire boiler etc., are given.
Withdrawn	Year taken out of stock, or next owning company.
New owner's No.	Number allotted by company shown in the withdrawal column.
Remarks	Additional information or reference to the notes at the end of the locomotive list.

Dimensions are confined to cylinder diameter and stroke and driving wheel diameter for the 'as built' condition (but in some of the more numerous classes there were variants not recorded here). The tables of dimensions also serve to group locomotives by classes, particularly where the railways concerned did not use a formal system of classification, or did not use such a system until a later date.

Most locomotives in Ireland were straightforward with two inside cylinders and saturated round top boilers. Exceptions as new are noted below the dimensional tables and conversions are noted in the locomotive lists. Narrow gauge locomotives had two outside cylinders and are not specially so noted. The following abbreviations are used in the locomotive lists:

B.Sat	Belpaire saturated boiler.		T.Sat	Taper saturated boiler.
B.Sh	Belpaire superheated boiler.		DEW	Dundalk Engineering Works (former GNR works).
DW	Driving wheels (diameter).		L&NWR	London & North Western Railway.
Rbt	Rebuilt.		LPHC	Londonderry Port & Harbour Commissioners.
RT.Sat	Round top saturated boiler.		W&O	Watson & Overend (contractors).
RT.Sh	Round top superheated boiler.		W.D	William Dargan (contractor).

* An asterisk is used to indicate an item or date which is not known or is doubtful.

INTRODUCTION

A century and one half has passed since a steam railway first carried passengers in Ireland. Today it is still possible to travel in steam hauled trains in Ireland, but for pleasure only.

In the span of 150 years just about 2,300 steam locomotives have worked in Ireland, with almost one-third having been built in the country.

The Irish Traction Group presents this register as a list of all known steam locomotives of the public railways and tramways, contractors and industrial lines. In addition it records references to unidentified steam locomotives, but it may never be possible to give fuller details of such locomotives, nor be certain that every locomotive has been accounted for in this volume. Non-steam traction in Ireland is not covered in this book.

The list has been built up over many years and the compiler is grateful to the undermentioned for their assistance:
R.N. Clements, D. Murray, K.A. Murray, R.C. Flewitt, G. Beesley, H. Richards, W.E. Shepherd, T.J. Edgington, W.H.G. Boot, G.S. Moore and G. Toms for general help.
S.V. Kennedy for kindly allowing inclusion of the list of names selected for possible use on the Great Southern Railways 800 Class 4-6-0 locomotives.
A.C. Baker, R. Wear, I. Biscoe, J.W. Lowe and J. Brownlie for help with industrial and contractors locomotives.
J.A. de Koningh (of Amsterdam, The Netherlands) for extra details of the locomotives used on the Shannon hydro-electric scheme.
P. Spencer for taking the trouble to check the data.
Neil Webster for his editing of the original draft and suggesting various changes.
The following organisations have very kindly made information available:

Irish Railway Record Society, Dublin.
Science Museum, London.
Museum of Science & Industry, Manchester.
Mitchell Library, Glasgow.

National Railway Museum, York.
Merseyside County Museum, Liverpool.
Coras Iompair Eireann/Irish Rail
Northern Ireland Railways

In addition numerous books and periodicals have been of great value, amongst these being:

Railway Observer (Railway Correspondence & Travel Society).
Journal of the Stephenson Locomotive Society.

Railway Magazine.
Locomotive Magazine.

The recording of industrial and contractors locomotives owes so much to the publication in 1962 of 'Irish Industrial and Contractors Locomotives' by Union Publications, a useful starting point in the complilation of this volume.

Irish Traction Group, Stockport, 1993.

LOCOMOTIVE OWNING RAILWAY COMPANIES & TRAMWAYS

The heading 'Company' includes national authorities and boards.

The heading 'Period' indicates the years during which the company possessed steam locomotives and not necessarily the legal period of existence.

Where no initials are shown the name of the company is used in the lists where too few locomotives are listed, or to avoid confusion; BR for Ballycastle Railways is specially avoided to prevent any confusion with British Railways.

Initials	Company	Period	Gauge (ft.-in.)	Page
A&EJR	Athenry & Ennis Junction Railway	1869-72	5-3	
A&TR	Athenry & Tuam Railway	1870-72	5-3	
	Ballycastle Railway	1879-1924	3-0	
B&LR	Ballymena & Larne Railway	1877-89	3-0	
BBC&PJR	Ballymena, Ballymoney, Coleraine & Portrush Junction Railway	1855-60	5-3	
BC&RBR	Ballymena, Cushendall & Red Bay Railway	1874-84	3-0	
B&BR	Belfast & Ballymena Railway	1847-60	5-3	
B&CDR	Belfast & County Down Railway	1848-1948	5-3	
B&NCR	Belfast & Northern Counties Railway	1860-1903	5-3	
		1884-1903	3-0	
BCR	Belfast Central Railway	1868-85	5-3	
BH&BR	Belfast, Holywood & Bangor Railway	1865-84	5-3	
CK&AR	Castleblayney, Keady & Armagh Railway	1911-13	5-3	
C&VBT	Castlederg & Victoria Bridge Tramway	1884-1933	3-0	
	Castleisland Railway	1875-79	5-3	
C&LR	Cavan & Leitrim Railway	1895-1924	3-0	
CL&RLR&T	Cavan, Leitrim & Roscommon Light Railway & Tramway	1887-95	3-0	
C&WT	Cavehill & Whitewell Tramway	1882-95	4-8½	
CVR	Clogher Valley Railway	1894-1941	3-0	
CVT	Clogher Valley Tramway	1886-94	3-0	
CIE	Coras Iompair Eireann	1945-63	5-3	
		1945-60	3-0	
C&BR	Cork & Bandon Railway	1849-88	5-3	
C&MDR	Cork & Macroom Direct Railway	1865-1924	5-3	
C&MLR	Cork & Muskerry Light Railway	1887-1924	3-0	
C&YR	Cork & Youghal Railway	1859-66	5-3	
CB&SCR	Cork, Bandon & South Coast Railway	1888-1924	5-3	
CB&PR	Cork, Blackrock & Passage Railway	1850-1900	5-3	
		1899-1924	3-0	
CDRJC	County Donegal Railways Joint Committee	1906-59	3-0	
DR	Donegal Railway	1892-1906	3-0	
D&BJR	Dublin & Belfast Junction Railway	1848-75	5-3	
D&BST	Dublin & Blessington Steam Tramway	1887-1932	5-3	
D&DR	Dublin & Drogheda Railway	1843-75	5-3	
D&KR	Dublin & Kingstown Railway	1834-56	4-8½	
D&LER	Dublin & Lucan Electric Railway	1899-1912	3-6	
D&LST	Dublin & Lucan Steam Tramway	1881-99	3-0	
D&MR	Dublin & Meath Railway	1862-69	5-3	
D&SER	Dublin & South Eastern Railway	1907-24	5-3	
D&WR	Dublin & Wicklow Railway	1853-60	5-3	
DSDT	Dublin Southern Districts Tramways	1881-84	5-3	
DW&WR	Dublin, Wicklow & Wexford Railway	1860-1906	5-3	
		1861-80	3-6	
D&ER	Dundalk & Enniskillen Railway	1848-62	5-3	
D&GR	Dundalk & Greenore Railway	1873	5-3	
DN&GR	Dundalk, Newry & Greenore Railway	1873-1951	5-3	
GCP&BVT	Giants Causeway, Portrush & Bush Valley Tramway	1883-1930	3-0	
GNR	Great Northern Railway	1876-1953	5-3	
GNRB	Great Northern Railway Board	1953-58	5-3	
GSR	Great Southern Railway	1924	5-3	
GSR	Great Southern Railways	1925-44	5-3	
		1925-44	3-0	
GS&WR	Great Southern & Western Railway	1845-1924	5-3	
INWR	Irish North Western Railway	1862-75	5-3	
L&BER	Letterkenny & Burtonport Extension Railway	1902-13	3-0	
Lim&ER	Limerick & Ennis Railway	1859-61	5-3	
L&BR	Listowel & Ballybunion Railway	1887-1924	Monorail	
LMS(NCC)	London Midland & Scottish Railway (Northern Counties Committee)	1923-47	5-3	
		1923-47	3-0	
L&CR	Londonderry & Coleraine Railway	1848-61	5-3	
L&ER	Londonderry & Enniskillen Railway	1846-62	5-3	

Initials	Company	Period	Gauge	Page
L&LSR	Londonderry & Lough Swilly Railway	1862-85	5-3	
		1882-1954	3-0	
LL&CST	Lucan, Leixlip & Celbridge Steam Tramway	1892-97	3-0	
MGWR	Midland Great Western Railway	1847-1924	5-3	
MR(NCC)	Midland Railway (Northern Counties Committee)	1903-22	5-3	
		1903-22	3-0	
N&AR	Newry & Armagh Railway	1857-79	5-3	
N&ER	Newry & Enniskillen Railway	1853-57	5-3	
NW&RR	Newry, Warrenpoint & Rostrevor Railway	1848-86	5-3	
NIR	Northern Ireland Railways	1968-71	5-3	
NR	The Northern Railway	1875-76	5-3	
PT	Portstewart Tramway	1882-97	3-0	
	Railway Executive (Northern Counties Committee)	1948-49	5-3	
		1948-49	3-0	
S&SLR	Schull & Skibbereen Light Railway (West Carbery Tramways & Light Rlys)	1886-1924	3-0	
SL&NCR	Sligo, Leitrim & Northern Counties Railway	1877-1957	5-3	
T&CLR	Timoleague & Courtmacsherry Light Railway	1890-1924	5-3	
T&DLR	Tralee & Dingle Light Railway	1889-1924	3-0	
UR	Ulster Railway	1839-48	6-2	
		1846-76	5-3	
UTA	Ulster Transport Authority	1949-68	5-3	
		1949-54	3-0	
W&CIR	Waterford & Central Ireland Railway	1868-1900	5-3	
W&RR	Waterford & Kilkenny Railway	1846-68	5-3	
W&LR	Waterford & Limerick Railway	1847-95	5-3	
W&TR	Waterford & Tramore Railway	1853-1924	5-3	
W&WR	Waterford & Wexford Railway	1894-98	5-3	
WD&LR	Waterford, Dungarvan & Lismore Railway	1878-98	5-3	
WL&WR	Waterford, Limerick & Western Railway	1896-1900	5-3	
	Waterford, New Ross & Wexford Junction Railway	1870-73	5-3	
WCR	West Clare Railway	1886-1924	3-0	
	West Cork Railways	1866-79	5-3	
WDR	West Donegal Railway	1881-92	3-0	

In addition the Belfast Street Tramways Co. and the Dublin Tramways Co. both used a steam tram locomotive on a trial basis in 1877 but never owned any steam stock.

Two railways, the South Clare Railways and the Donoughmore Extension Railway, were regarded as the nominal owners of locomotives in the stock of the West Clare Railway and the Cork & Muskerry Light Railway respectively. The locomotives concerned are so noted in the appropriate place.

SPECIAL NOTE
The Athenry & Tuam Extension to Claremorris Railway is statistically credited with two locomotives from 1894-1924. They were actually W&LR/WL&WR/GS&WR property. Therefore this railway is NOT listed as a locomotive owning company.

ANALYSIS OF LOCOMOTIVES BY BUILDER

SUMMARY TABLE

This section lists Irish steam locomotives by builders, giving the abbreviations used in the company and contractors lists. The eight columns give totals against manufacturers in the following order:
New to railway companies.
Formerly used in Britain and then used by Irish companies (and includes 2 locomotives - 1 Avonside and 1 Krauss - used on pleasure lines).
New to tramway type lines (including conventional locomotives supplied to such lines).
New to contractors and industrial users.
Formerly used in Britain and then in Ireland by contractors or industrial users.
Formerly used elsewhere in Europe and then in Ireland by contractors or industrial users (includes 2 Krauss used on pleasure railways).
Total number of locomotives built by railway or manufacturer named.
Steam railmotors.

As far as can be ascertained the number of locomotives of unidentified build are added to the totals. The grand total is impossible to finalise because of these unidentified locomotives but it is probably just under 2,300.

In the case of contractors or industrial locomotives only the first Irish user is listed in this section - previous owners outside Ireland are not detailed.

Abbreviation	Railway Workshops or Locomotive Builder Location	Railway companies New	Ex-Britain	Tram-ways New	Contractors & Industrial New	Ex-Britain	Ex-others	Total Loco-motives	Rail-Motors
	IRISH RAILWAY COMPANIES								
B&CDR	Belfast, Queens Quay	1						1	
B&NCR	Belfast, York Road	5						5	
CIE	Dublin, Inchicore	1						1	
CB&SCR	Cork	1						1	
D&KR	Dublin, Grand Canal Street	10						10	
D&SER	Dublin, Grand Canal Street	4						4	
DW&WR	Dublin, Grand Canal Street	32						32	
GNR	Dundalk	39						39	
GNR-BS	Dundalk, Barrack Street	1						1	
GNR-ND	Belfast	9						9	
GSR-B	Dublin, Broadstone	12						12	
GSR-I	Dublin, Inchicore	46						46	
GS&WR	Dublin, Inchicore	358						358	1
INWR	Dundalk, Barrack Street	2						2	
MGWR	Dublin, Broadstone	120						120	
NCC	Belfast, York Road	32						32	
UR	Belfast	11						11	
W&LR	Limerick	5						5	
WL&WR	Limerick	1						1	
	TOTAL	**690**	**0**	**0**	**0**	**0**	**0**	**690**	**1**
	BRITISH RAILWAY COMPANIES								
BR	Derby (British Railways)	8						8	
LMS	Derby (London Midland & Scottish Railway)	17						17	
L&NWR	Crewe (London & North Western Railway	6	6					12	
MR	Derby (Midland Railway)	10						10	2
	TOTAL	**41**	**6**	**0**	**0**	**0**	**0**	**47**	**2**
	IRISH LOCOMOTIVE BUILDERS								
G	Grendon	38			3			41	
Spence	W. Spence				18			18	
	TOTAL	**38**	**0**		**21**			**59**	
	BRITISH LOCOMOTIVE BUILDERS								
A	Adams	3						3	
AW	Armstrong, Whitworth	11						11	
AP	Aveling & Porter				2			2	
AE	Avonside Engine Company	19	1		2	4		26	
WGB	W.G. Bagnall	5	1		3	6		15	
AB	Andrew Barclay	6			5	2		13	
BM	Barr, Morrison				1			1	
BP	Beyer, Peacock	319						319	
BH	Black, Hawthorn	11			2			13	
BE	Brush Electrical	2		1				3	
BCK	Bury, Curtis & Kennedy	42						42	
But	Butterley Co.					1		1	
Ch	Chaplin				3	4		7	
CWL	Clayton Waggons Ltd.							0	6
Cross	J. Cross	2						2	
DK	Dick, Kerr	3			1			4	
D	Dubs	45						45	
Fbn	W. Fairbairn	62			1			63	
FE	Falcon Engine & Car Works	3	6					9	
For	Forrester	5						5	
FH	Fossick & Hackworth	6						6	
JF	J. Fowler	4			1			5	
FW	Fox, Walker				1			1	
GR	Grant, Ritchie				1			1	
Gl	Gryll				2			2	
TG	T. Green	5		4				9	
GW	Gilkes, Wilson	2						2	
RWH	R. & W. Hawthorn	7						7	
H(L)	Hawthorn (Leith)	1	1					2	
HL	Hawthorn, Leslie	3						3	
Hick	B. Hick					1		1	
Hor	Horsley Iron Works		1					1	
HC	Hudswell, Clarke	9	3		11	4		27	

Abbreviation	Railway Workshops or Locomotive Builder Location	Railway companies New	Railway companies Ex-Britain	Tramways New	Contractors & Industrial New	Contractors & Industrial Ex-Britain	Contractors & Industrial Ex-others	Total Locomotives	Rail-Motors
HH	H. Hughes			1				1	
HE	Hunslet Engine Co.	18	1		16	5		40	
JJ	J. Jones	2						2	
KS	Kerr, Stuart	5			5	4		14	
K	Kitson	48	16		1			65	3
L	R.B. Longridge	12						12	
Lewin	S. Lewin				2	1		3	
MAF	Manlove, Alliott & Fryer								1
MW	Manning, Wardle	2			3	9		14	6
MA	Murdock, Aitken					1		1	
NW	Nasmyth, Wilson	34						34	
N	Neilson								
NR	Neilson Reid	92				1		93	
NBL	North British Locomotive Co.	44						44	3
P	Peckett	2			8	4		14	
Robey	Robey				1			1	
Roth	Rothwell	4						4	
Sen	Sentinel Waggon Works	3				3		6	5
SR	Sharp, Roberts								
SB	Sharp Bros.	206		6	4			216	
SS	Sharp, Stewart								
RS	Robert Stephenson	27			6	1		34	
S&S	Stothert & Slaughter								
SG	Slaughter, Grunning	9						9	
Tay	Chas. Tayleur								
VF	Vulcan Foundry	46						46	
Wal	Walker Bros.			1				1	
W	Wilkinson			6				6	
EBW	E.B. Wilson	1						1	
YE	Yorkshire Engine Co.	2						2	
	TOTAL	1132	5	44	82	51		1314	24
	U.S. LOCOMOTIVE BUILDERS								
B&W	Burnham & Williams (Baldwin)	2						2	
	TOTAL	2						2	
	OTHER FOREIGN LOCOMOTIVE BUILDERS								
	Borsig						18	18	
JC	J. Cockerill				3			3	
	Hannoversche						19	19	
	Henschel						34	34	
	Jung						1	1	
	Krauss		1				5	6	
	Linke Hoffman						10	10	
OK	Orenstein & Koppel				9	4		13	
RMW	Rhine Metal Works						21	21	
T(B)	Tubize (Belgium)						1	1	
	TOTAL		1		12	4	109	126	
	BUILDERS NOT KNOWN	4	4		30*			38*	
	GRAND TOTALS	1907	16	44	145*	55	109	2276*	27

* Must remain approximate (all shown 'New to Ireland' but some of course may have been used else where beforehand). The 30* comprise an estimate of the locomotives not identified in the Contractors and Industrial Locomotives section and the Miscellaneous Locomotives section.

The systems listed as Tramways were:

	Belfast Street Tramways	D&LST	Dublin & Lucan Steam Tramway
C&VBT	Castlederg & Victoria Bridge Tramway	DSDT	Dublin Southern Districts Tramways
C&WT	Cavehill & Whitewell Tramway		Dublin Tramways Co.
CVR	Clogher Valley Railway	GCP&BVT	Giants Causeway, Portrush & Bush Valley Tramway
CVT	Clogher Valley Tramway	PT	Portstewart Tramway
D&BST	Dublin & Blessington Steam Tramway		

There was one steam locomotive known to have been built in Ireland for export (see T. Grendon), but of course it does not appear in the above totals.

CHRONOLOGICAL SUMMARY BY BUILDER

Except where shown in parentheses, all locomotives in this section were 5-3 gauge.
Numbers shown are those carried at the time of construction.
The totals for each locomotive builder include railmotors where applicable.

IRISH RAILWAY COMPANIES

B&CDR (Belfast, Queens Quay) — TOTAL 1

Year	Type	Numbers
1881	0-4-2	8

B&NCR, MR(NCC), LMS(NCC) (Belfast, York Road) — TOTAL 37

Year	Type	Numbers
1870	2-4-0	5
1871	2-4-0	4
1873	0-4-2	26
1901	4-4-0	34
1902	4-4-0	3
1903	4-4-0	4
1904	4-4-0	9
1905	4-4-0	20
1906	4-4-0	5
1907	4-4-0	17
1908	2-4-2T	112 (3-0)
1909	2-4-2T	112 (3-0)
1914	0-4-0ST	16
1919	2-4-2T	103 (3-0)
1920	2-4-2T	104 (3-0)
1924	4-4-0	1, 2
1925	4-4-0	79-81 (LMS Lot 26)
1926	4-4-0	3
1929	4-4-0	84
1931	4-4-0	4
1934	4-4-0	85
	2-6-0	94/5
1935	4-4-0	86
	2-6-0	96/7
1936	4-4-0	87
1937	2-6-0	98
1938	2-6-0	99
1939	2-6-0	100/1
1940	2-6-0	102
1942	2-6-0	103/4

CB&SCR (Cork) — TOTAL 1

Year	Type	Numbers
1901	4-4-0T	7

D&KR, DW&WR, D&SER (Dublin, Grand Canal Street) — TOTAL 46

Year	Type	Numbers
1841	2-2-2WT	*Princess, Belleisle* (4-8½)
1842	2-2-2WT	*Shamrock* (4-8½)
1843	2-2-2WT	*Erin* (4-8½)
1844	2-2-2WT	*Albert* (4-8½)
1845	2-2-2WT	*Burgoyne* (4-8½)
1847	2-2-2WT	*Cyclops* (4-8½)
1848	2-2-2WT	*Vulcan, Jupiter* (4-8½)
1851	2-2-2WT	*Comet* (4-8½)
1869	2-2-2WT	27/8
1871	2-2-2WT	29
1873	2-2-2WT	30/1
1874	2-2-2WT	36
1879	2-2-2WT	4
1880	2-2-2WT	40
1882	2-2-2WT	41
1885	2-4-0T	2
1886	2-4-0T	45
1887	2-2-2WT	27
	2-4-0T	28
1888	2-4-0T	46
1889	2-4-0T	47
	0-4-2	48
1890	2-4-0T	9
1891	2-4-0T	1, 49
1894	2-4-0T	6
1895	2-4-0T	7
1896	2-4-0T	10/1
1898	2-4-2T	3
1899	0-6-0	17
1900	0-6-0	36
1901	2-4-2T	12
1902	2-4-2T	40
1903	2-4-2T	8
1905	0-6-0	13/4
1906	2-4-2T	29
1907	2-4-2T	27
1909	2-4-2T	30
1910	0-6-0	18
1911	4-4-2T	20

UR, GNR (Belfast) — TOTAL 20

Year	Type	Numbers
1867	2-4-0	8, 12
1869	2-4-0	10/3
1871	0-4-2	7
1872	0-4-2	6
	0-6-0	37
1873	0-6-0	38
1874	0-4-2	5, 39
	2-4-0	23
1876	2-4-0	1
	0-6-0	14/5
1877	0-6-0	3
1878	0-6-0	16
1880	0-4-2	4
1881	0-4-2	2
1882	0-4-2	9
1884	2-2-2	11

INWR, GNR (Dundalk, Barrack Street) — TOTAL 3

Year	Type	Numbers
1873	2-4-0	31
1874	2-4-0	30
1876	0-6-0	44 (GNR)

GNR (Dundalk) — TOTAL 39

Year	Type	Numbers
1887	4-4-0T	100, 2
1888	4-4-0T	3, 4
1889	4-4-0T	5, 6
1890	0-6-0	60
1891	4-4-0T	7
	0-6-0	33
1893	4-4-0T	8, 91/2
1894	0-6-0	32
1895	0-6-0	29, 55
	2-4-2T	93
1896	0-6-0	56
	2-4-2T	94
1898	2-4-2T	90/5
1899	0-6-0	78
1900	0-6-0	100
1902	2-4-2T	13/4
1903	0-6-0	11
1904	0-6-0	10
	4-4-0	88/9
1906	4-4-0	104/5
1908	0-6-0	78, 108
1911	4-4-0	25, 43
1937	0-6-0	78-82

MGWR, GSR (Dublin, Broadstone) — TOTAL 132

Year	Type	Numbers
1879	0-6-0	49, 50
1880	0-6-0	51-4
	0-6-0T	100-3
1883	2-4-0	41/2
1884	2-4-0	1, 4, 5, 6
1885	0-6-0	55-60
1886	2-4-0	45/7
	0-6-0	85, 104
1887	2-4-0	43/4/6/8
	0-6-0	61/8, 71

Year	Type	Numbers
1888	0-6-0	62-5/7, 72
1889	2-4-0	7, 10
	0-6-0	66/9, 70
1890	2-4-0	8, 9, 11/2
	0-6-0T	105
1891	0-6-0	74/5, 80/4
1892	0-6-0	73/6/7/9, 82/3
1893	2-4-0	13/4/8
	0-6-0	78, 81
1894	2-4-0	17/9, 20
1895	2-4-0	15/6
1896	2-4-0	21-3
1897	2-4-0	24/7-9, 31
1898	2-4-0	30/2-4
1900	4-4-0	2, 26, 36/7
1901	4-4-0	3, 25
1902	4-4-0	128/9
1903	4-4-0	127
1904	4-4-0	126
1905	4-4-0	124/5
1909	4-4-0	7, 10
1910	4-4-0	4, 5
1911	4-4-0	6
1912	4-4-0	9
1913	4-4-0	8, 12
1915	4-4-0	11
1921	0-6-0	39-41
1922	0-6-0	36-8, 42/3
1923	0-6-0	86-95
1925	2-6-0	372-5 (GSR)
1926	2-6-0	376-81 (GSR)
1927	2-6-0	382/3 (GSR)

TOTAL 406

GS&WR, GSR, CIE (Dublin, Inchicore)

Year	Type	Numbers
1852	0-4-2	57/8
1853	2-2-2	59
1854	0-6-0	60/1
	0-4-2	62/3
1855	2-4-0	64-6
1856	0-6-0	67-9, 72-44
1857	0-2-4T	*Sprite*
1858	2-2-2	77-9
1859	2-2-2	76, 80/1
1860	0-4-2	82-4
1861	0-4-2	85-7
	2-2-2	88-90
1862	0-4-2	91-3
	2-2-2	94/5
1863	2-2-2	96
	0-4-2	97-9
1865	0-4-2	136-8
1866	2-4-0	1, 9, 16
	0-6-0	112/3
1867	2-6-0	4, 11
	2-2-2	27, 30
	0-6-0	103/11/8
1868	2-4-0	14/8, 56/7
	0-6-0	105/10
1869	2-4-0	3, 12, 58/9
	0-4-4T	33
	0-6-0	114/5
1870	2-4-0	20, 60/1
	0-4-4T	31/2/4
1871	0-4-4T	27, 30
	0-6-0	155/6/4-62
1872	2-4-0	17/9
	0-6-0	157/8
1873	0-4-4T	*Sprite*
	2-4-0	21-6
	0-6-0	102/4/67/8
1874	0-6-0	106/17/69-74
1875	0-4-4T	35-8
	2-4-0	64/5
	0-6-4T	(one for Castleisland Railway)
	0-6-0	108/42/79/80
1876	2-4-0	66-9
	0-4-4T	201/2
1877	4-4-0	2, 5, 6, 7
	0-6-0	109/19-21/43
1878	4-4-0	43-6
	0-6-0	144-6
1879	0-4-4T	28/9, 39, 40
	0-6-0	181/2
	0-6-4T	203/4
1880	4-4-0	8, 10/3/5
	0-6-0	183/4
	0-6-4T	205/6
1881	0-6-4T	91/2
	0-6-0	107/23-6/39-41
1882	0-6-0	101/22/7/8/30/1/87/8
1883	0-4-4T	47-50
	4-4-0	52-4
	-	*Pat* (Cork Coal Gantry locomotive)
1884	4-4-0	55
	0-4-4T	51, 70-2, 81-4
1885	4-4-0	93-6
	0-6-0	133-5/91
1886	4-4-0	9, 16, 85-9
	0-4-4T	77-80
1887	0-4-4T	73-6
	4-4-0	97/8
	0-6-0T	207-10
1888	4-4-0	4, 11/4/8, 56-9
	0-6-0	132/6-8
1889	0-6-0	103/14/29/49
1890	4-4-0	1, 3, 12, 20
	0-6-0T	99
	0-6-0	110
1891	4-4-0	60-3
	0-6-0T	100
	0-6-0	111/8/47
1892	2-4-2T	33/4, 41
1893	2-4-2T	42
1894	2-4-2T	35/6
	4-4-2T	37/8
	0-4-2T	*Fairy*
1895	4-4-0	64/5
	0-6-0T	201/2
1896	0-6-0	105/16
1898	0-6-0	192-5
1899	0-6-0	196-9
1900	4-4-2T	27, 30/1
	4-4-0	301-4
1901	4-4-2T	32, 317-20
	0-6-0T	217-20
1902	0-6-0	240-2
	4-4-0	305-8
1903	0-6-0	200/23/9/32/43/53-6, 351-4
1904	4-4-0	321
	Railmotor	1
1905	4-4-0	322-8
	4-6-0	362-5
1906	4-4-0	329-32
1907	4-4-0	333-6
	4-6-0	366/7
1908	4-4-0	337-40
1909	2-6-0	368-71
1912	0-6-0	249-52
1913	0-6-0	257-60
	4-4-0	341
1914	0-6-0	261-4
	0-4-2ST	*Sambo*
1915	4-8-0T	900
1916	4-6-0	400
1921	4-6-0	401/2/6
1924	4-6-0	500
	4-8-0T	901
1926	4-6-0	501/2
1928	2-6-0	384-9
	2-6-2T	850
1929	2-6-0	390/1
	0-6-0	700-4
1930	2-6-0	393-8
1933	0-6-2T	670-4
1934	0-6-0	710-4
1935	0-6-0	715-9
1936	4-4-0	342-6
1939	4-6-0	800/1
1940	4-6-0	802
1957	0-6-6-0T	CC1

TOTAL 6

W&LR, WL&WR (Limerick)

Year	Type	Numbers
1888	0-6-0	7
1890	0-6-0	6
1892	0-4-2T	3
1893	0-6-0	5
1894	0-4-4T	15
1899	0-4-4T	27

Note: It has been recorded that the running numbers were also regarded as the works numbers by the W&LR/WL&WR.

BRITISH RAILWAY COMPANIES

L&NWR (Crewe)

Year	Order No.	Railway	Nos.	Type	Remarks
1873	E39ø	D&GR	1, 2, 3	0-6-0ST	(Crewe motion Nos. 1509-11)
1876	E72ø	DN&GR	4, 5	0-6-0ST	(Crewe motion Nos. 1962/3)
1883	E7	DW&WR	60/1	2-4-2T	(Crewe motion Nos. 2683, 2677 - built 4-8½ gauge)
1884	E9	DW&WR	63	2-4-2T	(Crewe motion No. 2726 - built 4-8½ gauge)
1885	E18	DW&WR	59	2-4-2T	(Crewe motion No. 2856 - built 4-8½ gauge)
1896	E88	DW&WR	62/4	2-4-2T	(Crewe motion Nos. 3604/5 - built 4-8½ gauge)
1898	E120	DN&GR	6	0-6-0ST	(Crewe motion No. 3877)

Note: ø First series E orders; others were second series E orders.

MR, LMS, BRITISH RAILWAYS (Derby)

TOTAL 37

Year	Order Loco	Order Tender	LMS Lot	Railway	Nos.	Type	Remarks
1905	2833	2834		MR(NCC)	63-6	4-4-0	
1905	2915			MR(NCC)	90/1	Railmotors	
1908	3385	3386		MR(NCC)	67/8	4-4-0	
1914	4369	4370		MR(NCC)	69, 70	4-4-0	
1922	5648	5650		MR(NCC)	14/5	4-4-0	
1923	5649	5650		LMS(NCC)	71-3	0-6-0	
1933	8207	8209	103	LMS(NCC)	90-3	2-6-0	
1938		9857		LMS(NCC)			10 3500 gallon tenders
1946	669		178	LMS(NCC)	5, 6, 7, 8	2-6-4T	
1947	1674		190	LMS(NCC)	1-4, 9, 10	2-6-4T	
1949	3283		203	UTA	50-3	2-6-4T	
1950	4332		212	UTA	54-7	2-6-4T	

IRISH LOCOMOTIVE BUILDERS

T. GRENDON (Drogheda)

TOTAL 41

Year	Railway or user	Nos.	Type	Year	Railway or user	Nos.	Type
1845	D&DR	13-15	2-2-2	1851*	*	*	2-2-2T
1847	D&DR	16	2-2-2WT	1855	D&ER	7	0-6-0
1847	D&DR	17	2-2-2	1855	MGWR	36, 37	0-6-0
1847	MGWR	7-11	2-2-2	1856	D&DR	4	2-4-0
1848	D&ER	(two)	2-2-2	1856	D&ER	8	0-6-0
1848	D&ER	(two)	0-4-2	1856	MGWR	38, 39	0-6-0
1848*	Dargan	(one)	2-2-2	1856	MGWR	40, 41	2-4-0
1849	GS&WR	51, 52	0-4-2	1857	MGWR	2-6	2-4-0
1850	NW&RR	3	2-2-2T	1859	L&CR	8	0-4-2
1851	NW&RR	1, 2	2-2-2T	1860	MGWR	1	2-4-0
1851*	MGWR	30	2-2-2	1862	Greene & King*		4-cpld
1851*	MGWR	33 (in 1854)	2-2-2	1868	B&NCR	3	2-4-0

Note: Grendon built the only steam locomotive known to have been exported from Ireland. This was a 2-4-0 sub-contracted from R. Stephenson (Prog. No. 930 in their list) to the order of the Maua Railway of Brazil in 1856 (it is not counted in the Grendon total given above).
Grendon is also credited with the building of one 0-6-0 in 1855, but it cannot be traced in any railway's list, if indeed it was ever built. (From the details given it would have been built to a Stephenson long boiler pattern and may therefore have been a sub-contract job).

W. SPENCE (Dublin, Cork Street Foundry)

TOTAL 18

1887 to 1921 built 18 0-4-0T (1-10 gauge) for Arthur Guinness, Nos. 7-24 (see pp. ??? for individual dates).

BRITISH LOCOMOTIVE BUILDERS

W.B. ADAMS (Bow, London)

TOTAL 3

Year	Railway	Nos.	Type	Year	Railway	Nos.	Type
1849	C&BR	1, 2	0-2-2WT	1850	L&CR	4	2-2-0WT

ARMSTRONG, WHITWORTH (Newcastle-upon-Tyne)

TOTAL 11

Year	Order	Works Nos.	Railway	Nos.	Type	Remarks
1922	E13	175-9	MGWR	44-8	0-6-0	
1922	E18	185-90	GS&WR	403-5/7-9	4-6-0	
1922	E23	466/7	MR(NCC)		4-4-0	Ordered 1920 but built at Derby to order 5648.

AVELING & PORTER (Rochester, Kent)

TOTAL 2

1875 and 1878 built two 2-2-0TG (Prog. Nos. 1105 and 1432) 3-6 gauge for Haulbowline Dockyard.

AVONSIDE ENGINE CO. (Bristol)

TOTAL 26

Year	Order	Works Nos.	Railway/user	Nos./Names	Type	Remarks
1869	MG	777-80	MGWR	9, 10, 73, 74	2-4-0	
1870	MI	802/3	MGWR	8, 75	2-4-0	
1872	CI	965/6	W&CIR	10, 11	0-4-2	
1872*			N&AR			Two tenders
1876	WL	1125-8	W&LR	19, 26, 27, 33	0-4-2	
1876	WC	1169	W&CIR	12	0-4-2T	
1877	SLI	1197/8	SL&NCR	Pioneer, Sligo	0-6-2T	

Year	Order	Works Nos.	Railway/user	Nos./Names	Type	Remarks
1880	WD	1211-4	MGWR	96-99	0-6-0	Built 1878 to order of WD&LR but taken by MGWR.
1882	AGE	1337	Guinness	6	0-4-0T (1-10)	
1907	1645	1522	Pearson	*Scott*	0-6-0ST (4-8½)	
1908	1778	1547	Shane's Castle	*Nancy*	0-6-0T (3-0)	Not taken to Ireland until 1972.
1912	2210	1618	Pearson	*Courtney*	0-6-0ST (4-8½)	
1919	4015	1833	Pearson	146	0-6-0ST (4-8½)	
1920	4465	1872	Pearson	152	0 6-0ST (4-8½)	
1928	8000	2021	LP&HC	3	0-6-0ST	

Note: AE No. 1243 is listed in some sources as W&LR 0-6-0T No. 34 but this was an older locomotive by an unknown manfacturer.

W.G. BAGNALL (Stafford)   TOTAL 15

Year	Works Nos.	Railway/user	Nos./Names	Type	Remarks
1886	730/8	WCR	1, 2	0-6-0T (3-0)	
1887	793/4	WCR	3, 4	0-6-0T (3-0)	
1889	1116	Braddock	*Brancher*	0-4-0ST (3-0)	
1893	1416	Fergus Reclamation	F R S No. 2	0-4-0ST (2-0)	See Note
1897	1480	Best	*Crosshaven*	0-4-0ST (3-0)	
1898	1551	Fisher & LeFanu	*Mourne*	0-4-0ST (3-0)	
1900	1631	Portrush Columnar Basalt		0-4-0ST (2-6)	
1907	1844	H. & J. Martin		0-4-0ST (3-0)	
1908	1881	WCR	11	4-6-0T (3-0)	
1911	1945	Irish Industrial Minerals	*King George*	0-6-0T (2-0)	
1919	2081/6	H. & J. Martin		0-4-0ST (3-0)	
1926	2292	LMS(NCC)	18	0-6-0T	See Note

Notes: 1416 - Bagnall records do not specify that this locomotive was sent to Ireland (or anywhere else), but give Barrington as the consignee. He was engineer to the Fergus Reclamation Syndicate and as the locomotive was marked F R S No. 2 it may well have worked in Co. Clare.
2292 - New to LMS (4-8½ gauge), Lot 37 (Derby order No. 6616).

A. BARCLAY (Kilmarnock)   TOTAL 13

Year	Works Nos.	Railway/user	Nos./Names	Type
1887	297	Best	*Tullibardine*	0-4-0ST (3-0)
1893	703	Fergus Reclamation Syndicate		0-4-0ST (2-0)
1896	770	Carnlough Lime Co.	*Otter*	0-4-0ST (3-6)
1902	933-6	L&BER	1-4	4-6-0T (3-0)
1905	1022	C&MDR	5	0-6-2T
1908	1137	W&TR	4	0-4-2T
1915	1408	Pearson	*Adams*	0-6-0ST (4-8½)
1949	2263-5	Bord na Mona	1-3	0-4-0WT (3-0)

BARR, MORRISON (Kilmarnock)   TOTAL 1
1882 built one 0-4-0ST (named *Barnesmore*) for T.S. Dixon (3-0 gauge).

BEYER, PEACOCK (Gorton, Manchester)   TOTAL 319

Year	BP Order		Works Nos.	Railway	Nos./Name	Type
	Loco	Tender				
1857	145		53	B&CDR	5	2-4-0T
1858	225		75/6	D&DR	11, 20	0-4-2
1858	291		55	B&CDR	6	2-4-0T
1859	309		104	B&CDR	8	2-4-0T
1859	324		105/6	D&DR	14, 15	2-2-2
1859	332		107	D&ER	11	2-2-2
1859	384	385	151	UR	1	2-2-2
1860	427		185	D&DR	13	2-2-2
1861	432		195	D&DR	16	2-2-2
1860		442		D&ER	One tender	
1861	535	536	223/4	D&ER	13, 14	2-2-2
1861	537	538	225/6	UR	22, 23	2-2-2
1862	635		257	D&DR	10	0-4-2
1863	704	705	365/6	B&NCR	36, 37	0-6-0
1863	729	730	367-70	UR	26-29	2-4-0
1863	774		430	D&DR	21	0-4-2
1866	961	962	632/3	D&BJR	18, 19	2-4-0
1866	963	964	634-7	UR	33-36	0-4-2
1867	2045		747-50	GS&WR	147-50	0-6-0
1868	2102	2179	780-3	GS&WR	151-4	0-6-0
1868	2239	2240	835	D&BJR	20	2-4-0
1868	2268	2269	850/1	B&NCR	40, 41	2-4-0
1871	2632		1042	D&DR	12	0-4-2
1872	2858	2859	1159/60	D&BJR	21, 22	0-6-0
1872	2865		1161	D&DR	5	0-6-0
1873	2960	2961	1251/2	GS&WR	177, 178	0-6-0
1875	3347		1539/40	Northern	3, 42	2-4-0
1877	3525		1687	B&LR	1	2-4-0T (3-0)
1877	3560		1700/1	B&LR	2, 3	0-6-0T (3-0)
1878	3568		1707	BCR	3	2-4-0T
1878	3586	3587	1712	B&NCR	31	0-6-0
1878	3588	3589	1713/4	B&NCR	8, 22	2-4-0
1877	3628		1749-52	GNR	25, 24, 80, 59	2-4-0
1878	3647	3648	1789	B&CDR	4	0-6-0
1878	3714		1828	B&LR	4	2-4-0T (3-0)
1879	3783	3784	1870/1	GNR (N.D)	42, 43	0-6-0

Year	BP Order Loco	Tender	Works Nos.	Railway	Nos./Name	Type
1880	3874	3875	1920	B&NCR	30	0-6-0
1880	3876	3877	1921/2	B&NCR	45, 46	2-4-0
1880	3890		1935	BCR	4	4-4-0T
1880	3897		1947	B&LR	5	2-6-0ST (3-0)
1880	3924	3925	1960-3	MGWR	2, 3, 25, 26	2-4-0
1881	3924	3925	1964/5	MGWR	36, 37	2-4-0
1880	3933		1968/9	GNR	86, 87	2-4-0
1881	3970	3971	2029/30	GS&WR	189, 190	0-6-0
1881	6006		2046	C&BR	6	0-6-0ST
1881	6100		2103/4	GNR	84, 85	2-4-0
1882	6142		2116/7	GNR	79, 83	0-6-0
1882	6166		2137/8	SL&NCR	Fermanagh, Leitrim	0-6-4T
1882	6179		2142	NW&RR	5	2-4-0T
1882	6188		2156	C&BR	12	0-6-0ST
1883	6230		2233-6	B&NCR	25, 47-49	2-4-0T
1883	6254		2261-3	DW&WR	42-44	2-4-0T
1882	6291		2304	B&LR	6	0-6-0T (3-0)
1883	6309	6310	2342/3	GNR	46, 47	2-4-0
1883	6350		2394/5	GNR	61, 64	0-6-0
1885	6466		2515-8, 2655/6	GNR	117, 118, 17, 18, 45, 48	4-4-0
1885	6467		2519/20	GNR	88, 89	4-2-2
1885	6562		2623-5	GNR	97-99	4-4-0T
1885	6585	6586	2648	B&NCR	23	2-4-0
1886	6799		2784-6	GNR	80-82	0-6-0
1887	6877		2818-20	GNR	19, 20, 119	4-4-0
1887	6963		2902	C&BR	5	0-6-0ST
1888	6981		2904-6	GNR	28, 145, 146	0-6-0
1889	7130		3017-9	GNR	115, 116, 21	4-4-0
1890	7172	7173	3058/9, 3200/1	B&NCR	33, 50-52	2-4-0
1890	7315	7316	3273-5	GNR	31, 149, 150	0-6-0
1890	7375		3288	CB&SCR	16	0-6-0ST
1891	7442		3358-61	B&CDR	18, 19, 21, 22	2-4-2T
1892	7494		3455/6	GNR	82, 83	4-4-0
1892	7504	7505	3457/8	B&NCR	53, 54	0-6-0
1892	7511		3511-3	B&CDR	23-25	2-4-0
1892	7591	7592	3514	B&CDR	26	0-6-0
1892	7617	7618	3521	B&NCR	21	2-4-0
1893	7745		3583	GNR	36	0-6-0
1894	7745		3584	GNR	59	0-6-0
1894	7793	7794	3604	B&CDR	6	2-4-0
1894	7805		3607-9	GNR	151-3	0-6-0
1894	7846		3629	CB&SCR	17	0-6-0ST
1895	7853	7854	3632/3	B&NCR	50, 55	2-4-0
1895	7883		3664/5	GNR	72, 73	4-4-0
1895	7884		3666	GNR	54	4-4-0
1895	7932		3677	SL&NCR	Lurganboy	0-6-4T
1895	7959	7960	3680/1	B&NCR	56, 57	2-4-0
1895	8030		3797	GNR	57	0-6-0
1896	8030		3798	GNR	58	0-6-0
1896	8031		3799-3801	GNR	70, 71, 74	4-4-0
1896	8074		3853/4	B&CDR	7, 5	2-4-2T
1897	8096		3868/9/82/3	B&CDR	8, 27-29	2-4-2T
1897	8146	8147	3885-8	B&NCR	59-62	4-4-0
1898	8166		3926-8	GNR	75-77	4-4-0
1898	8307	8308	4059	B&NCR	24	4-4-0
1899	8427		4073/4	SL&NCR	Lissadell, Hazlewood	0-6-4T
1901	8614		4231-3	B&CDR	30, 3, 15	4-4-2T
1904	9116		4565/6	GNR	120, 121	4-4-0
1904	9159		4585/6	B&CDR	11, 12	4-4-2T
1904	9165		4592	SL&NCR	Sir Henry	0-6-4T
1904	9196	9197	4594	B&CDR	14	0-6-0
1905	9305	9307	4645/6	DW&WR	67, 68	4-4-0
1905	9306	9307	4647/8	DW&WR	65, 66	0-6-0
1905	9374		4720	SL&NCR	Enniskillen	0-6-4T
1906	9414		4736/7	GNR	106, 107	4-4-0
1906	9428		4752	CB&SCR	11	4-6-0T
1908	9743		5093/4	GNR	22, 23	0-6-4T
1909	9905		5262-4	B&CDR	1, 17, 20	4-4-2T
1909	9910		5265	CB&SCR	14	4-6-0T
1909	033		5327/8	GNR	45, 46	4-4-0
1910	034		5329	GNR	24	4-4-0
1910	0170		5413	CB&SCR	15	4-6-0T
1911	0228		5465-7	GNR	50, 129, 44	4-4-0
1911	0229		5468/9	GNR	12, 42	4-4-0
1911	0328		5531/2	GNR	166, 167	0-6-4T
1912	0407		5616	CB&SCR	20	4-6-0T
1913	0471		5628-32	GNR	170-4	4-4-0

12

Year	BP Order Loco	Tender	Works Nos.	Railway	Nos./Name	Type
1913	0472		5633-7	GNR	37, 40, 41, 137, 138	0-6-0
1913	0646		5737-41	GNR	185-9	4-4-2T
1914	0754		5822	CB&SCR	19	4-6-0T
1914	0784	0785	5842	B&CDR	10	0-6-0
1915	0854	0857	5896-5900	GNR	180-4	0-6-0
1915	0855	0857	5901-3	GNR	190-2	4-4-0
1915	0856	0857	5904-8	GNR	196-8, 200, 199	4-4-0
1917	0975		5943	SL&NCR	Lough Gill	0-6-4T
1919	01034		5954	CB&SCR	4	4-6-0T
1920	01160		5999-6002	B&CDR	22-25	4-6-4T
1920	01870		6034/77	CB&SCR	8, 13	4-6-0T
1921	01881 ø		6035-9	GNR	1-5	4-4-2T
1920	01885	01886	6040-7	GNR	6-8, 13, 14, 20, 47, 48	0-6-0
1921	01885	01886	6048-54	GNR	49, 96, 97, 201, 202, 117, 118	0-6-0
1921	01925	01926	6072	B&CDR	4	0-6-0
1921	01930		6073/4	B&CDR	13, 18	4-4-2T
1921	02045		6097/8	B&CDR	19, 21	4-4-2T
1922	02160	02161	6112/3	D&SER	15, 16	2-6-0
1923	02298		6134	B&CDR	29	0-6-4T
1924	02417		6201/2	B&CDR	8, 16	4-4-2T
1924	02427		6204/5	D&SER	34, 35	4-4-2T
1929	147		6630/1	GNR	62, 63	4-4-2T
1930	147		6632-4	GNR	64-66	4-4-2T
1932	1524		6731-5	GNR	83-87	4-4-0
1945	1425		7139	B&CDR	9	4-4-2T
1948	1556	1656	7244-8	GNR	201-5	4-4-0
1948	1557	1657	7249-53	GNR	145-9	0-6-0
1948	1558	1658	6961-5	GNR	206-10	4-4-0
1949	1427		7138, 7242	SL&NCR	Lough Melvin, Lough Erne	0-6-4T
1955		1668		GNR	Five tenders	
1956		1668		GNR	Two tenders	

Note: ø Originally ordered from Nasmyth, Wilson.

BLACK, HAWTHORN (Gateshead)   TOTAL 13

Year	Works Nos.	Railway/user	Nos./Names	Type
1868	59	BCR	1	0-6-0ST
1874	301/2	BC&RBR	1, 2	0-4-2ST (3-0)
1875	303	BC&RBR	3	0-4-2ST (3-0)
1874	336	BCR	2	0-6-0ST
1879	513	Butler & Fry	Lady Boyd	0-6-0ST (3-0)
1879	514	Belfast Harbour Commissioners	2	0-4-0ST (3-0)
1880	554/5	Ballycastle Railway	1, 2	0-6-0ST (3-0)
1882	684	L&LSR	1	0-6-2WT (3-0)
1883	742/3	L&LSR	2, 3	0-6-2T (3-0)
1885	834	L&LSR	4	0-6-0T (3-0)

BRUSH ELECTRICAL (Loughborough)   TOTAL 3

Year	Works No.	Railway	No.	Type	Year	Works No.	Railway	No.	Type
1898	274	C&MLR	7	4-4-0 (3-0)	1904	307	C&MLR	8	4-4-0T (3-0)
1899	284	D&BST	9	2-4-2T					

BURY, CURTIS & KENNEDY (Liverpool)   TOTAL 42

Year	Railway	Nos./Names	Type	Year	Railway	Nos./Names	Type
1845	GS&WR	21, 22	2-2-2	1847	GS&WR	43-7	0-4-2
1845	GS&WR	41, 42	0-4-2	1848	B&CDR	1-4	2-2-2
1846	GS&WR	23-9	2-2-2	1848	GS&WR	37-40	2-2-2
1847	B&BR	Vulcan	0-4-2	1848	GS&WR	48-50	0-4-2
1847	B&BR	Gladiator, Hercules, Queen, Prince	2-2-2	1848	NW&RR	1, 2	2-2-2
1847	GS&WR	30-6	2-2-2	1849	NW&RR	3	2-2-2

BUTTERLEY Co. (Ripley, Derbyshire)   TOTAL 1
A 2-2-2 was supplied by Butterley to Jeffs in 1841* (4-6).

A. CHAPLIN (Glasgow)   TOTAL 7

Year	Works No.	User	No.	Type
1863	370	Edwards Bros		0-4-0TG
1872	1505	Belfast Harbour Commissioners	1	0-4-0TG
*	*	T.W. Chester		0-4-0TG (4-8½)
*	*	C.M. Holland		0-4-0TG
1878	1939	Sir J. Jackson		0-4-0TG (4-8½)
1879	2090	E.J. Jackson		0-4-0TG (4-8½)
1887	2416	Board of Works, Dublin		0-4-0TG (3-6)

CLAYTON WAGGONS (Lincoln)   TOTAL 6
1928 built 6 steam railcars for GSR (Nos. 358-63).

J. CROSS (St. Helens, Lancashire)   TOTAL 2
1865 built 2 2-4-0T (Cross Nos. 17/8) for West Cork Railways (Nos. 1, 2).

DICK, KERR (Kilmarnock)

TOTAL 4

Year	Railway/user	Nos.	Type	Remarks
1886	S&SLR	1-3	0-4-0T (3-0)	Tramway type locomotives
1905	Marconi		0-4-0ST (2-0)	

DUBS (Glasgow)

TOTAL 45

Year	D. Order	Works Nos.	Railway	Nos.	Type
1865	17E	17/8	C&MDR	1, 2	2-4-0T
1866	122E	122/3	INWR	32, 33	2-4-0
1867	124E	124	INWR	34	0-4-2
1867	185E	185-90	MGWR	67-72	0-4-2
1867	235E	235	C&MDR	3	2-4-0T
1871	462E	462	INWR	35	0-6-0
1872	595E	595	INWR	36	0-6-0
1874	760E	760	C&BR	1	2-4-0T
1875	861E	861	C&BR	2	2-4-0T
1876	905E	905-9	MGWR	30-4	2-4-0
1877	1072E	1072	C&BR	8	2-4-0T
1881	1505E	1505	C&MDR	4	2-4-0T
1883	1877E	1877	C&BR	13	2-4-0T
1886	2194E	2194	W&LR	9	4-4-0
1886	2195E	2195	W&LR	24	0-6-0
1887	2323E	2323	C&BR	4	2-4-0T
1889	2477E	2477	W&LR	10	2-4-0
1890	2662E	2662	W&LR	22	2-4-0
1891	2777E	2777	CB&SCR	3	4-4-0T
1892	2880E	2880/1	W&LR	20, 23	2-4-0
1892	2890E	2890-2	WCR	5-7	0-6-2T (3-0)
1893	3025E	3025/6	W&LR	43, 44	2-4-0
1893	3042E	3042/3	W&LR	45, 46	0-6-0
1893	3048E	3048	CB&SCR	10	4-4-0T
1894	3109E	3109/10	W&LR	47, 48	2-4-0
1894	3169E	3169	WCR	8	2-6-2T (3-0)
1895	3222E	3222/3	W&LR	49, 50	0-6-0

W. FAIRBAIRN (Manchester)

TOTAL 63

Year	Railway	Nos.	Type	Year	Railway	Nos.	Type
1847	MGWR	1-6	2-2-2	1855	W&KR	1	2-4-0
1848	MGWR	12-17	2-2-2	1855	W&LR	21	2-4-0
1850	B&CDR	1 TANK	2-2-2WT	1855	W&TR	1, 2	2-2-2WT
1851	B&CDR	2 TANK	2-2-2WT	1856	GS&WR	75	0-4-2
1851	MGWR	27-29	2-2-2WT	*	Dargan		0-4-2
1852	MGWR	31	2-4-0	1859	B&CDR	9, 10	0-4-2
1853	D&WR	1, 2, 4, 5	2-2-2WT	1859	Lim&ER	1	0-4-2
1853	D&WR	3	2-4-0	1859	N&AR	1	*
1853	MGWR	32, 34	2-4-0	1859	UR	2	2-2-2
1853	W&LR	11, 12	2-4-0	1860	DW&WR	12-14	2-4-0
1854	MGWR	35	2-4-0	1860	MGWR	43-7	0-4-2
1854	W&LR	17-20	2-4-0	1861	B&NCR	34	2-4-0
1854	W&TR	(one)	0-4-2	1861	MGWR	48	0-4-2
1855	BBC&PJR	5-7	2-2-2WT	1862	C&BR	7	0-4-0ST
1855	D&DR	19	2-4-0	1862	DR	24, 25	2-2-2
1855	GS&WR	70, 71	2-4-0				

FALCON RAILWAY PLANT WORKS (Loughborough)

TOTAL 9

Year	Works Nos.	Railway	Nos.	Type	Remarks
1887	125-30	D&BST	1-6	0-4-0WT	Order of numbers uncertain.
1888	136-8	C&MLR	1-3	2-4-0T (3-0)	Order of numbers uncertain.

FORRESTER (Liverpool)

TOTAL 5

Year	Railway	Names	Type
1834	D&KR	*Kingstown, Dublin, Vauxhall*	2-2-0 (4-8½)
1836	D&KR	*Victoria, Comet*	2-2-0WT (4-8½)

FOSSICK & HACKWORTH (Stockton, Co. Durham)

TOTAL 6

Year	Railway	Nos.	Type	Year	Railway	Nos.	Type
1862	D&MR	1, 5, 6	0-4-2	1862	D&MR	7	2-4-0
1862	D&MR	2, 3	2-2-2				

J. FOWLER (Leeds)

TOTAL 5

Year	Works Nos.	Railway/user	Nos.	Type	Remarks
1866	*	BH&BR	3	2-4-0T	Four locomotives, JF Nos. 706-9 ordered by BH&BR but delivered as shown;
1866	*	B&CDR	1	2-4-0T	recorded as 'Irish Midland' in Fowler records.
1866	*	W&KR	6, 7	2-4-0T	
1880	4027	H.C. Drinkwater		0-6-0T (2-0)	No record of use in Ireland, but Drinkwater had Irish contracts at the time.

FOX, WALKER (Bristol)

TOTAL 1

1878 built 0-4-0ST (FW No. 369) for a Co. Antrim customer, probably an iron ore mine near Ballymena (3-0).

GILKES, WILSON (Middlesbrough)

TOTAL 2

1862 built 2 0-6-0T (GW Nos. 141*, 142*) for L&LSR Nos. 1, 2 (sub-contracted from Fossick & Hackworth).

GRANT, RITCHIE (Kilmarnock)

TOTAL 1

1886 built 0-6-0ST (GR No. 164) for Collen Bros (*Express*) (3-0 gauge).

T. GREEN (Leeds)

Year	Works Nos.	Railway	Nos.	Type
1892	170	LL&CST	7	0-4-0T (3-0)
1892	179	D&BST	7	2-4-2T
1892	180	C&MLR	5	0-4-4T (3-0)
1893	200	C&MLR	6	0-4-4T (3-0)
1896	215	D&BST	8	0-4-2T
1898	229	WCR	9	2-6-2T (3-0)
1900	234	WCR	2	2-6-2T (3-0)
1901	236	WCR	4	2-6-2T (3-0)
1906	367	D&BST	2	2-4-2T

Note: No. 170 is often quoted as Green's No. 169.

GRYLL (Llanelly)

TOTAL 2

May have been the builder of 2 2-4-0 in 1846 (4-8½ gauge) from Bromhead & Hemming (*Victoria*, *Albert*). It is quite possible that they were actually produced by an unidentified builder.

R. & W. HAWTHORN (Newcastle-upon-Tyne)

TOTAL 7

Year	Works Nos	Railway	Nos.	Type	Remarks
1852	810	MGWR	24	0-4-0	Tender works No. T448
1862	1170-5	MGWR	49-54	2-2-2	Tenders works Nos. T652-7

HAWTHORN (Leith)

TOTAL 2

Year	Railway	Name	Type		Year	Railway	No.	Type
1854	N&ER	*Newry*	0-4-0T		1862	W&LR	42	0-6-0WT (built 4-8½ gauge)

HAWTHORN, LESLIE (Newcastle-upon-Tyne)

TOTAL 3

Year	Works Nos.	Railway	Nos.	Type
1910	2801/2	L&LSR	13, 14	4-6-2T (3-0)
1928	3690	GNR	31	0-6-0CT

B. HICK (Bolton, Lancashire)

TOTAL 1

1838 built 0-4-2 *Soho*, later used by McCormick (originally 4-8½ gauge).

HORSLEY IRON WORKS (Tipton, Staffordshire)

TOTAL 1

1833 built 2-2-0 *Star*, later purchased by D&KR (4-8½ gauge).

HUDSWELL, CLARKE (Leeds)

TOTAL 27

Year	Works Nos.	Railway/user	Nos./Name	Type
1883	261	SL&NCR	*Erne*	4-4-0T
1892	397	Best	*Whittledene*	0-4-0ST (3-0)
1899	518/9	L&LSR	5, 6	4-6-2T (3-0)
1901	562/77	L&LSR	7, 8	4-6-2T (3-0)
1903	672	Naylor Bros.	1	0-6-0ST (4-8½)
1904	698	C&VBT	4	2-6-0T (3-0)
1905	746/7	L&LSR	11, 12	4-8-0 (3-0)
1906	759	Sir Robert MacAlpine	13	0-4-0ST (3-0)
1907	794	Sir Robert MacAlpine	14	0-6-0T (3-0)
1910	914	CVR	7	0-4-0T (3-0)
1912	978	C&VBT	5	0-4-4T (3-0)
1912	985/6	L&BER	5, 6	4-8-4T (3-0)
1914	1079	Guinness	2	0-4-0ST
1915	1094	British Portland Cement		0-4-0T
1915	1152	Guinness	3	0-4-0ST
1918	1166	War Department	*	0-4-0WT (2-0)
1917	1298	Sutton Sands		0-6-0WT (2-0)
1918	1310/1/3	War Department	3200/1/3	0-6-0WT (2-0)
1923	1497	Pearson	*Charlton*	0-6-0ST (4-8½)
1923	1505	Pearson	158	0-6-0ST (4-8½)
1924	1508	Pearson	159	0-6-0ST (4-8½)

H. HUGHES (Loughborough)

TOTAL 1

A Hughes tram locomotive 0-4-0T *Pioneer*, new in 1876 was tried on both the Belfast Street Tramways and Dublin Southern District Tramways in 1877 (both 5-3 gauge) but was not purchased by either, being returned to the builder.

HUNSLET ENGINE Co. (Leeds)

TOTAL 40

Year	Hunslet Order No.	Works Nos.	Railway/user	Nos./Name	Type
1871	930	71	Lowry	*Deer Hill*	0-4-0ST (3-0)
1872	1020	74	Pearson	*Huddersfield*	0-4-0ST (3-0)
1876	2460	156	Smith & Finlayson	*Waterford*	0-4-0ST
1878	2990	178	A.L. Tottenham	*Faugh-a-Ballagh*	0-4-0ST
1878	3540	202/3	C.M. Holland	*Maghera*, *Pioneer*	0-6-0ST
1878	3780	208	W.M. Murphy	*Spondon*	0-4-0ST (3-0)
1881	5590	268	River Fergus Reclamation	*Fergus*	0-4-ST (2-6)
1883	6600	315	R. Worthington	*Flirt*	0-4-0ST
1883	6800	319	R. Worthington	*Liffey*	0-4-0ST
1884	7700	352	R. Worthington	*Beauty*	0-6-0ST
1885	8360	382	R. Worthington	*Slaney*	0-6-0ST
1886	8960	404	T.S. Dixon	*Isabella*	0-4-0ST (3-0)

Year	Hunslet Order No.	Works Nos.	Railway/user	Nos./Name	Type	
1887	9900	431-3	L&BR	1-3	3-cpld (Monorail)	
1888	10480	457	Fisher & LeFanu	*Limerick*	0-6-0ST	
1889	11080	477-9	T&DLR	1-3	2-6-0T (3-0)	
1889	11230	482	R. Worthington	*Newmarket*	0-6-0T	
1890	12280	514	T&DLR	4	0-4-2T (3-0)	
1890	12660	520	T&CLR	*St. Molaga*	0-4-2T	
1892	13870	555	T&DLR	5	2-6-2T (3-0)	
1892	14060	557/8	T.H. Falkiner	*Shamrock, Rose*	0-6-0ST	
1892	14520	564	T.S. Dixon	*Bruckless*	0-4-0ST (3-0)	
1893	15570	591	R. Worthington	*Lady Mary*	0-6-0T	
1894	16470	609	W&WR	*Cambria*	0-4-0ST	
1894	16480	610	W&WR	*Erin*	0-6-0ST	
1894	16550	611	T&CLR	*Argadeen*	2-6-0T	
1898	20620	677	T&DLR	6	2-6-0T (3-0)	
1903	26420	832	T.S. Dixon	*Coolmore*	0-4-0ST (3-0)	
1904	27480	859	R. Worthington	*Kells*	0-4-0ST	
1910	32850	1051	T&DLR	8	2-6-0T (3-0)	
1912	34160	1098	WCR	1	4-6-0T (3-0)	
1919	36710	1200	C&MLR	4	4-4-0T (3-0)	
1922	40880	1432/3	WCR	3, 7	4-6-0T (3-0)	
1928	43200	1569	LMS(NCC)	19	0-6-0T	See Note

Note: 1569 was new to LMS (4-8½), Lot 52.

J. JONES (Newton-le-Willows, Lancashire)   TOTAL 2
1855 built 2 2-4-0 for LER (Nos. 13, 14).

KERR, STUART (Stoke-on-Trent)   TOTAL 14

Year	KS Order	Works Nos.	Railway/user	Nos./Name	Type	
1899	4933	659	G. Pauling		0-4-0ST (3-0)	
1899	4934	660	G. Pauling		0-4-0ST (3-0)	
1900	3110	741	R. Faris		0-4-2T (3-0)	See note
1903	988	766	G.A. Watson	*Doonagore*	0-4-2T (4-8½)	See note
1902	403	800	T&DLR	7	2-6-0T (3-0)	
1903	856	818	WCR	10	4-6-0T (3-0)	
1903	876	836	T&DLR	8	2-6-0T (3-0)	
1904	989	845/6	L&LSR	9, 10	4-6-2T (3-0)	
1905	7822	889	Dublin Port & Dock Board	*Brian Boru*	0-4-0ST (3-0)	
1910	4597	1100	Sulphate of Ammonia	*Moorhen*	0-4-0ST (2-0)	
1915	45	2464	Kynock Ltd.		0-4-0ST (2-0)	
1922	L23	4252	D. Thompson & Sons		0-4-0ST (2-0)	
1922	L16	4265	J. Howard		0-4-0ST (2-0)	

Note: Works Nos. 741 and 766 were built to orders 3052 and 3499 respectively.

KITSON (Leeds)   TOTAL 68
(a) Main series locomotives

Year	K. Order	Works Nos.	Railway/user	Nos./Name	Type	
1852		288-91	L&ER	5-8	2-2-0WT	
1853		320/1	W&KR	6, 7	2-2-2	(Tenders Nos. 322/3)
1860		796	J. Watson		0-6-0T	See note
1864		1213	W&LR	28	2-2-2	(Tender No. 1214)
1872		1783/4	W&LR	3, 7	0-4-2	(Tender No. 1785 only)
1886	59	2901-4	MGWR	35, 38-40	2-4-0	
1891	125	3370-2/80-2	MGWR	106-08,112-14	0-6-0T	
1893	139	3527-9	MGWR	115-17	0-6-0T	
1895	151	3584-6/99, 3600	MGWR	135-9	0-6-0	
1895	152	3587/8	W&LR	51, 52	0-4-4T	
1896	160	3616/7	WL&WR	16, 17	4-4-2T	
1896	161	3618/9	WL&WR	53, 54	4-4-0	
1897	174	3686/7	DW&WR	4, 5	0-6-2T	
1897	176	3689/90	WL&WR	18, 21	4-4-2T	
1897	177	3691-3	WL&WR	56-58	0-6-0	
1897	178	3694	WL&WR	55	4-4-0	
1900	214	3908	WL&WR	2	0-6-0	
1900	225	3974/5	MGWR	141, 142	0-6-0	(ordered by WL&WR)
1905	298	4296/7	B&CDR	1, 2	Railmotor	
1906	320	4383	B&CDR	3	Railmotor	
1908	350	4565/6	Ballycastle	3, 4	4-4-2T (3-0)	

Note: 796 was originally intended for Bahia & North Western Railway (Brazil).

(b) Tram locomotives (numbered in a separate Kitson series)

Year	Works Nos.	Railway/tramway	Nos.	Type
1881	15	C&WT	3	0-4-0T (4-8½)
1881	36/7	DSDT	1, 2	0-4-0T
1882	49, 54	C&WT	1, 2	0-4-0T (4-8½)
1882	56	Portstewart	1	0-4-0T (3-0)
1882	57	D&LST	1	0-4-0T (3-0)

Year	Works Nos.	Railway/tramway	Nos.	Type
1883	74, 81	D&LST	2, 3	0-4-0T (3-0)
1883	84	Portstewart	2	0-4-0T (3-0)
1884	105	D&LST	4	0-4-0T (3-0)
1884	106/7	C&VBT	1, 2	0-4-0T (3-0)
1884	108	D&LST	5	0-4-0T (3-0)
1887	224	D&LST	6	0-4-0T (3-0)
1888	235	C&MLR	4	0-4-2T (3-0)
1891	257	C&VBT	3	0-4-0T (3-0)
1900	302	B&NCR	3	0-4-0T (3-0) (For Portstewart Tramway)

R.B. LONGRIDGE (Bedlington, Northumberland)

TOTAL 12

Year	Railway	Nos.	Type		Year	Railway	Nos.	Type
1846	L&CR	*	2-4-0		1851	MGWR	18-21	2-2-2
1846	L&ER	1	2-4-0		1852	MGWR	22, 23	2-2-2
1846	L&ER	2	2-2-2		1852	MGWR	25, 26	2-4-0
1847	L&ER	3	2-4-0					

S. LEWIN (Poole, Dorset)

TOTAL 3

Year	User	Nos.	Type		Year	User	Nos.	Type
1875	*		0-6-0T (2-6)		1876	Guinnness	2, 3	0-4-0WT (1-10)

MANLOVE, ALLIOTT & FRYER (Nottingham)

TOTAL 1

In 1881 a Perrett type combined steam tramcar (possibly the example that was new in 1876) was tried on the Dublin & Lucan Steam Tramway but soon disappeared from Ireland.

MANNING, WARDLE (Leeds)

TOTAL 20

Year	MW Order	Works Nos.	Railway/user	Nos./Names	Type
1859	22	4	Brassey & Field	Rutland	0-6-0ST (originally 4-8½)
1860	200	18	Brassey & Field	Malvern	0-6-0ST (originally 4-8½)
1867	3270	237	Braddock	Glenloe	0-6-0ST (originally 4-8½)
1868	4000	261/2	B&CDR	12, 13	2-4-0
1870	4750	287	Haulbowline Dockyard		0-4-0ST (3-6)
1876	11140	614	Scott	Lancashire Witch	0-4-0ST (3-0)
1880	16560	773	T. Dowling	Bantry	0-4-0ST
1887	26000	1038	T.H. Falkiner	Lizzie	0-4-0ST (3-0)
1889	27050	1099	Fisher & LeFanu	Blackburn	0-6-0ST
1891	30500	1220	Braddock	Corrib	0-6-0ST
1897	39300	1357	Haulbowline Dockyard		0-4-0ST (3-6)
1898	41300	1399	Fisher & LeFanu*	*	0-6-0ST (4-8½)
*	*	*	Fisher & LeFanu	*	0-4-0ST (4-8½)
1906	58550	1684-7	GNR	4-7	Railmotor
1906	58800	1692/3	DW&WR	1, 2	Railmotor

MURDOCK, AITKEN (Glasgow)

TOTAL 1

1841 built 1 0-4-0 named Glenelrig (4-6 gauge), used by Jeffs.

NASMYTH, WILSON (Patricroft, Lancashire)

TOTAL 34

Year	Works Nos.	Railway	Nos.	Type	
1888	341	S&SLR	4	4-4-0T (3-0)	
1904	697-700	DR	12-15	4-6-4T (3-0)	
1907	828-32	CDRJC	16-20	2-6-4T (3-0)	
1911	929-33	GNR	9, 109/12, 38, 39	0-6-0	(Tender Nos. T433-7)
1911	950	GNR	165	0-6-0	(Tender No. T438)
1912	956-8	CDRJC	2A, 3A, 21	2-6-4T (3-0)	
1921	1115-9	GNR	1-5	4-4-2T	Built by BP (Works Nos. 6035-9)
1924	1423-7	GNR	21, 30, 115, 116, 139	4-4-2T	
1924	1428/31	GNR	15, 18	0-6-0	(Tender Nos. T1428/31)
1925	1429/30/2	GNR	16, 17, 19	0-6-0	(Tender Nos. T1429/30/2)
1924	1435-9	GNR	142-44, 147, 148	4-4-2T	

NEILSON (Glasgow)
NEILSON, REID (Glasgow)

TOTAL 93

Year	N/NR Order	Works Nos.	Railway/user	Nos./Names	Type
1859		542-4	C&YR	1-3	2-4-0ST
1860		599, 600	C&YR	4, 5	2-4-0ST
1861		602	T.W. Chester		0-4-0ST
1861		689-91	C&YR	6-8	2-2-2ST
1861		692/3	D&ER	15, 16	0-4-2
1862		855	D&DR	8	2-2-2ST
1862		885/6	C&YR	9, 10	2-4-0ST
1863		937-42	MGWR	55-60	0-4-2
1863		950/1	INWR	28, 29	0-4-2
1864		1042-7	MGWR	61-66	0-4-2
1865	E288	1122-7	DW&WR	Kate Kierney, Elfin, Kelpie, Ariel, Oberon, Titania	2-2-2WT
1865	E289	1144	DW&WR	Banshee	2-2-2WT
1871	E368	1575-80	MGWR	7, 76-80	0-4-2
1872	E391	1717-22	MGWR	81-86	0-4-2
1873	E405	1782/3	DW&WR	34, 35	2-2-2WT

Year	N/NR Order	Works Nos.	Railway/user	Nos./Names	Type
1873	E406	1784-95	MGWR	13-24	2-4-0
1893	E703	4573-8	DR	4-9	4-6-0T (3-0)
1894	E728	4740/1	CB&SCR	18, 9	4-4-0T
1899	E819	5557-60	GNR	133-136	4-4-0
1899	E820	5561-4	CB&PR	4-7	2-4-2T (3-0)
1901	E843	5753-5	GNR	101-103	0-6-0 (no tenders)
1901	E844	5756-8	GNR	130-132	4-4-0 (no tenders)
1902	E870	6103/4	DR	10, 11	4-4-4T (3-0)
1902	E877	6156/7	GNR	124, 125	4-4-0
1903	E891	6313-8	GS&WR	309-14	4-4-0

NORTH BRITISH LOCOMOTIVE Co. (Glasgow)   TOTAL 47

Year	NBL Order	Works Nos.	Railway	Nos.	Type	Remarks
1903	E895	15766/7	GNR	122, 123	4-4-0	(originally NR order)
1903	E896	15890/1	GNR	152, 153	0-6-0	(originally NR order)
1903	E1212	15943-9	GS&WR	355-361	0-6-0	(originally SS order)
1903	L3	16021-4	GS&WR	211-214	0-6-2T	
1904	L19	16128-31	MGWR	143-146	0-6-0	
1904	L59	16190/1	GNR	113, 114	4-4-0	
1904	L60	16433/4	GNR	154, 155	0-6-0	
1904	L74	16510/1	GNR	156, 157	4-4-0	
1905	L87	16607-9	GNR	1-3	Railmotor	
1906	L141	17082-4	GNR	158-160	0-6-0	(no tenders)
1907	L216	17814-6	GNR	126-128	4-4-0	
1908	L269	18286-91	GNR	110, 111, 161-164	0-6-0	
1924	L786	23096-23100	LMS(NCC)	74-78	4-4-0	(Derby order 6095)
1925	L797	23171/2	LMS(NCC)	82, 83	4-4-0	(LMS Lot 25, Derby order 6332)

PECKETT (Bristol)   TOTAL 14

Year	Works nos	Railway/user	Nos./Name	Type
1898	679/80	Pearson	75, 76	0-6-0ST (4-8½)
1899	806	Pearson	99	0-6-0ST (4-8½)
1903	1003	Fisher & LeFanu	*Cashel*	0-4-0ST (3-0)
1904	1026	British Aluminium	1	0-4-0T (3-0)
1906	1085	S&SLR	1	4-4-0T (3-0)
1906	1097	British Aluminium	2	0-4-0T (3-0)
1908	1189	P.J. Kinlen		0-4-0ST (3-0)
1914	1356	S&SLR	3	4-4-0T (3-0)
1914	1357	British Aluminium	3	0-4-0T (3-0)
1915	1412	Sutton Sands		0-6-0ST (2-0)
1920	1556	Allman & Co.		0-4-0ST
1948	2088	Courtaulds	*Patricia*	0-4-0ST
1950	2113	Courtaulds	*Wilfred*	0-4-0ST

ROBEY (Lincoln)   TOTAL 1
Built at unknown date a 10 hp locomotive (4-8½ gauge) used by Derrylea Peat Co.

ROTHWELL (Leeds)   TOTAL 4
1850 built 4 0-4-2 for GS&WR (Nos. 53-56).

SENTINEL WAGGON WORKS (Shrewsbury)   TOTAL 11

Year	Works Nos.	Railway/user	Nos.	Type
1925	5750	LMS(NCC)	401	Coach
1925	5751	LMS(NCC)	91	4-wheel
1927	6463	Cementation Co.	3	4-wheel (2-0)
1927	6844/5	GSR	354, 355	Coach
1927	6846/7	GSR	1, 2	4-wheel
1927	6870	Cementation Co.	4	4-wheel (2-0)
1927	6912/3	GSR	356, 357	Coach
1946	9149	Bord Solathair an Lectreachais		4-wheel (2-6)

SHARP, ROBERTS (Manchester)   TOTAL 216
SHARP BROS. (Manchester)
SHARP, STEWART (Manchester until 1887, then Glasgow)
(Note - distribution of Sharp's numbers up to about No. 600 is not entirely certain, in particular orders E150, E165 and E166).

Year	SS Order	Works Nos.	Railway/user	Nos./Names	Type	Remarks
1834		B, C, D	D&KR	*Hibernia, Britannia, Manchester*	2-2-0 (4-8½)	
1839		48/9	UR	*Express, Fury*	2-2-2 (6-2)	
1839		57	UR	*Spitfire*	2-2-2 (6-2)	
1841		130/3/55/6	UR	*Etna, Firefly, Achilles, Ajax*	2-2-2 (6-2)	
1842		206/7	UR	*Samson, Hercules*	0-4-2 (6-2)	
1843	E113	235	D&DR	2	2-2-2	
1843	E114	239	D&DR	1	0-4-2	
1844	E126	254-6	D&DR	3-5	2-2-2	
1844	E125	258/9	D&DR	6, 7	0-4-2	
1844	E135	272/3	D&DR	8, 9	2-2-2	
1844	E134	277	D&DR	10	2-2-2	See note
1844	E133	278	D&DR	11	0-4-2	
1845	E143	279	W. Dargan	*Lady Macneil*	0-4-2	

Year	SS Order	Works Nos.	Railway/user	Nos./Names	Type	Remarks
1846	E150	330-3/9/40	GS&WR	1-6	2-2-2	
1846	E162	343/4	UR	Cyclops, Pluto	2-2-2	
1846	E150	357/8/61/2	GS&WR	7-10	2-2-2	
1846	E150	366/7	UR	Lucifer, Jupiter	2-2-2	
1847	E150	392/4	UR	Cerberus, Vulcan	2-2-2	
1847	E150	393/5, 459/60/5/6	GS&WR	11-16	2-2-2	
1848	E150	490-3	GS&WR	17-20	2-2-2	
1847	E165	509-12	B&BR	Hawk, Kite, Falcon, Swallow	2-2-2	
1847	E166	513	B&BR	Eagle	0-4-2	
1848	E181	529/30/4/5	D&BJR	1-4	2-2-2	
1850	E234	655/6	CB&PR	1, 2	2-2-2WT	
1850	E239	662	CB&PR	3	2-2-2WT	
1851	E233	674	B&BR	Ostrich	0-4-2	
1852	E254	698/9	C&BR	5, 6	0-4-2	
1852	E256	706	D&ER	4	2-2-2	
1852	E181	707	D&BJR	5	2-2-2	
1853	E181	708/9/11	D&BJR	6-8	2-2-2	
1853	E260	716/7	L&CR	3, 4	2-2-0WT	
1853	E266	718/9/22/3	L&CR	7, *, 5, 6	2-2-0WT	
1853	E259	736/7/40	W&LR	13-15	0-4-2	
1853	E268	738	D&BJR	9	0-4-2	See Note
1853	E265	741/2	UR	14, 15	0-4-2	
1854	E274	764	W&LR	16	0-4-2	
1854	E268	774-6	D&BJR	10-12	0-4-2	
1854	E276	785/6	D&ER	5, 6	2-2-2	
1854	E280	787	D&BJR	13	2-2-2	
1854	E284	809/10	D&DR	12, 18	2-2-2	
1855	E279	878-81	BBC&PJR	1-4	2-2-2	
1856	E302	936-41	B&BR	12-17	2-4-0	
1857	E319	975	UR	16	0-4-2	
1857	E320	989	UR	17	2-2-2	
1857	E325	992	D&BJR	14	0-4-2	
1857	E327	993/4	B&BR	18, 19	0-6-0	
1857	E326	1006	D&BJR	15	0-4-2	
1857	E320	1007/8	UR	18, 19	2-2-2	
1858	E340	1052/3	D&ER	9, 10	0-4-2	
1858	E347	1081/2	D&BJR	16, 17	2-2-2WT	
1860	E366	1156	UR	3	0-4-2	
1860	E373	1210/1	DW&WR	15, 16	0-4-2	
1861	E398	1274	UR	4	0-4-2	
1861	E399	1275/6	UR	20, 21	2-2-2	
1861	E400	1277	B&NCR	35	0-6-0	
1862	E419	1345/6	W&LR	4, 5	0-4-2	
1863	E456	1473	D&DR	22	2-2-2	
1864	E453	1478-80	DW&WR	24-26	2-4-0	
1864	E454	1481-3	DW&WR	17, 19, 18	0-4-2	
1864	E450	1484	D&DR	2	2-2-2	
1864	E455	1489/90/5	DW&WR	21, 20, 22	0-4-2	
1865	E455	1496	DW&WR	23	0-4-2	
1864	E463	1529	W&LR	6	0-4-2	
1866	E518	1649/51/2	UR	30-32	0-4-2	(Built 1865)
1865	E498	1653	W&LR	29	0-4-0ST	
1867	E531	1797/8	B&NCR	38, 39	0-6-0	
1870	E560	2001	B&NCR	32	0-6-0	
1871	E594	2143	B&NCR	28	0-6-0	
1872	E588	2155-8	GS&WR	163-166	0-6-0	
1872	E608	2218/9	B&NCR	40, 41	2-4-0	
1873	E625	2269	B&NCR	7	0-6-0	
1873	E628	2304/5	DW&WR	32, 33	2-4-0	
1873	E630	2310/1	GS&WR	175, 176	0-6-0	
1873	E641	2335/6	B&NCR	6, 11	2-4-0	
1875	E661	2444	B&NCR	42	0-4-0ST	
1875	E687	2477	Guinness	1	0-4-0T (1-10)	
1875	E682	2487	B&NCR	43	0-6-0	
1876	E704	2560/1	UR	40, 41	0-4-2	
1876	E713	2627-9	B&NCR	10, 27, 29	2-4-0	
1876	E714	2630	B&NCR	44	0-6-0	
1876	E724	2645	L&LSR	4	0-6-0T	
1876	E728	2654/5	DW&WR	38, 39	0-4-2	
1876	E729	2656	DW&WR	37	0-4-2	
1877	E731	2677-80	GNR	62, 63, 65, 25	0-6-0	
1878	E755	2743	N&AR	*	0-4-2	
1878	E746	2764/5	Guinness	4, 5	0-4-0T (1-10)	
1878	E762	2818-21	WD&LR	1-4	0-4-2	
1879	E769	2836	L&LSR	5	0-6-0T	
1879	E766	2837/8	GS&WR	185, 186	0-6-0	
1879	E772	2842-4	GNR	27, 66, 67	0-6-0	

Year	SS Order	Works Nos.	Railway/user	Nos./Names	Type
1880	E780	2879	B&CDR	2	0-4-2
1880	E789	2924/5	GNR	26, 34	0-6-0
1881	E816	3021-3	WDR	2, 3, 1	2-4-0T (3-0)
1884	E864	3233	W&CIR	1	0-4-2
1886	E882	3358	B&CDR	10	0-4-2
1886	E884	3369/70	CVT	1, 2	0-4-2T (3-0)
1887	E884	3371-4	CVT	3-6	0-4-2T (3-0)
1887	E900	3392	B&CDR	9	0-4-2
1888	E921	3432	B&CDR	13	0-4-2
1890	E964	3615	B&CDR	16	0-4-2
1891	E972	3665	WD&LR	6	0-4-2
1891	E980	3693-5	MGWR	109-111	0-6-0T
1892	E1004	3813	WD&LR	7	0-4-2
1893	E1019	3909-11	DW&WR	52-54	4-4-2T
1895	E1046	4057-61	MGWR	130-134	0-6-0

Notes: An extra tender was supplied with order E134, perhaps for D&DR No. 12.
738 was diverted from order E259.
SS 1070, order E343, one 2-2-2T ordered by W&TR was repudiated in 1858 - for details see W&TR.

R. STEPHENSON (Newcastle-upon-Tyne until 1902, then Darlington)   TOTAL 34

Year	RS Order	Works Nos.	Railway/user	Nos./Name	Type
*	*	*	*	Gilsland	
1856		1048	MGWR	42	0-4-0 (4-8½)
1859		1190	Smith & Knight		2-4-0
1860		1280	Smith & Knight		0-6-0
1864		1609/10	L&LSR		0-6-0
1874		2088/9	Glenariffe Iron Ore & Harbour Co.	3, 4	0-6-0ST
1876		2284-90, 2305-7	MGWR	86-95	2-4-0T (3-0)
1884		2379	W&LR	1	0-6-0 See note
1887		2612-9	CL&RLR&T	1-8	4-4-0T (3-0)
1891		2738	Londonderry Port & Harbour Comm.	1	0-6-0ST
1896		2836	Londonderry Port & Harbour Comm.	2	0-6-0ST
1904	E14	3136	C&LR	9	0-6-4T (3-0)
1905	E15	3137/8	GNR	98, 99	0-6-2T
1911	E71	3454/5	GNR	168, 169	0-6-2T

Note: Works No. 2379 was new in 1879. It was originally built to 5-0 gauge for an unidentified customer but never delivered.

STOTHERT & SLAUGHTER (Bristol)
SLAUGHTER, GRUNING (Bristol)   TOTAL 9

Year	Railway	Nos.	Type		Year	Railway	Nos.	Type
1847	W&LR	1-6	2-2-2		1862	W&TR	3	0-4-2WT See note
1852	W&KR	4, 5	2-4-0					

Note: 3 given as builders progressive number 452 in some lists.

CHAS. TAYLEUR (Newton-le-Willows, Lancashire)
VULCAN FOUNDRY (Newton-le-Willows, Lancashire)   TOTAL 46

Year	VF Order	Works Nos.	Railway	Nos.	Type	Remarks
1848		241-3	W&KR	1-3	4-2-2T	(new 1846)
1849	200	321	C&BR	3	2-2-2	(Tender order No. 201)
1851	200	322	C&BR	4	2-2-2	(Tender order No. 201)
1854	836	392	D&WR	6	2-2-2ST	
1854	837	393	D&WR	7	2-2-2ST	
1855	832	394	D&WR	8	2-4-0ST	
1855	833	395	D&WR	9	2-4-0ST	
1855		407/8	D&WR	10, 11	2-2-2ST	
1864	998	508	B&CDR	11	2-4-0ST	
1864		509/10	N&AR	6, 7	0-4-2ST	
1865	90	537/8	B&CDR	12, 13	2-4-0ST	
1866	270	561	B&CDR	3	2-4-0ST	
1867	470	590	B&CDR	5	2-4-0ST	
1867	790	591	W&KR	8	2-4-0	
1868	790	592	W&KR	9	2-4-0	
1874	570	706-9	W&LR	25, 30-32	2-4-0	
1875	595	746	B&CDR	14	0-6-0	
1876	789	793	BH&BR	3	2-4-0ST	
1876	861	797	BH&BR	6	2-4-0ST	
1877	23	806	West Cork	3	2-4-0ST	
1881	135	910-3	W&LR	8, 35-37	2-4-0	
1882	664	990/1	W&LR	38, 39	2-4-0	
1883	775	1010/1	W&LR	40, 41	0-6-0	
1886	555	1162	W&LR	12	4-4-0	
1891	996	1310/1	DW&WR	50, 51	0-6-0	
1891	60	1315/6	W&LR	13, 14	2-4-2T	
1895	540	1448/9	DW&WR	55, 56	4-4-0	
1896	760	1455/6	DW&WR	57, 58	4-4-0	
1897	150	1558	W&CIR	4	0-4-2	

Note: Some lists of Vulcan Foundry built locomotives include Nos. 203 and 204 as one 0-4-0 and one 2-2-2 for the Ulster Railway in 1845 (15 x 20 in. cylinders, 5-0 driving wheels, 5-3 gauge). No such orders can be traced in existing UR records nor can any other user in Ireland be located.

WALKER Bros. (Wigan) — TOTAL 1
1928 supplied 1 0-4-0VB (Walker No. 114) to CVR, No. 8 (3-0 gauge).

W. WILKINSON (Wigan) — TOTAL 6

Year	Works Nos.	Tramway	Nos.	Type
1883	28/9	GCP&BVT	1, 2	0-4-0VB (3-0)
1883	30/1	DSDT	3, 4	0-4-0VB
1887	54	GCP&BVT	3	0-4-0VB (3-0)
1896	63	GCP&BVT	4	0-4-0VB (3-0)

E.B. WILSON (Leeds) — TOTAL 1
1857 built 1 0-4-2 (EBW No. 578) for W&KR, No. 2.

YORKSHIRE ENGINE Co. (Sheffield) — TOTAL 2
1870 built 2 2-4-0ST (YE order EI9, YE Nos. 151/2) for BH&BR, Nos. 4, 5.

U.S. LOCOMOTIVE BUILDER

BURNHAM & WILLIAMS (Baldwin Loco) (Philadelphia, USA) — TOTAL 2
1900 supplied 2 0-6-2ST (B&W Nos. 18027/8) to CB&SCR, Nos. 19, 20.

OTHER FOREIGN LOCOMOTIVE BUILDERS

(a) Locomotives not used on Shannon Hydro-electric Scheme

J. COCKERILL (Belgium) — TOTAL 3
1926 supplied 3 0-4-0VB (JC Nos. 3092/3/6) to Comlucht Suicre Eireann (Carlow Nos. 1-3).

KRAUSS (Germany) — TOTAL 3
1926 built 1 0-4-0 (prog. No. 8378). Belfast Corporation Transport Department *Jean* (1-3 gauge).
1932 supplied 2 locomotives (1-1 gauge) used at the Cork Industrial Fair & Exhibition, 1932.

ORENSTEIN & KOPPEL (Germany) — TOTAL 13

Year	Works Nos.	User	Nos./Name	Type
1904	1240	R. Worthington	*Armagh*	0-4-0WT (2-0)
*	*	Whyte	(two)	0-4-0WT (2-0)
1908	2488	Irish Industrial Minerals	*Derwent*	0-4-0WT (2-0)
1934	12473/4	Comlucht Suicre Eireann (Mallow)	1, 2	0-4-0T
1934	12475/6	Comlucht Suicre Eireann (Thurles)	1, 2	0-4-0T
1934	12477/8	Comlucht Suicre Eireann (Tuam)	1, 2	0-4-0T
1935	12662	Comlucht Suicre Eireann (Mallow)	3	0-4-0T
1935	12663	Comlucht Suicre Eireann (Thurles)	3	0-4-0T
1935	12664	Comlucht Suicre Eireann (Tuam)	3	0-4-0T

TUBIZE (Belgium) — TOTAL 1
1885 built 1 Lartigue type vertical boiler monorail locomotive used on the construction of the L&BR.

(b) Locomotives used on the Shannon Hydro-electric Scheme — TOTAL 106
All 0-4-0T built in Germany

Borsig	18	(2-11½ gauge)
Hannoversche	19	(2-11½ gauge).
Henschel	34	(2-11½ & 1-11½ gauges).
Jung	1	(1-11½ gauge)
Krauss	3	(2-11½ gauge).
Linke Hoffman	10	(1-11½ gauge).
Rhine Metal Works	21	(2-11½ gauge).

GENERAL NOTES
Railway company locomotives of unknown builder are accounted for as follows:

New to companies	DW&WR (1 - Hodgsons Tramway), L&ER (2)
Ex Britain	W&LR (1)
Unknown source	D&MR (1) - probably ex contractor
Ex contractors	L&CR (1), N&AR (1), W&TR (1)

Contractors and industrial locomotives of unknown origin are listed separately on pages

Locomotives built by HAIGH FOUNDRY (Wigan) - lists of locomotives built by this company have been published showing two for an "Irish Contractor" in 1837 and a further six in 1842. The contractor was Mullins & McMahon of Dublin and the work was in England and so these locomotives have no relevance to this list - they may in reality be fictional.

Under each Railway/Tramway Company in this section details are given of locomotives built new for that company, followed by a full list of all locomotives operated.

PART I - GREAT NORTHERN RAILWAY

Constituent and absorbed railways which contributed locomotives to the Great Northern Railway.

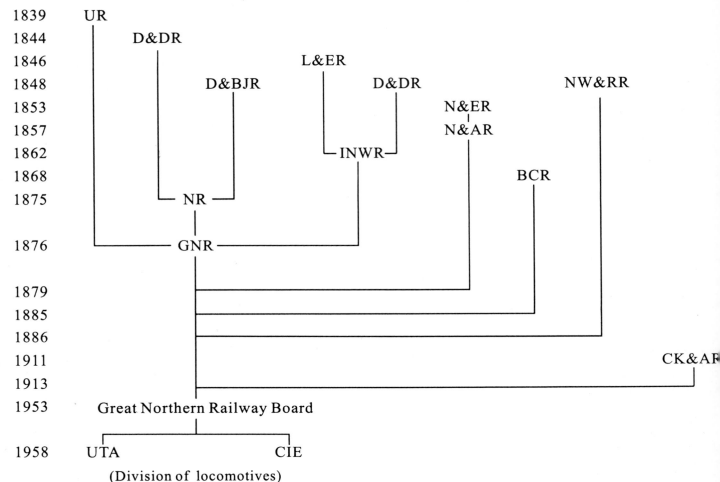

1839	UR
1844	D&DR
1846	L&ER
1848	D&BJR	D&DR	NW&RR
1853	N&ER
1857	N&AR
1862	INWR
1868	BCR
1875	NR
1876	GNR
1879	
1885	
1886	
1911	CK&AR
1913	
1953	Great Northern Railway Board
1958	UTA	CIE

(Division of locomotives)

ULSTER RAILWAY

6-2 Gauge.
Stock: 9 new locomotives built 1839-42.

Type	Years built	No. in class	Cylinders	Driving wheels	Locomotive names
2-2-2	1839	2	13 x 18	6-0	*Express, Fury*
2-2-2	1839	1	14 x 18	6-0	*Spitfire*
2-2-2	1841	4	14 x 18	5-6	*Etna, Firefly, Achilles, Ajax*
0-4-2	1842	2	14 x 20	5-0	*Samson, Hercules*

Name	Type	Date	Builder	Rebuilt	Later No.	Withdrawn	Remarks
Express	2-2-2	1839	SR		(1)	1859	Converted to 5-3 1848.
Fury	2-2-2	1839	SR		(2)	1859	Converted to 5-3 1848.
Spitfire	2-2-2	1839	SR	1846* 2-2-2WT		1849	Altered to 5-3 gauge for use by W. Dargan on construction of B&BR. Exchanged with B&BR *Hawk* in 1849.
Etna	2-2-2	1841	SR		(3)	1859	Converted to 5-3 1848.
Firefly	2-2-2	1841	SR		(4)	1859	Converted to 5-3 1848.
Achilles	2-2-2	1841	SR			1849	Sold to Coates & Young, Belfast. Altered to 5-3 and sold to L&ER in 1852.
Ajax	2-2-2	1841	SR			1849	Sold to Coates & Young, Belfast. Altered to 5-3 and sold to L&ER in 1852.
Samson	0-4-2	1842	SR		5	1872	Altered to 5-3 1848.
Hercules	0-4-2	1842	SR		6	1873	Altered to 5-3 1848.

5-3 Gauge.
Stock: 46 new locomotives built 1846-74.
6 locomotives converted from 6-2 gauge as listed above.
1 secondhand locomotive acquired 1849.

Type	Years	No. in Class	Cylinders	Driving wheels	Locomotive Nos.
2-2-2	1846-7	6	15 x 20	5-6	7-12
0-4-2	1853	2	16 x 24	4-6	14, 15
0-4-2	1857-61	3	16 x 24	4-6	3, 4, 16
2-2-2	1857-8	3	15 x 20	5-6	17-19
2-2-2	1859-61	3	15 x 20	5-6	1, 22, 23
2-2-2	1859-62	3	15 x 20	5-6	2, 24, 25
2-2-2	1861	2	15 x 20	5-6	20, 21
2-4-0	1863	4	16 x 22	6-1	26-29
0-4-2	1866	3	16 x 22	5-0	30-32
0-4-2	1866	4	17 x 24	5-0	33-36
2-4-0	1867-9	4	15 x 20	5-6	8, 10, 12, 13
0-4-2	1871-6	6	16 x 22	5-0	5-7, 39-41
0-6-0	1872-3	2	17 x 24	5-0	37, 38
2-4-0	1874	1	16 x 22	5-6	23

Names and Numbers
The UR tended to refer to a locomotive by name, but in several instances a name was not applied until sometime (even years in some cases) after delivery. Where necessary a date of naming is added in the notes column. Numbers were not applied until about 1852.

No.	Name	Type	Date	Builder	Rebuilt	Withdrawn	Remarks
7	*Cyclops*	2-2-2	1846	SB		1870	
8	*Lucifer*	2-2-2	1846	SB		1865	
9	*Pluto*	2-2-2	1846	SB		GNR	
10	*Jupiter*	2-2-2	1846	SB		1867	
11	*Cerberus*	2-2-2	1847	SB		GNR	
12	*Vulcan*	2-2-2	1847	SB		1865	
13	*Spitfire*	2-2-2	(B&BR *Hawk*)			1867	Taken in exchange in 1849 for *Spitfire* when latter passed into B&BR stock.
14	*Callan*	0-4-2	1853	SS		1874	Not named until 1866.
15	*Neagh*	0-4-2	1853	SS		1874	Not named until 1866*.
16	*Bann*	0-4-2	1857	SS		GNR	Not named until 1866.
17	*Shamrock*	2-2-2	1857	SS	1865 2-4-0	GNR	Not named until 1866.
18	*Rose*	2-2 2	1857	SS	1863 2-4-0	GNR	Not named until 1866.
19	*Thistle*	2-2-2	1858	SS	1864 2-4-0	GNR	Not named until 1865-6.
1	*Lagan*	2-2-2	1859	BP		1875	
2	*Blackwater*	2-2-2	1859	Fbn		GNR	
3	*Erne*	0-4-2	1860	SS		GNR	
4	*Owenreagh*	0-4-2	1861	SS		GNR	
20	*Ulidia*	2-2-2	1861	SS		GNR	
21	*Dalriada*	2-2-2	1861	SS		GNR	
22	*Iveagh*	2-2-2	1861	BP		GNR	
23	*Tyrone*	2-2-2	1861	BP		1873	

No.	Name	Type	Date	Builder	Rebuilt	Withdrawn	Remarks
24	*Breffney*	2-2-2	1862	Fbn		GNR	
25	*Clanaboy*	2-2-2	1862	Fbn		GNR	
26	*Ulster*	2-4-0	1863	BP		GNR	
27	*Munster*	2-4-0	1863	BP		GNR	
28	*Leinster*	2-4-0	1863	BP		GNR	
29	*Connaught*	2-4-0	1863	BP		GNR	
30	*Nore*	0-4-2	1866	SS		GNR	New in 1864. Built for São Paulo Railway
31	*Ovoca*	0-4-2	1866	SS		GNR	New in 1864. Built for São Paulo Railway
32	*Foyle*	0-4-2	1866	SS		GNR	New in 1864. Built for São Paulo Railway
33	*Shannon*	0-4-2	1866	BP		GNR	
34	*Liffey*	0-4-2	1866	BP		GNR	
35	*Carntual*	0-4-2	1866	BP		GNR	
36	*Donard*	0-4-2	1866	BP		GNR	
8	*Lucifer*	2-4-0	1867	UR		GNR	
12	*Vulcan*	2-4-0	1867	UR		GNR	
10	*Jupiter*	2-4-0	1869	UR		GNR	
13	*Spitfire*	2-4-0	1869	UR		GNR	
7	*Cyclone*	0-4-2	1871	UR		GNR	
6	*Tornado*	0-4-2	1872	UR		GNR	
37	*Stromboli*	0-6-0	1872	UR		GNR	
38	*Volcano*	0-6-0	1873	UR		GNR	
5	*Typhoon*	0-4-2	1874	UR		GNR	
23	*Tyrone*	2-4-0	1874	IJR		GNR	
39	*Tempest*	0-4-2	1874	UR		GNR	
40	*Siroco*	0-4-2	1876	SS		GNR	
41	*Simoom*	0-4-2	1876	SS		GNR	

38 locomotives taken into GNR stock 1876 (Nos. 2-13, 16-41) - numbers not initially altered by GNR.

DUBLIN & DROGHEDA RAILWAY

Stock: 33 new locomotives built 1843-72.
1 secondhand locomotive acquired 1844.

Type	Years built	No. in class	Cylinders	Driving wheels	Locomotive Nos. (+ subsequently renumbered)
0-4-2	1843-4	4	15 x 20	5-0	1, 6+, 7, 11
2-2-2	1843	1	15 x 18	5-0	2
2-2-2	1844	6	14 x 18	5-6	3-5, 8-10
2-2-2	1845-7	4	14 x 18	5-6	13-15, 17+
2-2-2WT	1847	1	14 x 18	5-6	16
2-2-2	1854	2	15 x 20	5-6	12+, 18
2-4-0	1855	1	15 x 20	5-6	19
2-4-0	1856	1	15 x 20	5-6	4
0-4-2	1858-62	3	16 x 22	5-0	10, 11, 20
2-2-2	1859-61	4	15 x 20	6-0	13-16
2-2-2T	1862	1	12 x 18	5-0	8
0-4-2	1863	1	16 x 22	5-0	21
2-2-2	1863-4	2	15 x 20	5-6	2, 22
2-4-0	1871	1	16 x 22	6-0	12
0-6-0	1872	1	17 x 24	5-0	5

No.	Original name	Later name	Type	Date	Builder	Renumbered	Rebuilt	Withdrawn	Remarks
1	*Nora Creina*	*Nestor**	0-4-2	1843	SB			NR	
2	*St. Patrick*		2-2-2	1843	SB			1863-4*	
3	*Fag-an-Bealach*		2-2-2	1844	SB		1846 2-2-2T	NR	
4	*Albert*		2-2-2	1844	SB		1846 2-2-2WT	1856	
5	*Victoria*		2-2-2	1844	SB			1871	
6	*Dublin*	*Samson**	0-4-2	1844	SB			NR	
7	*Princess*		0-4-2	1844	SB			1871	
8	*Alice*		2-2-2	1844	SB			1862	
9	*Alfred*	*Saturn*	2-2-2	1844	SB		1868 2-4-0	NR	
10	*Queen*		2-2-2	1844	SB		1848 2-4-0*	1862	See Note
11	*Prince*		0-4-2	1844	SB			1857	
12	*Firefly*		2-2-2	(Jeffs)			1846 2-2-2T	1853*	See Note
13	*McNeil*		2-2-2	1845	G			1860	
14			2-2-2	1845	G			1859	
15	*Hibernia*		2-2-2	1845	G			1859	
16			2-2-2WT	1847	G		* 2-2-2	1861	
17	*Drogheda*	*Venus*	2-2-2	1847	G	7 (1871)		NR	
12		*Apollo*	2-2-2	1854	SS	17 (1871)		NR	
18		*Diana**	2-2-2	1854	SS			NR	
19		*Pluto*	2-4-0	1855	Fbn			NR	
4		*Drogheda*	2-4-0	1856	G			NR	
11		*Ajax**	0-4-2	1858	BP			NR	
20		*Vulcan**	0-4-2	1858	BP			NR	
14		*Jupiter**	2-2-2	1859	BP			NR	
15		*Aurora**	2-2-2	1859	BP			NR	

No.	Original name	Later name	Type	Date	Builder	Renumbered	Rebuilt	Withdrawn	Remarks
13		Ulysses*	2-2-2	1860	BP			NR	
16		Jupiter*	2-2-2	1861	BP			NR	
10		Mercury* or Ajax*	0-4-2	1862	BP			NR	
8			2-2-2ST	1862	N			NR	
21		Neptune*	0-4-2	1863	BP		1873 0-6-0	NR	
22		Neptune*	2-2-2	1863	SS		1865	NR	See Note
2		Mars*	2-2-2	1864	SS			NR	
12		Achilles*	2-4-0	1871	BP			NR	
5		Hercules*	0-6-0	1872	BP			NR	

Notes

Naming - all the original names were removed. The later series came into use post 1870, but many are not known with certainty.

10 was originally built with outside cylinders as a "Bodmer's Expansion" locomotive. Altered in 1848 to conventional arrangement.

12 was purchased in 1843 from Jeffs (see Contractors List, Butterley Co. locomotive). Gauge altered 1844 from 4-6 to 5-3 by Grendon. Sold to Moore 1853 (see Contractors List)

22 was altered to 6-0 driving wheels in 1865.

22 locomotives taken into Northern Railway stock 1875, numbers not altered.

DUBLIN & BELFAST JUNCTION RAILWAY

Stock: 22 new locomotives built 1848-72.

Type	Years built	No. in class	Cylinders	Driving wheels	Locomotive Nos.
2-2-2	1848-54	9	15 x 20	5-6	1-8, 13
0-4-2	1853-7	2	16 x 24	4-6	9, 14
0-4-2	1854-7	4	16 x 22	5-0	10-12, 15
2-2-2WT	1858	2	12 x 18	5-0	16, 17
2-4-0	1866-8	3	16 x 22	6-0	18-20
0-6-0	1872	2	17 x 24	5-1½	21, 22

No.	Type	Date	Builder	Rebuilt	Withdrawn	NR No.	No.	Type	Date	Builder	Rebuilt	Withdrawn	NR No.
1	2-2-2	1848	SB	1872 2-4-0	NR	30	12	0-4-2	1854	SS		NR	33
2	2-2-2	1848	SB		NR	23	13	2-2-2	1854	SS		NR	27
3	2-2-2	1848	SB		NR	24	14	0-4-2	1857	SS		NR	36
4	2-2-2	1848	SB		NR	25	15	0-4-2	1857	SS		NR	34
5	2-2-2	1853	SB		NR	26	16	2-2-2WT	1858	SS		NR	28
6	2-2-2	1853	SB		1875		17	2-2-2WT	1858	SS		NR	29
7	2-2-2	1853	SB		1873		18	2-4-0	1866	BP		NR	37
8	2-2-2	1853	SB		1873		19	2-4-0	1866	BP		NR	38
9	0-4-2	1853	SS		NR	35	20	2-4-0	1866	BP		NR	39
10	0-4-2	1854	SS		NR	31	21	0-6-0	1872	BP		NR	40
11	0-4-2	1854	SS		NR	32	22	0-6-0	1872	BP		NR	41

19 locomotives taken into NR stock 1875 (Nos. 1-5, 9-22) and renumbered as shown.

LONDONDERRY & ENNISKILLEN RAILWAY

Stock: 12 new locomotives built 1846-55.
3 secondhand locomotives acquired 1847-52.

Type	Years built	No. in class	Cylinders	Driving wheels	Locomotive Nos.
2-4-0	1846	1	15 x 24	4-11	1
2-2-2	1846	1	15 x 24	6-1	2
2-4-0	1847	1	15 x 24	5-6	3
2-2-0WT	1850	1	9 x 15	5-0	4
2-2-0WT	1852	4	10 x 16	5-2	5-8
2-2-0WT	1852	2	11 x 18	5-2	11, 12
2-4-0	1855	2	15 x 20	4-7	13, 14
Outside cylinders: all 2-2-0WT and 2-4-0 Nos. 13 & 14.					

No.	Type	Date	Builder	Rebuilt	Withdrawn	INWR No.	Remarks
1	2-4-0	1846	L	1857* 4-7 DW	INWR	17	Doubtful if numbered at first.
2	2-2-2	1846	L	1854* 2-4-0	1860		Doubtful if numbered at first. Sold to D&ER (No. 2) in 1860
3	2-4-0	1847	L		1851		Doubtful if numbered at first. Transferred to L&CR (No. 2).
3	2-4-0	(L&CR *)			INWR	18	Doubtful if numbered at first. Transferred from L&CR in 1851.
4	2-2-0WT	1850	A		INWR	19	
5	2-2-0WT	1852	K		INWR	20	
6	2-2-0WT	1852	K		INWR	21	
7	2-2-0WT	1852	K		INWR	22	
8	2-2-0WT	1852	K		INWR	23	
9	2-2-2	(1852)			1857		Purchased from Coates & Young, Belfast. See UR (either Achilles or Ajax).

No.	Type	Date	Builder Rebuilt		Withdrawn	INWR No.	Remarks
10	2-2-2	(1852)			1857		Purchased from Coates & Young, Belfast. See UR (either *Achilles* or *Ajax*).
11	2-2-0WT	1852	*		INWR	24	
12	2-2-0WT	1852	*		INWR	25	
13	2-4-0	1855	JJ		INWR	26	
14	2-4-0	1855	JJ		INWR	27	

11 locomotives taken into INWR stock 1862 (Nos. 1, 3-8, 11-14) and renumbered as shown.

DUNDALK & ENNSKILLEN RAILWAY
IRISH NORTH WESTERN RAILWAY

Stock: 25 new locomotives built 1848-74.
12 locomotives ex Londonderry & Enniskillen Railway 1860-2.
2 secondhand locomotives acquired 1866.

Type	Years built	No. in class	Cylinders	Driving wheels	Locomotive Nos.
2-2-2	1848	2	14 x 18	5-6	*, *
0-4-2	1848	2	14 x 18	4-4	*, *
2-2-2	1852-4	3	15 x 20	5-7	4-6
0-6-0	1855-6	2	16 x 24	5-0	7, 8
0-4-2	1858	2	16 x 22	5-0	9, 10
2-2-2	1859-61	3	15 x 20	5-6	11, 13, 14
0-4-2	1861-3	5	16 x 24	5-3	15, 16, 28, 29, 34
2-4-0	1866	2	15 x 21	6-0	32, 33
0-6-0	1871-2	2	17 x 24	5-0	35, 36
2-4-0	1873	1	15 x 21	5-6	31
2-4-0	1874	1	16 x 21	6-0	30
Outside cylinders: Nos. 30 & 31 0-6-0ST (secondhand).					

No.	Type	Date	Builder	Renumbered	Rebuilt	Withdrawn	NR No.	Remarks
*	2-2-2	1848	G	1 (1850)		NR	43	Used by W. Dargan 1849-50.
*	2-2-2	1848	G	2 (1850)		1874		Used by W. Dargan 1849-50.
*	0-4-2	1848	G	3 (1850)		NR	45	Used by W. Dargan 1849-50.
*	0-4-2	1848	G			1850		Used by W. Dargan 1849 and retained.
4	2-2-2	1852	SS			NR	46	
5	2-2-2	1854	SS			NR	47	
6	2-2-2	1854	SS			NR	48	
7	0-6-0	1855	G			NR	49	
8	0-6-0	1856	G			NR	50	
9	0-4-2	1858	SS			NR	51	
10	0-4-2	1858	SS			NR	52	
11	2-2-2	1859	BP		1875 2-4-0	NR	53	
12	2-4-0	(L&ER 2)				NR	54	Purchased 1860 from L&ER.
13	2-2-2	1861	BP			NR	55	
14	2-2-2	1861	BP			NR	56	
15	0-4-2	1861	N			NR	57	
16	0-4-2	1861	N			NR	58	
17	2-4-0	(L&ER 1)				NR	59	
18	2-4-0	(L&ER 3)			1871* 2-2-2	NR	60	May have been rebuilt in 1869 or 1870*.
19	2-2-0WT	(L&ER 4)				1873		
20	2-2-0WT	(L&ER 5)				NR	62	
21	2-2-0WT	(L&ER 6)				NR	63	
22	2-2-0WT	(L&ER 7)				1873		
23	2-2-0WT	(L&ER 8)				1875		
24	2-2-0WT	(L&ER 11)				NR	66	
25	2-2-0WT	(L&ER 12)				NR	67	
26	2-4-0	(L&ER 13)				NR	68	
27	2-4-0	(L&ER 14)				NR	69	
28	0-4-2	1863	N			NR	70	
29	0-4-2	1863	N			NR	71	
30	0-6-0ST	(Brassey)		19 (1873)		NR	61	See note.
31	0-6-0ST	(Brassey)		22 (1873)		NR	64	See note.
32	2-4-0	1866	D			NR	74	
33	2-4-0	1866	D			NR	75	
34	0-4-2	1867	D			NR	76	
35	0-6-0	1871	D			NR	77	
36	0-6-0	1872	D			NR	78	
31	2-4-0	1873	INWR			NR	73	
30	2-4-0	1874	INWR			NR	72	

Notes

30 & 31 purchased in 1866 from Brassey & Field (see Contractors List MW 4 and 18). It is not possible to state which locomotive became INWR No. 30 or which locomotive became INWR No. 31.

34 locomotives taken into NR stock 1876 (Nos. 1, 3-22, 24-36) and renumbered as shown (one 0-6-0 under construction - completed as GNR No. 44).

THE NORTHERN RAILWAY

Stock: 2 new locomotives built 1875.
22 locomotives taken into stock from Dublin & Drogheda Railway 1875.
19 locomotives taken into stock from Dublin & Belfast Junction Railway 1875.
34 locomotives taken into stock from Irish North Western Railway 1876.

Type	Years built	No. in class	Cylinders	Driving wheels	Locomotive Nos.
2-4-0	1875	2	16 x 22	5-7	3, 42

Nos.	Former Railway	Former Nos.	Withdrawn		Nos.	Former Railway	Former Nos.	Withdrawn
1, 2	D&DR	1, 2	GNR	Nos. unchanged	31-4	D&BJR	10-12, 15	GNR
3	D&DR	3	1875	No. unchanged	35/6	D&BJR	9, 14	GNR
4-22	D&DR	4-22	GNR	Nos. unchanged	37-41	D&BJR	18-22	GNR
23-6	D&BJR	2-5	GNR		43	INWR	1	GNR
27-9	D&BJR	13, 16, 17	GNR		45-64	INWR	3-22	GNR
30	D&BJR	1	GNR		66-78	INWR	24-36	GNR

Note
Nos. 44 and 65 were not used by NR. No. 42 was used for a new locomotive 1875.

No.	Type	Date	Builder	Withdrawn
3	2-4-0	1875	BP	GNR
42	2-4-0	1875	BP	GNR

76 locomotives taken into GNR stock in 1876 (Nos. 1-43, 45-64, 66-78) and numbers not altered.

NEWRY & ENNISKILLEN RAILWAY / NEWRY & ARMAGH RAILWAY

Stock: 5 new locomotives built 1854-78.
4 secondhand locomotives acquired 1853-64.

Type	Years built	No. in class	Cylinders	Driving wheels	Locomotive Nos.
0-4-0T	1854	1	13 x 18	4-6	2
*	1859*	1	*	*	1
0-4-2ST	1864	2	16 x 22	5-1	6, 7
0-4-2	1878	1	16 x 22	5-0	*
Outside cylinders: 6, 7.					

No.	Name	Type	Date	Builder	Rebuilt	Withdrawn	GNR No.	Remarks
3	Eniskillen*	2-2-0WT	(L&CR *)		1866 2-2-2WT	1874		Purchased 1853. Sold to Connor & Manisty(see Contractors List).
2	Newry	0-4-0T	1854	H(L)	* 0-4-2T	GNR	86	
1		*	1859	Fbn		1864		Possibly secondhand 1859. Sold 1864(to Watson & Overend?).
1		0-6-0		(W&O)		GNR	83	Purchased 1864(see Contractors List RS 1190).
4		0-6-0		(W&O)		GNR	84	Purchased 1864(see Contractors List RS 1280).
5		2-4-0T	*	*		GNR	85	Purchased 1864. Source and builder not identified - allegedly obtained from Watson & Overend(see Contractors List).
6		0-4-2ST	1864	VF	1872 0-4-2	GNR	81	
7		0-4-2ST	1864	VF	1865 0-4-2	GNR	82	
*		0-4-2	1878	SS		1880		Refused by GNR. Sold to J. B. Cooper(Manager of BCR) - see BCR.

It seems that *Eniskillen** and *Newry* were not numbered until 1858-59.
6 locomotives taken into GNR stock 1879 (Nos. 1. 2, 4-7) and renumbered as shown.

BELFAST CENTRAL RAILWAY

Stock: 4 new locomotives built 1868-80.
1 secondhand locomotive acquired 1883.

Type	Years built	No. in class	Cylinders	Driving wheels	Locomotive Nos.
0-6-0ST	1868-74	2	14 x 20	3-6	1, 2
2-4-0T	1878	1	14 x 20	5-0	3
4-4-0T	1880	1	15 x 20	5-0	4

No.	Type	Date	Builder	Withdrawn	GNR No.	Remarks
1	0-6-0ST	1868	BH	GNR	93	
2	0 6-0ST	1874	BH	GNR	94	
3	2-4-0T	1878	BP	GNR	95	
4	4-4-0T	1880	BP	GNR	96	
*	0-4-2	(1883)		1885		Purchased from J.B. Cooper (see N&AR). Refused by GNR in 1885 and sold in 1886 to B&NCR (No. 50).

4 locomotives taken into GNR stock 1885 and renumbered as shown.

NEWRY, WARRENPOINT & ROSTREVOR RAILWAY

Stock: 7 new locomotives built 1848-82.
1 secondhand locomotive acquired 1866.

Type	Years built	No. in class	Cylinders	Driving wheels	Locomotive Nos.
2-2-2	1848-9	3	15 x 20	5-8	*
2-2-2T	1850	1	9 x 12	4-0	3
2-2-2T	1851	2	11 x 16	5-0	1, 2
2-4-0T	1882	1	14 x 20	5-0	*Warrenpoint*

No.	Name	Type	Date	Builder	Withdrawn	GNR No.	Remarks
1		2-2-2	1848	BCR	1850-2*		See note.
2		2-2-2	1848	BCR	1850-2*		See note.
3		2-2-2	1849	BCR	1850*		See note.
3	*Victoria*	2-2-2T	1850	G	1885		May possibly have been named *Newry* at some time.
1	*Rostrevor*	2-2-2T	1851	G	GNR	100	Possibly not named until 1883 - perhaps the numbers were
2	*Mourne**	2-2-2T	1851	G	1886		removed
4	*Drogheda*	4-cpld	(Grendon)		1882		See note.
-	*Warrenpoint*	2-4-0T	1882	BP	GNR	90	Possibly numbered 5.

Notes

1-3 were presumably numbered such from new. Purchased by Dargan and transferred by him to his W&LR haulage contract in 1851-2 (No. 3 became W&LR No. 8 and the others Nos. 9 and 10).

4 was purchased from Grendon in 1866 (see Contractors List, Grendon locomotive). Sold to McRea & McFarland (see Contractors List).

2 locomotives taken into GNR stock 1886 (*Rostrevor* and *Warrenpoint*) and renumbered as shown.

CASTLEBLAYNEY, KEADY & ARMAGH RAILWAY

Stock: 2 secondhand locomotives acquired 1911.

Name	Type	GNR No.	Remarks
Kells	0-4-0ST	203	Purchased from R. Worthington 1911 (HE 859 - see Contractors List).
Mulligan	0-6-0T	204	Purchased from R. Worthington 1911 (HE 482 - see Contractors List).

2 locomotives taken into GNR stock 1913 and renumbered in 1915 as shown.

GREAT NORTHERN RAILWAY
GREAT NORTHERN RAILWAY BOARD

Stock: 270 new locomotives built 1876-1948 (11 for Northern Division (ND) numbered separately when new).
76 locomotives taken into stock from Northern Railway 1876.
38 locomotives taken into stock from Ulster Railway 1876.
6 locomotives taken into stock from Newry & Armagh Railway 1879.
4 locomotives taken into stock from Belfast Central Railway 1885.
2 locomotives taken into stock from Newry, Warrenpoint & Rostrevor Railway 1886.
2 locomotives taken into stock from Castleblayney, Ready & Armagh Railway 1913.
1 locomotive purchased from Sligo, Leitrim & Northern Counties Railway 1940.
7 new steam railmotors built 1905-6.

Class	Type	Years built	No. in class	Cylinders	Driving wheels	Locomotive Nos. (+ later renumbered)
E	0-6-0	1876	1	17 x 24	5-0	44+
G	2-4-0	1877-83	6	16 x 22	5-7	24, 25, 46+, 47, 59+, 80+
B	0-6-0	1877	4	16 x 24	4-7	25+, 62, 63, 65
		1879-80	5	17 x 24	4-7	26, 27, 34, 66+, 67
H	2-4-0	1880-1	4	16 x 22	6-1½	84-87
A	0-6-0	1882-91	15	17 x 24	4-7¾	28, 31, 33, 60, 61, 64+, 79+, 80, 81, 82+, 83+, 145, 146, 149, 150
JS	4-2-2	1885	2	16 x 22	6-7	88, 89
J	4-4-0	1885-9	12	16 x 22	5-7	17-21, 45+, 48+, 115-119
BT	4-4-0T	1885	3	14 x 18	4-7	97, 98, 99+
		1887-93	10	15 x 18	4-7	2-8, 91+, 92+, 100+
P	4-4-0	1892-5	4	17 x 24	6-7	72, 73, 82+, 83+ (see note)
		1892-1906	8	17 x 24	5-7	51-54, 88, 89, 104, 105 (see note)
AL	0-6-0	1893-6	11	17 x 24	4-7	29, 32, 36, 55-59, 151-153+
JT	2-4-2T	1895-6	2	16 x 22	5-7	93, 94
		1898-1902	3	17 x 22	5-7	13+, 14+, 90
		1898	1	16½ x 22	5-7	95
PP	4-4-0	1896-1911	14	18 x 24	6-7	12, 25, 42-46, 50, 70, 71, 74, 106, 107, 129 (see note)

PP		1898	3	18½ x 24	6-7	75-77 (see note)
Q	4-4-0	1899-1904	13	18½ x 26	6-7	120-25, 130-36
PG	0-6-0	1899-1904	7	18½ x 24	4-7	10, 11, 78+, 100-103
QG	0-6-0	1903-4	4	18 x 26	4-7	152-155
QL	4-4-0	1904-10	8	18½ x 26	6-7	24, 113, 114, 126-28, 156, 157
QGT	0-6-2T	1905	2	18½ x 26	4-7	98, 99
LQG	0-6-0	1906-8	11	18½ x 26	4-7	78+, 108, 110, 111, 158-64
RT	0-6-4T	1908-11	4	17 x 24	4-3	22, 23, 166, 167
NQG	0-6-0	1911	5	18 x 26	4-7	9, 38, 39, 109, 112
NLQG	0-6-0	1911	1	18½ x 26	4-7	165
QGT2	0-6-2T	1911	2	18½ x 26	4-7	168, 169
S	4-4-0	1913	5	19 x 26	6-7	170-174
SG	0-6-0	1913	5	19 x 26	5-1	37+, 40+, 41+, 137+, 138+
T	4-4-2T	1913	5	18 x 24	5-9	185-189
S2	4-4-0	1915	3	19 x 26	6-7	190-192
SG2	0-6-0	1915-25	10	19 x 26	5-1	15-9, 180-4
U	4-4-0	1915-48	10	18 x 24	5-9	196-205
SG3	0-6-0	1920-1	15	19½ x 26	5-1	6-8, 13, 14, 20, 47-49, 96, 97, 117, 118, 201+, 202+
T2	4-4-2T	1921-30	20	18 x 24	5-9	1-5, 21, 30, 62-66, 115, 116, 139, 142-44 147+, 148+
CRANE	0-6-0CT	1928	1	14 x 20	3-4	31
V	4-4-0	1932	5	17¼ x 26 (1) 19 x 26 (2)	6-7	83-87
UG	0-6-0	1937-48	10	18 x 24	5-1	78-82, 145-49
VS	4-4-0	1948	5	15¼ x 26 (3)	6-7	206-210
C	0-6-0	1876-9	6	17 x 24	4-7	ND 3+, 14-16+, 42+, 43+
H	2-4-0	1876	1	16 x 22	5-6	ND I+
K	0-4-2	1880-2	3	16 x 22	4-6	ND 2+, 4+, 9+
G	2-2-2	1884	1	15 x 20	5-6	ND 11+

Notes

P Class was divided into two groups (according to coupled wheel diameters):-

    P 5-6   (Nos. 51-54, 88, 89, 104, 105).

    P 6-6   (Nos. 72, 73, 82, 83).

From 1928 PP class was divided into two groups (according to boiler diameter) - PP 4-3 or PP 4-6.

GNR locomotive classification system.

The class letters shown above were developed from a drawing of crank axles prepared in 1883. The cranks were listed from A to N as follows:

A	Beyer Peacock	24 in.		H	Beyer, Peacock/UR	22 in. (double frame)
B	Sharp, Stewart	24 in.		J	Beyer, Peacock	22 in. (including Nos. 84-7, later H and Nos. 44-6 ex D&BJR)
C	UR/GNR	24 in.				
D	D&BJR 0-6-0	24 in.		K	Sharp, Stewart	22 in.
E	Dubs	24 in.		L	Dubs/INWR	22 in.
F	Beyer, Peacock	24 in. (double frame)		M	UR	20 in. (double frame)
G	Beyer, Peacock	22 in.		N	Beyer, Peacock	20 in. (singles)

Various other classes then followed as O to X, but not in any particular order.

O	Longridge INWR	22 in.		T	Grendon	18 in.
P	Sharp, Stewart	20 in. (double frame)		U	Sharp, Stewart	20 in. (2-2-2 1854)
Q	Sharp, Stewart	20 in. (double frame)		V	Manning, Wardle	17 in. (0-6-0ST)
R	Sharp, Stewart	18 in. (double frame)		W	Jones	20 in. (2-4-0)
S	Sharp, Stewart	22 in. ex D&BJR 0-4-2		X	Vulcan Foundry	22 in. (0-4-2 ex N&AR)

Letters O, P, Q, R and T were subsequently used again.

O	Beyer, Peacock	20 in. (2-4-0T NW&RR)		R	Beyer, Peacock	20in. 4-4-0T ex BCR (previously O and then BP)
P	Beyer, Peacock	24 in.		T	Beyer, Peacock	18 in. 4-4-0T later BT
Q	Beyer, Peacock	26 in.				

These letters developed into a class letter system as follows:

A	0-6-0	24 in.; also AL 0-6-0		P	4-4-0	24 in.; also PP 4-4-0 and PG 0-6-0
B	0-6-0	24 in.		Q	4-4-0	26 in.; also QG, LQG, NQG, NLQG 0-6-0, QL 4-4-0, QGT, QGT2 0-6-2T
C	0-6-0	24 in.				
D	0-6-0	24 in.		RT	0-6-4T	24 in.
E	0-6-0	24 in.		S	4-4-0	26 in.; also S2 4-4-0 , SG , SG2, SG3 0-6-0
G	2-4-0	22 in.		T	4-4-2T	24 in.; also T2 4-4-2T
H	2-4-0	22 in.		U	4-4-0	24 in.; also UG 0-6-0
J	4-4-0	22 in.; also JS 4-2-2, JT 2-4-2T		V	4-4-0	26 in.; also VS 4-4-0

When locomotives of classes P, PG, PP, Q, QG, QL, LQG, NQG, NLQG, QGT and QGT2 were superheated an "s" suffix was added to the class letter, but class T became T1.

76 locomotives taken into stock from NR in 1876 (not renumbered in 1876).

No.	Name	Type	Class	Renumbered	Rebuilt	Withdrawn	Remarks
1	*Nestor**	0-4-2	P	1A (1887)		1892	
2	*Mars**	2-2-2	Q	23 (1877), 23A (1888)		1894	
3		2-4-0	G	23 (1888), 23A (1908)		1911	
4	*Drogheda*	2-4-0				1888	
5	*Hercules**	0-6-0	A	29 (1889), 29A (1895)		1911	
6	*Samson**	0-4-2	P	2 (1877), 2A (1887)		1892	
7	*Venus**	2-2-2	T	7A (1890)		1891	
8		2-2-2ST				1885-7*	
9	*Saturn*	2-4-0				1885	
10	*Mercury**	0-4-2	G	10A (1904)		1905	May have been *Ajax*.
11	*Ajax**	0-4-2	G			1903	
12	*Achilles*	2-4-0	G	12A (1911)		1911	
13	*Ulysses**	2-2-2	N	13A (1895)		1896	
14	*Jupiter**	2-2-2	N	14A (1895)		1896	
15	*Aurora*	2-2-2	N	15A (1898)		1901	
16	*Jupiter**	2-2-2	N	16A (1898)		1898	
17	*Apollo**	2-2-2	U	17A (1885)		1886	
18	*Diana**	2-2-2	U	18A (1883)		1886	
19	*Pluto*	2-4-0				1887	
20	*Vulcan**	0-4-2	G	9 (1887), 9A (1911), 201(1914)		1915	
21	*Neptune**	0-6-0	A	32 (1889), 21A (1894)		1908	
22	*Neputne**	2-2-2				1888*	
23		2-2-2				1876	
24		2-2-2				1877	
25		2-2-2				1877	
26		2-2-2				1879	
27		2-2-2				1879	
28		2-2-2WT	R			1885-7*	
29		2-2-2WT	R			1889	
30		2-4-0				1885	
31		0-4-2	B	31A (1889)		1903	
32		0-4-2	S			1885-7*	
33		0-4-2	S			1890	
34		0-4-2				1880	
35		0-4-2		35A (1898)		1900	
36		0-4-2			1879 0-6-0	1893	
37		2-4-0	J	44 (1898), 44A (1911)		1914	
38		2-4-0	J	45 (1898), 45A (1910), 201 (1915)		1920	
39		2-4-0	J	46 (1898), 46A (1910)		1911	
40		0-6-0	D	40A (1913), 40 (1913)	1913	1937	
41		0-6-0	D	41A (1913), 41 (1913)	1915	1934	
42		2-4-0	G	42A (1911)		1912	
43		2-2-2				1886-7*	
45		0-4-2				1885	
46		2-2-2				1880-3*	
47		2-2-2				1880-3*	
48		2-2-2				1885	
49		0-6-0				1885	
50		0-6-0		59 (1885), 59A (1894)		1903	
51		0-4-2		51A (1891-2*)		1895	
52		0-4-2				1885	
53		2-4-0	G	54 (1892), 22 (1895), 22A (1908)	1889	1914	
54		2-4-0				1890	
55		2-2-2	N	13 (1895), 13A (1902)	1890	1910	
56		2-2-2	N	14 (1895), 14A (1902)		1907	
57		0-4-2	B	102 (1895), 102A (1901)		1907	
58		0-4-2	B	103 (1895), 103A (1898)		1902	
59		2-4-0		79 (1877)		1879	
60		2-2-2				1892	
61		0-6-0ST	V	61A (1883), 91 (1885)		1891	
62		2-2-0WT				1876	
63		2-2-0WT				1876	
64		0-6-0ST	V	64A (1883), 92 (1885)		1891	
66		2-2-0WT				1879	
67		2-2-0WT				1879	
68		2-4-0	W	68A (1892)		1894	
69		2-4-0	W	69A (1892)		1896	
70		0-4-2	B	100 (1896), 100A (1898)		1901	
71		0-4-2	B	101 (1896), 101A (1899)		1904	
72		2-4-0	J	43 (1895), 43A (1911), 202 (1914)		1921	
73		2-4-0				1892	
74		2-4-0	L	124 (1895), 124A (1902)		1906	
75		2-4-0	L	125 (1895), 125A (1902)		1904	
76		0-4-2	A	44 (1888), 78 (1898), 78A (1898) 78 (1906), 78A (1908)		1909	
77		0-6-0	E	38 (1898), 38A (1911), 193 (1913)	1915	1948	
78		0-6-0	E	39 (1898), 39A (1911), 194 (1913)	1915	1948	

38 locomotives taken into stock from UR in 1876. (Not renumbered in 1876, but survivors were altered by the addition of 100 to numbers in 1885).

(Lens of Sutton)

▲ GNR 2-4-2T JT Class No. 90 (1898 GNR Dundalk)

(M.P. Rowledge)

▼ GNR 0-6-0 SG3 Class No. 47 (1920 Beyer, Peacock)

(Real Photos)

▲ GNR 2-4-0 H Class No. 86 (1880 Beyer, Peacock)

(M.P. Rowledge)

▼ GNR 0-6-0 PG Class No. 100 (1900 GNR Dundalk)

No.	Name	Type	Class	Renumbered	Rebuilt	Withdrawn
2	*Blackwater*	2-2-2				1880
3	*Erne*	0-4-2				1877
4	*Owenreagh*	0-4-2				1879
5	*Typhoon*	0-4-2	K	105 (1885), 105A (1906)		1911
6	*Tornado*	0-4-2	K	106 (1885), 106A (1906)		1906
7	*Cyclone*	0-4-2	K	107 (1885), 107A (1906)		1908
8	*Lucifer*	2-4-0	H	108 (1885), 108A (1893) 113 (1895), 113A (1904)		1906
9	*Pluto*	2-2-2				1882
10	*Jupiter*	2-4-0	M	110 (1885), 122 (1895) 122A (1898), 112A (1899)		1905
11	*Cerberus*	2-2-2				1884
12	*Vulcan*	2-4-0	H	112 (1885), 122 (1899), 122A (1904)		1905
13	*Spitfire*	2-4-0		113 (1885)		1888
16	*Bann*	0-4-2				1877
17	*Shamrock*	2-4-0		117 (1885), 117A (1885)		1886-7*
18	*Rose*	2-4-0		118 (1885), 118A (1885)		1887
19	*Thistle*	2-2-2		119 (1885), 119A (1885)		1886-7*
20	*Ulidia*	2-2-2	H	120 (1885), 120A (1904)	1879 2-4-0	1906
21	*Dalriada*	2-2-2	H	121 (1885), 121A (1904)	1877 2-4-0	1914
22	*Iveagh*	2-2-2		122 (1885), 110 (1895), 110A (1899)		1900
23	*Tyrone*	2-4-0	H	123 (1885)		1903
24	*Breffney*	2-2-2		124 (1885)		1895
25	*Clanaboy*	2-2-2		125 (1885), 75 (1895)		1897
26	*Ulster*	2-4-0	H	126 (1885), 126A (1907)		1909
27	*Munster*	2-4-0	H	127 (1885), 127A (1907)		1911
28	*Leinster*	2-4-0	H	128 (1885), 128A (1907)		1914
29	*Connaught*	2-4-0	H	129 (1885), 129A (1911)		1912
30	*Nore*	0-4-2	K	130 (1885)		1894
31	*Ovoca*	0-4-2	K	131 (1885), 131A (1901)		1909
32	*Foyle*	0-4-2	K	132 (1885), 132A (1901)		1904
33	*Shannon*	0-4-2	F	133 (1885), 109 (1899), 109A (1911)		1913
34	*Liffey*	0-4-2	F	134 (1885), 110 (1899), 110A (1908)		1911
35	*Carntual*	0-4-2	F	135 (1885), 111 (1899), 111A (1908)		1909
36	*Donard*	0-4-2	F	136 (1885), 112 (1899), 112A (1911)		1912
37	*Stromboli*	0-6-0	C	137 (1885), 137A (1913), 137 (1914)		1939
38	*Volcano*	0-6-0	C	138 (1885), 138A (1913), 138 (1914)		1948
39	*Tempest*	0-4-2	K	139 (1885), 104 (1895), 104A (1906)		1908
40	*Siroco*	0-4-2	K	140 (1885), 108 (1895)		1907
41	*Simoom*	0-4-2	K	141 (1885), 130 (1895), 78 (1901)		1906

11 locomotives built for the Northern Division 1876-84

No.	Name	Type	Class	Date	Builder	Renumbered	Withdrawn
14	*Vesuvius*	0-6-0	C	1876	GNR-ND	114 (1885), 144 (1886)	1924
15	*Hecla*	0-6-0	C	1876	GNR-ND	115 (1885), 147 (1889)	1924
1	*Lagan*	2-4-0	H	1876	GNR-ND	101 (1885), 114 (1886), 114A (1904)	1913
3	*Etna*	0-6-0	C	1877	GNR-ND	103 (1885), 139 (1895)	1925
16	*Teneriffe*	0-6-0	C	1878	GNR-ND	116 (1885), 148 (1889)	1925
42	*Torrent*	0-6-0	C	1879	BP	142 (1885)	1925
43	*Avalanche*	0-6-0	C	1879	BP	143 (1885)	1925
4	*Owenreagh*	0-4-2	K	1880	GNR-ND	104 (1885), 104A (1895)	1899
2	*Blackwater*	0-4-2	K	1881	GNR-ND	102 (1885), 102A (1894), 100A (1901)	1901
9	*Pluto*	0-4-2	K	1882	GNR-ND	109 (1885), 109A (1899)	1907
11	*North Star*	2-2-2	G	1884	GNR-ND	111 (1885), 111A (1899)	1901

259 new locomotives built 1876-1948.
15 absorbed/secondhand locomotives acquired 1879-1940.

Most were inside cylinder with round top saturated boilers, conversions to superheating being indicated in the following list by the "s" suffix to the class letter in the rebuilt column (except T, which became T1). The following classes were built with superheaters, Belpaire boilers, etc:

Belpaire boiler:	4-4-0 VS
Superheater	4-4-0 S, S2, U, V, VS; 0-6-0 SG, SG2, SG3; 4-4-2T T2
Compound (3-cylinder Smith)	4-4-0 V
Outside cylinders (2):	0-6-0CT No. 31
Multi-cylindered (3)	4-4-0 V, VS

(CIE, DEW (Dundalk Engineering Works) or UTA in withdrawal column refer to allocation of GNR locomotives when the stock was divided in October 1958.

No.	Name	Type	Class	Date	Builder	Renumbered	Rebuilt	Withdrawn	Remarks
44		0-6-0	E	1876	GNR-BS	76 (1888), 37 (1898), 37A (1913), 37 (1913)	1915	1948	See note.
24		2-4-0	G	1877	BP	24A (1910)		1914	
25	*Meath*	0-6-0	B	1877	SS	6 (1877), 30 (1889)		1925	
25		2-4-0	G	1877	BP	25A (1911)		1913	
59		2-4-0	G	1877	BP	50 (1885), 50A (1911)		1914	
62	*Tyrone*	0-6-0	B	1877	SS			1930	

No.	Name	Type	Class	Date	Builder	Renumbered	Rebuilt	Withdrawn	Remarks
63	Donegal	0-6-0	B	1877	SS			1930	
65	Derry	0-6-0	B	1877	SS			1930	
80		2-4-0	G	1877	BP	49 (1885), 49A (1913) 49 (1914)		1921	
27	Dublin	0-6-0	B	1879	SS			1930	
66	Monaghan	0-6-0	B	1879	SS	27 (1930), 149 (1932)		1938	
67	Fermanagh	0-6-0	B	1879	SS			1930	
81		0-4-2	X	(N&AR 6)		81A (1886)		1887	
82		0-4-2	X	(N&AR 7)		82A (1886)		1896	
83		0-6-0		(N&AR 1)		83A (1882)		1886	
84		0-6-0		(N&AR 4)		84A (1881)		1881	
85		2-4-0T		(N&AR 5)		85A (1881)		1894	
86	Newry	0-4-2T		(N&AR 2)		86A (1880)		1884	See note.
26	Armagh	0-6-0	B	1880	SS			1932	
34	Louth	0-6-0	B	1880	SS			1932	
86		2-4-0	H	1880	BP			1932	
87		2-4-0	H	1880	BP			1931	
84		2-4-0	H	1881	BP			1932	
85		2-4-0	H	1881	BP			1932	
79	Cavan	0-6-0	A	1882	BP	69 (1937)		1940	See note.
83	Newry	0-6-0	A	1882	BP	69 (1892)		1937	
46		2-4-0	G	1883	BP	48 (1898), 48A (1913) 48 (1913)		1921	
47		2-4-0	G	1883	BP	47A (1913), 47 (1914)		1921	
61	Sligo	0-6-0	A	1883	BP			1935	
64	Down	0-6-0	A	1883	BP	67 (1930)		1937	
17		4-4-0	J	1885	BP			1924	
18		4-4-0	J	1885	BP			1924	
45	Pansy	4-4-0	J	1885	BP	15 (1898)		1924	See note.
48		4-4-0	J	1885	BP	16 (1898)		1924	
88	Victoria	4-2-2	JS	1885	BP			1904	
89	Albert	4-2-2	JS	1885	BP			1904	
93		0-6-0ST		(BCR 1)				1892	
94		0-6-0ST		(BCR 2)				1895*	
95		2-4-0T	O	(BCR 3)				1898	
96		4-4-0T	BP	(BCR 4)		96A (1906), 195 (1913)		1950	See note.
97	Lisburn	4-4-0T	BT	1885	BP			1921	See note.
98		4-4-0T	BT	1885	BP	98A (1905)		1910	
99	Windsor	4-4-0T	BT	1885	BP	99A (1905), 96 (1906)		1921	See note.
117	Shamrock	4-4-0	J	1885	BP			1921	
118	Rose	4-4-0	J	1885	BP			1921	See note.
80	Antmim	0-6-0	A	1886	BP			1936	
81	Leitrim	0-6-0	A	1886	BP			1936	
82	Kildare	0-6-0	A	1886	BP	68 (1892)		1948	
90	Warrenpoint	2-4-0T	O	(NW&RR 5*)				1898	
100	Rostrevor	2-2-2T		(NW&RR 1*)		100A (1887)		1892	
2		4-4-0T	BT	1887	GNR			1921	
19		4-4-0	J	1887	BP			1924	
20		4-4-0	J	1887	BP			1921	
100		4-4-0T	BT	1887	GNR	1 (1888), 119 (1921)	1921 0-6-0T	1935	
119	Thistle	4-4-0	J	1887	BP			1921	See note.
3		4-4-0T	BT	1888	GNR			1921	
4		4-4-0T	BT	1888	GNR			1921	
28	Wexford	0-6-0	A	1888	BP			1956	
145	Carlow	0-6-0	A	1888	BP			1937	
146	Wicklow	0-6-0	A	1888	BP			1937	
5		4-4-0T	BT	1889	GNR			1921	
6		4-4-0T	BT	1889	GNR			1920	
21		4-4-0	J	1889	BP			1924	
115	Lily	4-4-0	J	1889	BP			1924	
116	Violet	4-4-0	J	1889	BP			1924	
31	Galway	0-6-0	A	1890	BP			1927	See note.
60	Dundalk	0-6-0	A	1890	GNR			CIE	
149	Roscommon	0-6-0	A	1890	BP			1931	See note.
150	Longford	0-6-0	A	1890	BP			CIE	
7	Ardee	4-4-0T	BT	1891	GNR			1920	See note.
33	Belfast	0-6-0	A	1891	GNR			CIE	
51	Hyacinth	4-4-0	P	1892	BP		1925 Ps	1950	See note.
52	Snowdrop	4-4-0	P	1892	BP		1923 Ps	1950	See note.
53		4-4-0	P	1892	BP		1924 Ps	1950	
82	Daisy	4-4-0	P	1892	BP	27 (1931)	1932 Ps	CIE	See note.
83	Narcissus	4-4-0	P	1892	BP	26 (1931)	1931 Ps	1957	See note.
8		4-4-0T	BT	1893	GNR			1921	
36	Waterford	0-6-0	AL	1893	BP			1957	
91		4-4-0T	BT	1893	GNR	13 (1920)		1921	
92		4-4-0T	BT	1893	GNR	14 (1920), 4 (1921)		1921	
32	Drogheda	0-6-0	AL	1894	GNR			UTA	
59	Kilkenny	0-6-0	AL	1894	BP			CIE	

No.	Name	Type	Class	Date	Builder	Renumbered	Rebuilt	Withdrawn	Remarks
151	Westmeath	0-6-0	AL	1894	BP	141 (1896)		1957	
152	Limerick	0-6-0	AL	1894	BP	140 (1896)		1957	
153	Clare	0-6-0	AL	1894	BP	35 (1895)		CIE	
29	Enniskillen	0-6-0	AL	1895	GNR			CIE	
54		4-4-0	P	1895	BP		1927 Ps	1950	
55	Portadown	0-6-0	AL	1895	GNR			CIE	
57	Cork	0-6-0	AL	1895	BP			CIE	
72	Daffodil	4-4-0	P	1895	BP		1931 Ps	CIE	See note.
73	Primrose	4-4-0	P	1895	BP		1931 Ps	CIE	See note.
93	Sutton	2-4-2T	JT	1895	GNR		1917	1955	See note.
56	Omagh	0-6-0	AL	1896	GNR			UTA	
58	Kerry	0-6-0	AL	1896	BP			CIE	
70	Precursor	4-4-0	PP	1896	BP		1920 PP 4-6 1930 PPs 4-3	1957	
71	Bundoran	4-4-0	PP	1896	BP		1920 PP 4-6 1930 PPs 4-6 1943 PPs 4-3	CIE	
74	Rostrevor	4-4-0	PP	1896	BP		1917 PP 4-6 1930 PPs 4-6	UTA	
94	Howth	2-4-2T	JT	1896	GNR		1919	1956	
75	Jupiter	4-4-0	PP	1898	BP		1919 PP 4-6 1931 PPs 4-3	CIE	
76	Hercules	4-4-0	PP	1898	BP		1919 PP 4-6 1931 PPs 4-6	UTA	
77	Achilles	4-4-0	PP	1898	BP		1920 PP 4-6 1931 PPs 4-6	1957	
90	Aster	2-4-2T	JT	1898	GNR			1957	
95	Crocus	2-4-2T	JT	1898	GNR			1955	
78	Strabane	0-6-0	PG	1899	GNR	151 (1901)	1921 PGs	UTA	
133	Apollo	4-4-0	Q	1899	NR		1919 Qs	1957	
134	Adonis	4-4-0	Q	1899	NR		1921 Qs	1951	
135	Cyclops	4-4-0	Q	1899	NR		1922 Qs	UTA	
136	Minerva	4-4-0	Q	1899	NR		1920 Qs	CIE	
100	Clones	0-6-0	PG	1900	GNR		1924 PGs	UTA	
101	Balmoral	0-6-0	PG	1901	NR		1927 PGs	UTA	
102	Bellek	0-6-0	PG	1901	NR		1928 PGs	UTA	
103	Dunleer	0-6-0	PG	1901	NR		1929 PGs	UTA	
130	Saturn	4-4-0	Q	1901	NR		1922 Qs	CIE	
131	Uranus	4-4-0	Q	1901	NR		1920 Qs	CIE	
132	Mercury	4-4-0	Q	1901	NR		1922 Qs	CIE	
13	Tulip	2-4-2T	JT	1902	GNR	91 (1920)		CIE	
14	Viola	2-4-2T	JT	1902	GNR	92 (1920)		1956	
124	Cerberus	4-4-0	Q	1902	NR		1924 Qs	1957	
125	Daphne	4-4-0	Q	1902	NR		1924 Qs	UTA	
11	Dromore	0-6-0	PG	1903	GNR		1924 PGs	UTA	
122	Vulcan	4-4-0	Q	1903	NBL		1924 Qs	UTA	
123	Lucifer	4-4-0	Q	1903	NBL		1923 Qs	CIE	
152	Lurgan	0-6-0	QG	1903	NBL		1926 QGs	CIE	
153	Scarva	0-6-0	QG	1903	NBL		1928 QGs	CIE	
10	Bessbrook	0-6-0	PG	1904	GNR		1925 PGs	UTA	
88	Victoria	4-4-0	P	1904	GNR		1927 Ps	1956	
89	Albert	4-4-0	P	1904	GNR		1923 Ps	1956	
113	Neptune	4-4-0	QL	1904	NBL		1924 QLs	1957	See note.
114	Theseus	4-4-0	QL	1904	NBL		1923 QLs	1932	See note.
120	Venus	4-4-0	Q	1904	BP		1923 Qs	1957	
121	Pluto	4-4-0	Q	1904	BP		1924 Qs	UTA	
154	Lambeg	0-6-0	QG	1904	NBL		1928 QGs	CIE	
155	Navan	0-6-0	QG	1904	NBL		1926 QGs	CIE	
156	Pandora	4-4-0	QL	1904	NBL		1925 QLs	UTA	
157	Orpheus	4-4-0	QL	1904	NBL		1922 QLs	UTA	See note.
98		0-6-2T	QGT	1905	RS		1932 QGTs	1957	
99		0-6-2T	QGT	1905	RS		1935 QGTs	CIE	
104	Ovoca	4-4-0	P	1906	GNR		1924 Ps	1956	
105	Foyle	4-4-0	P	1906	GNR		1925 Ps	CIE	
106	Tornado	4-4-0	PP	1906	BP		1928 PPs 4-3 1944 PPs 4-6	CIE	
107	Cyclone	4-4-0	PP	1906	BP		1929 PPs 4-6	UTA	
158	Balleybay	0-6-0	LQG	1906	NBL		1921 LQGs	CIE	
159	Cootehill	0-6-0	LQG	1906	NBL		1929 LQGs	CIE	See note.
160	Culloville	0-6-0	LQG	1906	NBL		1926 LQGs	UTA	
126	Diana	4-4-0	QL	1907	NBL		1923 QLs	1957	
127	Erebus	4-4-0	QL	1907	NBL		1928 QLs	UTA	See note.
128	Mars	4-4-0	QL	1907	NBL		1923 QLs	1957	
22		0-6-4T	RT	1908	BP			UTA	
23		0-6-4T	RT	1908	BP			UTA	
78	Pettigo	0-6-0	LQG	1908	GNR	119 (1937)	1929 LQGs	UTA	
108	Pomeroy	0-6-0	LQG	1908	GNR		1928 LQGs	UTA	
110	Laytown	0-6-0	LQG	1908	NBL		1930 LQGs	CIE	

34

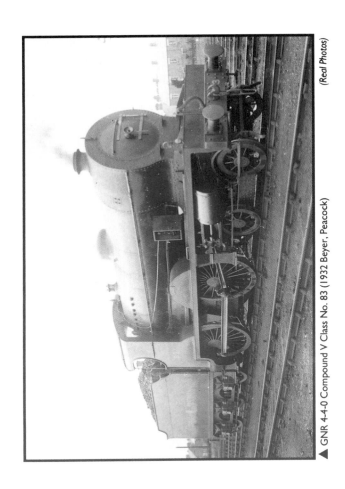

▲ GNR 4-4-0 Compound V Class No. 83 (1932 Beyer, Peacock)   (Real Photos)

▼ GNR 0-6-0 UG Class No. 79 (1937 GNR Dundalk)   (Real Photos)

▲ GNR 4-4-2T T2 Class No. 1 (1921 Beyer, Peacock)   (Real Photos)

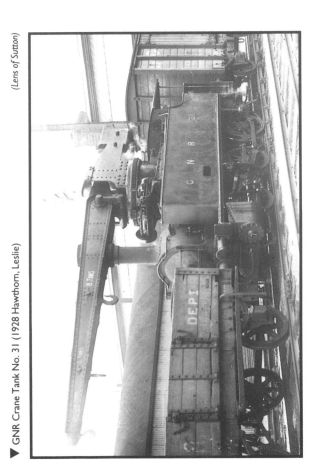

▼ GNR Crane Tank No. 31 (1928 Hawthorn, Leslie)   (Lens of Sutton)

35

No.	Name	Type	Class	Date	Builder	Renumbered	Rebuilt	Withdrawn	Remarks
111	*Malahide*	0-6-0	LQG	1908	NBL		1928 LQGs	UTA	
161	*Adavoyle*	0-6-0	LQG	1908	NBL		1929 LQGs	CIE	
162	*Ballyroney*	0-6-0	LQG	1908	NBL		1927 LQGs	UTA	
163	*Banbridge*	0-6-0	LQG	1908	NBL		1927 LOGs	CIE	
164	*Fintona*	0-6-0	LQG	1908	NBL		1930 LQGs	CIE	
45	*Siroco*	4-4-0	PP	1909	BP		1928 PPs 4-6	1957	
46	*Typhoon*	4-4-0	PP	1909	BP		1927 PPs 4-3	UTA	
							1945 PPs 4-6		
24	*Juno*	4-4-0	QL	1910	BP		1924 QLs	1957	
9	*Kells*	0-6-0	NQG	1911	NW		1930 NQGs	UTA	
							1945 LQGs		
12	*Ulster*	4-4-0	PP	1911	BP		1930 PPs 4-3	CIE	See note.
							1943 PPs 4-6		
25	*Liffey*	4-4-0	PP	1911	GNR		1927 PPs 4-3	1957	See note.
							1932 PPs 4-6		
38	*Kesh*	0-6-0	NQG	1911	NW		1931 NQGs	CIE	
39	*Beragh*	0-6-0	NQG	1911	NW		1931 NQGs	UTA	
							1956 LQGs		
42	*Munster*	4-4-0	PP	1911	BP		1929 PPs 4-3	UTA	
							1942 PPs 4-6		
43	*Lagan*	4-4-0	PP	1911	GNR		1928 PPs 4-3	UTA	
							1941 PPs 4-6		
44	*Leinster*	4-4-0	PP	1911	BP		1928 PPs 4-3	CIE	
							1944 PPs 4-6		
50	*Donard*	4-4-0	PP	1911	BP		1929 PPs 4-3	UTA	
							1939 PPs 4-6		
109	*Moira*	0-6-0	NQG	1911	NW		1930 LQGs	UTA	
112	*Keady*	0-6-0	NQG	1911	NW		1931 NQGs	CIE	
129	*Connaught*	4-4-0	PP	1911	BP		1929 PPs 4-3	1957	
165	*Newbliss*	0-6-0	NLQG	1911	NW		1929 LQGs	UTA	
166		0-6-4T	RT	1911	BP			UTA	
167		0-6-4T	RT	1911	BP			UTA	
168		0-6-2T	QGT2	1911	RS			1957	
169		0-6-2T	QGT2	1911	RS			1957	
37		0-6-0	SG	1913	BP	47 (1913), 177 (1913)		CIE	
40		0-6-0	SG	1913	BP	48 (1913), 178 (1913)		CIE	
41		0-6-0	SG	1913	BP	49 (1913), 179 (1913)		CIE	
137		0-6-0	SG	1913	BP	175 (1913)		UTA	
138		0-6-0	SG	1913	BP	176 (1913)		UTA	
170	*Errigal*	4-4-0	S	1913	BP		1939	CIE	See note.
171	*Slieve Gullion*	4-4-0	S	1913	BP		1938	CIE	See note.
172	*Slieve Donard*	4-4-0	S	1913	BP		1938	UTA	See note.
173	*Galtee More*	4-4-0	S	1913	BP		1938	UTA	See note.
174	*Carrantuohill*	4-4-0	S	1913	BP		1939	CIE	See note.
185		4-4-2T	T	1913	BP		1924 T1 RT. Sh	UTA	
186		4-4-2T	T	1913	BP		1923 T1 RT. Sh	UTA	
187		4-4-2T	T	1913	BP		1926 T1 RT. Sh	UTA	
188		4-4-2T	T	1913	BP		1927 T1 RT. Sh	CIE	
189		4-4-2T	T	1913	BP		1926 T1 RT. Sh	UTA	
203		0-4-0ST		(CK&AR *Kells*)				1930	See note.
204		0-6-0T		(CK&AR *Mulligar*)				1930	See note.
180		0-6-0	SG2	1915	BP			CIE	
181		0-6-0	SG2	1915	BP			CIE	
182		0-6-0	SG2	1915	BP			UTA	
183		0-6-0	SG2	1915	BP			UTA	
184		0-6-0	SG2	1915	BP			CIE	
190	*Lugnaquilla*	4-4-0	S2	1915	BP		1939	UTA	See note.
191	*Croagh Patrick*	4-4-0	S2	1915	BP		1939	CIE	See note.
192	*Slievenamon*	4-4-0	S2	1915	BP		1938	UTA	See note.
196	*Lough Gill*	4-4-0	U	1915	BP			UTA	See note.
197	*Lough Neagh*	4-4-0	U	1915	BP			CIE	See note.
198	*Lough Swilly*	4-4-0	U	1915	BP			CIE	See note.
199	*Lough Derg*	4-4-0	U	1915	BP			CIE	See note.
200	*Lough Melvin*	4-4-0	U	1915	BP			UTA	See note.
6		0-6-0	SG3	1920	BP			UTA	
7		0-6-0	SG3	1920	BP			UTA	
8		0-6-0	SG3	1920	BP			CIE	
13		0-6-0	SG3	1920	BP			UTA	
14		0-6-0	SG3	1920	BP			CIE	
20		0-6-0	SG3	1920	BP			UTA	
47		0-6-0	SG3	1920	BP			CIE	
48		0-6-0	SG3	1920	BP			CIE	
1		4-4-2T	T2	1921	BP			CIE	See note.
2		4-4-2T	T2	1921	BP			UTA	See note.
3		4-4-2T	T2	1921	BP			CIE	
4		4-4-2T	T2	1921	BP			UTA	
5		4-4-2T	T2	1921	BP			UTA	
49		0-6-0	SG3	1921	BP			UTA	

No.	Name	Type	Class	Date	Builder	Renumbered	Rebuilt	Withdrawn	Remarks
96		0-6-0	SG3	1921	BP			CIE	
97		0-6-0	SG3	1921	BP			UTA	
117		0-6-0	SG3	1921	BP			CIE	
118		0-6-0	SG3	1921	BP			CIE	
201		0-6-0	SG3	1921	BP	40 (1948)		UTA	
202		0-6-0	SG3	1921	BP	41 (1948)		UTA	
15		0-6-0	SG2	1926	NW			CIE	
18		0-6-0	SG2	1924	NW			UTA	
21		4-4-2T	T2	1924	NW			UTA	
30		4-4-2T	T2	1924	NW			UTA	
115		4-4-2T	T2	1924	NW			CIE	See note.
116		4-4-2T	T2	1924	NW			CIE	See note.
139		4-4-2T	T2	1924	NW			CIE	
142		4-4-2T	T2	1924	NW			UTA	
143		4-4-2T	T2	1924	NW			CIE	
144		4-4-2T	T2	1924	NW			CIE	
147		4-4-2T	T2	1924	NW	67 (1948)		CIE	
148		4-4-2T	T2	1924	NW	69 (1948)		UTA	
16		0-6-0	SG2	1925	NW			UTA	
17		0-6-0	SG2	1925	NW			UTA	
19		0-6-0	SG2	1925	NW			CIE	
31		0-6-0CT	CRANE	1928	HL			DEW	
62		4-4-2T	T2	1929	BP			CIE	
63		4-4-2T	T2	1929	BP			CIE	
64		4-4-2T	T2	1930	BP			UTA	
65		4-4-2T	T2	1930	BP			CIE	
66		4-4-2T	T2	1930	BP			UTA	
83	*Eagle*	4-4-0	V	1932	BP		1949 B. Sh	UTA	
84	*Falcon*	4-4-0	V	1932	BP		1947 B. Sh	CIE	
85	*Merlin*	4-4-0	V	1932	BP		1950 B. Sh	CIE	
86	*Peregrine*	4-4-0	V	1932	BP		1948 B. Sh	UTA	
87	*Kestrel*	4-4-0	V	1932	BP		1946 B. Sh	UTA	
78		0-6-0	UG	1937	GNR			UTA	
79		0-6-0	UG	1937	GNR			UTA	
80		0-6-0	UG	1937	GNR			CIE	
81		0-6-0	UG	1937	GNR			CIE	
82		0-6-0	UG	1937	GNR			UTA	
69		0-6-0	A	(SL&NCR *Sligo*)				1941	See note.
145		0-6-0	UG	1948	BP			CIE	
146		0-6-0	UG	1948	BP			UTA	
147		0-6-0	UG	1948	BP			CIE	
148		0-6-0	UG	1948	BP			CIE	
149		0-6-6	UG	1948	BP			UTA	
201	*Meath*	4-4-0	U	1948	BP			UTA	
202	*Louth*	4-4-0	U	1948	BP			UTA	
203	*Armagh*	4-4-0	U	1948	BP			CIE	
204	*Antrim*	4-4-0	U	1948	BP			CIE	
205	*Down*	4-4-0	U	1948	BP			UTA	
206	*Liffey*	4-4-0	VS	1948	BP			CIE	
207	*Boyne*	4-4-0	VS	1948	BP			CIE	
208	*Lagan*	4-4-0	VS	1948	BP			UTA	
209	*Foyle*	4-4-0	VS	1948	BP			CIE	
210	*Erne*	4-4-0	VS	1948	BP			UTA	

83 locomotives were taken into CIE stock and 83 locomotives were taken into UTA stock when assets were divided in October 1958, with the Dundalk Works crane locomotive passing to Dundalk Engineering Co., who took over the works.

GNR	Class	CIE	UTA	GNR	Class	CIE	UTA	GNR	Class	CIE	UTA	GNR	Class	CIE	UTA
1	T2	ø		20	SG3		33	47	SG3	47N		73	Ps	ø	
2	T2		2x	21	T2		ø	48	SG3	48N		74	PPs		74x
3	T2	3N		22	RT		ø	49	SG3		36	75	PPs	ø	
4	T2		4x	23	RT		23	50	PPs		50x	76	PPs	ø	
5	T2		5x	27	Ps	ø		55	AL	55N		78	UG		45
6	SG3		30	29	AL	ø		56	AL		56x	79	UG		46
7	SG3		31	30	T2		30x	57	AL	ø		80	UG	80N	
8	SG3	8N		31	CRANE	DEW		58	AL	ø		81	UG	81N	
9	LQGs		9x	32	AL		32x	59	AL	ø		82	UG		47
10	PGs		10x	33	A	ø		60	A	ø		83	V		83x
11	PGs		11x	35	AL	ø		62	T2	62N		84	V	ø	
12	PPs	ø		38	NQGs	38N		63	T2	ø		85	V	85N	
13	SG3		32	39	LQGs		39x	64	T2		64x	86	V		86x
14	SG3	14N		40	SG3		34	65	T2	65N		87	V		87x
15	SG2	15N		41	SG3		35	66	T2		66x	91	JT	91N	
16	SG2		38	42	PPs		42x	67	T2	67N		96	SG3	96N	
17	SG2		39	43	PPs		43x	69	T2	ø		97	SG3		37
18	SG2		40	44	PPs	44N		71	PPs	ø		99	OGTs	99N	
19	SG2	ø		46	PPs		46x	72	Ps	ø		100	PGs		100x

GNR	Class	CIE	UTA	GNR	Class	CIE	UTA	GNR	Class	CIE	UTA	GNR	Class	CIE	UTA
101	PGs		101x	132	Qs	132N		161	LQGs	161N		186	TI		186x
102	PGs		102x	135	Qs		135x	162	LQGs		162x	187	TI		187x
103	PGs		103x	136	Qs	ø		163	LQGs	163N		188	TI	ø	
105	Ps	105N		139	T2	ø		164	LQGs	164N		189	TI		189x
106	PPs	106N		142	T2		142x	165	LOGs		165x	190	S2		62
107	PPs		ø	143	T2	143N		166	RT		24	191	S2	191N	
108	LQGs		ø	144	T2	ø		167	RT		25	192	S2		63
109	LQGs		ø	145	UG	145N		170	S	170N		196	U		64
110	LQGs	ø		146	UG		48	171	S	171N		197	U	197N	
111	LQGs		111x	147	UG	147N		172	S		60	198	U	ø	
112	NQGs	112N		148	UG	148N		173	S		61	199	U	199N	
115	T2	ø		149	UG		49	174	S	174N		200	U		65
116	T2	116N		150	A	150N		175	SG		43	201	U		66
117	SG3	ø		151	PGs		151x	176	SG		44	202	U		67
118	SG3	ø		152	QGs	152N		177	SG	177N		203	U	203N	
119	LQGs		ø	153	QGs	153N		178	SG	178N		204	U	204N	
121	Qs		121x	154	QGs	154N		179	SG	179N		205	U		68
122	Qs		122x	155	QGs	155N		180	SG2	180N		206	VS	206N	
123	Qs	ø		156	QLs		156x	181	SG2	181N		207	VS	207N	
125	Qs		125x	157	QLs		ø	182	SG2		41	208	VS		58
127	QLs		127x	158	LQGs	158N		183	SG2		42	209	VS	209N	
130	Qs	ø		159	LQGs	159N		184	SG2	184N		210	VS		59
131	Qs	131N		160	LQGs		160x	185	TI		185x				

ø indicates not renumbered or allotted a new number.

Notes

Unless otherwise stated in the notes following locomotives were named when built. Names remained in use until 1912 for goods locomotives and 1914 for passenger locomotives, after which they were removed from all but the QL and S classes. Even these names were removed by 1925, except for No. 170, which retained it's name until 1930. The V Class of 1932 reintroduced the practice of naming of GNR locomotives.

1, 2, 115 & 116 were converted to oil burning in 1946. All reverted to coal in 1948.
7, 45, 73 & 97 were named in 1896.
12 was fitted with a Phoenix superheater when built. This was removed in 1915.
25 had a Ps Class boiler fitted in 1952.
31 was sold in 1928 to SL&NCR (named *Glencar A*).
38, 39 & 42 were fitted with Phoenix superheaters when built. These were removed in 1914.
44 was partly constructed by INWR (was to have been INWR No. 2).
51 & 52 were named in 1898*.
69 was sold in 1940 to SL&NCR (named *Sligo*).
72, 82 & 83 were named in 1897.
86A was sold in 1884 to Collen Bros. (see Contractors List).
93 was named in 1895.
96 is said to have been named *Windsor* (rather doubtful) until 1906.
99 was named in 1906 when renumbered 96.
113 was fitted with piston valves in 1922.
114 was fitted with piston valves in 1920.
118 & 119 were sold in 1921 to SL&NCR (named *Blacklion & Glencar* respectively).
127 was denamed in 1913, and the new name *Hercules* was affixed soon afterwards.
149 was sold in 1931 to SL&NCR (named *Sligo*). It returned to the GNR in 1940 as No. 69.
157 was fitted with piston valves in 1919.
159 was converted to oil burning in 1947, but reverted to coal in 1948.
170 & 174 had their names restored in 1939.
171 & 173 had their names restored in 1938.
172 had its name restored in 1938 and was converted to oil burning in 1938*, reverting to coal in 1941. It was again converted to oil burning in 1945 and reverted to coal in 1946.
190 was named in 1939 (the same name was allotted in 1915 but was not affixed).
191 was named in 1939 (selected name in 1915 was *Carlingford*).
192 was named in 1938 (selected name in 1915 was *Mount Hamilton*).
196 was named in 1953.
197 was named in 1949 *Lough Erne* in but this was altered to *Lough Neagh* before leaving the works.
198 was named in 1950. It was originally intended to have been named *Lough Melvin*.
199 was named in 1949.
200 was named in 1950. It was originally intended to have been named *Lough Swilly*.
203 & 204 were taken into GNR stock in 1913 but not numbered until 1915.

Freight Locomotive Classification

Load Class	Locomotive classes
A	A, AL, B
B	PG, QG, UG
C	LQGø, NOGø, NLQGø, SG, SG2
D	LQG, NQG, NLQG, SG3
E	C, D, E

ø = Before rebuilding.

Steam Railmotors
4-coupled (Nos. 1-3 Cyls 12 x 16, coupled wheels 3-7½) - outside cylinders.
           (Nos. 4-7 Cyls 12 x 16, coupled wheels 3-9) - outside cylinders.

No.	Date	Builder	Withdrawn	Seating	Remarks
1	1905	NBL	1913	16 1st; 39 3rd	Became coach No. 201 (Class J3)
2	1905	NBL	1913	16 1st; 39 3rd	Became coach No. 202 (Class J3)
3	1905	NBL	1913	16 1st; 39 3rd	Became coach No. 203 (Class J3)
4	1906	MW	1913	20 1st; 39 3rd	Became coach No. 204 (Class J2)
5	1906	MW	1913	20 1st; 39 3rd	Became coach No. 205 (Class J2)
6	1906	MW	1913	20 1st; 39 3rd	Became coach No. 206 (Class J2)
7	1906	MW	1913	20 1st; 39 3rd	Became coach No. 207 (Class J1)

Miscellaneous Locomotive

After acquiring the assets of the CK&AR in 1913, 2-0 gauge 0-4-0WT *Armagh* (OK 1240 - see Contractors List), was put to use in a quarry owned by the company (later at Goraghwood quarry), being scrapped c. 1915 - it is not absolutely certain that the GNR actually owned *Armagh* (it was not counted in the company's stock).

PART II - BELFAST & COUNTY DOWN RAILWAY/NORTHERN COUNTIES COMMITTEE/ULSTER TRANSPORT AUTHORITY/ NORTHERN IRELAND RAILWAYS

Constituent and absorbed railways which contributed locomotives to the Northern Counties Committee, Ulster Transport Authority and Northern Ireland Railways.

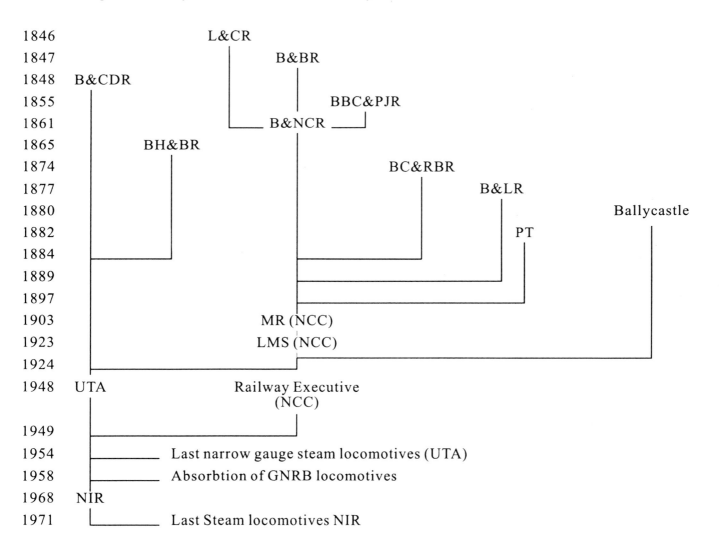

BELFAST, HOLYWOOD & BANGOR RAILWAY

Stock: 5 new locomotives built 1867-76.
2 secondhand locomotives acquired 1865.

Type	Years built	No. in class	Cylinders	Driving wheels	Locomotive Nos.
2-4-0T	1866	1	15 x 22	5-0	3
2-4-0T	1870	2	12 x 22	5-0	4, 5
2-4-0ST	1876	2	15 x 22	5-0	3, 6

No.	Type	Date	Builder	Withdrawn	B&CDR No.	Remarks
1	2-4-0ST	(B&CDR 11)		B&CDR	15	Purchased 1865 from B&CDR
2	2-4-0ST	(B&CDR 12)		B&CDR	16	Purchased 1865 from B&CDR
3	2-4-0T	1866	JF	1876		
4	2-4-0T	1870	YE	B&CDR	18	
5	2-4-0T	1870	YE	B&CDR	19	
3	2-4-0ST	1876	VF	B&CDR	17	
6	2-4-0ST	1876	VF	B&CDR	20	

6 locomotives taken into B&CDR stock 1884 and renumbered as shown.

BELFAST & COUNTY DOWN RAILWAY

Stock: 65 new locomotives 1848-1945.
6 secondhand locomotives acquired 1884 (2 of which were originally B&CDR stock).
3 new steam railmotors 1905-6.

Type	Years built	No. in class	Cylinders	Driving wheels	Locomotive Nos. (+ subsequently renumbered)
2-2-2	1848	4	15* x 20	5-6*	1, 2+, 3, 4
2-2-2WT	1850-1	2	10* x 15*	5-1	1 TANK+, 2 TANK+
2-4-0T	1857-8	2	15 x 22	5-6	5+, 6
2-4-0T	1859	1	12 x 18	5-0	8
0-4-2	1859	2	15 x 22	5-0	9, 10
2-4-0ST	1864-7	5	15 x 20	5-0	3, 5, 11, 12+, 13+
2-4-0T	1866	1	15 x 22	5-0	1
2-4-0	1868	2	15 x 20	5-0	12, 13
0-6-0	1875	1	17 x 24	5-0	14
0-6-0	1878	1	17 x 24	5-0	4
0-4-2	1880-90	5	15 x 22	5-1	2, 9+, 10, 13, 16
0-4-2	1881	1	*	*	8
2-4-2T	1891	4	18¼/26 x 24	5-1	18, 19, 21, 22
2-4-0	1892	3	16/23¼ x 24	6-0	23-25
0-6-0	1892	1	17 x 24	5-0	26
2-4-0	1894	1	16 x 24	6-0	6
2-4-2T	1896-7	6	16 x 24	5-6	5, 7, 8, 27, 28, 29
4-4-2T	1901-21	12	17 x 24	5-6	1, 3, 11-13, 15, 17-21, 30
0-6-0	1904-21	3	18 x 26	5-0	4, 10, 14
4-6-4T	1920	4	19 x 26	5-9	22-25
0-6-4T	1923	1	17 x 24	4-0	29
4-4-2T	1924-45	3	18 x 26	5-6	8, 9, 16
Belpaire boiler: 4-4-2T 1, 8, 9, 13, 16-21; 0-6-0 4, 10, 14; 4-6-4T 22-25; 0-6-4T 29.					
Beattie patent firebox: 2-4-0T 5 (later 7), 6, 8.					
Outside cylinders: 4-6-4T 22-25.					
Compound (2-Cyl. von Borries): 2-4-2T 18, 19, 21, 22; 2-4-0 23-25.					

No.	Type	Date	Builder	Renumbered	Rebuilt	Withdrawn	UTA No.	Remarks
1	2-2-2	1848	BCK			1865		
2	2-2-2	1848	BCK	8 (1880)	*	1897		Rebuilt 0-4-2* 1867-87 (1869 perhaps)
3	2-2-2	1848	BCK			1865.		
4	2-2-2	1848	BCK			1858		Sold to Moore (See Contractors List)
1	2-2-2WT	1850	Fbn	4 (1859)		1878		No. 1 TANK until 1859
2	2-2-2WT	1851	Fbn	5 (1859)		1866		No. 2 TANK until 1859
5	2-4-0T	1857	BP	7 (1859)		1896		
6	2-4-0T	1858	BP			1894		
8	2-4-0T	1859	BP			1880-3*		
9	0-4-2	1859	Fbn	9A (1887)		1888		A minute of 1859 suggests that these two were to be named *Samson* and *Hercules*. There is no evidence at all of naming.
10	0-4-2	1859	Fbn	10A (1886)		1887		
11	2-4-0ST	1864	VF			1904		
12	2-4-0ST	1865	VF			1865		Sold to BH&BR (No. 1)
13	2-4-0ST	1865	VF			1865		Sold to BH&BR (No. 2)
3	2-4-0ST	1866	VF	3A (1901)		1903*		
1	2-4-0T	1867	JF		1884 (0-4-2)	1909		

▲ B&CDR 4-4-2T No. 12 (1904 Beyer, Peacock)

(Real Photos)

▼ B&CDR 4-6-4T No. 24 (1920 Beyer, Peacock)

(Lens of Sutton)

▲ Fowler 2-4-0T. Builders view identified as one of the four ordered by the BH&BR 1866.

(University of Reading)

▼ B&CDR 2-4-0 No. 6 (1894 Beyer, Peacock)

(Real Photos)

No.	Type	Date	Builder	Renumbered	Rebuilt	Withdrawn	UTA No.	Remarks
5	2-4-0ST	1867	VF			1896*		
12	2-4-0	1868	MW			1904*		
13	2-4-0	1868	MW			1888		
14	0-4-0	1875	VF			1904		
4	0-4-0	1878	BP	4A (1921)		1922		
2	0-4-2	1880	SS		1902 (0-4-2T)	1937		
8	0-4-2	1881	B&CDR			1897		
15	2-4-0ST	(BH&BR 1)				1901		See B&CDR No. 12 (1865)
16	2-4-0ST	(BH&BR 2)				1894		See B&CDR No. 13 (1865)
17	2-4-0S	(BH&BR 3)				1909		
18	2-4-0T	(BH&BR 4)				1891		
19	2-4-0T	(BH&BR 5)				1891		
20	2-4-0ST	(BH&BR 6)				1909		
10	0-4-2	1886	SS		1902 (0-4-2T)	1914		
9	0-4-2	1887	SS	28 (1945)	1900 (0-4-2T)	UTA		
13	0-4-2	1888	SS		1901 (0-4-2T)	1921		
16	0-4-2	1890	SS		1901 (0-4-2T)	1924		
18	2-4-2T	1891	BP		1895 (4-4-2T)	1920		
19	2-4-2T	1891	BP		1898* (4-4-2T)	1920		
21	2-4-2T	1891	BP		1898* (4-4-2T)	1920		
22	2-4-2T	1891	BP		1898* (4-4-2T)	1920		
23	2-4-0	1892	BP			1921		
24	2-4-0	1892	BP	24A (1920)		1921		
25	2-4-0	1892	BP			1921		
26	0-6-0	1892	BP			UTA		
6	2-4-0	1894	BP		1943 B. Sat	UTA		
5	2-4-2T	1896	BP			UTA		
7	2-4-2T	1896	BP			UTA		
8	2-4-2T	1897	BP			1924		
27	2-4-2T	1897	BP			UTA		
28	2-4-2T	1897	BP			1937		
29	2-4-2T	1897	BP			1923		
3	4-4-2T	1901	BP		1931 B. Sat	UTA	203	
15	4-4-2T	1901	BP		1928 B. Sat	UTA	215	
30	4-4-2T	1901	BP		1924 B. Sat	UTA	230	
11	4-4-2T	1904	BP		1924 B. Sat	UTA	211	
12	4-4-2T	1904	BP		1928 B. Sat	UTA	212	
14	0-6-0	1904	BP			UTA	214	
1	4-4-2T	1909	BP			UTA	201	
17	4-4-2T	1909	BP			UTA	217	
20	4-4-2T	1909	BP			UTA	220	
10	0-6-0	1914	BP			UTA		
22	4-6-4T	1920	BP			UTA	222	
23	4-6-4T	1920	BP			UTA	223	
24	4-6-4T	1920	BP			UTA	224	
25	4-6-4T	1920	BP			UTA	225	
4	0-6-0	1921	BP			UTA	204	
13	4-4-2T	1921	BP			UTA	213	
18	4-4-2T	1921	BP			UTA	218	
19	4-4-2T	1921	BP			UTA	219	
21	4-4-2T	1921	BP			UTA	221	
29	0-6-4T	1923	BP			UTA	229	
8	4-4-2T	1924	BP			UTA	208	
16	4-4-2T	1924	BP			UTA	216	
9	4-4-2T	1945	BP			UTA	209	

29 locomotives taken into UTA stock 1948, B&CDR Nos. 1 & 3-30, most being renumbered as shown.

Steam Railmotors

No.	Date	Builder	Withdrawn	Seating	Remarks
1	1905	K	1924	60 3rd	Became coach No. 59
2	1905	K	1924	60 3rd	Became coach No. 72
3	1906	K	1924	76 3rd	Became coach No. 173

Note

All the above were 4-coupled railmotors (Cylinders 10 x 16, coupled wheels 3-7) - Belpaire boiler and outside cylinders.

LONDONDERRY & COLERAINE RAILWAY

Stock: 8 new locomotives 1846-59.
3 secondhand locomotives acquired 1848-59.

Type	Years built	No. in class	Cylinders	Driving wheels	Locomotive Nos.
2-4-0	1846	1	15 x 24	5-6	*
2-2-0WT	1853	6	11 x 18	5-3	3-7 and *
0-4-2	1859	1	14 x 20	5-0	8
Outside cylinders: all listed above except the 0-4-2.					

No.	Type	Date	Builder	Withdrawn	B&NCR No.	Remarks
*	2-4-0	1846	L	1851		Transferred to L&ER (No. 3)
*	*	*	*	1858*		Obtained 1848-9 from a Lough Foyle reclamation contractor
2	2-4-0	(L&ER 3)		B&NCR	27	Transferred from L&ER 1851
3	2-2-0WT	1853	SS	B&NCR	28	
4	2-2-0WT	1853	SS	B&NCR	29	
5	2-2-0WT	1853	SS	B&NCR	30	
6	2-2-0WT	1853	SS	B&NCR	31	
7	2-2-0WT	1853	SS	B&NCR	30	
*	2-2-0WT	1853	SS	1853		Sold to N&ER (No. 3)
1	2-2-2WT	(BBC&PJR *)		B&NCR	26	Purchased 1858-9; One of BBC&PJR Nos. 5, 6 or 7.
8	0-4-2	1859	G	B&NCR	33	

Note

It would seem that locomotives may not have been numbered at first on the L&CR as delivery of the SS 2-2-0WT was in the order 3, 4, 7, *, 5, 6, which suggests that numbers were not applied until 1854.

8 locomotives taken into B&NCR stock 1861 and renumbered as shown. 1 locomotive on order was taken directly into B&NCR stock (No. 34).

BALLYMENA, BALLYMONEY, COLERAINE & PORTRUSH JUNCTION RAILWAY

Stock: 7 new locomotives 1855.

Type	Years built	No. in class	Cylinders	Driving wheels	Locomotive Nos.
2-2-2	1855	4	15 x 20	5-6	1-4
2-2-2WT	1855	3	13 x 15	5-0	5-7

No.	Type	Date	Builder	Withdrawn	B&NCR No.	Remarks
1	2-2-2	1855	SS	B&NCR	20	
2	2-2-2	1855	SS	B&NCR	21	
3	2-2-2	1855	SS	B&NCR	22	
4	2-2-2	1855	SS	B&NCR	23	
5	2-2-2WT	1855	Fbn	*		One of these 2-2-2WT was sold to the L&CR in 1858 or 1859 and the other two passed into B&NCR stock as Nos. 24 and 25.
6	2-2-2WT	1855	Fbn	*		
7	2-2-2WT	1855	Fbn	*		

6 locomotives taken into B&NCR stock 1861 and renumbered as shown.

BALLYMENA, CUSHENDALL & RED BAY RAILWAY

3-0 Gauge.
Stock: 3 new locomotives 1874-5.

Type	Years built	No. in class	Cylinders	Driving wheels	Locomotive Nos.
0-4-2ST	1874-5	3	12 x 19	3-1	1-3

No.	Type	Date	Builder	B&NCR No.
1	0-4-2ST	1874	BH	60
2	0-4-2ST	1874	BH	61
3	0-4-2ST	1875	BH	62

3 locomotives taken into B&NCR stock 1884 and renumbered as shown.

BALLYMENA & LARNE RAILWAY

3-0 Gauge.
Stock: 6 new locomotives 1877-82.

Type	Years built	No. in class	Cylinders	Driving wheels	Locomotive Nos.
2-4-0T	1877-8	2	11 x 18	3-9	1, 4
0-6-0T	1877-82	3	13 x 18	3-9	2, 3, 6
2-6-0ST	1880	1	14 x 18	3-3	5

No.	Type	Date	Builder	B&NCR No.
1	2-4-0T	1877	BP	63
2	0-6-0T	1877	BP	65
3	0-6-0T	1877	BP	66
4	2-4-0T	1878	BP	64
5	2-6-0ST	1880	BP	68
6	0-6-0T	1882	BP	67

6 locomotives taken into B&NCR stock 1889 and renumbered as shown.

PORTSTEWART TRAMWAY

3-0 Gauge.
Stock: 2 new tram locomotives 1882-3.

Type	Years built	No. in class	Cylinders	Driving wheels	Locomotive Nos.
0-4-0T	1882-3	2	8 x 12	2-4¼	1, 2

No.	Type	Date	Builder	B&NCR No.
1	0-4-0T	1882	K	1
2	0-4-0T	1883	K	2

2 tram locomotives taken into B&NCR stock 1897, numbers not altered.

BELFAST & BALLYMENA RAILWAY
BELFAST & NORTHERN COUNTIES RAILWAY

B&BR Stock: 19 new locomotives 1847-57.
1 secondhand locomotive acquired 1847 (19 locomotives became B&NCR in 1861).
B&NCR Stock: 54 new 5-3 gauge locomotives built 1861-1902.
2 new 3-0 gauge locomotives built 1892.
6 locomotives taken into stock from Ballymena, Ballymoney, Coleraine & Portrush Junction Railway 1861.
8 locomotives taken into stock from Londonderry & Coleraine Railway 1861.
3 locomotives taken into stock from Ballymena, Cushendall & Red Bay Railway 1884.
6 locomotives taken into stock from Ballymena & Larne Railway 1889.
1 secondhand locomotive acquired 1886.
2 tram locomotives taken into stock from Portstewart Tramway 1897.
1 new tram locomotive built 1900.

Class	Type	Years built	No. in class	Cylinders	Driving wheels	Locomotive Nos. (+ subsequently renumbered)
	0-4-2	1847	1	16 x 22	5-0	*Vulcan*+
	2-2-2	1847	4	15 x 20	5-6	*Gladiator*+, *Hercules*+, *Queen*+, *Prince*+
	2-2-2	1847	4	15 x 20	5-6	*Hawk*, *Kite*+, *Falcon*+, *Swallow*+
	0-4-2	1847	1	15 x 22	5-0	*Eagle*+
	0-4-2	1851	1	16 x 24	4-6	*Ostrich*+
H	2-4-0	1856	6	15 x 20	5-6	12-17
L	0-6-0	1857-61	3	17 x 24	4-7	18, 19, 35
	2-4-0	1861	1	14 x 20	5-2	34
L1	0-6-0	1863	2	17 x 24	5-2	36, 37
K	0-6-0	1867-80	9	17 x 24	5-2	7, 28, 30-32, 38, 39, 43, 44
	2-4-0	1868	1	15 x 20	5-6	3
I	2-4-0	1868	2	15 x 20	5-7½	40+, 41+
	2-4-0	1870-1	2	15 x 20	5-6	4, 5
G	2-4-0	1872-8	9	16 x 22	5-7½	6, 8, 10, 11, 22, 27, 29, 40, 41
M	0-4-2	1873	1	17 x 24	5-2½	26
N	0-4-0ST	1875	1	16 x 22	4-0	42
F	2-4-0	1880-5	3	17 x 24	6-0	23, 45, 46
J	2-4-0T	1883	4	15 x 20	5-2½	25, 47, 48, 49
C	2-4-0	1890-5	7	16/23¼ x 24	6-0	21, 33, 50+, 51, 52, 56, 57
E	0-6-0	1892	2	17/25 x 24	5-2	53, 54
S	2-4-2T	1892	2	14¾/21 x 20	3-9	69+, 70+ (3-0 gauge)
D	2-4-0	1895	2	18/26 x 24	7-0	50, 55
B	4-4-0	1897-8	5	16/23¼ x 24	6-0	24, 59-62
A	4-4-0	1901-2	2	18/26 x 24	6-0	3, 34
Outside cylinders: 0-4-0ST N Class; 2-4-2T S Class.						
Compound (2-cyl von Borries) 2-4-0 C, D Classes; 4-4-0 A, B Classes; 0-6-0 E Class; 2-4-2T S Class.						

Class letters allotted to absorbed narrow gauge locomotives were O BC&RBR 0-4-2ST; P B&LR 2-4-0T; Q B&LR 0-6-0T; R B&LR 2-6-0ST.

B&BR locomotives were named only until 1852 when numbers were adopted.

5-3 gauge locomotives

No.	Name	Type	Class	Date	Builder	Renumbered	Rebuilt	Withdrawn	NCC No.	Remarks
1	*Hawk*	·2-2-2WT		(UR *Spitfire*)			1854 2-4-0T	1863		See note.
2	*Vulcan*	0-4-2		1847	BCK			1869		
3	*Gladiator*	2-2-2		1847	BCK		1855 2-4-0	1868		
4	*Hercules*	2-2-2		1847	BCK		1854 2-4-0	1871		
5	*Queen*	2-2-2		1847	BCK		1853 2-4-0	1869		
6	*Prince*	2-2-2		1847	BCK			1873		
	Hawk	2-2-2		1847	SB			1849		See note.
8	*Kite*	2-2-2		1847	SB			1878		
9	*Falcon*	2-2-2		1847	SB			1886		
10	*Swallow*	2-2-2		1847	SB			1876		
11	*Eagle*	0-4-2		1847	SB			1873		
7	*Ostrich*	0-4-2		1851	SB			1872		

44

No.	Name	Type	Class	Date	Builder	Renumbered	Rebuilt	Withdrawn	NCC No.	Remarks
12		2-4-0	H	1856	SS			MRNCC	12	
13		2-4-0	H	1856	SS			MRNCC	13	
14		2-4-0	H	1856	SS			MRNCC	14	
15		2-4-0	H	1856	SS			MRNCC	15	
16		2-4-0	H	1856	SS			MRNCC	16	
17		2-4-0	H	1856	SS			MRNCC	17	
18		0-6-0	L	1857	SS			MRNCC	18	
19		0-6-0	L	1857	SS			MRNCC	19	
20		2-2-2		(BBC&PJR 1)			1871 2-4-0	MRNCC	20	
21		2-2-2		(BBC&PJR 2)				1893		
22		2-2-2		(BBC&PJR 3)			1871 2-4-0	1877		
23		2-2-2		(BBC&YJR 4)			1870 2-4-0	1886		
24		2-2-2WT		(BBC&PJR *)				1898		
25		2-2-2WT		(BBC&PJR *)			1867 2-4-0	1883		
26		2-2-2WT		(L&CR 1)				1873		
27		2-4-0		(L&CR 2)				1876		
28		2-2-0WT		(L&CR 3)				1871		
29		2-2-0WT		(L&CR 4)			1869 2-4-0	1876		See note.
30		2-2-0WT		(L&CR 5)				1880		
31		2-2-0WT		(L&CR 6)				1878		
32		2-2-0WT		(L&CR 7)				1869		
33		0-4-2		(L&CR 8)				1871		
34		2-4-0		1861	Fbn			1901		See note.
35		0-6-0	L	1861	SS		1902	MRNCC	35	Reb. 5-0 Blr.
36		0-6-0	L1	1863	BP			MRNCC	36	
37		0-6-0	L1	1863	BP		1903	MRNCC	37	Reb. 5-0 Blr.
38		0-6-0	K	1867	SS			MRNCC	38	
39		0-6-0	K	1867	SS			MRNCC	39	
3		2-4-0	G	1868		3A (1902)		1902		
40		2-4-0	I	1868	BP	1 (1869)		MRNCC	1	
41		2-4-0	I	1868	BP	2 (1869)		MRNCC	2	
5		2-4-0		1870	B&NCR			MRNCC	5	
32		0-6-0	K	1870	SS			MRNCC	32	
4		2-4-0		1871	B&NCR			MRNCC	4	See note.
28		0-6-0	K	1871	SS			MRNCC	28	
40		2-4-0	G	1872	SS			MRNCC	40	
41		2-4-0	G	1872	SS			MRNCC	41	
6		2-4-0	G	1873	SS			MRNCC	6	
7		0-6-0	K	1873	SS			MRNCC	7	
11		2-4-0	G	1873	SS			MRNCC	11	
26		0-4-2	M	1873	B&NCR		1903	MRNCC	26	Reb. 5-0 Blr.
42		0-4-0ST	N	1875	SS			MRNCC	42	
43		0-6-0	K	1875	SS			MRNCC	43	
10		2-4-0	G	1876	SS			NRNCC	10	
27		2-4-0	G	1876	SS			MRNCC	27	
29		2-4-0	G	1876	SS			MRNCC	29	
44		0-6-0	K	1876	SS			MRNCC	44	
8		2-4-0	G	1878	BP			MRNCC	8	
22		2-4-0	G	1878	BP			MRNCC	22	
31		0-6-0	K	1878	BP			MRNCC	31	
30		0-6-0	K	1880	BP			MRNCC	30	
45		2-4-0	F	1880	BP			MRNCC	45	
46		2-4-0	F	1880	BP			MRNCC	46	
25		2-4-0T	J	1883	BP			MRNCC	25	
47		2-4-0T	J	1883	BP			MRNCC	47	
48		2-4-0T	J	1883	BP		1891 2-4-0ST	MRNCC	48	
49		2-4-0T	J	1883	BP		1891 2-4-0ST	MRNCC	49	
23		2-4-0	F	1885	BP			MRNCC	23	
50		0-4-2				9 (1887)		MRNCC	9	See note.
33	Galgorm Castle	2-4-0	C	1890	BP			MRNCC	33	
50		2-4-0	C	1890	BP	58 (1895)		MRNCC	58	
51		2-4-0	C	1890	BP			MRNCC	51	See note.
52		2-4-0	C	1890	BP			MRNCC	52	
21		2-4-0	C	1892	BP			MRNCC	21	
53		0-6-0	E	1892	BP			MRNCC	53	
54		0-6-0	E	1892	BP			MRNCC	54	
50	Jubilee	2-4-0	D	1895	BP		1897 4-4-0	MRNCC	50	
55	Parkmount	2-4-0	D	1895	BP		1897 4-4-0	MRNCC	55	
56		2-4-0	C	1895	BP			MRNCC	56	
57		2-4-0	C	1895	BP			MRNCC	57	
59		4-4-0	B	1897	BP			MRNCC	59	
60		4-4-0	B	1897	BP			MRNCC	60	
61		4-4-0	B	1897	BP			MRNCC	61	
62		4-4-0	B	1897	BP			MRNCC	62	
24		4-4-0	B	1898	BP			MRNCC	24	
34	Queen Alexandra	4-4-0	A	1901	B&NCR			MRNCC	34	
3	King Edward VII	4-4-0	A	1902	B&NCR			MRNCC	3	

Notes

1 was purchased in 1847 from UR (named *Spitfire* until 1849).
B&BR *Hawk* was sold to UR in 1849 to compensate UR. Fitted with 5-6 wheels on rebuilding. Sold 1863 to J. Killeen (see Contractors List).
4 may have been new in 1872.
29 incorporated parts of No. 32 on rebuilding.
34 was ordered by L&CR.
50 was purchased in 1886 from the Belfast Central Railway (originally built by SS in 1878).
51 ran as an oil burner between 1896 and 1901.
Reb. 5-0 Blr. refers to the fitting of a larger diameter boiler.

3-0 gauge locomotives

No.	Type	Class	Date	Builder	Renumbered		NCC No.	No.	Type	Class	Date	Builder	Renumbered		NCC No.
60	0-4-2ST	O		(BC&RBR 1)	101	(1897)	101	66	0-6-0T	Q		(B&LR 3)	107	(1897)	107
61	0-4-2ST	O		(BC&RBR 2)	102	(1897)	102	67	0-6-0T	Q		(B&LR 6)	108	(1897)	108
62	0-4-2ST	O		(BC&RBR 3)	103	(1897)	103	68	2-6-0ST	R		(B&LR 5)	109	(1897)	109
63	2-4-0T	P		(B&LR 1)	104	(1897)	104	69	2-4-2T	S	1892	BP	110	(1897)	110
64	2-4-0T	P		(B&LR 4)	105	(1897)	105	70	2-4-2T	S	1892	BP	111	(1897)	111
65	0-6-0T	Q		(B&LR 2)	106	(1897)	106								

62 5-3 gauge (Nos. 1-62) gauge and 11 3-0 gauge (Nos. 101-11) locomotives taken into MR(NCC) stock 1903, numbers not altered.

Portstewart Tramway (3-0 gauge).

Type	Years built	No. in class	Cylinders	Driving wheels	Locomotive Nos.
0-4-0T	1900	1	9½ x 12	2-3	3

No.	Type	Date	Builder	NCC No.
1	0-4-0T	(PT 1)		1
2	0-4-0T	(PT 2)		2
3	0-4-0T	1900	K	3

3 tram locomotives taken into MR(NCC) stock 1903, numbers not altered.

MIDLAND RAILWAY (NORTHERN COUNTIES COMMITTEE)

Stock: 62 5-3 gauge locomotives taken into stock from Belfast & Northern Counties Railway 1903.
11 3-0 gauge locomotives taken into stock from Belfast & Northern Counties Railway 1903.
3 tram locomotives taken into stock from Belfast & Northern Counties Railway 1903.
16 new 5-3 gauge locomotives built 1903-22.
4 new 3-0 gauge locomotives built 1903-22.
2 new steam railmotors built 1905.

Class	Type	Years built	No. in class	Cylinders	Driving wheels	Locomotive Nos. (+ subsequently renumbered)
A	4-4-0	1903-8	11	18/26 x 24	6-0	4, 5, 9, 17, 20, 63-8
S	2-4-2T	1908-20	4	14¾/21 x 20	3-9	103, 104, 112+, 113+ (3-0 gauge)
N	0-4-0ST	1914	1	16 x 22	4-0	16
U	4-4-0	1914-22	4	18 x 24	6-0	14, 15, 69, 70
Superheater	4-4-0 U Class.					
Outside cylinders:	0-4-0ST N Class; 2-4-2T S Class.					
Compound (2-cyl von Borries)	4-4-0 A Class; 2-4-2T S Class.					

62 5-3 gauge locomotives taken into stock 1903 (former numbers not altered):

No.	Name	Type	Class	Renumbered	Rebuilt	Withdrawn	Remarks
1		2-4-0	I			LMSNCC	
2		2-4-0	I			LMSNCC	
3	*King Edward VII*	4-4-0	A			LMSNCC	
4		2-4-0		4A (1903)		1905	
5		2-4-0		5A (1906)		1907	
6		2-4-0	G		1913 G1	LMSNCC	
7		0-6-0	K			LMSNCC	
8		2-4-0	G			LMSNCC	
9		0-4-2		9A (1904)		1905	
10		2-4-0	G		1910 G1	LMSNCC	
11		2-4-0	G			LMSNCC	
12		2-4-0	H			LMSNCC	
13		2-4-0	H			LMSNCC	
14		2-4-0	H			LMSNCC	
15		2-4-0	H			LMSNCC	
16		2-4-0	H	16A (1914)		1918	
17		2-4-0	H	17A (1907)		1908	
18		0-6-0	L		1908	LMSNCC	
19		0-6-0	L		1908; 1920	LMSNCC	Rbt. 5-0 boiler 1920
20		2-4-0		20A (1905)		1906	
21		2-4-0	C			LMSNCC	
22		2-4-0	G			LMSNCC	
23		2-4-0	F			LMSNCC	

(Real Photos)

▲ NCC 2-4-0 No. 4 (1871 B&NCR York Road)

(Real Photos)

▼ NCC 2-4-0 F Class No. 23 (1885 Beyer, Peacock)

(Real Photos)

▲ NCC 0-6-0 L Class No. 35 (1861 Beyer, Peacock)

(Real Photos)

▼ NCC 2-4-0 G Class No. 22 (1878 Beyer, Peacock)

47

No.	Name	Type	Class	Renumbered	Rebuilt	Withdrawn	Remarks
24		4-4-0	B			LMSNCC	
25		2-4-0T	J		1911 2-4-0ST	LMSNCC	
26		0-4-2	M			LMSNCC	
27		2-4-0	G		1910 G1	LMSNCC	
28		0-6-0	K			LMSNCC	
29		2-4-0	G			LMSNCC	
30		0-6-0	K		1922 K1	LMSNCC	
31		0-6-0	K			LMSNCC	
32		0-6-0	K		1917 K1	LMSNCC	
33	Galgorm Castle	2-4-0	C			LMSNCC	
34	Queen Alexandra	4-4-0	A			LMSNCC	
35		0-6-0	L			LMSNCC	
36		0-6-0	L1		1904	LMSNCC	Rbt. 5-0 boiler
37		0-6-0	L1			LMSNCC	
38		0-6-0	K		1912 K1	LMSNCC	Rbt. 5-0 boiler; Phoenix superheater 1912-*
39		0-6-0	K		1912 K1	LMSNCC	Rbt. 5-0 boiler
40		2-4-0	G			LMSNCC	
41		2-4 0	G			LMSNCC	
42		0-4-0ST	N			LMSNCC	
43		0-6-0	K		1920 K1	LMSNCC	Rbt. 5-0 boiler
44		0-6-0	K		1909 K1; 1921	LMSNCC	Rbt. 5-0 boiler 1921
45		2-4-0	F			LMSNCC	
46		2-4-0	F			LMSNCC	
47		2-4-0T	J		1914 2-4-0ST	LMSNCC	
48		2-4-0ST	J			LMSNCC	
49		2-4-0ST	J			LMSNCC	
50	Jubilee	4-4-0	D			LMSNCC	
51		2-4-0	C			LMSNCC	
52		2-4-0	C			LMSNCC	
53		0-6-0	E		1911 E1, 1921	LMSNCC	Rbt. 5-0 boiler 1921
54		0-6-0	E		1907 E1	LMSNCC	Rbt. 5-0 boiler
55	Parkmount	4-4-0	D			LMSNCC	
56		2-4-0	C			LMSNCC	
57		2-4-0	C			LMSNCC	
58		2-4-0	C			LMSNCC	
59		4-4-0	B			LMSNCC	
60		4-4-0	B		1921 B1	LMSNCC	Rbt. 5-0 boiler
61		4-4-0	B		1921 B1	LMSNCC	Rbt. 5-0 boiler
62		4-4-0	B			LMSNCC	

Note

Rbt. 5-0 boiler refers to the fitting of a larger diameter boiler in the year shown.

11 3-0 gauge locomotives taken into stock 1903 (former number not altered):

No.	Type	Class	Renumbered	Withdrawn	Remarks
101	0-4-2ST	O	101A (1920)	LMSNCC	
102	0-4-2ST	O	102A (1920)	LMSNCC	
103	0-4-2ST	O		1911	Believed sold to a Co. Antrim mine (see Contractors List)
104	2-4-0T	P		1920	
105	2-4-0T	P		LMSNCC	
106	0-6-0T	Q		LMSNCC	
107	0-6-0T	Q		LMSNCC	
108	0-6-0T	Q		LMSNCC	
109	2-6-0ST	R		LMSNCC	
110	2-4-2T	S		LMSNCC	
111	2-4-2T	S		LMSNCC	

18 5-3 and 2 3-0 gauge locomotives built 1903-22

No.	Type	Class	Date	Builder	Renumbered	Withdrawn	Remarks
4	4-4-0	A	1903	NCC		LMSNCC	
9	4-4-0	A	1904	NCC		LMSNCC	
20	4-4-0	A	1905	NCC		LMSNCC	
63	4-4-0	A	1905	MR		LMSNCC	
64	4-4-0	A	1905	MR		LMSNCC	
65	4-4-0	A	1905	MR		LMSNCC	
66	4-4-0	A	1905	MR		LMSNCC	
5	4-4-0	A	1906	NCC		LMSNCC	
17	4-4-0	A	1907	NCC		LMSNCC	
67	4-4-0	A	1908	MR		LMSNCC	
68	4-4-0	A	1908	MR		LMSNCC	
112	2-4-2T	S	1908	NCC	102 (1920)	LMSNCC	3-0 gauge
113	2-4-2T	S	1909	NCC	101 (1920)	LMSNCC	3-0 gauge
16	0-4-0ST	N	1914	NCC		LMSNCC	
69	4-4-0	U	1914	MR		LMSNCC	
70	4-4-0	U	1914	MR		LMSNCC	
103	2-4-2T	S	1919	NCC		LMSNCC	3-0 gauge
104	2-4-2T	S	1920	NCC		LMSNCC	3-0 gauge
14	4-4-0	U	1922	MR		LMSNCC	Originally to have been built by AW
15	4-4-0	U	1922	MR		LMSNCC	Originally to have been built by AW

48

Railmotors

No.	Date	Builder	Withdrawn	Seating	Remarks
90	1905	MR	1913	6 1st; 16 2nd: 24 3rd	Numbered in locomotive series. Became coach No. 79.
91	1905	MR	1913	6 19t; 16 2nd; 24 3rd	Numbered In locomotive series. Became coach No. 80.

Note

Both were single-driver railmotors (Cylinders 9 x 15 (outside), driving wheels 3-7).

Portstewart Tramway
3-0 gauge.
No changes to stock.

72 5-3 gauge (Nos. 1-70 and 14, 15 second locomotives), 13 3-0 gauge locomotives (Nos. 101-11, 101A, 102A) and 3 tram locomotives taken into LMS(NCC) stock 1923 (numbers not altered).

BALLYCASTLE RAILWAY

3-0 Gauge.
Stock: 4 new locomotives 1880-1908.
1 secondhand locomotive acquired 1882.

Type	Years built	No. in class	Cylinders	Driving wheels	Locomotive Nos.
0-6-0ST	1880	2	13 x 19	3-3	1, 2
4-4-2T	1908	2	14½ x 22	3-7	3, 4
Belpaire Boiler: 3 & 4.					

No.	Name	Type	Date	Builder	Withdrawn	NCC No.	Remarks
1	*Dalriada*	0-6-0ST	1880	BH	1924		Not taken into LMS(NCC) stock.
2	*Countess of Antrim*	0-6-0ST	1880	BH	1924		Not taken into LMS(NCC) stock.
3	*Lady Boyd*	0-6-0ST		1908			Purchased 1882 from Butler & Fry (see contractors List).
3		4-4-2T	1908	K	LMSNCC	113	
4		4-4-2T	1908	K	LMSNCC	114	

Line closed 1924. Reopened by LMS(NCC) later in 1924 and 2 locomotives taken into stock and renumbered as shown.

LONDON MIDLAND & SCOTTISH RAILWAY
(NORTHERN COUNTIES COMMITTEE)

Stock: 72 5-3 gauge locomotives taken into stock from Midland Railway (Northern Counties Committee) 1923.
13 3-0 gauge locomotives taken into stock from Midland Railway (Northern Counties Committee) 1923.
2 3-0 gauge locomotives taken into stock from Ballycastle Railway 1924.
2 locomotives transferred from London Midland & Scottish Railway 1944.
47 new locomotives built 1923-47 (and 18 rebuilt to new classes).
3 tram locomotives taken into stock from Midland Railway (Northern Counties Committee) 1923.
1 new railcar built 1925.

Class	Type	Years built	No. in class	Cylinders	Driving wheels	Locomotive Nos. (+ subsequently renumbered)
V	0-6-0	1923	3	18 x 24	5-2¼	71-73+
U1	4-4-0	1924-31	4	18 x 24	6-0	1-4
U2	4-4-0	1924-36	18	19 x 24	6-0	74-87; 70-73 rebuilt from U Class
B2	4-4-0	1925	1	18 x 24	6-0	24 (rebuilt from B - see also B3)
	Sentinel	1925	1	6¾ x 9	2-6	91
A1	4-4-0	1927-34	9	18 x 24	6-0	33, 34, 58, 62, 64-66, 68, 69 (rebuilt from A Class)
B3	4-4-0	1927-32	5	18 x 24	6-0	21, 24, 28, 60, 61 (rebuilt from B, B2 and C Classes)
W	2-6-0	1933-42	15	19 x 26	6-0	90-104
Y	0-6-0T	(1944)	2	18 x 26	4-7	18, 19 (transferred from LMS)
WT	2-6-4T	1946-7	10	19 x 26	6-0	1-10
Belpaire boiler: 4-4-0 U1, U2 Classes; 2-6-0 W Class; 2-6-4T WT Class; 0-6-0T Y Class.						
Superheater: 4-4-0 U1, U2 Classes, 0-6-0 V Class ; 2-6-0 W Class ; 2-6-4T WT Class .						
Outside cylinders: 2-6-0 W Class; 2-6-4T WT Class.						

72 5-3 gauge locomotives taken into stock 1923 (former numbers not altered):

No.	Name (date)	Type	Class	Renumbered	Rebuilt	Withdrawn	UTA No.	Remarks
1		2-4-0	I			1924		
2		2-4-0	I			1924		
3	*King Edward VII Binevenagh* (1932)	4-4-0	A	33 1926	1932 A1B.Sh	UTA	33	Name removed 1927 Rebuilt simple 1932
4	*Slemish* (1930)	4-4-0	A	62 1924	1928 A1 B.Sh	UTA	62	Rebuilt simple 1928
5		4-4-0	A	59 1925		1934		See note.
6		2-4-0	G1			1931		
7		0-6-0	K		1923 K1	1934		Rbt. 5-0 boiler
8		2-4-0	G			1930		

No.	Name (date)	Type	Class	Renumbered	Rebuilt	Withdrawn	UTA No.	Remarks
9	Slievebane (1933)	4-4-0	A	69 1925	1933 A1 B.Sh	UTA	69	Rebuilt simple 1933
10		2-4-0	G1			1931		
11		2-4-0	G			1933		
12		2-4-0	H			1924		
13		2-4-0	H			1924		
14		2-4-0	H	14A 1923		1924		
14		4-4-0	U	72 1923	1937 U2 B.Sh	UTA	72	See note.
15		2-4-0	H	15A 1923		1924		
15		4-4-0	U	73 1923	1937 U2 B.Sh	UTA	73	See note.
16		0-4-0ST	N			UTA	16	
17		4-4-0	A	58 1927	1934 A1 B.Sh	UTA	58	See note. Rebuilt simple 1934
18		0-6-0	L			1925		
19		0-6-0	L			1933		
20		4-4-0	A			1929		
21		2-4-0	C	51 1928	1928 C1	1938		Rbt. 5-0 boiler
22		2-4-0	G			1928		
23		2-4-0	F			1940		Reinstated 1941
						1942		
24	County Londonderry (1932)	4-4-0	B		1925 B2 / 1928 B3 B.Sh	1947		Rbt simple & 5-0 boiler 1925.
25		2-4-0ST	J			1934		
26		0-4-2	M			1925		
27		2-4-0	G1			1933		
28		0-6-0	K			1925		
29		2-4-0	G			1925		
30		0-6-0	K1			1938		
31		0-6-0	K		1927 K1	1947		Rbt. 5-0 boiler
32		0-6-0	K1			1933		
33	Galgorm Castle	2-4-0	C			1926		
34	Queen Alexandra Knocklayd (1932)	4-4-0	A		1928 A1 B. Sh	UTA	34	Name removed 1933 Rebuilt simple 1928
35		0-6-0	L			1925		
36		0-6-0	L1			1932		
37		0-6-0	L1			1928		
38		0-6-0	K1	44 1930	1930	1938		Used parts from No. 44 at 1930 rebuilding.
39		0-6-0	K1			1927		
40		2-4-0	G			1925		
41		2-4-0	G			1933		
42		0-4-0ST	N			1925		
43		0-6-0	K1			1938		
44		0-6-0	K1			1929		
45		2-4-0	F			1938		
46		2-4-0	F		1928 F1	1938		Rbt. 5-0 boiler
47		2-4-0ST	J			1932		
48		2-4-0ST	J			1933		
49		2-4-0ST	J			1934		
50	Jubilee	4-4-0	D		1926 D1	1946		Rbt. simple & superheater
51	County Down (1932)	2-4-0	C	21 1928	1926 B1 / 1928 B3 B. Sh	1947		Rbt. 5-0 boiler Rebuilt simple 1928
52		2-4-0	C		1928 C1	1931		Rbt. 5-0 boiler
53		0-6-0	E1			1934		
54		0-6-0	E1			1944		
55	Parkmount	4-4-0	D			1940		Reinstated 1942
						1944		
56		2-4-0	C			1942		
57	Galgorm Castle (1931)	2-4-0	C		1931 C1	1938		Rbt. 5-0 boiler
58	County Tyrone (1932)	2-4-0	C	28 1927	1927 B3 B.Sh	1938		Rebuilt simple 1927
59		4-4-0	B			1924		
60	County Donegal (1932)	4-4-0	B1		1932 B3 B.Sh	1946		Rebuilt simple 1932
61	County Antrim (1932)	4-4-0	B1		1932 B3 B.Sh	1946		Rebuilt simple 1932
62		4-4-0	B			1924		
63	Queen Alexandra (1932)	4-4-0	A			1936		See note.
64	Trostan (1932)	4-4-0	A		1929 A1 B.Sh	UTA	64	See note. Rebuilt simple 1929
65	Knockagh (1931)	4-4-0	A		1929 A1 B.Sh	UTA	65	Rebuilt simple 1929
66	Ben Madigan (1930)	4-4-0	A		1930 A1 B.Sh	UTA	66	Rebuilt simple 1930
67		4-4-0	A			1934		
68	Slieve Gallion (1932)	4-4-0	A		1927 A1 B.Sh	1947		Rebuilt simple 1927
69	Glenarm Castle (1932)	4-4-0	U	71 1923	1927 U2 B.Sh	UTA	71	
70		4-4-0	U		1924 U2 B.Sh	UTA	70	

Notes

Nos. 3, 33, 34, 50, 55 were all named before 1923.

Allotted names which were never affixed:

58	Lurigethan	63	Ben Bradagh	70	Portmuck Castle	73	Carra Castle
59	Craiggor	64	Slieveannora	72	Shane's Castle		

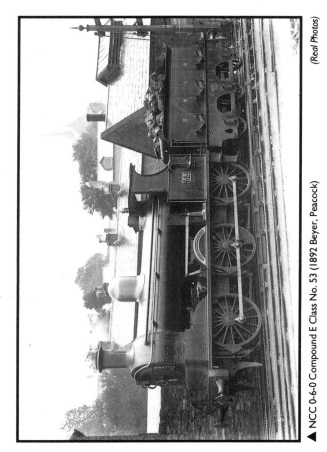

▲ NCC 0-6-0 Compound E Class No. 53 (1892 Beyer, Peacock)

(Real Photos)

▼ NCC 2-6-0 W Class No. 90 before naming (1933 LMS Derby)

(Real Photos)

▲ NCC 4-4-0 D Class No. 50 after conversion from Compound to Simple (1895 Beyer, Peacock)

(Lens of Sutton)

▼ NCC Sentinel Railcar No. 401 (1925)

(Lens of Sutton)

51

13 3-0 gauge locomotives taken into stock 1923 (former numbers not altered)

No.	Type	Class	Renumbered	Rebuilt	Withdrawn	UTA No.	Remarks
101	2-4-2T	S	41 1939	1928 S1	UTA	41	S1 has larger bunker
102	2-4-2T	S	42 1940	1930 S1	UTA	42	S1 has larger bunker
103	2-4-2T	S			1938		
104	2-4-2T	S	43 1942		UTA	43	
105	2-4-0T	P			1928		Sold to C&VBT (No. 3)
106	0-6-0T	Q			1933		
107	0-6-0T	Q			1931		
108	0-6-0T	Q			1932		
109	2-6-0ST	R			1934		
110	2-4-2T	S		1931 S2	1946		S2 is a 2-4-4T with B. Sat boiler
111	2-4-2T	S			UTA	44	Renumbered by RE(NCC) in 1948
101A	0-4-2ST	O			1923		
102A	0-4-2ST	O			1923		

49 new 5-3 gauge locomotives taken into stock 1923-47.
2 3-0 gauge locomotives taken into stock from Ballycastle Railway 1924.

No.	Name (date)	Type	Class	Date	Builder	Renumbered	Withdrawn	UTA No.	Remarks
71		0-6-0	V	1923	LMS	13 1923	UTA	13	See note.
72		0-6-0	V	1923	LMS	14 1923	UTA	14	See note.
73		0-6-0	V	1923	LMS	15 1923	UTA	15	See note.
1	Glenhesk (1932)	4-4-0	U1	1924	NCC		1947		
2	Glendun (1932)	4-4-0	U1	1924	NCC		1947		
74	Dunluce Castle (1931)	4-4-0	U2	1924	NBL		UTA	74	
75	Antrim Castle (1931)	4-4-0	U2	1924	NBL		UTA	75	
76	Olderfleet Castle (1932)	4-4-0	U2	1924	NBL		UTA	76	
77		4-4-0	U2	1924	NBL		UTA	77	See note.
78	Chichester Castle (1932)	4-4-0	U2	1924	NBL		UTA	78	
113		4-4-2T	T	(Ballycastle 3)			1940		Rebuilt 1926. Re-instated 1942
							1946		
114		4-4-2T	T	(Ballycastle 4)			1942		Rebuilt 1927
79	Kernbaan Castle (1931)	4-4-0	U2	1925	NCC		UTA	79	
80	Dunseverick Castle (1933)	4-4-0	U2	1925	NCC		UTA	80	
81	Carrickfergus Castle (1930)	4-4-0	U2	1925	NCC		UTA	81	
82	Dunananie Castle (1932)	4-4-0	U2	1925	NBL		UTA	82	
83	Carra Castle (1932)	4-4-0	U2	1925	NBL		UTA	83	
91		Sentinel		1925	Sen		1932		
3	Galgorm Castle / Glenaan (1932)	4-4-0	U1	1926	NCC		1946		Name removed 1931
84	Lisanoure Castle (1931)	4-4-0	U2	1929	NCC		UTA	84	
4	Glenariff	4-4-0	U1	1931	NCC	4A 1947	UTA	4A	
90	Duke of Abercorn (1934)	2-6-0	W	1933	LMS		UTA	90	See note.
91	The Bush (1935)	2-6-0	W	1933	LMS		UTA	91	See note.
92	The Bann (1936)	2-6-0	W	1933	LMS		UTA	92	See note.
93	The Foyle (1936)	2-6-0	W	1933	LMS		UTA	93	See note.
85		4-4-0	U2	1934	NCC		UTA	85	
94	The Maine (1936)	2-6-0	W	1934	NCC		UTA	94	
95	The Braid (1936)	2-6-0	W	1934	NCC		UTA	95	
86		4-4-0	U2	1935	NCC		UTA	86	See note.
96	Silver Jubilee	2-6-0	W	1935	NCC		UTA	96	
97	Earl of Ulster	2-6-0	W	1935	NCC		UTA	97	
87	Queen Alexandra	4-4-0	U2	1936	NCC		UTA	87	
98	King Edward VIII	2-6-0	W	1937	NCC		UTA	98	
99	King George VI	2-6-0	W	1938	NCC		UTA	99	
100	Queen Elizabeth	2-6-0	W	1939	NCC		UTA	100	Oil burner 1947-1948
101		2-6-0	W	1939	NCC		UTA	101	Oil burner 1947-1948. See note.
102		2-6-0	W	1940	NCC		UTA	102	
103	Thomas Somerset	2-6-0	W	1942	NCC		UTA	103	
104		2-6-0	W	1942	NCC		UTA	104	
18		0-6-0T	Y	(LMS 7456)			UTA	18	See note.
19		0-6-0T	Y	(LMS 7553)			UTA	19	See note.
5		2-6-4T	WT	1946	LMS		UTA	5	
6		2-6-4T	WT	1946	LMS		UTA	6	
7		2-6-4T	WT	1946	LMS		UTA	7	
8		2-6-4T	WT	1946	LMS		UTA	8	
1		2-6-4T	WT	1947	LMS		UTA	1	
2		2-6-4T	WT	1947	LMS		UTA	2	
3		2-6-4T	WT	1947	LMS		UTA	3	
4		2-6-4T	WT	1947	LMS		UTA	4	
9		2-6-4T	WT	1947	LMS		UTA	9	
10		2-6-4T	WT	1947	LMS		UTA	10	

58 5-3 gauge locomotives (Nos. 1-10, 13-16, 18, 19, 33, 34, 58, 62, 64-6, 69, 70-87, 90-104, 4A) and 4 3-0 gauge locomotives (Nos. 41-43, 111) taken into Railway Executive (Northern Counties Comittee) stock in 1948 when the LMS was Nationalised.

Notes

3, 4, 87, 96-100 and 103 were named when new.
Allotted names which were never affixed:
77 *Ballygalley Castle*
86 *King Edward VII*
90 *Earl of Ulster*
91 *Sorley Boy*
92 *Richard de Burgh*
93 *John de Courcy*
71-73 were delivered as such but were immediately altered to X, Y and Z and then to 13-5 respectively in early 1923.
18 was transferred from the LMS in 1944. It was new in 1926 (built by Bagnall) as No. 16539.
19 was transferred from the LMS in 1944. It was new in 1928 (built by Hunslet) as No. 16632.
101 ran as *King George VI* in July 1945.

LOCOMOTIVE PASSENGER LOADING CLASSIFICATION (1934).

Load class	Locomotive classes	Load
A	A, C, C1, D, F	135 tons
B	A1, B3, D1, E, K1, U	235 tons
C	U1, U2	255 tons
D	V (later V1)	300 tons
E	W (also WT from 1945)	330 tons

Tram Locomotives (3-0 gauge)

Tram locomotives Nos. 1, 2, and 3, withdrawn 1926,

The Portstewart tram line closed in 1926.

Railcar

4-wheeled chain drive power bogie (Cyls 6 x 9, driving wheels 2-6) - vertical boiler.

No.	Date	Builder	Withdrawn	Seating	Remarks
401	1925	Sentinel	1932	*	Numbered in the coaching stock series. Seating probably 55 3rd as on GSR vehicles.

RAILWAY EXECUTIVE (NORTHERN COUNTIES COMMITTEE)

Stock: 58 5-3 gauge locomotives taken into stock from LMS(NCC) 1948.
4 3-0 gauge locomotives taken into stock from LMS(NCC) 1948.

No changes were made before handing over to UTA in 1949, but S Class 2-4-2T No. 111 was renumbered 44 in 1948.

ULSTER TRANSPORT AUTHORITY

Stock: 29 locomotives taken into stock from Belfast & County Down Railway 1948.
58 5-3 gauge locomotives taken into stock from Railway Executive (Northern Counties Committee) 1949.
4 3-0 gauge locomotives taken into stock from Railway Executive (Northern Counties Committee) 1949.
83 locomotives taken into stock from Great Northern Railway Board 1958.
2 locomotives purchased from liquidator of Sligo, Leitrim & Northern Counties Railway 1959.
4 locomotives acquired from Coras Iompair Eireann 1963.
8 new locomotives 1949-50.

Class	Type	Years built	No. in class	Cylinders	Driving wheels	Locomotive Nos.
WT	2-6-4T	1949-50	8	19 x 26	6-0	50-7

The above locomotives were built with Belpaire boilers, superheaters and outside cylinders.

29 locomotives taken into stock from B&CDR 1948

B&CDR No.	UTA No.	Type	Withdrawn	Remarks	B&CDR No.	UTA No.	Type	Withdrawn	Remarks
1	201	4-4-2T	1962	Last ran 1949	17	217	4-4-2T	1956	Last ran 1953
3	203	4-4-2T	1956	Last ran 1952	18	218	4-4-2T	1956	Last ran 1951
4	204	0-6-0	1956	Last ran 1951	19	219	4-4-2T	1956	Last ran 1951
5		2-4-2T	1949		20	220	4-4-2T	1956	Last ran 1951
6		2-4-0	1956	Last ran 1951	21	221	4-4-2T	1956	Last ran 1950
7		2-4-2T	1949		22	222	4-6-4T	1956	Last ran 1953
8	208	4-4-2T	1956	Last ran 1953	23	223	4-6-4T	1956	Last ran 1952
9	209	4-4-2T	1956	Last ran 1953	24	224	4-6-4T	1956	Last ran 1952
10		0-6-0	1956	Last ran 1950	25	225	4-6-4T	1956	Last ran 1952
11	211	4-4-2T	1956	Last ran 1952	26		0-6-0	1950	
12	212	4-4-2T	1956	Last ran 1951	27		2-4-2T	1950	
13	213	4-4-2T	1956	Last ran 1950	28		0-4-2T	1949	
14	214	0-6-0	1954	Last ran 1952	29	229	0-6-4T	1956	Last ran 1955
15	215	4-4-2T	1956	Last ran 1952	30	230	4-4-2T	1962	Last ran 1951
16	216	4-4-2T	1956	Last ran 1951					

58 5-3 and 4 3-0 gauge locomotives taken into stock from RE(NCC) 1949, numbers not altered by UTA

No.	Name	Type	Class	Rebuilt		Withdrawn	Remarks
1		2-6-4T	WT			NIR	
2		2-6-4T	WT			NIR	
3		2-6-4T	WT			NIR	
4		2-6-4T	WT			NIR	
5		2-6-4T	WT			NIR	
6		2-6-4T	WT			NIR	
7		2-6-4T	WT			NIR	
8		2-6-4T	WT			NIR	
9		2-6-4T	WT			NIR	
10		2-6-4T	WT			NIR	
13		0-6-0	V	V1	1953	1964	Rebuilt B.Sh
14		0-6-0	V	V1	1951	1961	Rebuilt B.Sh
15		0-6-0	V	V1	1953	1961	Rebuilt B.Sh
16		0-4-0ST	N			1951	
18		0-6-0T	Y			1956	
19		0-6-0T	Y			1963	
33	Binevenagh	4-4-0	A1			1949	
34	Knocklayd	4-4-0	A1			1950	
41		2-4-2T	S1			1954	3-0 gauge
42		2-4-2T	S1			1954	3-0 gauge
43		2-4-2T	S			1954	3-0 gauge
44		2-4-2T	S			1954	3-0 gauge
58		4-4-0	A1			1954	
62	Slemish	4-4-0	A1			1954	
64	Trostan	4-4-0	A1			1954	
65	Knockagh	4-4-0	A1			1950	
66	Ben Madigan	4-4-0	A1			1954	
69	Slievebane	4-4-0	A1			1954	
70		4-4-0	U2			1956	
71	Glenarm Castle	4-4-0	U2			1956	
72		4-4-0	U2			1961	
73		4-4-0	U2			1956	
74	Dunluce Castle	4-4-0	U2			1963	
75	Antrim Castle	4-4-0	U2			1956	
76	Olderfleet Castle	4-4-0	U2			1960	
77		4-4-0	U2			1956	
78	Chichester Castle	4-4-0	U2			1960	
79	Kenbaan Castle	4-4-0	U2			1956	
80	Dunseverick Castle	4-4-0	U2			1961	
81	Carrickfergus Castle	4-4-0	U2			1957	
82	Dunananie Castle	4-4-0	U2			1956	
83	Carra Castle	4-4-0	U2			1956	
84	Lisanoure Castle	4-4-0	U2			1961	
85		4-4-0	U2			1960	
86		4-4-0	U2			1960	
87	Queen Alexandra	4-4-0	U2			1957	
90	Duke of Abercorn	2-6-0	W			1956	
91	The Bush	2-6-0	W			1965	
92	The Bann	2-6-0	W			1957	
93	The Foyle	2-6-0	W			1965	
94	The Maine	2-6-0	W			1965	
95	The Braid	2-6-0	W			1964	
96	Silver Jubilee	2-6-0	W			1961	
97	Earl of Ulster	2-6-0	W			1965	
98	King Edward VIII	2-6-0	W			1964	
99	King George VI	2-6-0	W			1965	
100	Queen Elizabeth	2-6-0	W			1959	
101	Lord Masserene (1949)	2-6-0	W			1956	Name originally allotted was *Viscount Masserene and Ferrard*
102		2-6-0	W			1956	
103	Thomas Somerset	2-6-0	W			1959	
104		2-6-0	W			1965	
4A	Glenariff	4-4-0	U1			1949	

New locomotives 1949-50

No.	Type	Class	Date	Builder	Withdrawn		No.	Type	Class	Date	Builder	Withdrawn	
50	2-6-4T	WT	1949	BR	NIR		54	2-6-4T	WT	1950	BR	NIR	See note
51	2-6-4T	WT	1949	BR	NIR		55	2-6-4T	WT	1950	BR	NIR	See note
52	2-6-4T	WT	1949	BR	NIR		56	2-6-4T	WT	1950	BR	NIR	
53	2-6-4T	WT	1949	BR	NIR		57	2-6-4T	WT	1950	BR	NIR	

Notes

54 was fitted with an enlarged bunker in 1965.

55 ran with a tender (Mogul W Class type) on trial in 1965 and was fitted with an enlarged bunker later the same year.

▲ NCC 0-4-2ST O Class No. 101 narrow gauge ex BC&RBR No. 1 (1874 Black, Hawthorn) *(Real Photos)*

▼ NCC Portstewart tram locomotives (1882-97 Kitson)

(Lens of Sutton)

▲ UTA 2-6-4T WT Class No. 56 (1950 British Railways Derby) with enlarged bunker and another as built on the last regular steam workings in Ireland

(Lens of Sutton)

▼ NCC 2-6-0ST R Class No. 109 narrow gauge ex B&LR No. 5 (1880 Beyer, Peacock) *(Real Photos)*

83 locomotives taken into stock from GNRB 1958 (renumbered where shown)

GNR No.	Type	Class	UTA No.	Withdrawn	Remarks
2	4-4-2T	T2	2x	1960	
4	4-4-2T	T2	4x	1960	
5	4-4-2T	T2	5x	1964	
6	0-6-0	SG3	30	1961	
7	0-6-0	SG3	31	1965	
9	0-6-0	LQGs	9x	1960	
10	0-6-0	PGs	10x	1964	
11	0-6-0	PGs	11x	1960	
13	0-6 0	SG3	32	1965	
16	0-6-0	SG2	38	1965	
17	0-6-0	SG2	39	1961	
18	0-6-0	SG2	40	1965	
20	0-6-0	SG3	33	1965	
21	4-4-2T	T2		1958	
22	0-6-4T	RT		1958	
23	0-6-4T	RT	23	1963	
30	4-4-2T	T2	30x	1961	
32	0-6-0	AL	32x	1960	
39	0-6-0	LQGs	39x	1960	
40	0-6-0	SG3	34	1965	
41	0-6-0	SG3	35	1965	
42	4-4-0	PPs	42x	1960	
43	4-4-0	PPs	43x	1960	
46	4-4-0	PPs		1958	
49	0-6-0	SG3	36	1965	
50	4-4-0	PPs	50x	1960	
56	0-6-0	AL	56x	1960	
64	4-4-2T	T2	64x	1960	
66	4-4-2T	T2	66x	1960	
69	4-4-2T	T2		1958	
74	4-4-0	PPs	74x	1963	Renumbered 42x (1960)
76	4-4-0	PPs		1958	
78	0-6-0	UG	45	1965	
79	0-6-0	UG	46	1963	
82	0-6-0	UG	47	1965	
83	4-4-0	V	83x	1960	*Eagle*
86	4-4-0	V	86x	1961	*Peregrine*
87	4-4-0	V	87x	1960	*Kestrel*
97	0-6-0	SG3	37	1967	
100	0-6-0	PGs	100x	1961	
101	0-6-0	PGs	101x	1960	
102	0-6-0	PGs	102x	1960	
103	0-6-0	PGs	103x	1960	
107	4-4-0	PPs		1958	
108	0-6-0	LQGs		1958	
109	0-6-0	LQGs		1958	
111	0-6-0	LQGs	111x	1963	
119	0-6-0	LQGs		1958	
121	4-4-0	Qs		1958	
122	4-4-0	Qs	122x	1960	
125	4-4-0	Qs		1958	
127	4-4-0	QLs	127x	1960	
135	4-4-0	Qs	135x	1963	
142	4-4-2T	T2	142x	1960	
146	0-6-0	UG	48	NIR	
149	0-6-0	UG	49	NIR	
151	0-6-0	PGs	151x	1961	
156	0-6-0	QLs	156x	1960	
157	4-4-0	QLs		1958	
160	0-6-0	LQGs		1958	
162	0-6-0	LQGs		1958	
165	0-6-0	LQGs	165x	1961	
166	0-6-4T	RT	24	1963	
167	0-6-4T	RT	25	1963	
172	4-4-0	S	60	1965	*Slieve Donard*
173	4-4-0	S	61	1964	*Galtee More*
175	0-6-0	SG	43	1965	
176	0-6-0	SG	44	1965	
182	0-6-0	SG2	41	1963	
183	0-6-0	SG2	42	1961	
185	4-4-2T	T1	185x	1960	
186	4-4-2T	T1	186x	1960	
187	4-4-2T	T1	187x	1964	
189	4-4-2T	T1	189x	1960	
190	4-4-0	S2	62	1965	*Lugnaquilla*
192	4-4-0	S2	63	1965	*Slievenamon*
196	4-4-0	U	64	1961	*Lough Gill*
200	4-4-0	U	65	1961	*Lough Melvin*
201	4-4-0	U	66	1965	*Meath*
202	4-4-0	U	67	1965	*Louth*
205	4-4-0	U	68	1965	*Down*
208	4-4-0	VS	58	1965	*Lagan*
210	4-4-0	VS	59	1963	*Erne*

Where no UTA number is shown the former GNR number was not altered at all. 35 locomotives as shown had 'x' added to the GNR number (as they were to remain in traffic only until in need of heavy repairs). GNR classification and names were retained. 34 locomotives were renumbered into the UTA list as shown below.

UTA Nos.	GNR Class	Former GNR Nos.
23-5	RT	23, 166, 167
30-7	SG3	6, 7, 13, 20, 40, 41, 49, 97
38-42	SG2	16, 17, 18, 182, 183
43/4	SG	175, 176
45-9	UG	78, 79, 82, 146, 149
58/9	VS	208, 210
60/1	S	172, 173
62/3	S2	190, 192
64-8	U	196, 200, 201, 202, 205

2 locomotives acquired from the liquidator of SL&NCR 1959

UTA No.	Name	Type	UTA Class	Withdrawn	Remarks
26	*Lough Melvin*	0-6-4T	Z	NIR	SL&NCR name retained
27	*Lough Erne*	0-6-4T	Z	NIR	SL&NCR name retained

4 locomotives acquired from CIE 1963 (Former GNRB locomotives. Numbers, names and classifications not altered)

No.	Name	Type	Class	Withdrawn	No.	Name	Type	Class	Withdrawn
170	*Errigal*	4-4-0	S	1965	174	*Carrantuohill*	4-4-0	S	1965
171	*Slieve Gullion*	4-4-0	S	1965	207	*Boyne*	4-4-0	VS	1965

22 locomotives taken into NIR stock 1968. (Nos. 1-10, 26/7, 48-57)

NORTHERN IRELAND RAILWAYS

Stock: 22 locomotives taken into stock from Ulster Transport Authority 1968.

No.	Type	Class	Withdrawn	Remarks	No.	Type	Class	Withdrawn	Remarks
1	2-6-4T	WT	1968		27	0-6-4T	Z	1970	*Lough Erne*
2	2-6-4T	WT	1968		48	0-6-0	UG	1968	
3	2-6-4T	WT	1970		49	0-6-0	UG	1968	
4	2-6-4T	WT	1971	See note	50	2-6-4T	WT	1970	See note
5	2-6-4T	WT	1970		51	2-6-4T	WT	1971	See note
6	2-6-4T	WT	1970		52	2-6-4T	WT	1968	
7	2-6-4T	WT	1968		53	2-6-4T	WT	1971	See note
8	2-6-4T	WT	1968		54	2-6-4T	WT	1970	
9	2-6-4T	WT	1968		55	2-6-4T	WT	1970	
10	2-6-4T	WT	1970		56	2-6-4T	WT	1970	See note
26	0-6-4T	Z	1968	*Lough Melvin*	57	2-6-4T	WT	1968	

Note

4, 50, 51, 53 & 56 were fitted with enlarged bunkers in 1968.

Steam working on NIR ceased in 1971.

PART III - GREAT SOUTHERN RAILWAYS & CORAS IOMPAIR EIREANN

Constituent and absorbed railways which contributed locomotives to the Great Southern Railways and Coras Iompair Eireann.

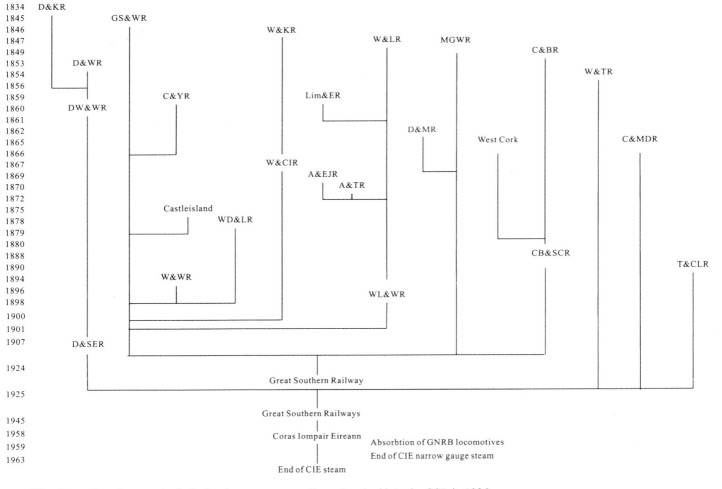

The above chart does not include the six narrow gauge lines absorbed into the GSR in 1925.

CORK & YOUGHAL RAILWAY

Stock: 10 new locomotives 1859-62.

Type	Years built	No. in class	Cylinders	Driving wheels	Locomotive Nos.
2-4-0ST	1859-62	7	15 x 24	5-9	1-5, 9, 10
2-2-2ST	1861	3	15 x 22	6-0	6-8

No.	Name	Type	Date	Builder	GS&WR No.
1	Lewis	2-4-0ST	1859	N	61
2	Roney	2-4-0ST	1859	N	62
3	Carlisle	2-4-0ST	1859	N	63
4	Chambers	2-4-0ST	1860	N	64
5	Pike	2-4-0ST	1860	N	65
6	Fermoy	2-2-2ST	1861	N	68
7	Stuart de Decies	2-2-2ST	1861	N	69
8		2-2-2ST	1861	N	70
9	Hartington	2-4-0ST	1862	N	66
10	Arnott	2-4-0ST	1862	N	67

10 locomotives taken into GS&WR stock 1866 and renumbered as shown.

CASTLEISLAND RAILWAY

Stock: 1 new locomotive 1875.

Type	Years built	No. in class	Cylinders	Driving wheels	Locomotive Nos.
0-6-4T	1875	1	10 x 18	3-8½	

No.	Type	Date	Builder	GS&WR No.	Remarks
	0-6-4T	1875	GS&WR	90	Not numbered by Castleisland Railway. Combined locomotive and carriage.

1 locomotive taken into GS&WR stock 1879 and numbered as shown.

WATERFORD, DUNGARVAN & LISMORE RAILWAY

Stock: 6 new locomotives 1878-92.
1 secondhand locomotive acquired 1883.

Type	Years built	No. in class	Cylinders	Driving wheels	Locomotive Nos.
0-4-2	1878-92	6	17 x 24	4-9½	1-4, 6, 7.

No.	Type	Date	Builder	GS&WR No.	Remarks
1	0-4-2	1878	SS	211	
2	0-4-2	1878	SS	212	
3	0-4-2	1878	SS	213	
4	0-4-2	1878	SS	214	
5	2-4-0ST	(GS&WR 71)		215	Purchased 1883
6	0-4-2	1891	SS	216	
7	0-4-2	1892	SS	217	

Note

The WD&LR originally ordered 4 0-6-0 from AE. These were refused and in 1880 they were purchased by the MGWR - see MGWR Nos. 96-9.

7 locomotives taken into GS&WR stock 1898 and allotted numbers 211-7.

WATERFORD & WEXFORD RAILWAY

Stock: 2 new locomotives 1894.

Type	Years built	No. in class	Cylinders	Driving wheels	Locomotive Nos.
0-4-0ST	1894	1	10 x 15	2-10	Cambria
0-6-0ST	1894	1	12 x 18	3-1	Erin
Outside cylinders: 0-4-0ST Cambria					

Name	Type	Date	Builder	Withdrawn
Cambria	0-4-0ST	1894	HE	GS&WR
Erin	0-6-0ST	1894	HE	GS&WR

2 locomotives taken into GS&WR stock 1898 (names retained, no numbers allotted).

▲ NCC 2-4-2T Compound S Class No. 111 (1892 Beyer, Peacock) (R.G. Jarvis)

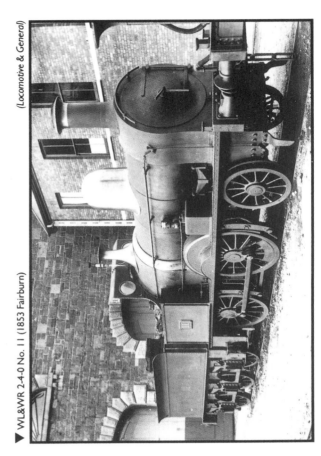

▼ WL&WR 2-4-0 No. 11 (1853 Fairburn) (Locomotive & General)

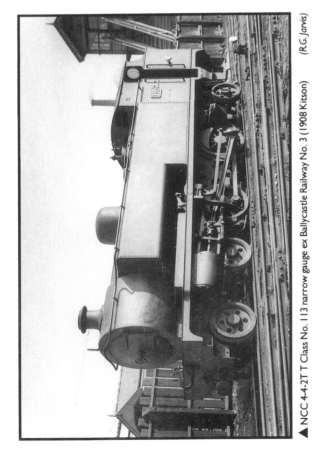

▲ NCC 4-4-2T T Class No. 113 narrow gauge ex Ballycastle Railway No. 3 (1908 Kitson) (R.G. Jarvis)

▼ G&SWR 0-4-2 No. 217 ex WD&LR No. 7 (1892 Sharp, Stewart) (Real Photos)

WATERFORD & KILKENNY RAILWAY
WATERFORD & CENTRAL IRELAND RAILWAY

Stock: 18 new locomotives 1846-97.

Type	Years built	No. in class	Cylinders	Driving wheels	Locomotive Nos. (+ subsequently renumbered)
4-2-2T	1846	3	14 x 20	5-6	1+, 2, 3.
2-4-0	1852	2	15 x 22	5-1	4+, 5+
2-2-2	1853	2	15 x 22	5-9	6+, 7+
2-4-0	1855	1	15 x 21	5-6	1
0-4-2	1857	1	16 x 24	4-9	2+
2-4-0T	1867	2	15 x 22	5-0	6, 7
2-4-0	1867-8	2	15 x 22	5-3	8, 9
0-4-2	1873	2	16 x 24	5-3	10, 11
0-4-2T	1876	1	14 x 22	4-6	12
0-4-2	1884	1	16 x 24	5-3	1
0-4-2	1897	1	16 x 24	5-3	4

Locomotives built 1846-57

The W&KR was operated by the W&LR from 1861-7, the locomotives being included in the latter's stock.

Original W&KR No.	W&LR No.	2nd W&KR No.	Type	Date	Builder	Withdrawn	GS&WR No.	Remarks
1			4-2-2T	1848	Tay	1859		Ready 1846. Renumbered 8 in 1857*. Sold to Carlisle & Hutchings
2			4-2-2T	1848	Tay	*		Ready 1846.
3			4-2-2T	1848	Tay	*		Ready 1846.
4	23	2	2-4-0	1852	S&S	GS&WR	251	
5	24	3	2-4-0	1852	S&S	GS&WR		Not allotted a GS&WR number.
6	25	4	2-2-2	1853	K	1892		
7	27	5	2-2-2	1853	K	1892		
1	26		2-4-0	1855	Fbn	W&LR		Retained by W&LR in 1867.
2	22	1	0-4-2	1857	EBW	1892		

Locomotives built 1867-97

No.	Type	Date	Builder	Rebuilt	GS&WR No.	Remarks
6	2-4-0T	1867	JF	1872 2-4-0	253	Two of JF Nos. 706-9 built to the order of BH&BR.
7	2-4-0T	1867	JF	1869 2-4-0	254	
8	2-4-0	1867	VF		255	
9	2-4-0	1868	VF		256	
10	0-4-2	1873	AE		257	
11	0-4-2	1873	AE		258	
12	0-4-2T	1876	AE		259	
1	0-4-2	1884	SS		250	May have been No. 13 when new
4	0-4-2	1897	VF		252	

11 locomotives (Nos. 1-4, 6-12) taken into GS&WR stock 1900 and renumbered as shown.

LIMERICK & ENNIS RAILWAY

Stock: 1 new locomotive 1859.
2 secondhand locomotives acquired 1859.

Type	Years built	No. in class	Cylinders	Driving wheels	Locomotive Nos.
0-4-2	1859	1	16 x 22	5-0	1

No.	Name	Type	Date	Builder	W&LR No.	Remarks
1		0-4-2	1859	Fbn	1	
2		0-4-2			2	Purchased 1859 from W. Dargan (see Miscellaneous List).
3	Pioneer	0-4-2			3	Purchased 1859 from W. Dargan (see Contractors List).

3 locomotives taken into W&LR stock 1861, numbers not altered.

ATHENRY & ENNIS JUNCTION RAILWAY

Stock: 3 secondhand locomotives acquired 1869-70.

No.	Name	Type	W&LR No.	Remarks
1	Drumconora	2-2-2	30	Purchased 1869 from MGWR (No. 8).
2	Lough Cutra	2-2-2	31	Purchased 1869 from MGWR (No. 9 or 10*).
3	Gort	0-4-2	24	Purchased 1870 from D&MR (No. 5). Ran as A&TR No. 4 in 1872.

3 locomotives taken into W&LR stock 1872 and renumbered as shown.

ATHENRY & TUAM RAILWAY

Stock: 3 secondhand locomotives acquired 1870-1.
1 locomotive transferred from Athenry & Ennis Junction Railway 1872.

No.	Name	Type	W&LR No.	Remarks
1		0-4-2	22	Purchased 1870 from D&MR (No. 1).
2		0-4-2	23	Purchased 1870 from D&MR (No. 2).
3		0-4-2	25	Purchased 1871 from GS&WR (No. 102).
4	Gort	0-4-2		Ran as A&TR No. 4 during 1872 only and then returned to A&EJR.

3 locomotives taken into W&LR stock 1872 and renumbered as shown.

WATERFORD & LIMERICK RAILWAY
WATERFORD, LIMERICK & WESTERN RAILWAY

Stock: 76 new locomotives 1847-1900.
22 secondhand locomotives acquired 1853-83.

Type	Years built	No. in class	Cylinders	Driving wheels	Locomotive Nos.
2-2-2	1847	6	15 x 22	5-9	1-6
2-4-0	1853-4	4	15 x 21	5-0	11, 12, 17, 18
0-4-2	1853-4	4	16 x 24	4-6	13-16
2-4-0	1854-5	3	15 x 21	5-6	19-21
0-4-2	1862-4	3	16 x 24	4-6	4-6
2-2-2	1864	1	15 x 22	5-10½	28
0-4-0ST	1865	1	12 x 17	3-10	29
0-4-2	1872	2	16 x 24	4-6	3, 7
2-4-0	1874-82	10	16 x 24	5-6	8, 25, 30-32, 35-39
0-4-2	1876	4	16 x 24	5-6	19, 26, 27, 33
0-6-0T	(1878)	1	15 x 18	4-0	34
0-6-0	1883	2	17½ x 26	5-1½	40, 41
0-6-0WT	(1862)	1	15 x 21	3-6	42
0-6-0	(1879)	1	17 x 24	4-6	1
4-4-0	1886	1	16½ x 24	5-1	9
4-4-0	1886	I	17½ x 26	5-6	12
0-6-0	1886	1	17 x 24	4-6	24
0-6-0	1888-93	3	16 x 24	4-7	5-7
2-4-0	1888-94	8	17 x 24	6-0	10, 20, 22, 23, 43, 44, 47, 48
2-4-2T	1891	2	16 x 24	5-6	13, 14
0-4-2T	1892	1	16 x 24	4-7	3
0-6-0	1893	2	17 x 24	5-1½	45, 46
0-4-4T	1894	1	16 x 24	4-7	15
0-6-0	1895	2	17½ x 24	5-1½	49, 50
0-4-4T	1895	2	16 x 24	5-6	51, 52
4-4-2T	1896-7	4	16 x 24	5-6	16-18, 21
4-4-0	1896-7	3	17 x 24	6-0	53-55
0-6-0	1897-1900	4	17 x 24	5-2	2, 56-58
0-4-4T	1899	1	16 x 24	5-4	27
Belpaire boiler: 0-6-0 2					
Outside cylinders: 2-2-2 1-6; 0-6-0WT 42					

No.	Name	Type	Date	Builder	Withdrawn	GS&WR No.	Remarks
1	Glengall	2-2-2	1847	S&S	1861		See note
2	Bessborough	2-2-2	1847	S&S	1862		See note
3	Waterford	2-2-2	1847	S&S	1860		See note
4	Limerick	2-2-2	1847	S&S	1860		See note
5	Suir	2-2-2	1847	S&S	1862		See note
6	Shannon	2-2-2	1847	S&S	1862		See notes. Rebuilt to 2-2-2T 1857*
7		2-2-2	(W. Dargan)		1871		Purchased 1853 from W. Dargan. See Miscellaneous List.
8		2-2-2	(W. Dargan)		1880		Purchased 1853 from W. Dargan. New to NW&RR (No. 3).
9		2-2-2	(W. Dargan)		1885		Purchased 1853 from W. Dargan. New to NW&RR (No. 1 or 2*).
10		2-2-2	(W. Dargan)		1888		Purchased 1853 from W. Dargan. New to NW&RR (No. 1 or 2*).
11		2-4-0	1853	Fbn		GS&WR 264	
12		2-4-0	1853	Fbn	1885		
13		0-4-2	1853	SS	1891		
14		0-4-2	1853	SS	1891		
15		0-4-2	1853	SS	1894		
16		0-4-2	1854	SS	1896		
17		2-4-0	1854	Fbn	1896		
18		2-4-0	1854	Fbn	1897		

No.	Name	Type	Date	Builder	Withdrawn	GS&WR No.	Remarks
19		2-4-0	1854	Fbn	1874		
20		2-4-0	1854	Fbn	1892		
21		2-4-0	1855	Fbn	1897		
22		0-4-2	(W&KR 2)		1867		Returned to W&KR (No. 1)
23		2-4-0	(W&KR 4)		1867		Returned to W&KR (No. 2)
24		2-4-0	(W&KR 5)		1867		Returned to W&KR (No. 3)
25		2-2-2	(W&KR 6)		1867		Returned to W&KR (No. 4)
26		2-4-0	(W&KR 1)		1875		
27		2-2-2	(W&KR 7)		1867		Returned to W&KR (No. 5)
1		0-4-2	(Lim&ER 1)		1883		
2		0-4-2	(Lim&ER 2)		1900		
3	Pioneer	0-4-2	(Lim&ER 3)		1874		Renumbered 27 (1872)
4		0-4-2	1862	SS	GS&WR	223	
5		0-4-2	1862	SS	1893		
6		0-4-2	1864	SS	1890		
28	South of Ireland	2-2-2	1864	K	GS&WR	280	
29		0-4-0ST	1865	SS	GS&WR	228	
3		0-4-2	1872	K	1892		
7		0-4-2	1872	K	1888		
22		0-4-2	(A&TR 1)		1890		
23		0-4-2	(A&TR 2)		1892		
24	Gort	0-4-2	(A&EJR 3)		1886		
25		0-4-2	(A&TR 3)		1873-4*		
30	Drumconora	2-2-2	(A&EJR 1)		1873		
31	Lough Cutra	2-2-2	(A&EJR 2)		1872-3*		
25	Verbera	2-4-0	1874	VF	GS&WR	277	Originally named Limerick
30	Lily	2-4-0	1874	VF	GS&WR	281	Originally named Waterford
31	Myrtle	2-4-0	1874	VF	GS&WR	282	Originally named Ennis
32	Dahlia	2-4-0	1874	VF	GS&WR	283	Originally named Tuam
19	Kincora	0-4-2	1876	AE	GS&WR	272	
26		0-4-2	1876	AE	GS&WR	278	
27		0-4-2	1876	AE	1899		
33		0-4-2	1876	AE	GS&WR	284	
34		0-6-0T	*	*	GS&WR	229	Purchased 1878 from AE. Origin unknown but claimed to be 7-0¼ gauge when new.
8	Primrose	2-4-0	1881	VF	GS&WR	261	
35		2-4-0	1881	VF	GS&WR	285	Originally named Duncannon
36	Violet	2-4-0	1881	VF	GS&WR	286	
37	Camelia	2-4-0	1881	VF	GS&WR	287	
38	Hyacinth	2-4-0	1882	VF	GS&WR	288	
39	Shamrock	2-4-0	1882	VF	GS&WR	289	Originally named North Star
40	Vulcan	0-6-0	1883	VF	GS&WR	230	
41	Titan	0-6-0	1883	VF	GS&WR	231	
42		0-6-0WT	1862	H(L)	GS&WR	232	Purchased 1883. Built for Anglesey Central Railway, then Neath & Brecon Railway No. 3 Miers.
1		0-6-0	1879	RS	GS&WR	221	Purchased 1883 from maker (arrived 1884). Rebuilt to 0-6-0 ST 1899.
9	Garryowen	4-4-0	1886	D	GS&WR	262	
12	Earl of Bessborough	4-4-0	1886	VF	GS&WR	265	Rebuilt to 2-4-0 1894.
24	Sarsfield	0-6-0	1886	D	GS&WR	227	
7	Progress	0-6-0	1888	W&LR	GS&WR	226	Renamed Wasp 1893.
10	Sir James	2-4-0	1889	D	GS&WR	263	
6	Ant	0-6-0	1890	W&LR	GS&WR	225	
22	Era	2-4-0	1890	D	GS&WR	275	
13	Derry Castle	2-4-2T	1891	VF	GS&WR	266	
14	Lough Derg	2-4-2T	1891	VF	GS&WR	267	
3	Zetland	0-4-2T	1892	W&LR	GS&WR	260	
20	Galtee More	2-4-0	1892	D	GS&WR	273	
23	Sleive-Na-Mon	2-4-0	1892	D	GS&WR	276	
5	Bee	0-6-0	1893	W&LR	GS&WR	224	
43	Knockma	2-4-0	1893	D	GS&WR	290	
44	Nephin	2-4-0	1893	D	GS&WR	291	
45	Colleen Bawn	0-6-0	1893	D	GS&WR	233	
46	Erin Go Bragh	0-6-0	1893	D	GS&WR	234	
15	Roxborough	0-4-4T	1894	W&LR	GS&WR	268	
47	Carrick Castle	2-4-0	1894	D	GS&WR	292	
48	Granston	2-4-0	1894	D	GS&WR	293	
49	Dreadnought	0-6-0	1895	D	GS&WR	235	
50	Hercules	0-6-0	1895	D	GS&WR	236	

▲ GS&WR 0-6-0 No. 226 ex WL&WR No. 7 (1888 WL&WR Limerick) (Real Photos)

▼ GS&WR 0-4-2 No. 101 (1845 Bury, Curtis & Kennedy) (Real Photos)

▲ WL&WR 0-6-0WT No. 42 (1862 Hawthorn) (Locomotive & General)

▼ WL&WR 2-4-0 No. 47 later GS&WR No. 292 (1894 Dubs) (Real Photos)

No.	Name	Type	Date	Builder	Withdrawn	GS&WR No.	Remarks
53	*Jubilee*	4-4-0	1896	K	GS&WR	296	
54	*Killemnee*	4-4-0	1896	K	GS&WR	297	
18	*Geraldine*	4-4-2T	1897	K	GS&WR	271	
21	*Blarney Castle*	4-4-2T	1897	K	GS&WR	274	
55	*Bernard*	4-4-0	1897	K	GS&WR	298	
56	*Thunderer*	0-6-0	1897	K	GS&WR	237	
57	*Cyclops*	0-6-0	1897	K	GS&WR	238	
58	*Goliath*	0-6-0	1897	K	GS&WR	239	
27	*Thomond*	0-4-4T	1899	WL&WR	GS&WR	279	
2	*Shannon*	0-6-0	1900	K	GS&WR	222	

Notes

Naming became fairly general from 1886 onwards, all new locomotives then being named and many older locomotives had names affixed. Locomotives taken into stock from the Lim&ER and A&EJR retained their names. The 2-4-0s of 1874 and 1881-2 may all have had names when new in addition to those shown (one was *Cahir*, number unknown), but these names were removed at an early date. All names were removed by the GS&WR after 1901. 2-2-2 Nos. 1-6 were named only until about 1853. It is not certain exactly which names applied to each number, but it is likely that the order given is correct. One of Nos. 1-6 was converted to a tank locomotive - No. 6 is most probable.

WL&WR Nos. 47 and 48 were counted statistically as the property of the Athenry & Tuam Extension to Claremorris Railway 1894-1924 (but also included in WL&WR and GS&WR totals as well!).

There were 2 0-6-0 locomotives on order in 1900 which were purchased by the MGWR in 1901. They were to have been WL&WR Nos. 4 *Shamrock* and 11 *Samson* - see MGWR Nos. 141 and 142.

58 locomotives (Nos. 1-58) taken into GS&WR stock in 1901 and renumbered as shown.

GREAT SOUTHERN & WESTERN RAILWAY

Stock: 458 new locomotives built 1845-1924.
10 locomotives taken into stock from Cork & Youghal Railway 1866.
1 locomotive taken into stock from Castleisland Railway 1879.
7 locomotives taken into stock from Waterford, Dungarvan & Lismore Railway 1898.
2 locomotives taken into stock from Waterford & Wexford Railway 1898.
11 locomotives taken into stock from Waterford & Central Ireland Railway 1900.
58 locomotives taken into stock from Waterford, Limerick & Western Railway 1901.
1 locomotive taken into stock from Fenit Harbour Commissioners 1901.
1 locomotive taken into stock from Dublin & Blessington Steam Tramway 1921*.
1 new steam railmotor built 1905.

Class	Type	Years built	No. in class	Cylinders	Driving wheels	Locomotive Nos. (+ subsequently renumbered)
	2-2-2	1845	2	14 x 20	5-8	21, 22
	0-4-2	1845	2	14 x 24	5-0	41+, 42+
	2-2-2	1846-8	20	15 x 20	5-6	1-20
	2-2-2	1846-7	14	15 x 20	6-0	23-36
	0-4-2	1847	2	15 x 24	5-0	43+ 44+
	0-4-2	1847-8	6	16 x 24	5-0	45-50+
	2-2-2	1848	4	15 x 20	5-8	37-40
	0-4-2	1849	2	15 x 24	5-0	51+, 52+
	0-4-2	1850	4	15 x 24	5-0	53-56+
	0-4-2	1852	2	15 x 24	5-0	57+, 58+
	2-2-2	1853	1	15 x 20	6-0	59+
	0-6-0	1854	2	17 x 24	5-0	60+, 61+
	0-4-2	1854	2	16 x 24	5-2	62+, 63+
	2-4-0	1855	3	14½ x 22	5-2	64-66+
	2-4-0	1855	2	15 x 21	5-6	70+ 71+
	0-6-0	1856	6	16 x 24	4-6	67+, 68+, 69+, 72-4+
	0-4-2	1856	1	16 x 22	5-0	75+
	0-2-4T	1857	1	6½ x 12	4-6	*Sprite*
	2-2-2	1858	3	15 x 20	6-6	77-9+
	2-2-2	1859-63	9	15 x 22	6-6	76+ 80+, 81+, 88-90+, 94-6+. (See note)
	0-4-2	1860-2	9	16 x 24	4-6	82-7+, 91-3+
	0-4-2	1863-5	6	16 x 24	5-0	97-9+, 136-8. (See note)
1	2-4-0	1866-74	9	15 x 22	5-7½	1, 4, 9, 11, 14, 16-9
101	0-6-0	1866-1903	118	17 x 24} 18 x 24}	5-1¾	101-200, 223/9/32/40-3/53-6 and replacement 103 5/10/1/4/47/9 (See note)
56	2-2-2	1867	2	15 x 20	6-0	27+, 30+
	0-6-0	1867	1	17 x 24	5-1¼	118
56	2-4-0	1868-70	6	16 x 22	6-6	56-61
1	2-4-0	1869-70	3	16 x 22	5-7½	3, 12, 20
33	0-4-4T§	1869-70	2	15 x 20	5-7½	33, 34
27	0-4-4T§	1870-1	4	15 x 20	5-7½	27, 30-32
21	2-4-0	1873-6	10	16 x 20	5-7½	21-6, 66-9

Class	Type	Years built	No. in class	Cylinders	Driving wheels	Locomotive Nos. (+ subsequently renumbered)
SPRITE	0-4-4T§	1873	1	9 x 12	5-0	*Sprite*
64	2 4-0	1875	2	17 x 22	6-6½	64, 65
35	0-4-4T§	1875	4	15 x 20	5-7½	35-8
201	0-6-4T§	1876	2	18 x 24	4-6½	201+, 202+
2	4-4-0	1877-80	12	16 x 20	5-8½	2, 5-8, 10, 13, 15, 43-6
28	0-4-4T§	1879	4	16 x 20	5-8½	28, 29, 39, 40
203	0-6-4T§	1879-80	4	18 x 24	4-6½	203-6
90	0-6-4T§	1881	2	10 x 18	3-8½	91, 92 (See note)
47	0-4-4T§	1883-7	20	16 x 20	5-8½	47-51, 70-84
52	4-4-0	1883-90	20	17 x 22	6-7	1, 3, 4, 9, 11, 12, 14, 16, 18, 20, 52-9, 97/8
60	4-4-0	1885-95	15	18 x 24	6-7	60-5, 85-9, 93-6
207	0-6-0T	1887-1901	10	18 x 24	4-6½	201, 202, 207-10, 217-20
99	0-6-0T	1890-1	2	10 x 18	3-8½	99, 100
42	2-4-2T	1892-4	6	16 x 20	5-8½	33-6, 41, 42
37	4-4-2T	1894-1901	6	16 x 20	5-8½	37, 38, 317-20
FAIRY	0-4-2T	1894	1	9 x 12	5-0	*Fairy*
301	4-4-0	1900	4	18 x 26	6-7	301-4
27	4-4-2T	1900-1	4	17 x 22	5-8½	27, 30-2
305	4-4-0	1902	4	18 x 26	6-7	305-8
309	4-4-0	1903	6	18½ x 26	6-7	309-14
351	0-6-0	1903	4	18 x 26	5-1¾	351-4
355	0-6-0	1903	7	19 x 26	5-1¾	355-61
211	0-6-2T	1903	4	18 x 26	4-6½	211-4
321	4-4-0	1904-6	12	18½ x 26	6-7	321-32
362	4-6-0	1905-7	6	19¼ x 26	5-1¾	362-7
333	4-4-0	1907-8	8	18 x 26	5-8½	333-40
368	2-6-0	1909	4	19 x 26	5-1¾	368-71
249	0-6-0	1912	4	18 x 26	5-1¾	249-52
341	4-4-0	1913	1	19 x 26	6-7	341
257	0-6-0	1913-4	8	19 x 26	5-1¾	257-64
SAMBO	0-4-2ST	1914	1	16 x 20	4-6½	*Sambo*
900	4-8-0T	1915	1	19¼ x 26	4-6½	900
400	4-6-0	1916-22	10	14 x 26 (4)	6-7	400-9
500	4-6-0	1924	1	19½ x 28	5-8½	500

Belpaire boiler: 4-4-0 341; 2-6-0 368; 4-6-0 400, 500; 4-8-0T 900.	
Superheater: 0-6-0 257; 4-4-0 341; 4-6-0 400-6, 500.	
Outside cylinders (2): *Sprite* (1857); 4-6-0 500.	
Outside cylinders (4): 4-6-0 400.	

Notes

§ These locomotives had back tanks only.

Nos. 76, 80 & 81 were ordered as Nos. 80-2.

Nos. 136-8 were ordered as Nos. 100-2.

Nos. 103/11 were built with 15 in. cylinders, other locomotives built 1866-74 were 17 in. when new. From No. 171 onwards (1874) 18 in. cylinders were used. These eventually became standard. Wheel diameter was originally 5-1½ but increased to 5-1¾ with thicker tyres.

A further 90 class locomotive had been built in 1875 for the Castleisland Railway (becoming No. 90 on being taken into GS&WR stock in 1879). These were combined locomotives and carriages (Nos. 90 and 92) or van (No. 91).

Locomotives taken into GS&WR stock 1866-1921*

(i) Locomotives built 1845-65

At first locomotives had only names but about 1847 numbers came into use, the names being dispensed with. It is not possible to link any particular name with any particular locomotive. It seems that animal names were applied to Bury locomotives (*Camel, Lion, Dromedary, Stag, Antelope* are known) and birds to Sharp locomotives (*Pheasant* is known) - other names were *Buffalo, Leopard, Urus, Grouse.*

59 out of the 100 locomotives existing in 1864 were renumbered that year, the only time that a major renumbering of purely GS&WR locomotives ever took place.

First No.	1864 No.	Type	Date	Builder	Withdrawn	Remarks
21	21	2-2-2	1845	BCK	1873	
22	22	2-2-2	1845	BCK	1873	
41	100	0-4-2	1845	BCK	1873	
42	101	0-4-2	1845	BCK	1880	
1	1	2-2-2	1846	SS	1866	
2	2	2-2-2	1846	SS	1873	
3	3	2-2-2	1846	SS	1865	
4	4	2-2-2	1846	SS	1867	
5	5	2-2-2	1846	SS	1875	
6	6	2-2-2	1846	SS	1872	
7	7	2-2-2	1846	SS	1874	
8	8	2-2-2	1846	SS	1874	

First No.	1864 No.	Type	Date	Builder	Withdrawn	Remarks
9	9	2-2-2	1846	SS	1866	
10	10	2-2-2	1846	SS	1874	May have been sold (See Contractors List)
23	23	2-2-2	1846	BCK	1872	
24	24	2-2-2	1846	BCK	1872	Sold to C&BR (No. 8)
25	25	2-2-2	1846	BCK	1872	
26	26	2-2-2	1846	BCK	1872	
27	27	2-2-2	1846	BCK	1867	
28	28	2-2-2	1846	BCK	1873	Ran until 1876
29	29	2-2-2	1846	BCK	1871	
11	11	2-2-2	1847	SB	1867	
12	12	2-2-2	1847	SB	1865	
13	13	2-2-2	1847	SB	1874	Sold (See Contractors List)
14	14	2-2-2	1847	SB	1868	
15	15	2-2-2	1847	SB	1876	
16	16	2-2-2	1847	SB	1866	
30	30	2-2-2	1847	BCK	1867	
31	31	2-2-2	1847	BCK	1867	
32	32	2-2-2	1847	BCK	1876	
33	33	2-2-2	1847	BCK	1865	
34	34	2-2-2	1847	BCK	1867	
35	35	2-2-2	1847	BCK	1868	
36	36	2-2-2	1847	BCK	1875	
43	102	0-4-2	1847	BCK	1871	Sold to A&EJR (No. 3)
44	103	0-4-2	1847	BCK	1865	Sold to C&BR (No. 8) in 1867
45	104	0-4-2	1847	BCK	1870	
46	105	0-4-2	1847	BCK	1865	
47	106	0-4-2	1847	BCK	1871	
17	17	2-2-2	1848	SB	1868	May have been sold 1870 (See Contractors List)
18	18	2-2-2	1848	SB	1868	
19	19	2-2-2	1848	SB	1870	'Spare locomotive' at Thurles until 1879
20	20	2-2-2	1848	SB	1868	
37	37	2-2-2	1848	BCK	1873	Rebuilt as 2-4-0 1852-3*
38	38	2-2-2	1848	BCK	1871	Rebuilt as 2-4-0 1852-3*. Sold to C&BR (No. 8)
39	39	2-2-2	1848	BCK	1868	Rebuilt as 2-4-0 1852-3*
40	40	2-2-2	1848	BCK	1875	Rebuilt as 2-4-0 1852-3
48	107	0-4-2	1848	BCK	1875	
49	108	0-4-2	1848	BCK	1874	
50	109	0-4-2	1848	BCK	1876	
51	111	0-4-2	1849	G	1865	
52	112	0-4-2	1849	G	1865	
53	112	0-4-2	1850	Roth	1866	
54	113	0-4-2	1850	Roth	1866	
55	114	0-4-2	1850	Roth	1865	Ran until 1868
56	115	0-4-2	1850	Roth	1865	Ran until 1868
57	117	0-4-2	1852	GS&WR	1873	
58	118	0-4-2	1852	GS&WR	1867	
59	43	2-2-2	1853	GS&WR	1873	
60	139	0-6-0	1854	GS&WR	1874	Ordered as a tank locomotive
61	140	0-6-0	1854	GS&WR	1876	Ordered as a tank locomotive
62	122	0-4-2	1854	GS&WR	1882	
63	123	0-4-2	1854	GS&WR	1879	
64	119	2-4-0	1855	GS&WR	1873	
65	120	2-4-0	1855	GS&WR	1873	
66	121	2-4-0	1855	GS&WR	1873	
70	41	2-4-0	1855	Fbn	1889	Rebuilt 1871
71	42	2-4-0	1855	Fbn	1887	Rebuilt 1871
67	141	0-6-0	1856	GS&WR	1878	
68	142	0-6-0	1856	GS&WR	1873	
69	143	0-6-0	1856	GS&WR	1874	
72	144	0-6-0	1856	GS&WR	1879	Rebuilt as 0-6-0T 1868
73	145	0-6-0	1856	GS&WR	1874	Rebuilt as 0-6-0T 1868
74	146	0-6-0	1856	GS&WR	1877	
75	116	0-4-2	1856	Fbn	1913	Rebuilt as 0-4-2ST 1885. Number removed and named *Sambo* 1890.
Sprite		0-2-4T	1857	GS&WR	1873	May have been No. 76 when built. Had a passenger compartment.
77	45	2-2-2	1858	GS&WR	1878	
78	46	2-2-2	1858	GS&WR	1878	
79	47	2-2-2	1858	GS&WR	1876	
76	44	2-2-2	1859	GS&WR	1878	Probably completed as No. 80
80	48	2-2-2	1859	GS&WR	1881	Probably completed as No. 82
81	49	2-2-2	1859	GS&WR	1882	
82	124	0-4-2	1860	GS&WR	1880	Ran until 1882. Sold (See Contractors List)
83	125	0-4-2	1860	GS&WR	1880	
84	126	0-4-2	1860	GS&WR	1883	

First No.	1864 No.	Type	Date	Builder	Withdrawn	Remarks
85	127	0-4-2	1861	GS&WR	1879	
86	128	0-4-2	1861	GS&WR	1882	
87	129	0-4-2	1861	GS&WR	1881	
88	50	2-2-2	1861	GS&WR	1878	
89	51	2-2-2	1861	GS&WR	1882	
90	52	2-2-2	1861	GS&WR	1882	
91	130	0-4-2	1862	GS&WR	1880	
92	131	0-4-2	1862	GS&WR	1880	Ran until 1881
93	132	0-4-2	1862	GS&WR	1884	
94	53	2-2-2	1862	GS&WR	1882	
95	54	2-2-2	1862	GS&WR	1878	
96	55	2-2-2	1863	GS&WR	1882	
97	133	0-4-2	1863	GS&WR	1883	
98	134	0-4-2	1863	GS&WR	1884	
99	135	0-4-2	1863	GS&WR	1881	
(100)	136	0-4-2	1865	GS&WR	1884	
(101)	137	0-4-2	1865	GS&WR	1884	
(102)	138	0-4-2	1865	GS&WR	1886	

(ii) Locomotives built or acquired 1866-1924

After the 1864 renumbering of the 'first period' stock locomotives fell ito distinctive groups according to general usage as follows:

1-100	Passenger (although 100 was used for a goods locomotive in 1864).
101-200	Goods.
201-220	Goods tank (apart from use of Nos. 211-7 for WD&LR locomotives in 1898 which were renumbered again in 1901).
221-299	Absorbed/amalgamated locomotives of 1898 and new goods locomotives 1902-14.
301-341	Passenger.
351-371	Goods.
400-409	Express passenger.
500	Mixed traffic
900	Heavy shunting.

The few locomotives of post 1865 that were renumbered are indicated in the remarks column. Likewise the very few names are also given in the remarks column.

GS&WR locomotive classification system

The earliest list of locomotives by class appeared in 1877 (but may be a little older):

Class 1	2-4-0	Express
Class 2	2-4-0	Light passenger
Class 2A	0-4-4T	Branch and light pasenger
Class 3	0-6-0	Goods

This system was superseded by the use of a number, normally that of the lowest numbered locomotive in the class, but in a few cases another number within the class was used to avoid conflict with a class number used before. Whilst a general class number was used, there were many sub-class identities for variations within a class. Sub-class numbers are not used in this list.

No.	Type	Class	Date	Builder	Rebuilt	Withdrawn	Remarks
1	2-4-0	1	1866	GS&WR	1871	1887	See note
9	2-4-0	1	1866	GS&WR	1874	1884	See note
16	2-4-0	1	1866	GS&WR	1873	1885	See note
61	2-4-0ST		(C&YR 1)			1883	Renumbered 71 (1870). Sold WD&LR (No. 5)
62	2-4-0ST		(C&YR 2)			1884	Renumbered 72 (1870)
63	2-4-0ST		(C&YR 3)			1885	Renumbered 73 (1870)
64	2-4-0ST		(C&YR 4)			1887	Renumbered 74 (1870)
65	2-4-0ST		(C&YR 5)			1887	Renumbered 75 (1870)
66	2-4-0ST		(C&YR 9)			1887	Renumbered 76 (1870)
67	2-4-0ST		(C&YR 10)			1884	Renumbered 77 (1870)
68	2-2-2ST		(C&YR 6)	1879 2-4-0ST		1885	Renumbered 78 (1870)
69	2-2-2ST		(C&YR 7)	1879 2-4-0ST		1884	Renumbered 79 (1870)
70	2-2-2ST		(C&YR 8)	1879 2-4-0ST		1886	Renumbered 80 (1870)
112	0-6-0	101	1866	GS&WR	1911	GSR	
113	0-6-0	101	1866	GS&WR	1903	GSR	
4	2-4-0	1	1867	GS&WR	1872	1888	See note
11	2-4-0	1	1867	GS&WR	1872	1888	See note
27	2-2-2	56	1867	GS&WR	1870 2-4-0	1888	Renumbered 62 (1870). Renewal of old No. 27
30	2-2-2	56	1867	GS&WR	1871 2-4-0	1890	Renumbered 63 (1870). Renewal of old No. 30
103	0-6-0	101	1867	GS&WR		1886	
111	0-6-0	101	1867	GS&WR		1888	
118	0-6-0		1867	GS&WR		1890	Never absorbed into 101 Class
147	0-6-0	101	1867	BP		1888	
148	0-6-0	101	1867	BP	1907	GSR	
149	0-6-0	101	1867	BP		1887	
150	0-6-0	101	1867	BP	1920	GSR	
14	2-4-0	1	1868	GS&WR	1872	1887	See note
18	2-4-0	1	1868	GS&WR	1871	1888	See note
56	2-4-0	56	1868	GS&WR		1887	
57	2-4-0	56	1868	GS&WR		1887	

No.	Type	Class	Date	Builder	Rebuilt	Withdrawn	Remarks
105	0-6-0	101	1868	GS&WR		1895	
110	0-6-0	101	1868	GS&WR		1890	
151	0-6-0	101	1868	BP	1904	GSR	
152	0-6-0	101	1868	BP	1901	GSR	
153	0-6-0	101	1868	BP	1904	GSR	
154	0-6-0	101	1868	BP	1915	GSR	
3	2-4-0	1	1869	GS&WR		1890	
12	2-4-0	1	1869	GS&WR		1889	
33	0-4-4T	33	1869	GS&WR		1889	Single Fairlie type
58	2-4-0	56	1869	GS&WR		1886	
59	2-4-0	56	1869	GS&WR		1885	
114	0-6-0	101	1869	GS&WR		1889	Shorter wheelbase than standard 101 Class
115	0-6-0	101	1869	GS&WR		GSR	Shorter wheelbase than standard 101 Class
20	2-4-0	1	1870	GS&WR		1888	
31	0-4-4T	27	1870	GS&WR		1896	
32	0-4-4T	27	1870	GS&WR		1896	
34	0-4-4T	33	1870	GS&WR		1889	Single Fairlie type
60	2-4-0	56	1870	GS&WR		1891	
61	2-4-0	56	1870	GS&WR		1891	
27	0-4-4T	27	1871	GS&WR		1899	
30	0-4-4T	27	1871	GS&WR		1899	
155	0-6-0	101	1871	GS&WR		GSR	Shorter wheelbase than standard 101 Class
156	0-6-0	101	1871	GS&WR		GSR	Shorter wheelbase than standard 101 Class
159	0-6-0	101	1871	GS&WR	1912	GSR	
160	0-6-0	101	1871	GS&WR	1907	GSR	
161	0-6-0	101	1871	GS&WR		GSR	
162	0-6-0	101	1871	GS&WR	1909	GSR	
17	2-4-0	1	1872	GS&WR	1890*	1909	
19	2-4-0	1	1872	GS&WR		1890	
157	0-6-0	101	1872	GS&WR	1912	GSR	
158	0-6-0	101	1872	GS&WR	1905	GSR	
163	0-6-0	101	1872	SS	1923	GSR	
164	0-6-0	101	1872	SS	1924	GSR	
165	0-6-0	101	1872	SS	1891; 1924	GSR	Compound 1891. Reverted to simple 1896.
166	0-6-0	101	1872	SS	1923	GSR	
21	2-4-0	21	1873	GS&WR		GSR	
22	2-4-0	21	1873	GS&WR		GSR	
23	2-4-0	21	1873	GS&WR		1912	
24	2-4-0	21	1873	GS&WR		1923	Civil war loss
25	2-4-0	21	1873	GS&WR		1923	Civil war loss
26	2-4-0	21	1873	GS&WR		GSR	
102	0-6-0	101	1873	GS&WR	1904	GSR	
104	0-6-0	101	1873	GS&WR	1908	GSR	
167	0-6-0	101	1873	GS&WR	1918	GSR	
168	0-6-0	101	1873	GS&WR	1920	GSR	
175	0-6-0	101	1873	SS	1924	GSR	
176	0-6-0	101	1873	SS	1922	GSR	
177	0-6-0	101	1873	BP	1921	GSR	
178	0-6-0	101	1873	BP	1912	GSR	
Sprite	0-4-4T	SPRITE	1873	GS&WR	1889	GSR	Combined locomotive and carriage (separated in 1889).
106	0-6-0	101	1874	GS&WR	1921	GSR	
117	0-6-0	101	1874	GS&WR	1904	GSR	
169	0-6-0	101	1874	GS&WR	1921	GSR	
170	0-6-0	101	1874	GS&WR	1917	GSR	
171	0-6-0	101	1874	GS&WR		GSR	
172	0-6-0	101	1874	GS&WR	1906	GSR	
173	0-6-0	101	1874	GS&WR	1902	GSR	
174	0-6-0	101	1874	GS&WR		GSR	
35	0-4-4T	35	1875	GS&WR		1892	
36	0-4-4T	35	1875	GS&WR		1892	
37	0-4-4T	35	1875	GS&WR		1893	
38	0-4-4T	35	1875	GS&WR		1893	
64	2-4-0	64	1875	GS&WR		1897	
65	2-4-0	64	1875	GS&WR		1897	
108	0-6-0	101	1875	GS&WR	1922	GSR	
142	0-6-0	101	1875	GS&WR	1907	GSR	
179	0-6-0	101	1875	GS&WR	1920	GSR	
180	0-6-0	101	1875	GS&WR	1912	GSR	
66	2-4-0	21	1876	GS&WR		GSR	
67	2-4-0	21	1876	GS&WR		GSR	
68	2-4-0	21	1876	GS&WR		GSR	
69	2-4-0	21	1876	GS&WR		1911	
201	0-6-4T	201	1876	GS&WR		1910	Number removed and named *Negro* 1896

▲ GS&WR 2-2-2 No. 48 (1859 GS&WR Inchicore)

(Real Photos)

▼ GS&WR 0-6-0 101 Class No. 170 with original small boiler (1874 GS&WR Inchicore)

(LCGB Ken Nunn Collection)

▲ GS&WR 2-2-2 No. 19 (1848 Sharp Brothers)

(Real Photos)

▼ GS&WR 2-4-0 I Class No. 20 (1870 GS&WR Inchicore)

(Real Photos)

No.	Type	Class	Date	Builder	Rebuilt	Withdrawn	Remarks
202	0-6-4T	201	1876	GS&WR	1896 0-6-0T	GSR	Side tanks added 1883. Number removed and named *Jumbo* 1896.
2	4-4-0	2	1877	GS&WR		GSR	
5	4-4-0	2	1877	GS&WR		GSR	
6	4-4-0	2	1877	GS&WR		GSR	
7	4-4-0	2	1877	GS&WR		GSR	
109	0-6-0	101	1877	GS&WR	1912	GSR	
119	0-6-0	101	1877	GS&WR		GSR	
120	0-6-0	101	1877	GS&WR	1920	GSR	
121	0-6-0	101	1877	GS&WR	1916	GSR	
143	0-6-0	101	1877	GS&WR	1906	GSR	
43	4-4-0	2	1878	GS&WR		GSR	
44	4-4-0	2	1878	GS&WR		GSR	
45	4-4-0	2	1878	GS&WR		GSR	
46	4-4-0	2	1878	GS&WR		GSR	
144	0-6-0	101	1878	GS&WR	1910	GSR	
145	0-6-0	101	1878	GS&WR	1922	GSR	
146	0-6-0	101	1878	GS&WR	1912	GSR	
28	0-4-4T	28	1879	GS&WR		1906	
29	0-4-4T	28	1879	GS&WR		1907	
39	0-4-4T	28	1879	GS&WR		1916	
40	0-4-4T	28	1879	GS&WR		GSR	Later counted as 47 Class
90	0-6-4T	90			1915 0-6-0T	GSR	Former Castleisland Railway locomotive and carriage (latter removed 1915).
181	0-6-0	101	1879	GS&WR	1920	GSR	
182	0-6-0	101	1879	GS&WR		GSR	
185	0-6-0	101	1879	SS	1916	GSR	
186	0-6-0	101	1879	SS	1910	GSR	
203	0-6-4T	203	1879	GS&WR		GSR	
204	0-6-4T	203	1879	GS&WR	1914 0-6-0T	GSR	Became 204 Class on rebuilding.
8	4-4-0	2	1880	GS&WR		GSR	
10	4-4-0	2	1880	GS&WR		GSR	
13	4-4-0	2	1880	GS&WR		GSR	
15	4-4-0	2	1880	GS&WR		GSR	
183	0-6-0	101	1880	GS&WR		GSR	
184	0-6-0	101	1880	GS&WR	1921	GSR	
205	0-6-4T	203	1880	GS&WR		GSR	Armoured for military use * -1923.
206	0-6-4T	203	1880	GS&WR		GSR	Armoured for military use 1922-1923.
91	0-6-4T	90	1881	GS&WR	1922 0-6-0ST	GSR	Carriage portion removed and became 91 Class.
92	0-6-4T	90	1881	GS&WR		GSR	Later became 92 Class
107	0-6-0	101	1881	GS&WR	1919	GSR	
123	0-6-0	101	1881	GS&WR	1907-8*	GSR	
124	0-6-0	101	1881	GS&WR	1901	GSR	
125	0-6-0	101	1881	GS&WR	1915	GSR	
126	0-6-0	101	1881	GS&WR	1904	GSR	
139	0-6-0	101	1881	GS&WR	1909	GSR	
140	0-6-0	101	1881	GS&WR	1909	GSR	
141	0-6-0	101	1881	GS&WR	1923	GSR	
189	0-6-0	101	1881	BP	1904	1923	Civil war loss
190	0-6-0	101	1881	BP	1916	GSR	
101	0-6-0	101	1882	GS&WR	1924	GSR	
122	0-6-0	101	1882	GS&WR	1901	GSR	
127	0-6-0	101	1882	GS&WR	1914	GSR	
128	0-6-0	101	1882	GS&WR	1914	GSR	
130	0-6-0	101	1882	GS&WR	1902	GSR	
131	0-6-0	101	1882	GS&WR	1909	GSR	
187	0-6-0	101	1882	GS&WR		GSR	
188	0-6-0	101	1882	GS&WR	1923	GSR	
47	0-4-4T	47	1883	GS&WR		GSR	
48	0-4-4T	47	1883	GS&WR		GSR	
49	0-4-4T	47	1883	GS&WR		GSR	
50	0-4-4T	47	1883	GS&WR		1911	
52	4-4-0	52	1883	GS&WR		GSR	
53	4-4-0	52	1883	GS&WR		GSR	
54	4-4-0	52	1883	GS&WR		GSR	
51	0-4-4T	47	1884	GS&WR		GSR	
55	4-4-0	52	1884	GS&WR		GSR	
70	0-4-4T	47	1884	GS&WR		GSR	
71	0-4-4T	47	1884	GS&WR		1907	
72	0-4-4T	47	1884	GS&WR		GSR	
81	0-4-4T	47	1884	GS&WR		GSR	
82	0-4-4T	47	1884	GS&WR		1906	
83	0-4-4T	47	1884	GS&WR		GSR	

No.	Type	Class	Date	Builder	Rebuilt	Withdrawn	Remarks
84	0-4-4T	47	1884	GS&WR		1908	
93	4-4-0	60	1885	GS&WR	1894; 1901	GSR	Compound 1894. Reverted to simple 1901.
94	4-4-0	60	1885	GS&WR		GSR	
95	4-4-0	60	1885	GS&WR		GSR	
96	4-4-0	60	1885	GS&WR		GSR	
133	0-6-0	101	1885	GS&WR	1904	GSR	
134	0-6-0	101	1885	GS&WR	1922	GSR	
135	0-6-0	101	1885	GS&WR	1903	GSR	
191	0-6-0	101	1885	GS&WR	1914	GSR	
9	4-4-0	52	1886	GS&WR		GSR	
16	4-4-0	52	1886	GS&WR		GSR	
77	0-4-4T	47	1886	GS&WR		GSR	
78	0-4-4T	47	1886	GS&WR		GSR	
79	0-4-4T	47	1886	GS&WR		1923	Civil war loss
80	0-4-4T	47	1886	GS&WR		GSR	
85	4-4-0	60	1886	GS&WR		GSR	
86	4-4-0	60	1886	GS&WR		GSR	
87	4-4-0	60	1886	GS&WR		GSR	
88	4-4-0	60	1886	GS&WR		GSR	
89	4-4-0	60	1886	GS&WR		GSR	
73	0-4-4T	47	1887	GS&WR		GSR	
74	0-4-4T	47	1887	GS&WR		GSR	
75	0-4-4T	47	1887	GS&WR		GSR	
76	0-4-4T	47	1887	GS&WR		GSR	
97	4-4-0	52	1887	GS&WR		GSR	
98	4-4-0	52	1887	GS&WR		GSR	
207	0-6-0T	207	1887	GS&WR		GSR	
208	0-6-0T	207	1887	GS&WR		GSR	
209	0-6-0T	207	1887	GS&WR		GSR	
210	0-6-0T	207	1887	GS&WR		GSR	
4	4-4-0	52	1888	GS&WR		GSR	
11	4-4-0	52	1888	GS&WR		GSR	
14	4-4-0	52	1888	GS&WR		GSR	
18	4-4-0	52	1888	GS&WR		GSR	
56	4-4-0	52	1888	GS&WR		GSR	
57	4-4-0	52	1888	GS&WR		GSR	
58	4-4-0	52	1888	GS&WR		GSR	
59	4-4-0	52	1888	GS&WR		GSR	
132	0-6-0	101	1888	GS&WR	1909	GSR	
136	0-6-0	101	1888	GS&WR	1905	GSR	
137	0-6-0	101	1888	GS&WR	1902	GSR	
138	0-6-0	101	1888	GS&WR	1903	GSR	
103	0-6-0	101	1889	GS&WR	1921	GSR	
114	0-6-0	101	1889	GS&WR	1907	GSR	
129	0-6-0	101	1889	GS&WR	1909	GSR	
149	0-6-0	101	1889	GS&WR	1903	GSR	
1	4-4-0	52	1890	GS&WR		GSR	
3	4-4-0	52	1890	GS&WR		GSR	
12	4-4-0	52	1890	GS&WR		GSR	
20	4-4-0	52	1890	GS&WR		GSR	
99	0-6-0T	99	1890	GS&WR		GSR	
110	0-6-0T	101	1890	GS&WR	1922	GSR	
60	4-4-0	60	1891	GS&WR		GSR	
61	4-4-0	60	1891	GS&WR		GSR	
62	4-4-0	60	1891	GS&WR		GSR	
63	4-4-0	60	1891	GS&WR		GSR	
100	0-6-0T	99	1891	GS&WR		GSR	
111	0-6-0	101	1891	GS&WR	1913	GSR	
118	0-6-0	101	1891	GS&WR		GSR	
147	0-6-0	101	1891	GS&WR	1907	GSR	
33	2-4-2T	42	1892	GS&WR		GSR	
34	2-4-2T	42	1892	GS&WR		GSR	
41	2-4-2T	42	1892	GS&WR		GSR	
42	2-4-2T	42	1893	GS&WR		GSR	
35	2-4-2T	42	1894	GS&WR		GSR	
36	2-4-2T	42	1894	GS&WR		GSR	
37	4-4-2T	37	1894	GS&WR		GSR	Ordered as 2-4-2T. Armoured for military use 1917- *.
38	4-4-2T	37	1894	GS&WR		GSR	Ordered as 2-4-2T.
Fairy	0-4-2T	FAIRY	1894	GS&WR		GSR	
64	4-4-0	60	1895	GS&WR		GSR	
65	4-4-0	60	1895	GS&WR		GSR	
201	0-6-0T	207	1895	GS&WR		GSR	
202	0-6-0T	207	1895	GS&WR		GSR	

No.	Type	Class	Date	Builder	Rebuilt	Withdrawn	Remarks
105							
	0-6-0	101	1896	GS&WR	1910	GSR	
116	0-6-0	101	1896	GS&WR	1908	GSR	
192	0-6-0	101	1898	GS&WR	1908	GSR	
193	0-6-0	101	1898	GS&WR	1910	GSR	
194	0-6-0	101	1898	GS&WR	1908	GSR	
195	0-6-0	101	1898	GS&WR	1909	GSR	
211	0-4-2	244	(WD&LR 1)			1909	Renumbered 244 (1901)
212	0-4-2	244	(WD&LR 2)			1906	Renumbered 245 (1901)
213	0-4-2	244	(WD&LR 3)		1898* 0-4-2ST	1914	Renumbered 246 (1901). Became 246 Class on rebuilding.
214	0-4-2	244	(WD&LR 4)			1905	Renumbered 247 (1901)
215	2-4-0ST		(WD&LR 5)			1898	Not renumbered
216	0-4-2	244	(WD&LR 6)			1913	Renumbered 248 (1901)
217	0-4-2	244	(WD&LR 7)			1910	Renumbered 249 (1901)
Cambria	0-4-0ST		(W&WR Cambria)			1921*	Not numbered. Sold to D&BST (No. 5).
Erin	0-6-0ST		(W&WR Erin)			GSR	Nominally No. 300
196	0-6-0	101	1899	GS&WR	1911	GSR	
197	0-6-0	101	1899	GS&WR	1912	GSR	
198	0-6-0	101	1899	GS&WR	1911	GSR	
199	0-6-0	101	1899	GS&WR	1913	GSR	
27	4-4-2T	27	1900	GS&WR		GSR	Armoured for military use 1922-1923
30	4-4-2T	27	1900	GS&WR		GSR	
31	4-4-2T	27	1900	GS&WR		GSR	
250	0-4-2		(W&CIR 1)			1905	Not renumbered
251	2-4-0		(W&CIR 2)			1901	Not renumbered
	2-4-0		(W&CIR 3)			1900	Not allotted a GS&WR number
252	0-4-2	252	(W&CIR 4)			1909	
253	2-4-0		(W&CIR 6)			1901	Not renumbered
254	2-4-0		(W&CIR 7)			1901	Not renumbered
255	2-4-0		(W&CIR 8)			1902	Not renumbered
256	2-4-0		(W&CIR 9)			1902	Not renumbered
257	0-4-2	257	(W&CIR 10)			1906	
258	0-4-2	257	(W&CIR 11)			1907	
259	0-4-2T		(W&CIR 12)			1902	Not renumbered
301	4-4-0	301	1900	GS&WR		GSR	Named Victoria (removed 1904*)
302	4-4-0	301	1900	GS&WR		GSR	Named Lord Roberts (removed 1904*)
303	4-4-0	301	1900	GS&WR		GSR	Named Saint Patrick (removed 1904*)
304	4-4-0	301	1900	GS&WR		GSR	Named Princess Ena (removed 1904*) - was to have been Shamrock.
32	4-4-2T	27	1901	GS&WR		GSR	
217	0-6-0T	207	1901	GS&WR		GSR	
218	0-6-0T	207	1901	GS&WR		GSR	
219	0-6-0T	207	1901	GS&WR		GSR	
220	0-6-0T	207	1901	GS&WR		GSR	
221	0-6-0ST	221	(WL&WR 1)			1909	
222	0-6-0	222	(WL&WR 2)		1924 RT.Sat	GSR	
223	0-4-2		(WL&WR 4)			1901	Not renumbered
224	0-6-0	224	(WL&WR 5)			1909	
225	0-6-0	224	(WL&WR 6)			1907	
226	0-6-0	224	(WL&WR 7)			1905	
227	0-6-0	227	(WL&WR 24)			1910	
228	0-4-0ST	228	(WL&WR 29)			GSR	
229	0-6-0T		(WL&WR 34)			1901	Not renumbered
230	0-6-0	230	(WL&WR 40)			1909	
231	0-6-0	230	(WL&WR 41)			1910	
232	0-6-0WT		(WL&WR 42)			1901	Not renumbered
233	0-6-0	233	(WL&WR 45)			1919	
234	0-6-0	233	(WL&WR 46)			1911	
235	0-6-0	233	(WL&WR 49)		1923	GSR	Later 235 Class
236	0-6-0	233	(WL&WR 50)			GSR	Later 235 Class
237	0-6-0	237	(WL&WR 56)			GSR	Later 222 Class
238	0-6-0	237	(WL&WR 57)			GSR	Later 222 Class
239	0-6-0	237	(WL&WR 58)			GSR	Later 222 Class
260	0-4-2T	260	(WL&WR 3)			1912	
261	2-4-0		(WL&WR 8)			1902	Not renumbered
262	4-4-0	262	(WL&WR 9)			1912	
263	2-4-0	263	(WL&WR 10)			1907	
264	2-4-0		(WL&WR 11)			1903*	Not renumbered
265	2-4-0	265	(WL&WR 12)			1907	
266	2-4-2T	266	(WL&WR 13)			1914	Sold to C&MDR (No. 6)
267	2-4-2T	266	(WL&WR 14)			GSR	Later 267 Class. Armoured for military use 1922-23.
268	0-4-4T	268	(WL&WR 15)			1914	
269	4-4-2T	269	(WL&WR 16)			GSR	

▲ GSR 4-4-0 2 Class No. 10 (1880 GS&WR Inchicore)　　　(J.M. Jarvis)

▼ GSR 4-4-0 52 Class No. 12 with Belpaire boiler (1890 GS&WR Inchicore)　　　(J.M. Jarvis)

▲ GSR 0-6-0 101 Class No. 139 with Belpaire boiler (1881 GS&WR Inchicore)　　　(J.M. Jarvis)

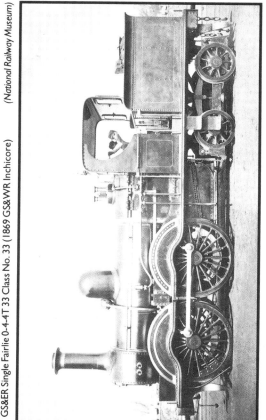

▼ GS&ER Single Fairlie 0-4-4T 33 Class No. 33 (1869 GS&WR Inchicore)　　　(National Railway Museum)

73

No.	Type	Class	Date	Builder	Rebuilt	Withdrawn	Remarks
270	4-4-2T	269		(WL&WR 17)		GSR	
271	4-4-2T	269		(WL&WR 18)		GSR	
272	0-4-2			(WL&WR 19)		1901	Not renumbered
273	2-4-0	263		(WL&WR 20)		1909	
274	4-4-2T	269		(WL&WR 21)	1924	GSR	
275	2-4-0	263		(WL&WR 22)		1913	
276	2-4-0	263		(WL&WR 23)		GSR	Later 276 Class
277	2-4-0			(WL&WR 25)		1902	Not renumbered
278	0-4-2	278		(WL&WR 26)		1910	
279	0-4-4T	279		(WL&WR 27)		GSR	
280	2-2-2			(WL&WR 28)		1902*	Not renumbered
281	2-4-0	281		(WL&WR 30)		1903	
282	2-4-0	281		(WL&WR 31)		1910	
283	2-4-0	281		(WL&WR 32)		1910	
284	0-4-2			(WL&WR 33)		1901	Not renumbered
285	2-4-0	281		(WL&WR 35)		1911	
286	2-4-0	281		(WL&WR 36)		1904	
287	2-4-0	281		(WL&WR 37)		1909	
288	2-4-0	281		(WL&WR 38)		1907	
289	2-4-0	281		(WL&WR 39)		1905	
290	2-4-0	263		(WL&WR 43)		GSR	Later 276 Class
291	2-4-0	263		(WL&WR 44)		GSR	Later 276 Class
292	2-4-0	263		(WL&WR 47)		1915	
293	2-4-0	263		(WL&WR 48)		GSR	Later 276 Class
294	0-4-4T	294		(WL&WR 51)		1910	
295	0-4-4T	294		(WL&WR 52)		GSR	Later 295 Class
296	4-4-0	296		(WL&WR 53)	1923	GSR	
297	4-4-0	296		(WL&WR 54)		GSR	
298	4-4-0	296		(WL&WR 55)		GSR	
299	0-6-0ST	299		(Fenit Harbour Comm.)		GSR	See Contractors List
317	4-4-2T	37	1901	GS&WR		GSR	Armoured for military use 1917-*, *-1923.
318	4-4-2T	37	1901	GS&WR		GSR	
319	4-4-2T	37	1901	GS&WR		GSR	
320	4-4-2T	37	1901	GS&WR		GSR	Temporarily named *Inchicore* for Cork Exhibition during 1901-2.
240	0-6-0	101	1902	GS&WR		GSR	
241	0-6-0	101	1902	GS&WR		GSR	
242	0-6-0	101	1902	GS&WR		GSR	
305	4-4-0	305	1902	GS&WR	1906 T.Sat	GSR	
306	4-4-0	305	1902	GS&WR	1906 T.Sat	GSR	
307	4-4-0	305	1902	GS&WR	1906 T.Sat	GSR	Marshall valve gear 1904, removed *.
308	4-4-0	305	1902	GS&WR	1904 T.Sat	GSR	
200	0-6-0	101	1903	GS&WR		GSR	
211	0-6-2T	211	1903	NBL	1907 0-6-0	GSR	
212	0-6-2T	211	1903	NBL	1907 0-6-0	GSR	
213	0-6-2T	211	1903	NBL		GSR	Later 213 Class
214	0-6-2T	211	1903	NBL		GSR	Later 213 Class
223	0-6-0	101	1903	GS&WR		GSR	
229	0-6-0	101	1903	GS&WR		GSR	
232	0-6-0	101	1903	GS&WR		GSR	
243	0-6-0	101	1903	GS&WR		GSR	
253	0-6-0	101	1903	GS&WR		GSR	
254	0-6-0	101	1903	GS&WR		GSR	
255	0-6-0	101	1903	GS&WR		GSR	
256	0-6-0	101	1903	GS&WR		GSR	
309	4-4-0	309	1903	NR	1913 T.Sat	GSR	Became 321 Class on rebuilding
310	4-4-0	309	1903	NR		GSR	Later 310 Class
311	4-4-0	309	1903	NR		GSR	Later 310 Class
312	4-4-0	309	1903	NR	1920 T.Sat	GSR	Became 321 Class on rebuilding
313	4-4-0	309	1903	NR		GSR	Later 310 Class
314	4-4-0	309	1903	NR		GSR	Later 310 Class
351	0-6-0	351	1903	GS&WR		GSR	
352	0-6-0	351	1903	GS&WR		GSR	
353	0-6-0	351	1903	GS&WR		GSR	
354	0-6-0	351	1903	GS&WR		GSR	
355	0-6-0	355	1903	NBL	* 2-6-0 1914 B.Sat	GSR	Altered about 1907
356	0-6-0	355	1903	NBL	1908 2-6-0 1924 B.Sat	GSR	
357	0-6-0	355	1903	NBL	* 2-6-0	GSR	Altered about 1907
358	0-6-0	355	1903	NBL	1907 2-6-0	GSR	
359	0-6-0	355	1903	NBL	1908 2-6-0	GSR	
360	0-6-0	355	1903	NBL	* 2-6-0 1921 B.Sat	GSR	Altered about 1907

No.	Type	Class	Date	Builder	Rebuilt	Withdrawn	Remarks
361	0-6-0	355	1903	NBL	* 2-6-0 1923 B.Sat	GSR	Altered about 1907
321	4-4-0	321	1904	GS&WR	1924 B.Sat	GSR	
322	4-4-0	321	1905	GS&WR	1924 B.Sat	GSR	
323	4-4-0	321	1905	GS&WR	1924 B.Sat	GSR	
324	4-4-0	321	1905	GS&WR		GSR	
325	4-4-0	321	1905	GS&WR		GSR	
326	4-4-0	321	1905	GS&WR		GSR	Superheated 1912. Removed 1913.
327	4-4-0	321	1905	GS&WR	1922	GSR	Heavier frames 1922
328	4-4-0	321	1905	GS&WR	1922	GSR	Heavier frames 1922
362	4-6-0	362	1905	GS&WR		GSR	
363	4-6-0	362	1905	GS&WR		GSR	
364	4-6-0	362	1905	GS&WR		GSR	
365	4-6-0	362	1905	GS&WR		GSR	
329	4-4-0	321	1906	GS&WR	1921	GSR	Heavier frames 1921
330	4-4-0	321	1906	GS&WR	1919	GSR	Heavier frames 1919
331	4-4-0	321	1906	GS&WR	1918	GSR	Heavier frames 1918
332	4-4-0	321	1906	GS&WR	1919	GSR	Marshall valve gear when new. Removed *. Heavier frames 1919
333	4-4-0	333	1907	GS&WR		GSR	
334	4-4-0	333	1907	GS&WR		GSR	
335	4-4-0	333	1907	GS&WR		GSR	
336	4-4-0	333	1907	GS&WR		GSR	
366	4-6-0	362	1907	GS&WR		GSR	
367	4-6-0	362	1907	GS&WR		GSR	
337	4-4-0	333	1908	GS&WR		GSR	
338	4-4-0	333	1908	GS&WR		GSR	
339	4-4-0	333	1908	GS&WR		GSR	
340	4-4-0	333	1908	GS&WR		GSR	
368	2-6-0	368	1909	GS&WR		GSR	
369	2-6-0	368	1909	GS&WR		GSR	
370	2-6 0	368	1909	GS&WR		GSR	
371	2-6-0	369	1909	GS&WR		GSR	
249	0-6-0	249	1912	GS&WR		GSR	Reclassified 351 Class in 1923
250	0-6-0	249	1912	GS&WR		GSR	Reclassified 351 Class in 1923
251	0-6-0	249	1912	GS&WR		GSR	Reclassified 351 Class in 1923
252	0-6-0	249	1912	GS&WR		GSR	Reclassified 351 Class in 1923
257	0-6-0	257	1913	GS&WR		GSR	
258	0-6-0	257	1913	GS&WR		GSR	
259	0-6-0	257	1913	GS&WR		GSR	
260	0-6-0	257	1913	GS&WR		GSR	
341	4-4-0	341	1913	GS&WR		GSR	Named Sir William Goulding
261	0-6-0	257	1914	GS&WR		GSR	
262	0-6-0	257	1914	GS&WR		GSR	
263	0-6-0	257	1914	GS&WR		GSR	
264	0-6-0	257	1914	GS&WR		GSR	
Sambo	0-4-2ST	SAMBO	1914	GS&WR		GSR	
900	4-8-0T	900	1915	GS&WR		GSR	
400	4-6-0	400	1916	GS&WR		GSR	
401	4-6-0	400	1921	GS&WR		GSR	
402	4-6-0	400	1921	GS&WR		GSR	
406	4-6-0	400	1921	GS&WR		GSR	
Imp	0-4-0T	IMP	(D&BST 2)			GSR	Purchased 1921*.
403	4-6-0	400	1922	AW		GSR	Ready 1922, but stored until 1923.
404	4-6 0	400	1922	AW		GSR	Ready 1922, but stored until 1923.
405	4-6-0	400	1922	AW		GSR	Ready 1922, but stored until 1923.
407	4-6-0	400	1922	AW	1924 B.Sh	GSR	Ready 1922, but stored until 1923.
408	4-6-0	400	1922	AW	1924 B.Sh	GSR	Ready 1922, but stored until 1923.
409	4-6-0	400	1922	AW		GSR	Ready 1922 but, stored until 1923.
500	4-6-0	500	1924	GS&WR		GSR	

Note
The date given as new for locomotives 1, 4, 9, 11, 14, 16 & 18 was the first 'conversion' from the pre-1865 locomotive and the second date represents the elimination of old parts to give a 'new' locomotive. The rebuilding dates for the 101 Class are those for a larger size of boiler (4-4 instead of 4-0 diameter. Nos. 200/23/9/32/40-3/53-6 were built with the larger boiler).

326 locomotives (Nos. 1-16, 18, 20-2/6/7, 30-8, 40-9, 51-68, 70/2-8, 80/1/3/5-9, 90-9, 100-88/90-9, 200-14/7-20/2/3/9/32/5-43/9-64/7/9-71/4/6/9/90/1/3/5-9, 301-14/7-41/51-71, 400-9, 500, 900, Erin, Fairy, Imp, Jumbo, Sambo, Sprite) taken into Great Southern Railway stock in 1924, becoming Great Southern Railways stock in 1925, not being renumbered.

Departmental Stock
The GS&WR in 1921-3 listed 11 such locomotives (1 2-6-0, 5 0-6-0, 1 0-6-4T, 1 0-4-4T, 3 0-4-2T) and 12 in 1924 (2 2-6-0, 4 0-6-0, 1 0-6-4T, 1 0-6-0T, 1 0-4-4T, 3 0-4-2T). The locomotives consistently regarded as departmental stock were No. 92, Sprite, Fairy and Sambo.

Locomotive *Pat*

A 4-wheeled locomotive built in 1883 by the GS&WR for the coal gantry at Cork (cylinders 6½ x 7½, driving wheels 3-7½). It was always counted as an item of plant and never included in the locomotive stock.

Two narrow gauge locomotives

In 1888 the GS&WR sold 2 narrow gauge (actual gauge unknown) locomotives, with other plant, to H. & J. Martin at Queenstown (Cobh). No other details are available.

Locomotive Load Classification (1912)
Inchicore Works Classification (1924)

Type	Class	Works class	Load class	Remarks	Type	Class	Works class	Load class	Remarks	Type	Class	Works class	Load class	Remarks
4-8-0T	900	A1			4-4-0	52	D10	E		0-6-0T	Jumbo	J6		
4-6-0	500	B1			4-4-0	2	D11	E		0-6-0	101	J7	B	
4-6-0	400	B2			2-6-0	355	E1	A		0-6-0	235	J8	B	J8
4-6-0	362	B3	A		2-6-0	368	E2	A		0-6-0	222	J9	B	J9
4-4-2T	27	C1	D		2-4-2T	267	F1	E		0-6-0ST	Erin	J10		
4-4-2T	269	C2	E		2-4-2T	42	F2	E		0-6-0ST	299	J11		
4-4-2T	37	C3	E		2-4-0	276	G1			0-6-0ST	91	J12		
4-4-0	333	D1	C	D1	2-4-0	21	G2	E		0-6-0T	90	J13		J13
4-4-0	333	D2	C	D2	0-6-4T	203	H1	F		0-4-4T	279	K1	D	
4-4-0	341	D3			0-6-4T	90	H2		H2	0-4-4T	295	K2	E	
4-4-0	321	D4	C		0-6-2T	213	I1	F		0-4-4T	47	K3	E	
4-4-0	310	D5	C		0-6-0	211	J1	AA		0-4-2T	Sprite	L1		
4-4-0	301	D6	C		0-6-0	257	J2	AA		0-4-2T	Fairy	L2		
4-4-0	305	D7	C		0-6-0	351	J3	AA		0-4-2ST	Sambo	L3		
4-4-0	60	D8	D		0-6-0T	207	J4	F		0-4-0T	Imp	M1		
4-4-0	296	D9	D		0-6-0T	204	J5	F		0-4-2ST	228	M2		

Classes included in the 1912 Load List which were extinct by 1924:

246 (0-4-2ST) - F
262 (4-4-0) - D
268 (0-4-4T) - E

Notes

D1 Nos. 333-6.
D2 Nos. 337-40.
H2 No. 92
J8 Nos. 235/6.
J9 Nos. 222/37-9.
J13 Nos. 90/9, 100

Steam Railmotor

Single driver railmotor (Cylinders 8¾ x 12, driving wheels 2-9) - outside cylinders.

No.	Date	Builder	Withdrawn	Seating	Remarks
1	1904	GS&WR	1912	6 1st; 48 3rd	Became tri-composite brake No. 1118. Scrapped 1914.

DUBLIN & MEATH RAILWAY

Stock: 6 new locomotives built 1862-4.
1 secondhand locomotive acquired 1862.

Type	Years built	No. in class	Cylinders	Driving wheels	Locomotive Nos.
0-4-2	1862	3	14 x 20	4-9	1, 5, 6
2-2-2	1862	2	*	*	2, 3
2 4-0	1864	1	16 x 20	5-1	7

No.	Type	Date	Builder	Withdrawn	Remarks
1	0-4-2	1862	FH	1869	Sold 1870 to A&TR (No. 1)
2	2-2-2	1862	FH	1869	{ One of Nos. 2 or 3 was sold in 1872* to T. Edwards (see Contractors List) and the other was
3	2-2-2	1862	FH	1869	{ scrapped in 1873.
4	*	*	*	1869	Purchased 1862 from unknown source (definitely 4-coupled). Disposed of in 1870*.
5	0-4-2	1862	FH	1869	Sold 1870 to A&EJR (No. 3)
6	0-4-2	1862	FH	1869	Sold 1870 to A&TR (No. 2)
7	2-4-0	1864	FH	MGWR	

1 locomotive (No. 7) taken into MGWR stock 1869 (renumbered 11). Remainder refused by MGWR and disposed of as shown.

MIDLAND GREAT WESTERN RAILWAY

Stock: 290 new locomotives 1847-1924.
1 secondhand locomotive acquired 1869.

Class	Type	Years built	No. in class	Cylinders	Driving wheels	Locomotive Nos. (+ subsequently renumbered)
	2-2-2	1847	6	14 x 20	5-6*	1-6
	2-2-2	1847	7	14 x 18	5-7	7-11, 30, 33
	2-2-2	1848	6	14 x 20	5-7	12, 13, 14+, 15, 16, 17+
	2-2-2	1851-2	6	15 x 20	5-7	18-23
	2-2-2WT	1851	3	11 x 15	5-1	27-29
	0-4-0	1852	1	15 x 20	5-0	24
	2-4-0	1852	2	16 x 20	5-1	25, 26
	2-4-0	1852-4	4	16 x 21	5-1	31+, 32, 34+, 35
	0-6-0	1855-6	4	16 x 24	5-1	36-9
	2-4-0	1856-60	8	15 x 20	5-7	1-6, 40, 41
	2-4-0	1856	1	14 x 20	5-6	42
	0-4-2	1860-1	6	16 x 24	5-1	43-48
	2-2-2	1862	6	15 x 22	6-6	49-54+
	0-4-2	1863	6	16 x 24	5-1	55-60
	0-4-2	1864-7	12	17 x 24	5-2	61-72
	2-4-0	1869-70	6	16 x 22	6-3	8-10, 73-75+
	0-4-2	1871-2	12	17 x 24	5-2	7+, 76-8, 79+, 80+, 81-4, 85+, 86+
	2-4-0	1873	12	15 x 22	5-8	13-24
	2-4-0	1876	5	16 x 22	5-8	30-4
L	0-6-0	1876	10	17 x 24	5-2	86-90, 91+, 92+, 93, 94, 95+
Ln	0-6-0	1878-9	6	18 x 24	5-1½	49-54
H	0-6-0	1878	4	18 x 24	4-9	96-9
D	2-4-0	1880-7	22	16 x 22	5-8	1+, 2-5, 6+, 25/6, 35+, 36/7, 38+, 39-48
P	0-6-0T	1880-90	5	18 x 24	4-6	100-3, 105
L	0-6-0	1885-9	20	17 x 24	5-3	55-72, 85, 104+
7-12	2-4-0	1889-90	6	17 x 24	6-3	7-10, 11+, 12
Lm	0-6-0	1885-93	22	18 x 24	5-3	73-84, 130-9
E	0-6-0T	1890-3	12	15 x 22	4-6	106-17
K	2-4-0	1893-7	20	17 x 24	5-8	13-24, 27-34
D Bogie	4-4-0	1900-1	6	16 x 22	5-8	2, 3, 25+, 26+, 36+, 37+
W	0-6-0	1900	2	17 x 24	5-2	141, 142
A	4-4-0	1902-5	6	18 x 26	6-3	124-9
B	0-6-0	1904	4	18 x 26	5-3	143-6
C	4-4-0	1909-15	9	18 x 26	6-3	4-6+, 7-12
F	0-6-0	1921-4	23	19 x 26	5-8	36-48, 86+, 87-95
Belpaire boiler: 4-4-0 A, C; 0-6-0 B, F, W.						
Superheater: 4-4-0 11; 0-6-0 F.						
Outside cylinders: 2-2-2 1-6 (1847)						

(i) Locomotives built 1847-52

Name 1847-53	1853 No.	Name post 1868	Type	Date	Builder	Renumbered	Rebuilt	Withdrawn	Remarks
Orion	1		2-2-2	1847	Fbn		1852 2-2-2T	1860	
Mars	2		2-2-2	1847	Fbn			1856	
Saturn	3		2-2-2	1847	Fbn			1856	
Mercury	4		2-2-2	1847	Fbn			1856	
Jupiter	5		2-2-2	1847	Fbn			1856	
Sirius	6		2-2-2	1847	Fbn			1856	
Dunsandle	7		2-2-2	1847	G			1871	
Vesta	8		2-2-2	1847	G			1869	Sold A&EJR (No. 1)
Venus	9		2-2-2	1847	G			1870	See note
Luna	10		2-2-2	1847	G			1870	See note
Juno	11		2-2-2	1847	G			1867	Sold - see note
Heron	12		2-2-2	1848	Fbn			1873	
Condor	13	Condor	2-2-2	1848	Fbn			1873	
Petrel	14	Heron*	2-2-2	1848	Fbn	86 (1873)		1875	
Pelican	15		2-2-2	1848	Fbn			1873	
Cygnet	16		2-2-2	1848	Fbn			1873	
Ouzel	17	Snipe	2-2-2	1848	Fbn	87 (1873)		1875	
Eclipse	18	Vulcan*	2-2-2	1851	L	90 (1873) 98 (1876)		1880	
Childers	19		2-2-2	1851	L		1854 2-4-0	1872-3*	
Arabian	20	Arabian	2-2-2	1851	L	91 (1873)	1854 2-4-0	1875	
Voltigeur	21	Eclipse	2-2-2	1851	L	88 (1873)	1854 2-4-0	1875	
Fairy	27	Bee	2-2-2WT	1851	Fbn	27A (1897)		1902*	
Titania	28	Elf	2-2-2WT	1851	Fbn	28A (1897)		1902*	
Ariel	29	Fairy	2-2-2WT	1851	Fbn	29A (1897)	1876 2-2-2ST	1902*	

Name 1847-53	1853 No.	Name post 1868	Type	Date	Builder	Renumbered	Rebuilt	Withdrawn	Remarks
Harkaway	22	Childers	2-2-2	1852	L	92 (1873)	1854 2-4-0	1875	
Birdcatcher	23	Cygnet	2-2-2	1852	L	89 (1873)		1875	
Hawthorn	24		0-4-0	1852	RWH			1873	
Cyclops	25	Cyclops	2-4-0	1852	L			1880	
Vulcan	26		2-4-0	1852	L			1880	
Pallas	30		2-2-2	1851	G			1875	Purchased 1852
	31	*	2-4-0	1852	Fbn	96 (1876)		1880	May have been named post 1868

Notes

Either No. 9 or No. 10 was sold to A&EJR (No. 2).
11 was sold to Edgworth & Stanford (see Contractors List).

(ii) Locomotives built 1852-76

No.	Name	Type	Date	Builder	Renumbered	Rebuilt	Withdrawn	Remarks
32		2-4-0	1853*	Fbn			1875	May have been new in 1852
33	Falcon	2-2-2	1854	G		1867 2-2-4T	1875	New 1848* but not sold by builder until 1854.
34	*	2-4-0	1853	Fbn	97 (1876)		1880	
35	Wren	2-4-0	1854	Fbn			1886	
36	Stockwell	0-6-0	1855	G			1881	
37	Voltigeur	0-6-0	1855	G			1881	
38	Birdcatcher	0-6-0	1856	G			1881-2*	
39	Harkaway	0-6-0	1856	G			1881-3*	
40	Emperor	2-4-0	1856	G			1880	
41	Regal	2-4-0	1856	G			1883	
42	Ouzel	2-4-0	1856	RS			1880	
2	Jupiter	2-4-0	1857	G			1880	
3	Juno	2-4-0	1857	G			1880	
4	Venus	2-4-0	1857	G			1884	
5	Mars	2-4-0	1857	G			1884	
6	Vesta	2-4-0	1857	G			1884	
1	Orion	2-4-0	1860	G			1884	
43	Regent	0-4-2	1860	Fbn			1879	
44	Duke	0-4-2	1860	Fbn			1879	
45	Marquis	0-4-2	1860	Fbn			1878	
46	Baron	0-4-2	1860	Fbn			1879	
47	Viscount	0-4-2	1860	Fbn			1878	
48	Earl	0-4-2	1860	Fbn			1878	
49	Queen	2-2-2	1862	RWH	45 (1879)		1881-6*	
50	Viceroy	2-2-2	1862	RWH	47 (1879)		1884-6*	
51	Leinster	2-2-2	1862	RWH	43 (1879)		1886	
52	Munster	2-2-2	1862	RWH	46 (1880)		1886-7*	
53	Ulster	2-2-2	1862	RWH	44 (1880)		1886-7*	
54	Connaught	2-2-2	1862	RWH	48 (1880)		1887	
55	Inny	0-4-2	1863	N			1885	
56	Liffey	0-4-2	1863	N			1885	
57	Lough Corrib	0-4-2	1863	N			1885	
58	Lough Gill	0-4-2	1863	N			1885	
59	Shannon	0-4-2	1863	N			1885	
60	Lough Owel	0-4-2	1863	N			1885	
61	Lynx	0-4-2	1864	N			1888	
62	Tiger	0-4-2	1864	N			1888	
63	Lion	0-4-2	1864	N			1888	
64	Leopard	0-4-2	1864	N			1888	
65	Wolf	0-4-2	1864	N			1888	
66	Elephant	0-4-2	1864	N			1889	
67	Dublin	0-4-2	1867	D			1888	
68	Mullingar	0-4-2	1867	D			1887	
69	Athlone	0-4-2	1867	D			1889	
70	Ballinasloe	0-4-2	1867	D			1888	
71	Galway	0-4-2	1867	D			1887	
72	Sligo	0-4-2	1867	D			1888	
11	Meath	0-4-2	(D&MR 7)		85 (1873)		1886	Taken into stock 1869
9	Emerald Isle	2-4-0	1869	AE			1890	
10	Faugh-a-Ballagh	2-4-0	1869	AE			1889	
73	Connemara	2-4-0	1869	AE	7 (1873)		1889	
74	Erin-Go-Bragh	2-4-0	1869	AE	11 (1873)		1890	
8	St. Patrick	2-4-0	1870	AE			1890	
75	Shamrock	2-4-0	1870	AE	12 (1873)		1890	
7	Comet	0-4-2	1871	N	73 (1873)		1892	
76	Lightning	0-4-2	1871	N			1892	
77	Star	0-4-2	1871	N			1892	
78	Planet	0-4-2	1871	N			1893	
79	Luna	0-4-2	1871	N	74 (1873)		1891	
80	Hector	0-4-2	1871	N	75 (1873)		1891	
81	Clancarty	0-4-2	1872	N			1893	
82	Clonbrock	0-4-2	1872	N			1892	
83	Lucan	0-4-2	1872	N			1892	

▲ CIE 4-4-0 333 Class No. 339 (1908 GS&WR Inchicore). The tender had been fitted with oil tanks in 1947.

(J.M. Jarvis)

▼ GS&WR 4-6-0 362 Class No. 365 (1905 GS&WR Inchicore)

(Real Photos)

▲ GSR 0-4-4T 47 Class No. 49 - it was unusual in having a side window cab (1883 GS&WR Inchicore)

(Real Photos)

▼ CIE 2-4-2T 33 Class No. 34 (1892 GS&WR Inchicore)

(Lens of Sutton)

No.	Name	Type	Date	Builder	Renumbered	Rebuilt	Withdrawn	Remarks
84	Dunkellan	0-4-2	1872	N			1891	
85	Mayo	0-4-2	1872	N	79 (1873)		1892	
86	Dunsandle	0-4-2	1872	N	80 (1873)		1891	
13	Rapid	2-4-0	1873	N			1893	
14	Racer	2-4-0	1873	N			1893	
15	Rover	2-4-0	1873	N			1895	
16	Rob Roy	2-4-0	1873	N			1895	
17	Reindeer	2-4-0	1873	N			1894	
18	Ranger	2-4-0	1873	N			1893	
19	Spencer	2-4-0	1873	N			1894	
20	Speedy	2-4-0	1873	N			1894	
21	Swift	2-4-0	1873	N			1896	
22	Samson	2-4-0	1873	N			1896	
23	Sylph	2-4-0	1873	N			1896	
24	Sprite	2-4-0	1873	N			1896	
30	Active	2-4-0	1876	D			1897	
31	Alert	2-4-0	1876	D			1897	
32	Ariel	2-4-0	1876	D			1898	
33	Arrow	2-4-0	1876	D			1898	
34	Aurora	2-4-0	1876	D			1898	

Note

The names listed against locomotives built in 1852-67 are those affixed from 1868.

(iii) Locomotives built 1876-1924

All locomotives built from mid-1876 were classified by number or letter (some of the earlier classes may have been given a class number in the style of the 1889-90 2-4-0 which were 7-12 Class). The letters are listed in the introductory table of dimensions.

No.	Name	Class	Type	Date	Builder	Renumbered	Rebuilt	Withdrawn	GSR No.	Remarks
86	Bullfinch	L	0-6-0	1876	RS		1894	GSR	577	
87	Buzzard	L	0-6-0	1876	RS	87A (1924)	1895	1924		
88	Buffalo	L	0-6-0	1876	RS	88A (1924)	1895	1924		
89	Bison	L	0-6-0	1876	RS	89A (1924)	1895	1924		
90	Beaver	L	0-6-0	1876	RS	90A (1924)	1894	1924		
91	Bear	L	0-6-0	1876	RS	64 (1924)	1895	GSR	579	
92	Bittern	L	0-6-0	1876	RS	135 (1924)	1895	GSR	575	
93	Butterfly	L	0-6-0	1876	RS		1894	1923		
94	Badger	L	0-6-0	1876	RS		1894	1923		Civil war loss
95	Bulldog	L	0-6-0	1876	RS	85 (1924)	1895	GSR	573	
49	Marquis	Ln	0-6-0	1879	MGWR		1899	GSR	563	
50	Viscount	Ln	0-6-0	1879	MGWR		1899	GSR	564	
2	Jupiter	D	2-4-0	1880	BP			1900		
3	Juno	D	2-4-0	1880	BP			1901		
25	Cyclops	D	2-4-0	1880	BP			1901		
26	Britannia	D	2-4-0	1880	BP			1900		
51	Regent	Ln	0-6-0	1880	MGWR		1899	GSR	565	Renamed Baron 1892-6*
52	Baron	Ln	0-6-0	1880	MGWR		1899	GSR	566	Renamed Regent 1892-6*
53	Duke	Ln	0-6-0	1880	MGWR		1899, 1919	GSR	567	See note
54	Earl	Ln	0-6-0	1880	MGWR		1898	GSR	568	
96	Avonside	H	0-6-0	1880	AE		1906 B.Sat 1922 B.Sh	GSR	619	See note
97	Hibernia	H	0-6-0	1880	AE		1907 B.Sat 1921 B.Sh	GSR	620	See note
98	Caledonia	H	0-6-0	1880	AE		1908 B.Sat 1919 B.Sh	GSR	621	See note
99	Cambria	H	0-6-0	1880	AE		1908 B.Sat 1918 B.Sh	GSR	622	See note See note
100	Giantess	P	0-6-0T	1880	MGWR			GSR	614	
101	Giant	P	0-6-0T	1880	MGWR		1902 B.Sat	GSR	615	
102	Pilot	P	0-6-0T	1880	MGWR			GSR	616	Armoured for military use 1922-3*
103	Pioneer	P	0-6-0T	1880	MGWR		1903 B.Sat	GSR	617	
36	Empress of Austria	D	2-4-0	1881	BP			1900		
37	Wolfdog	D	2-4-0	1881	BP			1900		
41	Regal	D	2-4-0	1883	MGWR		1904 B.Sat	1915		
42	Ouzel	D	2-4-0	1883	MGWR		1902 B.Sat	1921		
1	Orion	D	2-4-0	1884	MGWR	36 (1922)	1906 B.Sat	1922		Nominal renumbering
4	Venus	D	2-4-0	1884	MGWR			1910		
5	Mars	D	2-4-0	1884	MGWR			1910		
6	Vesta	D	2-4-0	1884	MGWR	44 (1911)	1905 B.Sat	1916		Renamed Ulster 1911
55	Inny	L	0-6-0	1885	MGWR		1902 B.Sat	GSR	594	
56	Liffey	L	0-6-0	1885	MGWR		1902 B.Sat	GSR	595	
57	Lough Corrib	L	0-6-0	1885	MGWR		1904 B.Sat	GSR	596	

No.	Name	Class	Type	Date	Builder	Renumbered	Rebuilt	Withdrawn	GSR No.	Remarks
58	*Lough Gill*	L	0-6-0	1885	MGWR		1903 B.Sat	GSR	597	
59	*Shannon*	L	0-6-0	1885	MGWR		1903 B.Sat	GSR	598	
60	*Lough Owel*	L	0-6-0	1885	MGWR		1913 B.Sat	GSR	599	
35	*Airedale*	D	2-4-0	1886	K	37 (1922)	1905 B.Sat	1922		Nominal renumbering
38	*Eagle*	D	2-4-0	1886	K	48 (1922)	1906 B.Sat	1923		
39	*Hawk*	D	2 4-0	1886	K		1905 B.Sat	1922		
40	*Lily*	D	2-4-0	1886	K		1905 B.Sat	1922		
45	*Queen*	D	2-4-0	1886	MGWR		1905 B.Sat	1922		
47	*Viceroy*	D	2-4-0	1886	MGWR		1906 B.Sat	1921		
85	*Meath*	L	0-6-0	1886	MGWR		1907 B.Sat	1924		
104	*Wren*	L	0-6-0	1886	MGWR	140 (1901)	1901 B.Sat	GSR	611	
43	*Leinster*	D	2-4-0	1887	MGWR		1905 B.Sat	1916		
44	*Ulster*	D	2-4-0	1887	MGWR			1911		
46	*Munster*	D	2-4-0	1887	MGWR		1908 B.Sat	1921		
48	*Connaught*	D	2-4-0	1887	MGWR	38 (1922)	1906 B.Sat	1922		Nominal renumbering
61	*Lynx*	L	0-6-0	1887	MGWR		1913 B.Sat	GSR	600	
68	*Mullingar*	L	0-6-0	1887	MGWR		1903 B.Sat	GSR	606	
71	*Galway*	L	0-6-0	1887	MGWR		1912 B.Sat	GSR	609	
62	*Tiger*	L	0-6-0	1888	MGWR		1904 B.Sat	GSR	601	
63	*Lion*	L	0-6-0	1888	MGWR		1903 B.Sat	GSR	602	
64	*Leopard*	L	0-6-0	1888	MGWR		1904 B.Sat	1923		Civil war loss
65	*Wolf*	L	0-6-0	1888	MGWR		1904 B.Sat	GSR	603	
67	*Dublin*	L	0-6-0	1888	MGWR		1903 B.Sat	GSR	605	
72	*Sligo*	L	0-6-0	1888	MGWR		1906 B.Sat	GSR	610	
7	*Connemara*	7-12	2-4-0	1889	MGWR			1909		
10	*Faug-a-Ballagh*	7-12	2-4-0	1889	MGWR	10A (1909)		1910		
66	*Elephant*	L	0-6-0	1889	MGWR		1910 B.Sat	GSR	604	
69	*Athlone*	L	0-6-0	1889	MGWR		1904 B.Sat	GSR	607	
70	*Ballinasloe*	L	0-6-0	1889	MGWR		1902 B.Sat	GSR	608	
8	*St. Patrick*	7-12	2-4-0	1890	MGWR	8A (1913)		1914		
9	*Emerald Isle*	7-12	2-4-0	1890	MGWR			1912		
11	*Erin-Go-Bragh*	7-12	2-4-0	1890	MGWR	41 (1915) 45 (1921)		1922		
12	*Shamrock*	7-12	2-4-0	1890	MGWR			1910		
105	*Hercules*	P	0-6-0T	1890	MGWR		1911 B.Sat	GSR	618	
74	*Luna*	Lm	0-6-0	1891	MGWR			GSR	576	
75	*Hector*	Lm	0-6-0	1891	MGWR			GSR	612	
80	*Dunsandle*	Lm	0-6-0	1891	MGWR			GSR	574	
84	*Dunkellan*	Lm	0-6-0	1891	MGWR			GSR	572	
106	*Lark*	E	0-6-0T	1891	K			GSR	551	
107	*Robin*	E	0-6-0T	1891	K			GSR	552	
108	*Swallow*	E	0-6-0T	1891	K			GSR	553	
109	*Fly*	E	0-6-0T	1891	SS			GSR	554	
110	*Bat*	E	0-6-0T	1891	SS			GSR	555	
111	*Wasp*	E	0-6-0T	1891	SS			GSR	556	
112	*Hornet*	E	0-6-0T	1891	K			GSR	557	
113	*Gnat*	E	0-6-0T	1891	K			GSR	558	
114	*Stork*	E	0-6-0T	1891	K			GSR	559	
73	*Comet*	Lm	0-6-0	1892	MGWR			GSR	582	
76	*Lightning*	Lm	0-6-0	1892	MGWR			GSR	569	
77	*Star*	Lm	0-6-0	1892	MGWR			GSR	589	
79	*Mayo*	Lm	0-6-0	1892	MGWR			GSR	578	
82	*Clonbrock*	Lm	0-6-0	1892	MGWR			GSR	583	
83	*Lucan*	Lm	0-6-0	1892	MGWR			GSR	571	
13	*Rapid*	K	2-4-0	1893	MGWR		1922 RT.Sh	GSR	659	Became Ks Class
14	*Racer*	K	2-4-0	1893	MGWR			GSR	650	
18	*Ranger*	K	2 4-0	1893	MGWR			GSR	652	
78	*Planet*	Lm	0-6-0	1893	MGWR			GSR	570	
81	*Clancarty*	Lm	0-6-0	1893	MGWR			GSR	613	
115	*Achill*	E	0-6-0T	1893	K			GSR	560	
116	*Cong*	E	0-6-0T	1893	K			GSR	561	
117	*Moy*	E	0-6-0T	1893	K			GSR	562	
17	*Reindeer*	K	2-4-0	1894	MGWR		1923 RT.Sh	GSR	661	Became Ks Class
19	*Spencer*	K	2-4-0	1894	MGWR			GSR	653	
20	*Speedy*	K	2-4-0	1894	MGWR			1923		Civil War loss
15	*Rover*	K	2-4-0	1895	MGWR		1921 RT.Sh	GSR	660	Became Ks Class
16	*Rob Roy*	K	2-4-0	1895	MGWR			GSR	651	
130	*Ajax*	Lm	0-6-0	1895	SS			GSR	584	
131	*Atlas*	Lm	0-6-0	1895	SS			GSR	585	
132	*Pluto*	Lm	0-6-0	1895	SS			GSR	586	
133	*Titan*	Lm	0-6-0	1895	SS			GSR	587	
134	*Vulcan*	Lm	0-6-0	1895	SS			GSR	588	
135	*Arran Isles*	Lm	0-6-0	1895	K			1923		Civil War loss
136	*Cavan*	Lm	0-6-0	1895	K			GSR	590	
137	*Maynooth*	Lm	0-6-0	1895	K			GSR	591	

No.	Name	Class	Type	Date	Builder	Renumbered	Rebuilt	Withdrawn	GSR No.	Remarks
138	*Nephin*	Lm	0-6-0	1895	K			GSR	592	
139	*Tara*	Lm	0-6-0	1895	K			GSR	593	
21	*Swift*	K	2-4-0	1896	MGWR		1921 RT.Sh	GSR	662	Became Ks Class
22	*Samson*	K	2-4-0	1896	MGWR		1923 RT.Sh	GSR	663	Became Ks Class
23	*Sylph*	K	2-4-0	1896	MGWR		1924 RT.Sh	GSR	664	Became Ks Class
24	*Sprite*	K	2-4-0	1897	MGWR		1918 RT.Sh	GSR	665	Became Ks Class
27	*Clifden*	K	2-4-0	1897	MGWR		1919 RT.Sh	GSR	666	Became Ks Class
28	*Clara*	K	2-4-0	1897	MGWR			GSR	654	
29	*Clonsilla*	K	2-4-0	1897	MGWR			GSR	655	
31	*Alert*	K	2-4-0	1897	MGWR		1924 RT.Sh	GSR	667	Became Ks Class
30	*Active*	K	2-4-0	1898	MGWR			GSR	656	
32	*Ariel*	K	2-4-0	1898	MGWR		1924 RT.Sh	GSR	668	Became Ks Class
33	*Arrow*	K	2-4-0	1898	MGWR			GSR	657	
34	*Aurora*	K	2-4-0	1898	MGWR			GSR	658	
2	*Jupiter*	D Bogie	4-4-0	1900	MGWR		1920 RT.Sh	GSR	534	Became Ds Class
26	*Britannia*	D Bogie	4-4-0	1900	MGWR	5 (1924)		GSR	532	
36	*Empress of Austria*	D Bogie	4-4-0	1900	MGWR	1 (1922)		GSR	530	
37	*Wolfdog*	D Bogie	4-4-0	1900	MGWR	35 (1922) 6 (1924)		GSR	533	
3	*Juno*	D Bogie	4-4-0	1901	MGWR		1919 RT.Sh	GSR	535	Became Ds Class
25	*Cyclops*	D Bogie	4-4-0	1901	MGWR	4 (1924)		GSR	531	
141	*Limerick*	W	0-6-0	1901	K			GSR	233	See note
142	*Athenry*	W	0-6-0	1901	K			GSR	234	See note
128	*Majestic*	A	4-4-0	1902	MGWR			GSR	549	
129	*Celtic*	A	4-4-0	1902	MGWR		1918 B.Sh	GSR	546	Became As Class
127	*Titanic*	A	4-4-0	1903	MGWR		1920 B.Sh	GSR	545	Became As Class
126	*Atlantic*	A	4-4-0	1904	MGWR			GSR	548	
143	*Canada*	B	0-6-0	1904	NBL		1916 B.Sh	GSR	646	
144	*Australia*	B	0-6-0	1904	NBL		1917 B.Sh	GSR	647	
145	*India*	B	0-6-0	1904	NBL		1918 B.Sh	GSR	648	
146	*Africa*	B	0-6-0	1904	NBL		1919 B.Sh	GSR	649	
124	*Mercuric*	A	4-4-0	1905	MGWR		1916 B.Sh 1924	GSR	550	Became As Class Became A1 Class
125	*Brittanic*	A	4-4-0	1905	MGWR		1917 B.Sh	GSR	547	Became As Class
7	*Connemara*	C	4-4-0	1909	MGWR		1917 B.Sh	GSR	540	Became C1 Class
10	*Faugh-a-Ballagh*	C	4-4-0	1909	MGWR		1921 B.Sh	GSR	543	Became C1 Class. Ran as an oil burner 1910-2.
4	*Ballynahinch*	C	4-4-0	1910	MGWR	25 (1924)	1924 B.Sh	GSR	538	Became Cs Class
5	*Croagh Patrick*	C	4-4-0	1910	MGWR	26 (1924)	1924 B.Sh	GSR	539	Became Cs Class
6	*Kylemore*	C	4-4-0	1911	MGWR	9 (1924)	1917 B.Sh	GSR	542	Became C1 Class
9	*Emerald Isle*	C	4-4-0	1912	MGWR	20 (1924)	1922 B.Sh	GSR	537	Became Cs Class
8	*St. Patrick*	C	4-4-0	1913	MGWR		1917 B.Sh	GSR	541	Became C1 Class
12	*Shamrock*	Cs	4-4-0	1913	MGWR			GSR	536	Built Cs Class
11	*Erin-Go-Bragh*	C1	4-4-0	1915	MGWR			GSR	544	Built C1 Class
39		F	0-6-0	1921	MGWR			GSR	633	
40		F	0-6-0	1921	MGWR			GSR	634	
41		F	0-6-0	1921	MGWR			GSR	635	
36		FA	0-6-0	1922	MGWR			GSR	636	
37		FA	0-6-0	1922	MGWR			GSR	637	
38		FA	0-6-0	1922	MGWR			GSR	638	
42		FA	0-6-0	1922	MGWR			GSR	639	
43		FA	0-6-0	1922	MGWR			GSR	640	
44		FA	0-6-0	1922	AW			GSR	641	
45		FA	0-6-0	1922	AW			GSR	642	
46		FA	0-6-0	1922	AW			GSR	643	
47		FA	0-6-0	1922	AW			GSR	644	
48		FA	0-6-0	1922	AW			GSR	645	
86		FB	0-6-0	1924	MGWR	35 (1924)		GSR	623	
87		FB	0-6-0	1924	MGWR			GSR	624	
88		FB	0-6-0	1924	MGWR			GSR	625	
89		FB	0-6-0	1924	MGWR			GSR	626	
90		FB	0-6-0	1924	MGWR			GSR	627	
91		FB	0-6-0	1924	MGWR			GSR	628	
92		FB	0-6-0	1924	MGWR			GSR	629	
93		FB	0-6-0	1924	MGWR			GSR	630	
94		FB	0-6-0	1924	MGWR			GSR	631	
95		FB	0-6-0	1924	MGWR			GSR	632	

139 locomotives (Nos. 1-99, 100-3/5-17/24-46) taken into Great Southern Railway stock 1924, becoming Great Southern Railways stock in 1925 and renumbered as shown.

Notes
All except the F Class locomotives were named when built.
96-9 were purchased 1880 from builders, having been built 1878 to order of WD&LR but refused due to late completion.

▲ GSR 4-8-0T 900 Class No. 901 (1924 Great Southern Railway Inchicore)

(Lens of Sutton)

▼ MGWR 2-4-0 D Class No. 6, later No. 44 (1884 MGWR Broadstone) showing old cab style   *(Real Photos)*

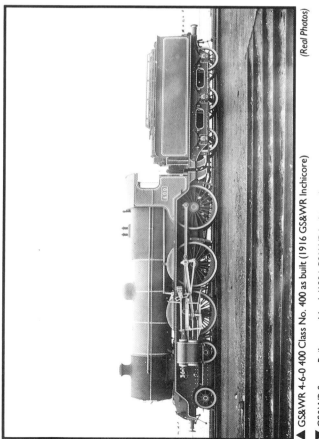

▲ GS&WR 4-6-0 400 Class No. 400 as built (1916 GS&WR Inchicore)

(Real Photos)

▼ GS&WR Steam Railmotor No. 1 (1904 GS&WR Inchicore)

(Real Photos)

141/2 were purchased 1901 from builders, having been built 1900 to order of WL&WR.
53 was fitted with Cusack-Morton firebox superheater in 1919.
99 was fitted with Cusack-Morton firebox superheater in 1914. Normal superheater boiler fitted 1918.
C1 Class locomotives had a larger diameter Belpaire boiler than Cs Class locomotives.

Contractors Locomotives
When C. Braddock surrendered his contract to build the Clifden line in 1892 his plant was taken over by the MGWR. It was then made available to T. H. Falkiner, who completed the branch. The locomotives concerned were WGB 1116, MW 237, MW 1220 and probably HE 203 (see Contractors List).

WEST CORK RAILWAYS

Stock: 3 new locomotives 1865-77.

Type	Years built	No. in class	Cylinders	Driving wheels	Locomotive Nos.
2-4-0T	1865	2	15 x 22	5-6	1, 2
2-4-0ST	1877	1	15 x 22	4-11½	3
Outside cylinders: 2-4-0T 1, 2					

No.	Name	Type	Date	Builder	C&BR No.	Remarks
1	*Patience*	2-4-0T	1865	Cross	9 ⎫	Names may have been other way round.
2	*Perseverence*	2-4-0T	1865	Cross	10 ⎬	
3		2-4-0ST	1877	VF	11	

3 locomotives taken into C&BR stock 1880 and renumbered as shown.

CORK & BANDON RAILWAY
CORK, BANDON & SOUTH COAST RAILWAY

Stock: 32 new locomotives built 1849-1920.
6 secondhand locomotives acquired 1865-85.
3 locomotives taken into stock from West Cork Railways in 1880.

Type	Years built	No. in class	Cylinders	Driving wheels	Locomotive Nos.
0-2-2WT	1849	2	8 x 12	5-0	1, 2
2-2-2	1849-51	2	14 x 20	5-6	3, 4
0-4-2	1852	2	16 x 22	5-0	5, 6
0-4-0ST	1862	1	14 x 22	4-6	7
2-4-0T	1874-87	5	15 x 22	5-0	1, 2, 4, 8, 13
0-6-0ST	1881-90	4	17 x 24	4-2	5, 6, 12, 16
4-4-0T	1891-3	2	16 x 22	5-6	3, 10
0-6-0ST	1894	1	17 x 24	4-6	17
4-4-0T	1894	2	16 x 22	5-6	9, 18
0-6-2ST	1900	2	18 x 24	4-8	19, 20
4-4-0T	1901	1	15 x 22	5-0	˙7
4-6-0T	1906-20	8	18 x 24	5-2½	4, 8, 11, 13-5, 19, 20

No.	Type	Date	Builder	Renumbered	Rebuilt	Withdrawn	GSR No.	Remarks
1	0-2-2WT	1849	A			1867*		Named *Rith Teineadh*
2	0-2-2WT	1849	A			1867*		Named *Sighe Gaoithe*
3	2-2-2	1849	VF			1890		Named *Faug A Ballagh*
4	2-2-2	1851	VF			1888		
5	0-4-2	1852	SB			1887		
6	0-4-2	1852	SB			1879		
7	0-4-0ST	1862	Fbn		* 0-4-2ST 1890 0-4-4T*	1899		Exact details of rebuilding unclear
8	0-4-2			1 (1867)		1874		Purchased 1865 from GS&WR (No. 103)
8	2-2-2					1872*		Purchased 1867 from Moore (see Contractors List)
8	2-4-0			2 (1872)		1877		Purchased 1871 from GS&WR (No. 38)
8	2-2-2					1874		Purchased 1872 from GS&WR (No. 24)
	2-4-0T	1874	D	1 (1875)		GSR	482	Not numbered until 1875
2	2-4-0T	1875	D		1908 4-4-0T	GSR	477	
8	2-4-0T	1877	D			1920		
9	2-4-0T		(W Cork 1)			1895		West Cork name retained
10	2-4-0T		(W Cork 2)			1893		West Cork name retained
11	2-4-0ST		(W Cork 3)			1904		
6	0-6-0ST	1881	BP			GSR	472	Fitted with 4-5 diam. wheels 1901
12	0-6-0ST	1882	BP			GSR	474	Fitted with 4-5 diam. wheels 1899
13	2-4-0T	1883	D			1919		
14	0-6-0				1893 4-4-0T	1908		Purchased 1885 from L&LSR (No. 4)
15	0-6-0			15A *	1898 4-4-0T	1910*		Purchased 1885 from L&LSR (No. 5). Not sold for scrap until 1921.
4A	2-4-0T	1887	D	4 (1888)		1919		Still in steam in 1924 as No. 9
5	0-6-0ST	1887	BP			GSR	475	
16	0-6-0ST	1890	BP			GSR	476	
3	4-4-0T	1891	D		1902* 4-4-2T	GSR	479	Armoured for military use 1922

84

▲ GSR 0-6-0T 551 Class No. 553 ex MGWR No. 108 (1891 Kitson)

(Real Photos)

▼ CB&SCR 4-4-0T No. 15 originally L&LSR 0-6-0T No. 5 (1879 Sharp, Stewart)

(Real Photos)

▲ GSR 0-6-0 573 Class No. 584 ex MGWR No. 130 (1895 Sharp, Stewart)

(J.M. Jarvis)

▼ CIE 4-4-0 540 Class No. 543 ex MGWR No. 10 (1909 MGWR Broadstone)

(J.M. Jarvis)

No.	Type	Date	Builder	Renumbered	Rebuilt	Withdrawn	GSR No.	Remarks
10	4-4-0T	1891	D		1906* 4-6-0T	GSR	471	Possibly 4-4-2T before becoming 4-6-0T
17	0-6-0ST	1894	BP			GSR	473	
9	4-4-0T	1894	N		1898 4-4-2T	GSR	480	
18	4-4-0T	1894	N		1900 4-4-2T	GSR	481	
19	0-6-2ST	1900	B&W			1914		
20	0-6-2ST	1900	B&W			1912		
7	4-4-0T	1901	CB&SCR			GSR	478	
11	4-6-0T	1906	BP			GSR	465	
14	4-6-0T	1909	BP			GSR	467	
15	4-6-0T	1910	BP			GSR	468	
20	4-6-0T	1912	BP			GSR	470	
19	4-6-0T	1914	BP			GSR	469	
4	4-6-0T	1919	BP			GSR	463	
8	4-6-0T	1920	BP			GSR	464	
13	4-6-0T	1920	BP			GSR	466	

20 locomotives (Nos. 1-20) taken into Great Southern Railway stock 1924, becoming Great Southern Railways stock in 1925 and renumbered as shown.

GREAT SOUTHERN RAILWAY

The Great Southern Railway was formed on 12th November 1924 by the amalgamation of the following railways (in advance of the fuller amalgamation of 1925):
Great Southern & Western Railway 326 locomotives
Midland Great Western Railway 139 locomotives
Cork, Bandon & South Coast Railway 20 locomotives

1 new locomotive was added to Great Southern Railway stock.

Class	Type	Years built	No. in class	Cylinders	Driving wheels	Locomotive Nos.
900	4-8-0T	1924	1	19¼ x 26	4-6½	901
Belpaire boiler: 4-8-0T 901						

No.	Type	Class	Date	Builder	Withdrawn
901	4-8-0T	900	1924	GSR-I	GSR

No locomotives were withdrawn in this short period and 486 locomotives passed into Great Southern Railways stock in 1925 (12 being counted as service stock - see GS&WR).

DUBLIN & KINGSTOWN RAILWAY

Stock: 18 new locomotives built 1834-51.
1 secondhand locomotive acquired 1835.

Type	Years built	No. in class	Cylinders	Driving wheels	Locomotive Names
2-2-0	1834	3	11 x 16	5-0	*Hibernia, Britannia, Manchester*
2-2-0	1834	3	11 x 18	5-0	*Kingstown, Dublin, Vauxhall*
2-2-0WT	1836	2	11 x 18	5-0	*Victoria, Comet*
2-2-2WT	1841-4	5	12 x 18	5-0	*Princess, Belleisle, Shamrock, Erin, Albert*
2-2-2WT	1845-8	4	14 x 20	5-6	*Burgoyne, Cyclops, Vulcan, Jupiter*
2-2-2WT	1851	1	13 x 18	5-0	*Comet*
Outside cylinders: All locomotives. (Sharp, Roberts locomotives had vertical cylinders).					

Name	Type	Date	Builder	Rebuilt	Withdrawn	Remarks
Hibernia	2-2-0	1834	SR		1842	
Britannia	2-2-0	1834	SR		1843	Sold to McCormick (See Contractors List)
Manchester	2-2-0	1834	SR		1846	Sold to McCormick (see Contractors List)
Kingstown	2-2-0	1834	For	1837 2-2-2WT	1847	Sold to McCormick and W. Dargan (see Contractors List)
Dublin	2-2-0	1834	For	1839 2-2-2WT	1846-7*	
Vauxhall	2-2-0	1834	For	1840 2-2-2WT	D&WR	
Star	2-2-0		Hor		1840	Purchased 1835 from builders (new in 1833). Previously worked on Liverpool & Manchester Railway (outside cylinders 11 x 18, driving wheels 5-0)
Victoria	2-2-0WT	1836	For	* 2-2-2WT	1846	Sold to McCormick and W. Dargan (see Contractors List)
Comet	2-2-0WT	1836	For	* 2-2-2WT	1851	
Princess	2-2-2WT	1841	D&KR		D&WR	
Belleisle	2-2-2WT	1841	D&KR		D&WR	
Shamrock	2-2-2WT	1842	D&KR		D&WR	
Erin	2-2-2WT	1843	D&KR		D&WR	
Albert	2-2-2WT	1844	D&KR		D&WR	
Burgoyne	2-2-2WT	1845	D&KR		D&WR	
Cyclops	2-2-2WT	1847	D&KR		D&WR	
Vulcan	2-2-2WT	1848	D&RR		D&WR	
Jupiter	2-2-2WT	1848	D&KR		D&WR	
Comet	2-2-2WT	1851	D&KR		D&WR	

11 locomotives (*Vauxhall, Princess, Belleisle, Shamrock, Erin, Albert, Burgoyne, Cyclops, Vulcan, Jupiter* and *Comet*) taken into D&WR stock 1856. Names not altered and numbers not allotted.

DUBLIN & WICKLOW RAILWAY
DUBLIN WICKLOW & WEXFORD RAILWAY
DUBLIN & SOUTH EASTERN RAILWAY

Stock: 98 new locomotives built and 2 conversions ex railmotors 1853-1924.
11 locomotives taken into stock from Dublin & Kingstown Railway 1856.
6 secondhand locomotives acquired 1902.

Type	Years built	No. in class	Cylinders	Driving wheels	Locomotive Nos. (+ subsequently renumbered)
2-2-2WT	1853	2	13 x 18*	5-0*	1, 2+
2-4-0	1853	1	13 x 18*	5-6*	3
2-2-2WT	1853	2	13 x 20	5-3	4, 5
2-2-2ST	1854-5	4	13 x 20	5-3¼	6, 7, 10, 11
2-4-0ST	1855	2	15 x 22	5-3	8, 9
2-4-0	1860	3	15 x 20	5-6	12, 13, 14+
0-4-2	1860	2	16 x 24	5-0	15, 16
0-4-2	1864-5	7	17 x 24	4-9	17-9, 20+, 21-3
2-4-0	1864-73	5	15 x 22	5-3	24-6, 32, 33
2-2-2WT	1865	7	14 x 20	5-6½	*Ariel, Kelpie, Kate Kearney, Banshee, Titania, Oberon, Elfin*
2-2-2WT	1869	2	14 x 20	5-6	27, 28
2-2-2WT	1871-87	7	15 x 20	5-6	4, 27, 29-31, 36, 40
2-2-2WT	1873	2	15 x 20	5-6	34, 35
0-4-2	1876	1	16 x 24	5-0½	37
0-4-2	1876	2	17 x 24	4- 9½	38, 39
2-4-0WT	1882	1	15 x 22	5-5	41
2-4-0T	1883	3	15 x 22	5-3	42-4
2-4-0T	1885-96	12	16 x 24	5-5	1, 2, 6, 7, 9-11, 28, 45-7, 49
0-4-2	1889	1	17 x 24	4-10½	48
0-6-0	1891	2	18 x 26	4-9	50, 51
4-4-2T	1893	3	18 x 26	5-3	52-4
4-4-0	1895-6	4	18 x 26	6-1	55-8
0-6-2T	1897	2	18½ x 26	4-9	4, 5
2-4-2T	1898-1909	7	17 x 24	5-6	3, 8, 12, 27, 29, 30, 40
0-6-0	1899	1	17 x 24	5-0	17
0-6-0	1900	1	17½ x 24	5-0	36
2-4-2T	(1902)	6	17 x 20	4-8½	59-64
0-6-0	1905-10	3	18 x 26	5-1	13, 14, 18
0-6-0	1905	2	18¼ x 26	5-1	65, 66
4-4-0	1905	2	18 x 26	6-1	67, 68
4-4-2T	1911-24	3	18 x 26	6-0	20, 34, 35
2-6-0	1922	2	19 x 26	5-1	15, 16
Belpaire boiler: 2-4-2T 27, 29, 30; 4-4-2T 34, 35; 2-6-0 15, 16.					
Superheater: 2-6-0 15, 16.					

No.	Name	Type	Date	Builder	Renumbered	Rebuilt	Withdrawn	GSR No.	Remarks
1		2-2-2WT	1853	Fbn			1892		
2		2-2-2WT	1853	Fbn	45 (1885)		1901		
3		2-4-0	1853	Fbn		1884 2-4-0T	1898		
4		2-2-2WT	1853	Fbn			1872		
5		2-2-2WT	1853	Fbn	5A (1897)		1900		
6		2-2-2ST	1854	VF	6A (1894)		1903		Sold to Sir Robert MacAlpine (see Contractors List)
7		2-2-2ST	1854	VF	7A (1895)		1902		
8		2-4-0ST	1855	VF		1895 2-4-0T	1903		
9		2-4-0ST	1855	VF		* 2-4-0T	1890		
10		2-2-2ST	1855	VF	10A (1896)		1902		
11		2-2-2ST	1855	VF	11A (1896)		1902		
	Vauxhall	2-2-2WT		(D&KR)			1856		
	Princess	2-2-2WT		(D&KR)			1884		Regauged to 5-3 1856
	Belleisle	2-2-2WT		(D&KR)			1864-72*		Regauged to 5-3 1856
	Shamrock	2-2-2WT		(D&KR)			1864-72*		Regauged to 5-3 1856
	Erin	2-2-2WT		(D&KR)			1864-72*		Regauged to 5-3 1856
	Albert	2-2-2WT		(D&KR)			1874		Regauged to 5-3 1856
	Burgoyne	2-2-2WT		(D&KR)			1864-72*		Regauged to 5-3 1856
	Cyclops	2-2-2WT		(D&KR)			1866		Regauged to 5-3 1856
	Vulcan	2-2-2WT		(D&KR)			1866		Regauged to 5-3 1856
	Jupiter	2-2-2WT		(D&KR)			1876		Regauged to 5-3 1856
	Comet	2-2-2WT		(D&KR)			1864-72*		Regauged to 5-3 1856

No.	Name	Type	Date	Builder	Renumbered	Rebuilt	Withdrawn	GSR No.	Remarks
12		2-4-0	1860	Fbn			1902		
13		2-4-0	1860	Fbn			1904		
14	Glen of the Downs	2-4-0	1860	Fbn	14A (1905) 31 (1907)		1923		Not named until renumbered 31.
15	Barrow	0-4-2	1860	SS	15A (1922)		GSR	ø	Allotted No. 48 (1922)
16	Killiney	0-4-2	1860	SS		1901 0-4-2T	1922		
17		0-4-2	1864	SS			1899		
18		0-4-2	1864	SS			1908		
19		0-4-2	1864	SS			GSR	ø	Civil War loss
20		0-4-2	1864	SS	22 (1911)		GSR	ø	
21	Kilcoole	0-4-2	1864	SS		1904 0-4-2T	GSR	ø	
22		0-4-2	1864	SS			1910		
24	Glenmore	2-4-0	1864	SS			GSR	422	
25	Glenart	2-4-0	1864	SS			GSR	ø	Civil War loss
26	Blackrock	2-4-0	1864	SS		1900 2-4-0T	GSR	ø	
23		0-4-2	1865	SS			1923		
	Ariel	2-2-2WT	1865	N			1894		
	Kelpie	2-2-2WT	1865	N			1889		Sold to R. Worthington (see Contractors List)
	Kate Kearney	2-2-2WT	1865	N			1886		
	Banshee	2-2-2WT	1865	N			1894		Sold to Fisher & LeFanu (see Contractors List)
	Titania	2-2-2WT	1865	N			1889		Sold to R. Worthington (see Contractors List)
	Oberon	2-2-2WT	1865	N			1891		Sold to W. Murphy (see Contractors List)
	Elfin	2-2-2WT	1865	N			1892		Sold to W. Murphy (see Contractors List)
27		2-2-2WT	1869	DW&WR			1887		See note
28		2-2-2WT	1869	DW&WR			1887		See note
29		2-2-2WT	1871	DW&WR			1906		
30		2-2-2WT	1873	DW&WR			1902		
31		2-2-2WT	1873	DW&WR			1905		
32	Glenmalure	2-4-0	1873	SS			GSR	ø	
33	Glendalough	2-4-0	1873	SS			GSR	ø	
34		2-2-2WT	1873	N			1923		
35		2-2-2WT	1873	N			1923		
36		2-2-2WT	1874	DW&WR	36A (1900)		1902		
37	Slaney	0-4-2	1876	SS			1923		
38	Nore	0-4-2	1876	SS			GSR	ø	
39	Suir	0-4-2	1876	SS			GSR	ø	Civil War loss
4		2-2-2WT	1879	DW&WR	4A (1897) 30 (1902)		1908		
40		2-2-2WT	1880	DW&WR			1906		
41	Delgany	2-4-0WT	1882	DW&WR		1903 2-4-0T	GSR	ø	
42	Ballybrack	2-4-0T	1883	BP			GSR	ø	
43	Shanganagh	2-4-0T	1883	BP			GSR	ø	
44	Dunleary	2-4-0T	1883	BP			GSR	ø	
2	Glenageary	2-4-0T	1885	DW&WR			GSR	ø	
45	St. Kiernan	2-4-0T	1886	DW&WR		1910 2-4-2T	GSR	432	
27		2-2-2WT	1887	DW&WR			1906		
28	St. Lawrence	2-4-0T	1887	DW&WR		1909 2-4-2T	GSR	431	
46	Princess Mary	2-4-0T	1888	DW&WR		1910 2-4-2T	GSR	433	
47	Stillorgan	2-4-0T	1889	DW&WR			GSR	425	
48		0-4-2	1889	DW&WR			1913		
9	Dalkey	2-4-0T	1890	DW&WR			GSR	424	
1		2-4-0T	1891	DW&WR			GSR		
49	Carrickmines	2-4-0T	1891	DW&WR			GSR	423	
50	Arklow	0-6-0	1891	VF		1912 B.Sat	GSR	447	
51	New Ross	0-6-0	1891	VF		1915 B.Sat	GSR	ø	Civil War loss
52	Duke of Connaught	4-4-2T	1893	SS		1920	GSR	458	
53	Duke of Abercorn	4-4-2T	1893	SS			GSR	460	
54	Duke of Leinster	4-4-2T	1893	SS		1913	GSR	459	
6		2-4-0T	1894	DW&WR			GSR	ø	
7		2-4-0T	1895	DW&WR			GSR	426	
55	Rathdown	4-4-0	1895	VF		1923 B.Sat	GSR	450	
56	Rathmines	4-4-0	1895	VF		1911 B.Sat	GSR	451	
10	St. Senanus	2-4-0T	1896	DW&WR		1903 2-4-2T	GSR	429	
11	St. Kevin	2-4-0T	1896	DW&WR		1900 2-4-2T	GSR	430	
57	Rathnew	4-4-0	1896	VF		1906 B.Sat	GSR	452	
58	Rathdrum	4-4-0	1896	VF		1915 B.Sat	GSR	543	See note
4	Lismore	0-6-2T	1897	K		1908 0-6-0 1924 B. Sat	GSR	448	
5	Clonmel	0-6-2T	1897	K		1908 0-6-0	GSR	449	
3	St. Patrick	2-4-2T	1898	DW&WR			GSR	428	
17	Wicklow	0-6-0	1899	DW&WR			GSR	440	
36	Wexford	0-6-0	1900	DW&WR			GSR	441	

▲ DW&WR 2-2-2WT No. 5A (1853 Fairburn)　　(Real Photos)

▼ GSR 2-4-2T 428 Class No. 433 ex D&SER No. 46 (1888 DW&WR, Grand Canal Street)　　(Lens of Sutton)

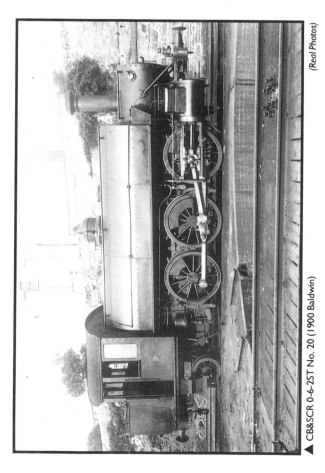

▲ CB&SCR 0-6-2ST No. 20 (1900 Baldwin)　　(Real Photos)

▼ CIE 4-6-0T 463 Class No. 464 ex CB&SCR No. 8 (1920 Beyer, Peacock)　　(M.P. Rowledge)

No.	Name	Type	Date	Builder	Renumbered	Rebuilt	Withdrawn	GSR No.	Remarks
12	*St. Brigid*	2-4-2T	1901	DW&WR			GSR	435	
40	*St. Selskar*	2-4-2T	1902	DW&WR			GSR	439	
59	*Earl of Fitzwilliam*	2-4-2T					1916		See note
60	*Earl of Courtown*	2-4-2T					1917		See note
61	*Earl of Wicklow*	2-4-2T					1916		See note
62	*Earl of Meath*	2-4-2T					1917		See note
63	*Earl of Carysfort*	2-4-2T					1917		See note
64	*Earl of Bessborough*	2-4-2T				1914	GSR	427	See note
8	*St. Brendan*	2-4-2T	1903	DW&WR			GSR	434	
13	*Waterford*	0-6-0	1905	DW&WR			GSR	442	
14	*Limerick*	0-6-0	1905	DW&WR			GSR	443	
65	*Cork*	0-6-0	1905	BP			GSR	445	
66	*Dublin*	0-6-0	1905	BP			GSR	446	
67	*Rathmore*	4-4-0	1905	BP			GSR	454	
68	*Rathcoole*	4-4-0	1905	BP			GSR	ø	Civil War loss
29	*St. Mantan*	2-4-2T	1906	DW&WR			GSR	437	
69		0-4-0T					GSR	*Elf*	Ex-railmotor No. 1 (1907)
70		0-4-0T					1918		Ex-railmotor No. 2 (1907). Sold to D&BST.
27	*St. Aidan*	2-4-2T	1907	D&SER			GSR	436	
30	*St. Iberius*	2-4-2T	1909	D&SER			GSR	438	
18	*Enniscorthy*	0-6-0	1910	D&SER			GSR	444	
20	*King George*	4-4-2T	1911	D&SER			GSR	455	
15		2-6-0	1922	BP			GSR	461	
16		2-6-0	1922	BP			GSR	462	
34		4-4-2T	1924	BP			GSR	456	
35		4-4-2T	1924	BP			GSR	457	

42 locomotives taken into GSR stock (Nos. 3-5, 7-18, 20/4/7-9, 30/4-6, 40/5-7/9, 50/2-8, 64-7/9) and allotted new numbers/name as shown. 19 (denoted by ø above) were still in D&SER stock, but were discarded by the GSR.

Notes

Names - Apart from the ex-D&KR locomotives which kept their names and the 1865 2-2-2WT which had only names, DW&WR/D&SER locomotives were not named until the practice started in 1898, being added to many at the time of rebuilding or when new until 1911, after which names were mostly removed from about 1917. At the Amalgamation only Nos. 2, 21, 37, 65-8 were still named.

27 was a renewal of ex-D&KR *Cyclops*.

28 was a renewal of ex-D&KR *Vulcan*.

58 was fitted with a larger diameter Belpaire boiler (5-0) than Nos. 55-7 (4-8).

59-64 were purchased in 1902 from London & North Western Railway. Former identities and disposal details are as follows:

DW&WR No.	L&NWR No.	Date	(L&NWR Scrap No.)	Disposal 1916-7
59	2070	1885	(3563)	Cramlington Colliery No. 13 (Scrapped 1923)
60	2502	1883	(3564)	Inland Waterways & Docks No. 42 (Scrapped 1919)
61	2496	1883	(3578)	Cramlington Colliery No. 14 (Scrapped 1929)
62	842	1896	(3583)	Inland Waterways & Docks No. 43 (Scrapped 1919)
63	1017	1884	(3584)	War Department, Shoeburyness No. 12 (Scrapped 1921-2*)
64	2251	1896	(3585)	Retained by D&SER, having been rebuilt with a larger boiler. Armoured for military use 1921-2.

(Nos. 59 and 61 were initially sold to J.F.Wake, Darlington).

0-6-0ST *Blackburn*

MW1099 was taken over with a contractor's plant (see Naylor Bros. in the Contractors List) in 1916, but was never included in D&SER stock totals. It was still in existance in 1925 but was not taken into GSR stock.

Hodgson's Tramway, Arklow (3-6 gauge)

2 'Agricultural type' locomotives taken over in 1861. 1 added to stock in 1861-3*.

No.	Type	Date	Builder	Withdrawn	Remarks
1	4-wheel			1876	Taken over from Wicklow Copper Mine Co. (See Contractors List)
2	4-wheel			1876	See Contractors List
3	4-wheel	1861-3*	Unknown	1880	(Cyl. 8 x 12, Driving wheels 1-6)

(Nos. 1, 2 definitely chain drive, No. 3 probably so).

Steam Railmotors

4 coupled railmotor (Cyl. 12 x 16, driving wheels 3-7). Belpaire boiler and outside cylinders (No. 1 Walschaerts valve gear, No. 2 Marshall's valve gear).

No.	Date	Builder	Withdrawn	Seating	Remarks
1	1906	MW	1907	16 1st, 39 3rd	Seperated from coach as 0-4-0T No. 69. Coach became No. 19.
2	1906	MW	1907	16 1st, 39 3rd	Seperated from coach as 0-4-0T No. 70. Coach became No. 20.

Note

Coaches became GSR Nos. 209D and 212D respectively.

WATERFORD & TRAMORE RAILWAY

Stock: 5 new locomotives built 1854-1908.
1 secondhand locomotive acquired 1854.

Type	Years built	No. in class	Cylinders	Driving wheels	Locomotive Nos.
0-4-2	1854	1	16 x 22	5-0	*
2-2-2WT	1855	2	13 x 19	5-0	1, 2
0-4-2WT	1861	1	15 x 21	5-0	3
0-4-2T	1908	1	15 x 22	4-6	4

No.	Type	Date	Builder	Withdrawn	GSR No.	Remarks
4	2-2-2WT	(W. Dargan)		1904		Purchased from Dargan 1854. Bury type but actual builder unknown, having originated on London & Birmingham Railway c.1838 and was later L&NWR No. 191. Sold but further use not identified
*	0-4-2	1854	Fbn	1855		
1	2-2-2WT	1855	Fbn	GSR	483	
2	2-2-2WT	1855	Fbn	GSR	484	
3	0-4-2WT	1861	SG	GSR	485	
4	0-4-2T	1908	AB	GSR	486	

4 locomotives (Nos. 1-4) taken into GSR stock 1925 and renumbered as shown.

The W&TR ordered a 2-2-2T in 1857 from SS (order E343, Prog. No. 1070). It had a Beattie pattern firebox. The company repudiated this locomotive and the builders later completed the locomotive as SS No. 1228, selling it in 1861 to the Waveney Valley Railway (*Perseverance*, later Great Eastern Railway No. 30).

CORK & MACROOM DIRECT RAILWAY

Stock: 5 new locomotives built 1865-1904.
1 secondhand locomotive acquired 1914.

Type	Years built	No. in class	Cylinders	Driving wheels	Locomotive Nos.
2-4-0T	1865-81	4	15 x 21	5-6	1-4
0-6-2T	1904	1	16 x 24	5-1	5
Belpaire boiler: 0-6-2T No. 5.					

No.	Type	Date	Builder	Withdrawn	GSR No.	Remarks
1	2-4-0T	1865	D	1905		
2	2-4-0T	1865	D	GSR	487	
3	2-4-0T	1867	D	GSR	488	
4	2-4-0T	1881	D	GSR	489	
5	0-6-2T	1904	AB	GSR	490	
6	2-4-2T			GSR	491	Purchased 1914 from GS&WR (No. 266).

5 locomotives (Nos. 2-6) taken into GSR stock 1925 and renumbered as shown.

TIMOLEAGUE & COURTMACSHERRY LIGHT RAILWAY

Stock: 2 new locomotives built 1890-4.
1 secondhand locomotive acquired 1890.

Type	Years built	No. in class	Cylinders	Driving wheels	Locomotive Nos.
0-4-2T	1890	1	10½ x 16	3-3	*St. Molaga*
2-6-0T	1894	1	14 x 18	3-6	*Argadeen*
Outside cylinders: 0-4-2T *St. Molaga*					

Name	Type	Date	Builder	Withdrawn	Remarks
St. Molaga	0-4-2T	1890	HE	GSR	
Slaney	0-6-0ST	(Worthington)		1920	Purchased 1890 from Rbt. Worthington (HE 382).
Argadeen	2-6-0T	1894	HE	GSR	

2 locomotives (*St. Molaga* and *Argadeen*) taken into GSR stock 1925 (retaining names, not having numbers allotted).

CORK, BLACKROCK & PASSAGE RAILWAY

Stock: 3 new 5-3 gauge locomotives built 1850.
4 new 3-0 gauge locomotives built 1899.

Type	Years built	No. in class	Cylinders	Driving wheels	Locomotive Nos.
2-2-2WT	1850	3	12 x 18	5-0	1-3
2-4-2T	1899	4	14½ x 22	4-6	4-7

No.	Type	Date	Builder	Withdrawn	Remarks
1	2-2-2WT	1850	SB	1900	5-3 gauge.
2	2-2-2WT	1850	SB	1900	5-3 gauge. Altered to saddle tank 1880*.
3	2-2-2WT	1850	SB	1900	5-3 gauge.
4	2-4-2T	1899	NR	GSR	3-0 gauge.
5	2-4-2T	1899	NR	GSR	3-0 gauge.
6	2-4-2T	1899	NR	GSR	3-0 gauge.
7	2-4-2T	1899	NR	GSR	3-0 gauge.

4 locomotives (Nos. 4-7) taken into GSR stock 1925 (numbers not altered).

SCHULL & SKIBBEREEN LIGHT RAILWAY
(WEST CARBERY TRAMWAYS & LIGHT RAILWAYS)

3-0 gauge.
Stock: 6 new locomotives built 1886-1914.

Type	Years built	No. in class	Cylinders	Driving wheels	Locomotive Nos.
0-4-0T	1886	3	9½ x 16	2-6	1-3
4-4-0T	1888	1	12 x 18	3-4	4
4-4-0T	1906-14	2	12 x 18	3-0½	1, 3
Belpaire boiler: 4-4-0T No. 4 (the first locomotive in the British Isles with a Belpaire boiler).					

No.	Name	Type	Date	Builder	Withdrawn	Remarks
1	Marion	0-4-0T	1886	DK	1905	
2	Ida	0-4-0T	1886	DK	GSR	
3	Ilen	0-4-0T	1886	DK	1914	
4	Erin	4-4-0T	1888	NW	GSR	
1	Gabriel	4-4-0T	1906	P	GSR	
3	Conciliation	4-4-0T	1914	P	GSR	Name soon removed. Named Kent 1920*

4 locomotives (Nos. 1-4) taken into GSR stock 1925 (numbers not altered).

WEST CLARE RAILWAY

3-0 gauge.
Stock: 16 new locomotives built 1886-1922.

Type	Years built	No. in class	Cylinders	Driving wheels	Locomotive Nos.
0-6-0T	1886	2	13 x 20	3-6	1, 2
0-6-0T	1887	2	14 x 20	3-6	3, 4
0-6-2T	1892	3	15 x 20	4-0	5-7
2-6-2T	1894-1901	4	15 x 20	3-6	. 2, 4, 8, 9
4-6-0T	1903	1	15 x 20	3-0	10
4-6-0T	1908	1	15 x 20	3-6	11
4-6-0T	1912	1	15 x 20	3-9	1
4-6-0T	1922	2	15 x 20	3-9	3, 7

No.	Name	Type	Date	Builder	Withdrawn	Remarks
1		0-6-0T	1886	WGB	1913	
2		0-6-0T	1886	WGB	1900	
3	Clifden	0-6-0T	1887	WGB	1915	Frames, tanks, nameplates from No. 4 in 1906.
4	Besborough	0-6-0T	1887	WGB	1901	
5	Slieve Callan	0-6-2T	1892	D	GSR	Driving wheels later reduced to 3-6.
6	Saint Senan	0-6-2T	1892	D	GSR	Driving wheels later reduced to 3-6.
7	Lady Inchiquin	0-6-2T	1892	D	1922	Driving wheels later reduced to 3-6.
8	Lisdoonvarna	2-6-2T	1894	D	GSR	
9	Fergus	2-6-2T	1898	TG	GSR	
2	Ennis	2-6-2T	1900	TG	GSR	
4	Liscannor	2-6-2T	1901	TG	GSR	
10	Lahinch	4-6-0T	1903	KS	GSR	
11	Kilkee	4-6-0T	1908	WGB	GSR	
1	Kilrush	4-6-0T	1912	HE	GSR	
3	Ennistymon	4-6-0T	1922	HE	GSR	
7	Malbay	4-6-0T	1922	HE	GSR	

11 locomotives taken into GSR stock 1925 (numbers not altered).

Nos. 5-7 (0-6-2T) and No.7 (4-6-0T) were nominally the property of the South Clare Railways.

▲ GSR 2-6-0 461 Class No. 461 ex D&SER No. 15 (1922 Beyer, Peacock)

(Locomotive & General)

▼ W&TR 2-2-2WT No. 2 later GSR No. 484 (1855 Fairburn)

(Real Photos)

▲ GSR 4-4-0 454 Class No. 454 ex D&SER No. 67 (1905 Beyer, Peacock)

(J.M. Jarvis)

▼ C&MDR 0-6-2T No. 5 later GSR No. 490 (1904 Barclay)

(Real Photos)

93

CAVAN, LEITRIM & ROSCOMMON LIGHT RAILWAY & TRAMWAY
CAVAN & LEITRIM RAILWAY

3-0 gauge.
Stock: 9 new locomotives built 1887-1904.

Type	Years built	No. in class	Cylinders	Driving wheels	Locomotive Nos.
4-4-0T	1887	8	14 x 20	3-6	1-8
0-6-4T	1904	1	15 x 20	3-3	9

No.	Name	Type	Date	Builder	Withdrawn	Remarks
1	Isabel	4-4-0T	1887	RS	GSR	
2	Kathleen	4-4-0T	1887	RS	GSR	
3	Lady Edith	4-4-0T	1887	RS	GSR	
4	Violet	4-4-0T	1887	RS	GSR	
5	Gertrude	4-4-0T	1887	RS	GSR	
6	May	4-4-0T	1887	RS	GSR	
7	Olive	4-4-0T	1887	RS	GSR	
8	Queen Victoria	4-4-0T	1887	RS	GSR	Name removed c.1921
9	King Edward	0-6-4T	1904	RS	GSR	

9 locomotives taken into GSR stock 1925 (numbers not altered).

CORK & MUSKERRY LIGHT RAILWAY

3-0 gauge.
Stock: 9 new locomotives built 1887-1919.

Type	Years built	No. in class	Cylinders	Driving wheels	Locomotive Nos.
2-4-0T	1887	3	11½ x 18	3-6	1-3
0-4-2T	1888	1	11 x 15	3-6	4
0-4-4T	1892-3	2	14 x 20	3-6	5, 6
4-4-0T	1898	1	14 x 22	4-0	7
4-4-0T	1904	1	12 x 18	4-0	8
4-4-0T	1919	1	13 x 20	3-6	4

No.	Name	Type	Date	Builder	Rebuilt	Withdrawn	Remarks
1	City of Cork	2-4-0T	1887	FE	* 4-4-0T	GSR	Altered about 1889.
2	Coachford	2-4-0T	1887	FE	* 4-4-0T	GSR	Altered about 1889.
3	St. Annes	2-4-0T	1887	FE	* 4-4-0T	1924	Altered about 1889.
4	Blarney	0-4-2T	1888	K		1911	
5	Donoughmore	0-4-4T	1892	TG		GSR	
6	The Muskerry	0-4-4T	1893	TG		GSR	Sometimes ran as Muskerry.
7	Peake	4-4-0T	1898	BE		GSR	
8	Dripsey	4-4-0T	1904	BE		GSR	
4	Blarney	4-4-0T	1919	HE		GSR	

7 locomotives (Nos. 1, 2, 4-8) taken into GSR stock 1925 (numbers not altered).
Nos. 5 and 6 were nominally owned by the Donoughmore Extension Railway.

TRALEE & DINGLE LIGHT RAILWAY

3-0 gauge.
Stock: 9 new locomotives Built 1889-1910.

Type	Years built	No. in class	Cylinders	Driving wheels	Locomotive Nos. (+ subsequently renumbered)
2-6-0T	1889-1910	5	13 x 18	3-0½	1,-3, 6, 8+
0-4-2T	1890	1	11 x 18	3-0½	4
2-6-2T	1892	1	13½ x 18	3-0½	5
2-6-0T	1902-3	2	12½ x 20	3-0	7, 8+

No.	Type	Date	Builder	Renumbered	Withdrawn	Remarks
1	2-6-0T	1889	HE		GSR	
2	2-6-0T	1889	HE		GSR	
3	2-6-0T	1889	HE		GSR	
4	0-4-2T	1890	HE		1908	
5	2-6-2T	1892	HE		GSR	Delivered as an oil burner but soon altered to coal burning.
6	2-6-0T	1898	HE		GSR	
7	2-6-0T	1902	KS		GSR	
8	2-6-0T	1903	KS	4 (1908)	GSR	
8	2-6-0T	1910	HE		GSR	

8 locomotives taken into GSR stock 1925 (numbers not altered).

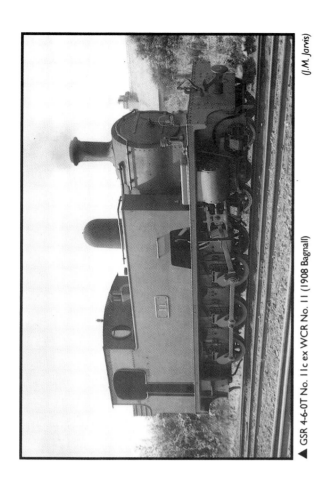

▲ GSR 4-6-0T No. 11c ex WCR No. 11 (1908 Bagnall)

(J.M. Jarvis)

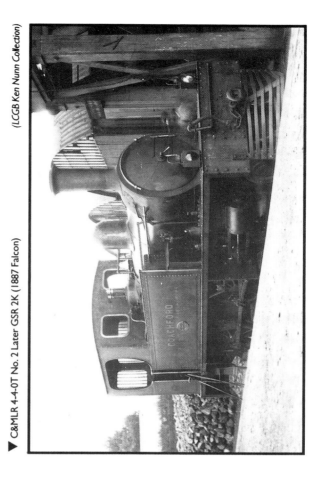

▼ C&MLR 4-4-0T No. 2 Later GSR 2K (1887 Falcon)

(LCGB Ken Nunn Collection)

▲ C&LR 4-4-0T No. 4 later GSR 4L (1887 Stephenson)

(Locomotive & General)

▼ GSR 2-4-2T No. 13L ex CB&PR No. 4 (1899 Neilson Reid)

(J.M. Jarvis)

GREAT SOUTHERN RAILWAYS

Stock:

539 5-3 gauge locomotives taken into stock 1925 from the following railways:

Great Southern Railway	486
Dublin & South Eastern Railway	42
Waterford & Tramore Railway	4
Cork & Macroom Direct Railway	5
Timoleague & Courtmacsherry Light Railway	2

43 3-0 gauge locomotives taken into stock 1925 from the following railways:

Cavan & Leitrim Railway	9
Cork, Blackrock & Passage Railway	4
Cork & Muskerry Light Railway	7
Schull & Skibbereen Light Railway	4
Tralee & Dingle Light Railway	8
West Clare Railway	11

In addition to the 582 locomotives a further 41 have been mentioned as taken into GSR stock to give a total of 623. These 41 extra appear to be:-
20 ex D&SER (Nos. 1, 2, 6,15A,19, 21/2/5/6, 32/3/8/9, 41-4, 51, 68 and *Blackburn*).
1 ex CB&SCR (2-4-0T No. 4),
1 ex T&CLR (0-6-0ST *Slaney*)
4 ex MGWR (0-6-0 Nos. 87A, 88A, 89A, 90A)
1 ex C&MLR (4-4-0T No. 3)
2 ex GS&WR ordered 4-6-0 Nos. 501/2,
12 ex MGWR purchased parts for 2-6-0 (South Eastern & Chatham Railway design, obtained from Woolwich Arsenal in 1923).

It will be noted that 14 locomotives were counted prematurely! The pre-amalgamation stock was condemned in early 1925, despite which MGWR 0-6-0 No. 87A continued to work until October 1925 and D&SER 2-4-0T No. 44 until 1927.

59 new locomotives (5-3 gauge) built 1925-40 and 1 secondhand acquired 1930

Class	Type	Years built	No. in class	Cylinders	Driving wheels	Locomotive Nos. (+ subsequently renumbered)
372	2-6-0	1925-9	20	19 x 28	5-6	372-91 (See note)
500	4-6-0	1926	2	19½ x 28	5-8½	501/2
280	Sentinel	1927	2	6¾ x 9	2-6	1+, 2+
850	2-6-2T	1928	1	17½ x 28	5-6	850
700	0-6-0	1929	5	18 x 24	5-1¾	700-4
393	2-6-0	1930	6	19 x 28	6-0	393-8 (See note)
670	0-6-2T	1933	5	18 x 24	5-6	670-4
710	0-6-0	1934-5	10	18 x 24	5-¾	710-9
342	4-4-0	1936	5	18 x 26	5-8½	342-6
800	4-6-0	1939-40	3	18½ x 28 (3)	6-7	800-2
Belpaire boiler: All classes except Sentinel 280 Class.						
Vertical boiler: Sentinel 280 Class.						
Superheater: All classes except 0-6-0 700 Clsss.						
Outside cylinders: 2-6-0 372, 393 Classes; 4-6-0 501/1; 2-6-2T 850 Class.						
Three cylinders: 4-6-0 800 Class.						
Vertical cylinders: Sentinel 280 Class.						

Note
27 sets of parts for locomotives were obtained in 1923-5 but only 26 were built as the 372 and 393 Classes, the other not being built at all.

GSR locomotive classification systems.
The primary method of classification was a simple numerical system inherited from the GS&WR which normally used the number of the lowest numbered locomotive in the class. A second system used by Inchicore Works, based on the Great Northern Railway (of England) method, consisted of a letter to indicate the wheel arrangement followed by a number; each wheel arrangement was arranged in descending order of tractive effort. This second system is given at the end of the GSR locomotive list, together with a Traffic Department 'Load Class'.

539 5-3 gauge locomotives taken into stock 1925 (9 which did not have GSR numbers are listed at the end):

No.	Type	GSR Class	Former Railway and No.	Rebuilt by GSR	Withdrawn	Remarks
1	4-4-0	52	GS&WR 1		CIE	
2	4-4-0	2	GS&WR 2	1932 B.Sat	CIE	
3	4-4-0	52	GS&WR 3		CIE	
4	4-4-0	52	GS&WR 4	1933 B.Sh	CIE	
5	4-4-0	2	GS&WR 5	1935 B.Sat	CIE	
6	4-4-0	2	GS&WR 6	1942-3* B.Sat	CIE	
7	4-4-0	2	GS&WR 7	1932 B.Sat	CIE	
8	4-4-0	2	GS&WR 8		CIE	
9	4-4-0	52	GS&WR 9		CIE	
10	4-4-0	2	GS&WR 10	1939 B.Sat	CIE	
11	4-4-0	52	GS&WR 11		CIE	
12	4-4-0	52	GS&WR 12	1932 B.Sh	CIE	
13	4-4-0	2	GS&WR 13	1933 B.Sat	CIE	
14	4-4-0	52	GS&WR 14	1932 B.Sh	CIE	
15	4-4-0	2	GS&WR 15	1937 B.Sat	CIE	
16	4-4-0	52	GS&WR 16	1933 B.Sh	CIE	

No.	Type	GSR Class	Former Railway and No.	Rebuilt by GSR	Withdrawn	Remarks
18	4-4-0	52	GS&WR 18	1933 B.Sh	CIE	
20	4-4-0	52	GS&WR 20	1941 B.Sh	CIE	
21	2-4-0	21	GS&WR 21		CIE	
22	2-4-0	21	GS&WR 22		CIE	
26	2-4-0	21	GS&WR 26		1928	
27	4-4-2T	27	GS&WR 27		CIE	
30	4-4-2T	27	GS&WR 30		CIE	
31	4-4-2T	27	GS&WR 31		CIE	
32	4-4-2T	27	GS&WR 32		CIE	
33	2-4-2T	33	GS&WR 33		CIE	
34	2-4-2T	33	GS&WR 34		CIE	
35	2-4-2T	33	GS&WR 35		CIE	
36	2-4-2T	33	GS&WR 36		CIE	
37	4-4-2T	37	GS&WR 37		CIE	
38	4-4-2T	37	GS&WR 38		CIE	
40	0-4-4T	47	GS&WR 40		1936	
41	2-4-2T	33	GS&WR 41		CIE	
42	2-4-2T	33	GS&WR 42		CIE	
43	4-4-0	2	GS&WR 43	1932 B.Sat	CIE	
44	4-4-0	2	GS&WR 44		CIE	
45	4-4-0	2	GS&WR 45	1931 B.Sat	CIE	
46	4-4-0	2	GS&WR 46		1935	
47	0-4-4T	47	GS&WR 47		CIE	
48	0-4-4T	47	GS&WR 48		1930	
49	0-4-4T	47	GS&WR 49		CIE	
51	0-4-4T	47	GS&WR 51		1934	
52	4-4-0	52	GS&WR 52	1931 B.Sh	CIE	
53	4-4-0	52	GS&WR 53		1925	
54	4-4-0	52	GS&WR 54	1930 B.Sh	CIE	
55	4-4-0	52	GS&WR 55	1932 B.Sh	CIE	
56	4-4-0	52	GS&WR 56	1932 B.Sh	CIE	
57	4-4-0	52	GS&WR 57		CIE	
58	4-4-0	52	GS&WR 58		CIE	
59	4-4-0	52	GS&WR 59		CIE	
60	4-4-0	60	GS&WR 60	1934 B.Sh	CIE	
61	4-4-0	60	GS&WR 61	1935 B.Sh	CIE	
62	4-4-0	60	GS&WR 62	1939 B.Sh	CIE	
63	4-4-0	60	GS&WR 63		CIE	
64	4-4-0	60	GS&WR 64	1941 B.Sh	CIE	
65	4-4-0	60	GS&WR 65	1931 B.Sat	CIE	
66	2-4-0	21	GS&WR 66		1928	
67	2-4-0	21	GS&WR 67		1928	
68	2-4-0	21	GS&WR 68		1928	
70	0-4-4T	47	GS&WR 70		1940	
72	0-4-4T	47	GS&WR 72		1940	
73	0-4-4T	47	GS&WR 73		1928	
74	0-4-4T	47	GS&WR 74		1930	
75	0-4-4T	47	GS&WR 75		1931	
76	0-4-4T	47	GS&WR 76		1931	
77	0-4-4T	47	GS&WR 77		1931	
78	0-4-4T	47	GS&WR 78		CIE	
80	0-4-4T	47	GS&WR 80		1931	
81	0-4-4T	47	GS&WR 81		1934	
83	0-4-4T	47	GS&WR 83		1928	
85	4-4-0	60	GS&WR 85		CIE	
86	4-4-0	60	GS&WR 86	1937 B.Sh	CIE	
87	4-4-0	60	GS&WR 87		CIE	
88	4-4-0	60	GS&WR 88	1935 B.Sh	CIE	
89	4-4-0	60	GS&WR 89	1925 B.Sat; 1936 B.Sh	CIE	
90	0-6-0T	90	GS&WR 90		CIE	
91	0-6-0ST	91	GS&WR 91		1930	
92	0-6-4T	92	GS&WR 92		CIE	
93	4-4-0	60	GS&WR 93	1933 B.Sh	CIE	
94	4-4-0	60	GS&WR 94	1934 B.Sh	CIE	
95	4-4-0	60	GS&WR 95	1941 B.Sh	CIE	
96	4-4-0	60	GS&WR 96	1935 B.Sh	CIE	
97	4-4-0	52	GS&WR 97		1930	
98	4-4-0	52	GS&WR 98	1936 B.Sh	CIE	
99	0-6-0T	99	GS&WR 99		1930	Later 90 Class
100	0-6-0T	100	GS&WR 100		CIE	Later 90 Class
101	0-6-0	101	GS&WR 101	1940 B.Sh	CIE	
102	0-6-0	101	GS&WR 102		CIE	
103	0-6-0	101	GS&WR 103		CIE	
104	0-6-0	101	GS&WR 104	1930 B.Sh	CIE	
105	0-6-0	101	GS&WR 105		CIE	
106	0-6-0	101	GS&WR 106	1937 B.Sh	CIE	
107	0-6-0	101	GS&WR 107	1935 B.Sh	CIE	
108	0-6-0	101	GS&WR 108	1931 B.Sh	CIE	

No.	Type	GSR Class	Former Railway and No.	Rebuilt by GSR	Withdrawn	Remarks
109	0-6-0	101	GS&WR 109		CIE	
110	0-6-0	101	GS&WR 110	1930 B.Sh	CIE	
111	0-6-0	101	GS&WR 111		CIE	
112	0-6-0	101	GS&WR 112		1929	
113	0-6-0	101	GS&WR 113		1930	
114	0-6-0	101	GS&WR 114		CIE	
115	0-6-0	101	GS&WR 115		1929	
116	0-6-0	101	GS&WR 116		CIE	
117	0-6-0	101	GS&WR 117		1930	
118	0-6-0	101	GS&WR 118	1927; 1933 B.Sh	CIE	1927 Rebuilt with larger diameter RT.Sat boiler.
119	0-6-0	101	GS&WR 119	1929	CIE	Rebuilt with larger diameter RT.Sat boiler.
120	0-6-0	101	GS&WR 120	1935 B.Sh	CIE	
121	0-6-0	101	GS&WR 121		CIE	
122	0-6-0	101	GS&WR 122	1942 B.Sh	CIE	
123	0-6-0	101	GS&WR 123	1932 B.Sh	CIE	
124	0-6-0	101	GS&WR 124		CIE	
125	0-6-0	101	GS&WR 125		CIE	
126	0-6-0	101	GS&WR 126	1938 B.Sh	CIE	
127	0-6-0	101	GS&WR 127	1931 B.Sh	CIE	
128	0-6-0	101	GS&WR 128	1933 B.Sh	CIE	
129	0-6-0	101	GS&WR 129	1933 B.Sh	1940	
130	0-6-0	101	GS&WR 130		CIE	
131	0-6-0	101	GS&WR 131		CIE	
132	0-6-0	101	GS&WR 132	1941 B.Sh	CIE	
133	0-6-0	101	GS&WR 133		CIE	
134	0-6-0	101	GS&WR 134		CIE	
135	0-6-0	101	GS&WR 135		CIE	
136	0-6-0	101	GS&WR 136	1936 B.Sh	CIE	
137	0-6-0	101	GS&WR 137	1931 B.Sh	CIE	
138	0-6-0	101	GS&WR 138		CIE	
139	0-6-0	101	GS&WR 139	1933 B.Sh	CIE	
140	0-6-0	101	GS&WR 140	1942 B.Sh	CIE	
141	0-6-0	101	GS&WR 141	1939 B.Sh	CIE	
142	0-6-0	101	GS&WR 142		1928	
143	0-6-0	101	GS&WR 143	1936 B.Sh	CIE	
144	0-6-0	101	GS&WR 144	1932 B.Sh	CIE	
145	0-6-0	101	GS&WR 145		1926	
146	0-6-0	101	GS&WR 146	1930 B.Sh	CIE	
147	0-6-0	101	GS&WR 147	1941 B.Sh	CIE	
148	0-6-0	101	GS&WR 148	1932 B.Sh	CIE	
149	0-6-0	101	GS&WR 149	1931 B.Sh	CIE	
150	0-6-0	101	GS&WR 150		CIE	
151	0-6-0	101	GS&WR 151		CIE	
152	0-6-0	101	GS&WR 152		CIE	
153	0-6-0	101	GS&WR 153	1932 B.Sh	CIE	
154	0-6-0	101	GS&WR 154	1941 B.Sh	CIE	
155	0-6-0	101	GS&WR 155		1929	
156	0-6-0	101	GS&WR 156	1936 B.Sh	CIE	Last 101 Class with original small boiler. Converted directly to larger B.Sh boiler.
157	0-6-0	101	GS&WR 157		CIE	
158	0-6-0	101	GS&WR 158	1941 B.Sh	CIE	
159	0-6-0	101	GS&WR 159	1931 B.Sh	CIE	
160	0-6-0	101	GS&WR 160	1931 B.Sh	CIE	
161	0-6-0	101	GS&WR 161	1925-7*	CIE	Rebuilt with larger diameter RT.Sat boiler.
162	0-6-0	101	GS&WR 162		CIE	
163	0-6-0	101	GS&WR 163	1936 B.Sh	CIE	
164	0-6-0	101	GS&WR 164	1932 B.Sh	CIE	
165	0-6-0	101	GS&WR 165		CIE	
166	0-6-0	101	GS&WR 166	1931 B.Sh	CIE	
167	0-6-0	101	GS&WR 167		CIE	
168	0-6-0	101	GS&WR 168	1935 B.Sh	CIE	
169	0-6-0	101	GS&WR 169		1928	
170	0-6-0	101	GS&WR 170	1941 B.Sh	CIE	
171	0-6-0	101	GS&WR 171	1929; 1933 B.Sh	CIE	1929 Rebuilt with larger diameter RT.Sat boiler.
172	0-6-0	101	GS&WR 172		CIE	
173	0-6-0	101	GS&WR 173		1933	
174	0-6-0	101	GS&WR 174	1929; 1933 B.Sh	CIE	1929 Rebuilt with larger diameter RT.Sat boiler.
175	0-6-0	101	GS&WR 175	1933 B.Sh	CIE	
176	0-6-0	101	GS&WR 176		CIE	
177	0-6-0	101	GS&WR 177		1926	
178	0-6-0	101	GS&WR 178		1926	
179	0-6-0	101	GS&WR 179	1934 B.Sh	CIE	
180	0-6-0	101	GS&WR 180		1928	
181	0-6-0	101	GS&WR 181	1936 B.Sh	CIE	
182	0-6-0	101	GS&WR 182	1929; 1938 B.Sh	CIE	1929 Rebuilt with larger diameter RT.Sat boiler.
183	0-6-0	101	GS&WR 183	1929; 1932 B.Sh	CIE	1929 Rebuilt with larger diameter RT.Sat boiler.
184	0-6-0	101	GS&WR 184		CIE	
185	0-6-0	101	GS&WR 185	1933 B.Sh	CIE	
186	0-6-0	101	GS&WR 186	1934 B.Sh	CIE	

No.	Type	GSR Class	Former Railway and No.	Rebuilt by GSR	Withdrawn	Remarks
187	0-6-0	101	GS&WR 187	1929*	CIE	1929* Rebuilt with larger diameter RT.Sat boiler.
188	0-6-0	101	GS&WR 188	1931 B.Sh	CIE	
190	0-6-0	101	GS&WR 190		CIE	
191	0-6-0	101	GS&WR 191		CIE	
192	0-6-0	101	GS&WR 192	1932 B.Sh	CIE	
193	0-6-0	101	GS&WR 193		CIE	
194	0-6-0	101	GS&WR 194	1931 B.Sh	CIE	
195	0-6-0	101	GS&WR 195		CIE	
196	0-6-0	101	GS&WR 196		CIE	
197	0-6-0	101	GS&WR 197	1930 B.Sh	CIE	
198	0-6-0	101	GS&WR 198	1931 B.Sh	CIE	
199	0-6-0	101	GS&WR 199	1932 B.Sh	CIE	
200	0-6-0	101	GS&WR 200	1941 B.Sh	CIE	
201	0-6-0T	201	GS&WR 201		CIE	
202	0-6-0T	201	GS&WR 202		CIE	
203	0-6-4T	203	GS&WR 203		1940	
204	0-6-0T	204	GS&WR 204		CIE	
205	0-6-4T	203	GS&WR 205		1928	
206	0-6-4T	203	GS&WR 206		1928	
207	0-6-0T	201	GS&WR 207		CIE	
208	0-6-0T	201	GS&WR 208		CIE	
209	0-6-0T	201	GS&WR 209		CIE	
210	0-6-0T	201	GS&WR 210		CIE	
211	0-6-0	211	GS&WR 211		CIE	
212	0-6-0	211	GS&WR 212		CIE	
213	0-6-2T	213	GS&WR 213		CIE	
214	0-6-2T	213	GS&WR 214		CIE	
217	0-6-0T	201	GS&WR 217		CIE	
218	0-6-0T	201	GS&WR 218		CIE	
219	0-6-0T	201	GS&WR 219		CIE	
220	0-6-0T	201	GS&WR 220		CIE	
222	0-6-0	222	GS&WR 222		CIE	
223	0-6-0	101	GS&WR 223		CIE	
228	0-4-0ST	228	GS&WR 228		1925	
229	0-6-0	101	GS&WR 229		CIE	
232	0-6-0	101	GS&WR 232		CIE	
233	0-6-0	234	MGWR 141		1929	Not renumbered.
234	0-6-0	234	MGWR 142	1932 RT.Sat	CIE	Same as 222 Class.
235	0-6-0	235	GS&WR 235		1928	
236	0-6-0	235	GS&WR 236	1925	CIE	
237	0-6-0	235	GS&WR 237	1926	CIE	
238	0-6-0	235	GS&WR 238	1925	1934	
239	0-6-0	235	GS&WR 239	1925	CIE	
240	0-6-0	101	GS&WR 240		CIE	
241	0-6-0	101	GS&WR 241		CIE	
242	0-6-0	101	GS&WR 242		CIE	
243	0-6-0	101	GS&WR 243		CIE	
249	0-6-0	351	GS&WR 249	1932 B.Sh	CIE	
250	0-6-0	351	GS&WR 250	1934 B.Sh	CIE	
251	0-6-0	351	GS&WR 251	1937 B.Sh	CIE	
252	0-6-0	351	GS&WR 252	1931 B.Sh	CIE	
253	0-6-0	101	GS&WR 253		CIE	
254	0-6-0	101	GS&WR 254	1933 B.Sh	CIE	
255	0-6-0	101	GS&WR 255	1936 B.Sh	CIE	
256	0-6-0	101	GS&WR 256	1931 B.Sh	CIE	
257	0-6-0	257	GS&WR 257		CIE	
258	0-6-0	257	GS&WR 258	1937 B.Sh	CIE	
259	0-6-0	257	GS&WR 259	1935 B.Sh	CIE	
260	0-6-0	257	GS&WR 260	1931 B.Sh	CIE	
261	0-6-0	257	GS&WR 261		CIE	
262	0-6-0	257	GS&WR 262	1934 B.Sh	CIE	
263	0-6-0	257	GS&WR 263	1936 B.Sh	CIE	
264	0-6-0	257	GS&WR 264	1932 B.Sh	CIE	
267	2-4-2T	267	GS&WR 267		1935	
269	4-4-2T	269	GS&WR 269	1925	CIE	
270	4-4-2T	269	GS&WR 270	1926	CIE	
271	4-4-2T	269	GS&WR 271	1926	CIE	
274	4-4-2T	269	GS&WR 274		CIE	
276	2-4-0	276	GS&WR 276	1925	CIE	
279	0-4-4T	279	GS&WR 279	1927	CIE	
290	2-4-0	276	GS&WR 290	1926	CIE	
291	2-4-0	276	GS&WR 291	1925	CIE	
293	2-4-0	276	GS&WR 293	1925	CIE	
295	0-4-4T	295	GS&WR 295	1926	CIE	
296	4-4-0	296	GS&WR 296		CIE	
297	4-4-0	296	GS&WR 297		1928	
298	4-4-0	296	GS&WR 298	1927	CIE	
299	0-6-0ST	299	GS&WR 299		CIE	
301	4-4-0	301	GS&WR 301	1931 B.Sh	CIE	

No.	Type	GSR Class	Former Railway and No.	Rebuilt by GSR	Withdrawn	Remarks
302	4-4-0	301	GS&WR 302	1932 B.Sh	CIE	
303	4-4-0	301	GS&WR 303	1933 B.Sh	CIE	
304	4-4-0	301	GS&WR 304	1932 B.Sh	CIE	
305	4-4-0	305	GS&WR 305	1930 B.Sh	CIE	
306	4-4-0	305	GS&WR 306	1931 B.Sh; 1935 B.Sh	CIE	Larger diameter boiler in 1935.
307	4-4-0	305	GS&WR 307	1937 B.Sh	CIE	
308	4-4-0	305	GS&WR 308		1933	
309	4-4-0	321	GS&WR 309	1935 B.Sh	CIE	Became 310 Class 1935.
310	4-4-0	310	GS&WR 310	1932 B.Sh	CIE	
311	4-4-0	310	GS&WR 311	1931 T.Sat; 1934 B.Sh	CIE	Became 321 Class 1931. 310 Class 1934.
312	4-4-0	321	GS&WR 312	1931 B.Sh	CIE	Became 310 Class 1931.
313	4-4-0	310	GS&WR 313	1934 B.Sh	CIE	
314	4-4-0	310	GS&WR 314	1930 B.Sh	CIE	
317	4-4-2T	37	GS&WR 317		CIE	
318	4-4-2T	37	GS&WR 318		CIE	
319	4-4-2T	37	GS&WR 319		CIE	
320	4-4-2T	37	GS&WR 320		CIE	
321	4-4-0	321	GS&WR 321	1933 B.Sh	CIE	
322	4-4-0	321	GS&WR 322	1937 B.Sh	CIE	
323	4-4-0	321	GS&WR 323	1932 B.Sh	CIE	
324	4-4-0	321	GS&WR 324		1928	
325	4-4-0	321	GS&WR 325		1928	
326	4-4-0	321	GS&WR 326		1927	
327	4-4-0	321	GS&WR 327	1935 B.Sh	CIE	
328	4-4-0	321	GS&WR 328	1929 B.Sat; 1932 B.Sh	CIE	
329	4-4-0	321	GS&WR 329	1929 B.Sat; 1932 B.Sh	CIE	
330	4-4-0	321	GS&WR 330	1930 B.Sh	CIE	
331	4-4-0	321	GS&WR 331	1929 B.Sat; 1932 B.Sh	CIE	
332	4-4-0	321	GS&WR 332	1927 B.Sh	CIE	Became 332 Class 1927 (when fitted with piston valves).
333	4-4-0	333	GS&WR 333	1930 B.Sh	CIE	
334	4-4-0	333	GS&WR 334	1932 B.Sh	CIE	
335	4-4-0	333	GS&WR 335	1933 B.Sh	CIE	
336	4-4-0	333	GS&WR 336	1930 B.Sh	CIE	
337	4-4-0	333	GS&WR 337	1930 B.Sh	CIE	
338	4-4-0	333	GS&WR 338	1927 B.Sh	CIE	Became 338 Class 1927 (when fitted with piston valves).
339	4-4-0	333	GS&WR 339	1933 B.Sh	CIE	
340	4-4-0	333	GS&WR 340	1932 B.Sh	CIE	
341	4-4-0	341	GS&WR 341		1928	Retained name *Sir William Goulding*.
351	0-6-0	351	GS&WR 351	1930 B.Sh	CIE	
352	0-6-0	351	GS&WR 352	1938 RT.Sh	CIE	
353	0-6-0	351	GS&WR 353	1930 B.Sh	1931	
354	0-6-0	351	GS&WR 354	1935 B.Sh	CIE	
355	2-6-0	355	GS&WR 355		1928	
356	2-6-0	355	GS&WR 356	1925 B.Sh	CIE	
357	2-6-0	355	GS&WR 357	1930 B.Sat; 1935 B.Sh	CIE	.Withdrawn 1931. Reinstated 1935.
358	2-6-0	355	GS&WR 358	1930 B.Sat; 1934 B.Sh	CIE	
359	2-6-0	355	GS&WR 359	1930 B.Sat; 1934 B.Sh	CIE	
360	2-6-0	355	GS&WR 360	1929 B.Sat; 1937 B.Sh	CIE	
361	2-6-0	355	GS&WR 361	1928 B.Sh	CIE	
362	4-6-0	362	GS&WR 362		1928	
363	4-6-0	362	GS&WR 363		1928	
364	4-6-0	362	GS&WR 364		1928	
365	4-6-0	362	GS&WR 365		1928	
366	4-6-0	362	GS&WR 366		1931	
367	4-6-0	362	GS&WR 367		1928	
368	2-6-0	368	GS&WR 368		1928	
369	2-6-0	368	GS&WR 369	1934 B.Sh	CIE	
370	2-6-0	368	GS&WR 370	1935 B.Sh	CIE	
371	2-6-0	368	GS&WR 371		1928	
400	4-6-0	400	GS&WR 400		1929	
401	4-6-0	400	GS&WR 401	1930 2-cyl; 1939	CIE	Caprotti valve gear 1930. Larger diameter B.Sh boiler 1939. Became 402 Class (1930)
402	4-6-0	400	GS&WR 402	1927 2-cyl	CIE	Became 402 Class (1927)
403	4-6-0	400	GS&WR 403	1934 2-cyl; 1936	CIE	Larger diameter B.Sh boiler 1936.
404	4-6-0	400	GS&WR 404		1930	Actually became No. 409 in 1930.
405	4-6-0	400	GS&WR 405	1933 2-cyl; 1937	CIE	Larger diameter B.Sh boiler 1937.
406	4-6-0	400	GS&WR 406	1930 2-cyl	CIE	Caprotti valve gear 1930. Became 402 Class (1930)
407	4-6-0	400	GS&WR 407	1937 2-cyl	CIE	
408	4-6-0	400	GS&WR 408		1930	
409	4-6-0	400	GS&WR 409	1925 B.Sh; 1935 2-cyl	CIE	Scrapped in place of No. 404. Post 1930 data really applies to No. 404.
422	2-4-0	422	D&SER 24		1928	
423	2-4-0T	423	D&SER 49		CIE	
424	2-4-0T	423	D&SER 9	1934 B.Sat	CIE	
425	2-4-0T	423	D&SER 47	1930 B.Sat	CIE	

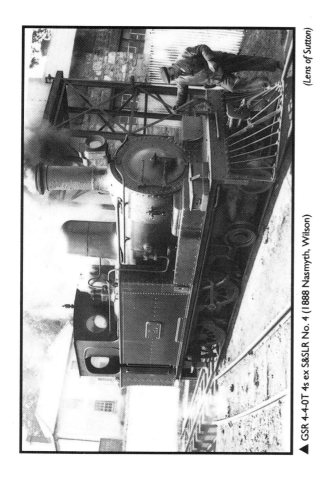

(Lens of Sutton)

▲ GSR 4-4-0T 4s ex S&SLR No. 4 (1888 Nasmyth, Wilson)

(LCGB Ken Nunn Collection)

▲ S&SLR 0-4-0T No. 2 (1886 Dick, Kerr)

(Real Photos)
(Real Photos)

▲ T&DLR 0-4-2T No. 4 showing double cab and enclosed motion for tramway operation (1890 Hunslet)

▲ GSR Sentinel Locomotive No. 1 Later No. 280 (1927)

No.	Type	GSR Class	Former Railway and No.		Rebuilt by GSR	Withdrawn	Remarks
426	2-4-0T	423	D&SER	7		1927	Not renumbered
427	2-4-2T	427	D&SER	64		1936	
428	2-4-2T	428	D&SER	3	1934 B.Sat	CIE	
429	2-4-2T	428	D&SER	10		1925	Not renumbered
430	2-4-2T	428	D&SER	11		CIE	
431	2-4-2T	428	D&SER	28		CIE	
432	2-4-2T	428	D&SER	45	1939 B.Sat	CIE	
433	2-4-2T	428	D&SER	46	1943 B.Sat	CIE	
434	2-4-2T	434	D&SER	8		CIE	
435	2-4-2T	434	D&SER	12		CIE	
436	2-4-2T	434	D&SER	27	1926 RT.Sat	CIE	
437	2-4-2T	434	D&SER	29	1937 RT.Sat	CIE	
438	2-4-2T	434	D&SER	30	1930 RT.Sat; 1933 B.Sat 1937 RT.Sat	CIE	
439	2-4-2T	434	D&SER	40		CIE	
440	0-6-0	440	D&SER	17		1929	
441	0-6-0	441	D&SER	36		1934	
442	0-6-0	442	D&SER	13		1930	
443	0-6-0	442	D&SER	14		CIE	
444	0-6-0	442	D&SER	18	1943 B.Sat	CIE	
445	0-6-0	442	D&SER	65		CIE	
446	0-6-0	442	D&SER	66	1940* B.Sat	CIE	
447	0-6-0	447	D&SER	50		1930	
448	0-6-0	448	D&SER	4		CIE	
449	0-6-0	448	D&SER	5	1926 B.Sat	1940	
450	4-4-0	450	D&SER	55		1929	
451	4-4-0	450	D&SER	56		1934	
452	4-4-0	450	D&SER	57		1933	
453	4-4-0	453	D&SER	58		1940	
454	4-4-0	454	D&SER	67	1935 B.Sat; 1939 B.Sat	CIE	Larger diameter boiler 1939.
455	4-4-2T	455	D&SER	20		CIE	
456	4-4-2T	455	D&SER	34	1935 RT.Sat; 1938 B.Sat 1941 RT.Sat	CIE	
457	4-4-2T	455	D&SER	35	1936 RT.Sat	CIE	
458	4-4-2T	458	D&SER	52		CIE	
459	4-4-2T	458	D&SER	54		CIE	
460	4-4-2T	458	D&SER	53	1926	CIE	
461	2-6-0	461	D&SER	15		CIE	
462	2-6-0	461	D&SER	16		CIE	
463	4-6-0T	463	CB&SCR	4	1943 B.Sh	CIE	
464	4-6-0T	463	CB&SCR	8		CIE	
465	4-6-0T	463	CB&SCR	11		CIE	
466	4-6-0T	463	CB&SCR	13		CIE	
467	4-6-0T	463	CB&SCR	14	1935 B.Sh	CIE	
468	4-6-0T	463	CB&SCR	15	1944 B.Sh	CIE	
469	4-6-0T	463	CB&SCR	19		CIE	
470	4-6-0T	463	CB&SCR	20		CIE	
471	4-6-0T	471	CB&SCR	10		1933	
472	0-6-0ST	472	CB&SCR	6		1940	
473	0-6-0ST	472	CB&SCR	17		1935	
474	0-6-0ST	474	CB&SCR	12		1925	Not renumbered.
475	0-6-0ST	475	CB&SCR	5		1939	
476	0-6-0ST	475	CB&SCR	16		1925	Not renumbered.
477	4-4-0T	477	CB&SCR	2		1930	
478	4-4-0T	477	CB&SCR	7		1934	
479	4-4-2T	479	CB&SCR	3		1930	
480	4-4-2T	479	CB&SCR	9		1935	
481	4-4-2T	479	CB&SCR	18		1935	Ran until summer 1936.
482	2-4-0T	482	CB&SCR	1		1930	
483	2-2-2WT	483	W&TR	1		1936	
484	2-2-2WT	483	W&TR	2		1928	
485	0-4-2WT	485	W&TR	3		1930	
486	0-4-2T	486	W&TR	4		1941	
487	2-4-0T	487	C&MDR	2		1928	
488	2-4-0T	487	C&MDR	3		1934	
489	2-4-0T	487	C&MDR	4		1928	
490	0-6-2T	490	C&MDR	5		1935	
491	2-4-2T	491	C&MDR	6		1934	Same as 267 Class.
500	4-6-0	500	GS&WR	500		CIE	Fitted with feedwater heater 1928. Part removed 1932, remainder 1940.
530	4-4-0	530	MGWR	1	1936 RT.Sh; 1939 B.Sh	CIE	
531	4-4-0	530	MGWR	4	1930 RT.Sh; 1934* B.Sh	CIE	
532	4-4-0	530	MGWR	5	1930 RT.Sh	CIE	
533	4-4-0	530	MGWR	6	1935* RT.Sh	CIE	
534	4-4-0	530	MGWR	2	1932 B.Sh	CIE	
535	4-4-0	530	MGWR	3	1935* RT.Sat	CIE	
536	4-4-0	536	MGWR	12	1925 RT.Sh; 1935 B.Sh 1938 B.Sh	CIE	Rebuilt to MGWR Cs Class 1925. Larger diameter boiler 1938.
537	4-4-0	536	MGWR	20	1935 B.Sh; 1940 B.Sh	CIE	Larger diameter boiler 1940.

No.	Type	GSR Class	Former Railway and No.		Rebuilt by GSR	Withdrawn	Remarks
538	4-4-0	536	MGWR	25	1936 B.Sh	CIE	Larger diameter boiler 1936.
539	4-4-0	536	MGWR	26	1935 B.Sh; 1939 B.Sh	CIE	Larger diameter boiler 1939.
540	4-4-0	540	MGWR	7		CIE	
541	4-4-0	540	MGWR	8		CIE	
542	4-4-0	540	MGWR	9		CIE	
543	4-4-0	540	MGWR	10		CIE	
544	4-4-0	540	MGWR	11	1926 B.Sh	CIE	Larger diameter boiler 1926.
545	4-4-0	545	MGWR	127		CIE	
546	4-4-0	545	MGWR	129		CIE	Withdrawn and reinstated 1933.
547	4-4-0	545	MGWR	125		CIE	
548	4-4-0	545	MGWR	126	1925 B.Sh	CIE	
549	4-4-0	545	MGWR	128	1926 B.Sh	1931	
550	4-4-0	545	MGWR	124		CIE	
551	0-6-0T	551	MGWR	106		CIE	
552	0-6-0T	551	MGWR	107		CIE	
553	0-6-0T	551	MGWR	108		CIE	Enlarged bunker 1941 (for Tramore line).
554	0-6-0T	551	MGWR	109		CIE	
555	0-6-0T	551	MGWR	110		CIE	Enlarged bunker 1936 (for Tramore line).
556	0-6-0T	551	MGWR	111		CIE	
557	0-6-0T	551	MGWR	112		CIE	
558	0-6-0T	551	MGWR	113		CIE	
559	0-6-0T	551	MGWR	114		CIE	
560	0-6-0T	551	MGWR	115		CIE	Enlarged bunker 1932 (for Tramore line).
561	0-6-0T	551	MGWR	116		CIE	
562	0-6-0T	551	MGWR	117		CIE	
563	0-6-0	563	MGWR	49		1928	Not renumbered.
564	0-6-0	563	MGWR	50		1925	Not renumbered.
565	0-6-0	563	MGWR	51		1926	Not renumbered.
566	0-6-0	563	MGWR	52		1926	Not renumbered.
567	0-6-0	563	MGWR	53	1925; 1942 B.Sh	CIE	Removal of experimental firebox superheater 1925. Later 567 Class.
568	0-6-0	563	MGWR	54		1925	Not renumbered.
569	0-6-0	573	MGWR	76		1925	Not renumbered.
570	0-6-0	573	MGWR	78		1925	Not renumbered.
571	0-6-0	573	MGWR	83		1925	Not renumbered.
572	0-6-0	573	MGWR	84		1925	Not renumbered.
573	0-6-0	573	MGWR	85		1927	Not renumbered.
574	0-6-0	573	MGWR	80	1940 B.Sh	CIE	
575	0-6-0	573	MGWR	135	1930 B.Sat; 1940 B.Sh	CIE	
576	0-6-0	573	MGWR	74	1931 B.Sh	CIE	
577	0-6-0	573	MGWR	86		1928	
578	0-6-0	573	MGWR	79		1926	Not renumbered.
579	0-6-0	573	MGWR	64		1928	Not renumbered .
582	0-6-0	573	MGWR	73	1932 B.Sh	CIE	
583	0-6-0	573	MGWR	82	1926 B.Sat; 1932 B.Sh	CIE	
584	0-6-0	573	MGWR	130	1937 B.Sh	CIE	
585	0-6-0	573	MGWR	131		CIE	
586	0-6-0	573	MGWR	132		CIE	
587	0-6-0	573	MGWR	133	1941 B.Sh	CIE	
588	0-6-0	573	MGWR	134	1940 B.Sh	CIE	
589	0-6-0	573	MGWR	77	1941 B.Sh	CIE	
590	0-6-0	573	MGWR	136	1936 B.Sh	CIE	
591	0-6-0	573	MGWR	137	1940 B.Sh	CIE	
592	0-6-0	573	MGWR	138		CIE	
593	0-6-0	573	MGWR	139		CIE	
594	0-6-0	594	MGWR	55	1942 RT.Sat	CIE	
595	0-6-0	594	MGWR	56	1934 B.Sh	CIE	
596	0-6-0	594	MGWR	57	1935 B.Sh	CIE	
597	0-6-0	594	MGWR	58	1930 B.Sh	CIE	
598	0-6-0	594	MGWR	59	1937 B.Sh	CIE	
599	0-6-0	594	MGWR	60	1936 B.Sh	CIE	
600	0-6-0	594	MGWR	61		CIE	
601	0-6-0	594	MGWR	62	1931 B.Sh	CIE	
602	0-6-0	594	MGWR	63	1933 B.Sh	CIE	
603	0-6-0	594	MGWR	65	1940 B.Sh	CIE	
604	0-6-0	594	MGWR	66	1933 B.Sh	CIE	
605	0-6-0	594	MGWR	67	1932 B.Sh	CIE	
606	0-6-0	594	MGWR	68	1933 B.Sh	CIE	
607	0-6-0	594	MGWR	69	1934 B.Sh	CIE	
608	0-6-0	594	MGWR	70	1932 B.Sh	CIE	
609	0-6-0	594	MGWR	71	1935 B.Sh	CIE	
610	0-6-0	594	MGWR	72	1931 B.Sh	CIE	
611	0-6-0	594	MGWR	140		1925	Not renumbered.
612	0-6-0	594	MGWR	75	1925 B.Sat; 1942 RT.Sat	CIE	1925 conversion started by MGWR.
613	0-6-0	594	MGWR	81	1925 B.Sat; 1940 B.Sh	CIE	1925 conversion started by MGWR.
614	0-6-0T	614	MGWR	100	1932 B.Sat; 1939 RT.Sat	CIE	
615	0-6-0T	614	MGWR	101		CIE	
616	0-6-0T	614	MGWR	102	1932 B.Sat; 1941 RT.Sat	CIE	

No.	Type	GSR Class	Former Railway and No.		Rebuilt by GSR	Withdrawn	Remarks
617	0-6-0T	614	MGWR	103	1939 B.Sat; 1944 RT.Sat	CIE	
618	0-6-0T	614	MGWR	105		CIE	
619	0-6-0	619	MGWR	96		CIE	
620	0-6-0	619	MGWR	97		CIE	
621	0-6-0	619	MGWR	98		CIE	
622	0-6-0	619	MGWR	99		CIE	
623	0-6-0	623	MGWR	35		CIE	
624	0-6-0	623	MGWR	87		CIE	
625	0-6-0	623	MGWR	88		CIE	
626	0-6-0	623	MGWR	89		CIE	
627	0-6-0	623	MGWR	90		CIE	
628	0-6-0	623	MGWR	91		CIE	
629	0-6-0	623	MGWR	92		CIE	
630	0-6-0	623	MGWR	93		CIE	
631	0-6-0	623	MGWR	94		CIE	
632	0-6-0	623	MGWR	95		CIE	
633	0-6-0	623	MGWR	39		CIE	
634	0-6-0	623	MGWR	40		CIE	
635	0-6-0	623	MGWR	41		CIE	
636	0-6-0	623	MGWR	36		CIE	
637	0-6-0	623	MGWR	37		CIE	
638	0-6-0	623	MGWR	38		CIE	
639	0-6-0	623	MGWR	42		CIE	
640	0-6-0	623	MGWR	43		CIE	
641	0-6-0	623	MGWR	44		CIE	
642	0-6-0	623	MGWR	45		CIE	
643	0-6-0	623	MGWR	46		CIE	
644	0-6-0	623	MGWR	47		CIE	
645	0-6-0	623	MGWR	48		CIE	
646	0-6-0	646	MGWR	143		1933	
647	0-6-0	646	MGWR	144		1930	
648	0-6-0	646	MGWR	145		1939	
649	0-6-0	646	MGWR	146		1939	
650	2-4-0	650	MGWR	14	1926 RT.Sh; 1935 B.Sh	CIE	
651	2-4-0	650	MGWR	16	1927 RT.Sh; 1935 B.Sh	CIE	
652	2-4-0	650	MGWR	18	1926 RT.Sh; 1935 B.Sh	CIE	
653	2-4-0	650	MGWR	19	1929 RT.Sh; 1942 B.Sh	CIE	
654	2-4-0	650	MGWR	28	1926 RT.Sh; 1942 B.Sh	CIE	
655	2-4-0	650	MGWR	29	1926 RT.Sh; 1941 B.Sh	CIE	
656	2-4-0	650	MGWR	30	1926 RT.Sh; 1934 B.Sh	CIE	
657	2-4-0	650	MGWR	33	1925 RT.Sh; 1929 RT.Sat	CIE	
658	2-4-0	650	MGWR	34	1925 RT.Sh; 1935 RT.Sat 1940 B.Sh	CIE	
659	2-4-0	650	MGWR	13	1932 B.Sh	CIE	
660	2-4-0	650	MGWR	15	1931 B.Sh	CIE	
661	2-4-0	650	MGWR	17	1933 B.Sh	CIE	
662	2-4-0	650	MGWR	21	1931 RT.Sat	CIE	
663	2-4-0	650	MGWR	22	1932 B.Sh	CIE	
664	2-4-0	650	MGWR	23	1930 RT.Sat; 1934 B.Sh 1941 RT.Sat	CIE	
665	2-4-0	650	MGWR	24		CIE	
666	2-4-0	650	MGWR	27	1930 RT.Sat; 1935 B.Sh 1941 RT.Sh	CIE	
667	2-4-0	650	MGWR	31	1934 B.Sh; 1939 RT.Sh 1943 B.Sh	CIE	
668	2-4-0	650	MGWR	32	1940 B.Sh	CIE	
900	4-8-0T	900	GS&WR	900		1928	
901	4-8-0T	900	GS&WR	901		1931	

Name	Type	GSR Class	Former Railway and No.		Rebuilt by GSR	Withdrawn	Remarks
Argadeen	2-6-0T	Argadeen	T&CLR		1929	CIE	
Elf	2-4-0T	Elf	D&SER	69	1925 0-4-0T	1931	Same as *Imp* on rebuilding.
Erin	0-6-0ST	Erin	GS&WR			1930	Nominally No. 300
Fairy	0-4-2T	Fairy	GS&WR			1927	Same as *Sprite*
Imp	0-4-0T	Imp	GS&WR			1928	
Jumbo	0-6-4T	Jumbo	GS&WR			CIE	
St. Molaga	0-4-2T	St. Molaga	T&CLR			CIE	
Sambo	0-4-2ST	Sambo	GS&WR			CIE	
Sprite	0-4-2T	Sprite	GS&WR			1927	Same as *Fairy*

Nos. 569-93 were originally allotted to MGWR Nos. 64, 73-86, 130-9 in that order. Nos. 612/3 were originally allotted to MGWR Nos. 141/2. Of other former MGWR classes the order of renumbering took into account sub-divisions as follows:

530 Class: 530-3 were D Class, 534/5 were Ds Class.

536 Class: 536 was C Class, 537-9 were Cs Class.

540 Class: 540-4 were C1 Class.

545 Class: 545-7 were As Class, 548/9 were A Class, 550 was A1 Class.

623 Class: 623-32 were FB Class, 633-5 were F Class, 636-45 were FA Class.

650 Class: 650-8 were K Class, 659-68 were Ks Class.

43 3-0 gauge locomotives taken into stock 1925 ('Section' suffix added to most existing numbers):

No.	Type	GSR Class	Former Railway	Renumbered	Withdrawn	Remarks
1 c	4-6-0T	1C	WCR		CIE	
2 c	2-6-2T	2C	WCR		CIE	
3 c	4-6-0T	3C	WCR		CIE	
4	2-6-2T	2C	WCR		1928	Section suffix not added.
5 c	0-6-2T	5C	WCR		CIE	
6 c	0-6-2T	5C	WCR		CIE	
7 c	4-6-0T	3C	WCR		CIE	
8	2-6-2T	2C	WCR		1925	Section suffix not added.
9 c	2-6-2T	2C	WCR		CIE	
10 c	4-6-0T	10C	WCR		CIE	
11 c	4-6-0T	11C	WCR		CIE	
1 k	4-4-0T	1K	C&MLR		1935	
2 k	4-4-0T	1K	C&MLR		1935	
4	4-4-0T	4K	C&MLR		1927	Section suffix not added.
5 k	0-4-4T	5K	C&MLR	9T (1935)	1936	
6 k	0-4-4T	5K	C&MLR	69 (1936)	CIE	Withdrawn 1935. Reinstated 1936. Reclassified 6S.
7 k	4-4-0T	7K	C&MLR		1935	
8 k	4-4-0T	8K	C&MLR		1935	
1	4-4-0T	1L	C&LR		CIE	Section suffix not added. Name retained *Isabel*.
2 L	4-4-0T	1L	C&LR		CIE	
3 L	4-4-0T	1L	C&LR		CIE	
4 L	4-4-0T	1L	C&LR		CIE	
5	4-4-0T	1L	C&LR		1925	Section suffix not added.
6	4-4-0T	1L	C&LR		1927	Section suffix not added.
7	4-4-0T	1L	C&LR		CIE	Section suffix not added.
8 L	4-4-0T	1L	C&LR		CIE	
9	0-6-4T	9L	C&LR		1934	Section suffix not added. Name retained *King Edward*.
4 P	2-4-2T	4P	CB&PR	10L (1934)	CIE	Withdrawn 1933. Reinstated 1934. Reclassified 10L.
5 P	2-4-2T	4P	CB&PR	11L (1934)	1936	Withdrawn 1933. Reinstated 1934. Reclassified 10L.
6 P	2-4-2T	4P	CB&PR	12L (1934)	CIE	Withdrawn 1933. Reinstated 1934. Reclassified 10L.
7 P	2-4-2T	4P	CB&PR	13L (1934)	CIE	Withdrawn 1933. Reinstated 1934. Reclassified 10L.
1	4-4-0T	1S	S&SLR		1937	Section suffix not added.
2	0-4-0T	2S	S&SLR		1926	Section suffix not added.
3 s	4-4-0T	3S	S&SLR		CIE	Name retained *Kent*.
4 s	4-4-0T	4S	S&SLR		CIE	
1 T	2-6-0T	1T	T&DLR		CIE	
2 T	2-6-0T	1T	T&DLR		CIE	
3 T	2-6-0T	1T	T&DLR		CIE	
4 T	2-6-0T	4T	T&DLR		CIE	
5 T	2-6-0T	5T	T&DLR		CIE	
6 T	2-6-0T	1T	T&DLR		CIE	
7	2-6-0T	4T	T&DLR		1928	Section suffix not added.
8 T	2-6-0T	1T	T&DLR		CIE	

Names
Except where indicated, or due to early withdrawal, names were removed by the GSR.

59 new locomotives (5-3 gauge) built 1925-40 and 1 secondhand acquired 1930

No.	Name	Type	Class	Date	Builder	Withdrawn	Remarks
372		2-6-0	372	1925	GSR-B	CIE	Built as MGWR No. 49, became GSR No. 410 but altered to No. 372 before entering service.
373		2-6-0	372	1925	GSR-B	CIE	
374		2-6-0	372	1925	GSR-B	CIE	
375		2-6-0	372	1925	GSR-B	CIE	
376		Z-6-0	372	1926	GSR-B	CIE	
377		2-6-0	372	1926	GSR-B	CIE	
378		2-6-0	372	1926	GSR-B	CIE	
379		2-6-0	372	1926	GSR-B	CIE	
380		2-6-0	372	1926	GSR-B	CIE	
381		2-6-0	372	1926	GSR-B	CIE	
501		4-6-0	500	1926	GSR-I	CIE	
502		4-6-0	500	1926	GSR-I	CIE	
1	Sentinel	Sentinel	280	1927	Sen	CIE	Renumbered 280 (1927)
2	Sentinel	Sentinel	280	1927	Sen	CIE	Renumbered 281 (1927)
382		2-6-0	372	1927	GSR-B	CIE	
383		2-6-0	372	1927	GSR-B	CIE	
384		2-6-0	372	1928	GSR-I	CIE	
385		2-6-0	372	1928	GSR-I	CIE	
386		2-6-0	372	1928	GSR-I	CIE	
387		2-6-0	372	1928	GSR-I	CIE	
388		2-6-0	372	1928	GSR-I	CIE	
389		2-6-0	372	1928	GSR-I	CIE	
850		2-6-0	372	1928	GSR-I	CIE	Locomotive diagram book allows for Nos. 851-3
390		2-6-0	372	1929	GSR-I	CIE	
391		2-6-0	372	1929	GSR-I	CIE	

No.	Name	Type	Class	Date	Builder	Withdrawn	Remarks
700		0-6-0	700	1929	GSR-I	CIE	
701		0-6-0	700	1929	GSR-I	CIE	
702		0-6-0	700	1929	GSR-I	CIE	
703		0-6-0	700	1929	GSR-I	CIE	
704		0-6-0	700	1929	GSR-I	CIE	
393		2-6-0	393	1930	GSR-I	CIE	
394		2-6-0	393	1930	GSR-I	CIE	
395		2-6-0	393	1930	GSR-I	CIE	
396		2-6-0	393	1930	GSR-I	CIE	
397		2-6-0	393	1930	GSR-I	CIE	
398		2-6-0	393	1930	GSR-I	CIE	
495		0-4-0ST	495			CIE	Purchased 1930 from Allman (see Contractors List)
670		0-6-2T	670	1933	GSR-I	CIE	
671		0-6-2T	670	1933	GSR-I	CIE	
672		0-6-2T	670	1933	GSR-I	CIE	
673		0-6-2T	670	1933	GSR-I	CIE	
674		0-6-2T	670	1933	GSR-I	CIE	
710		0-6-0	710	1934	GSR-I	CIE	
711		0-6-0	710	1934	GSR-I	CIE	
712		0-6-0	710	1934	GSR-I	CIE	
713		0-6-0	710	1934	GSR-I	CIE	
714		0-6-0	710	1934	GSR-I	CIE	
715		0-6-0	710	1935	GSR-I	CIE	
716		0-6-0	710	1935	GSR-I	CIE	
717		0-6-0	710	1935	GSR-I	CIE	
718		0-6-0	710	1935	GSR-I	CIE	
719		0-6-0	710	1935	GSR-I	CIE	
342		4-4-0	342	1936	GSR-I	CIE	
343		4-4-0	342	1936	GSR-I	CIE	
344		4-4-0	342	1936	GSR-I	CIE	
345		4-4-0	342	1936	GSR-I	CIE	
346		4-4-0	342	1936	GSR-I	CIE	
800	*Maedhbh*	4-6-0	800	1939	GSR-I	CIE	Original nameplates were *Maeve* (but soon altered).
801	*Macha*	4-6-0	800	1939	GSR-I	CIE	
802	*Tailte*	4-4-0	800	1940	GSR-I	CIE	

475 5-3 and 28 3-0 gauge locomotives taken into CIE stock 1945, numbers/names not altered. For numerical list see Coras Iompair Eireann.

400 Class Rebuilding

The seven rebuilt were altered from 4 to 2 cylinders. Nos. 401, 402 & 406 had new frames (cyl. 19½ x 28), whilst Nos. 403, 405, 407 & 409 had a new front end only (cyl. 19½ x 26).

800 Class Names

In addition to the names given for Nos. 800-2 a further seven are listed and may have been selected for use should further locomotives have been built *Deidre, Cliona, Emer, Aoife, Beara, Scathach* and *Dana*. The letters on the nameplates of Nos. 800-2 were in Irish script.

Departmental Stock 1925-44

The GSR listed 12 such locomotives in 1925 (0-6-0 6, 0-6-4T 1, 0-6-0T 1, 0-4-4T 1, 0-4-2T 3), 10 in 1926 (0-6-0 6, 0-6-4T 1, 0-4-2T 3), 3 in 1927-43 (0-6-0 1, 0-6-4T 1, 0-4-2T 1) and 3 in 1944 (0-6-4T 1, 0-6-0T 1, 0-4-2T 1). Those consistently regarded as departmental were No. 92, *Sambo, Sprite* and *Fairy,* joined by *Jumbo* in 1944. Others moved back to the capital list in 1927, but 1 0-6-0, exchanged as necessary, was counted as departmental until 1944.

Cork Coal Gantry Locomotive

Pat (ex-GS&WR) remained in use 1925-44 (not counted as stock).

'Inchicore Works' classification and GSR 'Load Class'

5-3 gauge locomotives

Wheel Arrangement	Inchicore Class	GSR Class	Former Railway	Former Class	GSR Load Class 1925	1931	Remarks
4-8-0T	A1	900	GS&WR	900	B		
4-6-0	B1	500	GS&WR	500	B	B	
4-6-0	B1A	800				H	
4-6-0	B2	400	GS&WR	400	E	C	
4-6-0	B2A	402				C	Rebuilt locomotives. (Nos. 401, 402, 406).
4-6-0	B3	362	GS&WR	362	C		
4-6-0T	B4	463	CB&SCR		H	HT	
4-6-0T	B5	471	CB&SCR		S	RT	
4-4-2T	C1						Allotted to proposed suburban tank (10 ordered).
4-4-2T	C2	455	D&SER		K	KT	(No. 455 was N in 1925 list).
4-4-2T	C3	458	D&SER		N	MT	
4-4-2T	C4	27	GS&WR	27	P	OT	
4-4-2T	C5	269	GS&WR	269	P	OT	
4-4-2T	C6	479	CB&SCR		S	RT	
4-4-2T	C7	37	GS&WR	37	S	RT	
4-4-0	D1	341	GS&WR	341	H		
4-4-0	D2	333	GS&WR	333	M	L	No. 338 later 'J'. Nos. 333-40 later D4 (1926) and No. 338 D4A (1928) and D3 (1937).

Wheel Arrangement	Inchicore Class	GSR Class	Former Railway	Former Class	GSR Load Class 1925	1931	Remarks
4-4-0	D3	321	GS&WR	321	L	J	Nos. 321-3; reclassified D2 (1926) and 'M.
4-4-0	D4	321	GS&WR	321	L	J	Nos. 324-32; reclassified D3 (1926) and then D2 (1927-32); Load Class altered to 'M. Nos. 309/12 reclassified D3 (1926) and then D10 (1930); Load Class altered to 'M'.
		342	GSR			L	Included in D4 with 333 Class.
4-4-0	D5	545	MGWR	A	J	J	
4-4-0	D6	540	MGWR	C1	L	J	
4-4-0	D7	536	MGWR	C	M	L	
4-4-0	D8	454	D&SER		N	M	
4-4-0	D9	450	D&SER		N	M	
4-4-0	D10	310	GS&WR	310	M	M	
4-4-0	D11	301	GS&WR	301	N	M	
4-4-0	D12	305	GS&WR	305	N	M	
4-4-0	D13	60	GS&WR	60	P		No. 89. Reclassifed D14 (1934).
4-4-0	D14	60	GS&WR	60	P	O	No. 89 added 1934.
4-4-0	D15	296	GS&WR	296	P	O	
4-4-0	D16	530	MGWR	D Bogie	Q	R	
4-4-0	D17	52	GS&WR	52	R	R	
4-4-0T	D18	477	CB&SCR		T	RT	
4-4-0	D19	2	GS&WR	2	S	R	
0-4-4T	E1	279	GS&WR	279	P	OT	
0-4-4T	E2	295	GS&WR	295	Q	PT	
0-4-4T	E3	47	GS&WR	47	S	RT	
2-4-2T	F1	434	D&SER		N	MT	
2-4-2T	F2	428	D&SER		O	NT	
2-4-2T	F3	427	D&SER		O	NT	
2-4-2T	F4	267	GS&WR	267	Q	PT	
2-4-2T	F5	491	C&MDR		Q	PT	
2-4-2T	F6	33	GS&WR	42	S	RT	
2-4-0T	G1	423	D&SER		O	NT	
2-4-0	G2	650	MGWR	K	Q	O	
2-4-0	G3	276	GS&WR	276	P	O	
2-4-0	G4	21	GS&WR	21	S		
2-4-0T	G5	487	C&MDR		T	RT	
2-4-0T	G6	482	CB&SCR		T		
2-4-0	G7	422	D&SER		Q		
0-6-4T	H1	203	GS&WR	203	J	KT	
0-6-4T	H2	92	GS&WR	92			Not classified for loads.
0-6-2T	I1	213	GS&WR	213	C	FT	
0-6-2T	I2	490	C&MDR		N	MT	
0-6-2T	I3	670				KT	
0-6-0	J1	448	D&SER		C	E	
0-6-0	J2	646	MGWR	B	B	B	
0-6-0	J3	211	GS&WR	211	C	E	
0-6-0	J4	257	GS&WR	257	C	C	Later 'E'.
0-6-0	J5	623	MGWR	F	C	E	
0-6-0	J6	619	MGWR	H	C	C	
0-6-0	J7	447	D&SER		E		
0-6-0	J8	442	D&SER		C	E	
0-6-0	J9	351	GS&WR	351	E	E	
0-6-0T	J10	614	MGWR	P	F	FT	
0-6-0T	J11	201	GS&WR	207	F	FT	
0-6-0T	J12	204	GS&WR	204	F	FT	
0-6-0T	J13	Jumbo	GS&WR	Jumbo		FT	
0-6-0	J14	441	D&SER		H	J	
0-6-0	J15	101	GS&WR	101	J	J	
0-6-0	J15A	700				J	
0-6-0	J15B	710				J	
0-6-0	J16	563	MGWR	Ln	J	J	Later 567 Class.
0-6-0	J17	234	MGWR	W	J	J	
0-6-0	J18	573	MGWR	Lm	K	J	
0-6-0	J19	594	MGWR	L	K	J	
0-6-0	J20	440	D&SER		M		
0-6-0ST	J21	475	CB&SCR		L	KT	
0-6-0	J22	235	GS&WR	235	M	L	
0-6-0ST	J23	474	CB&SCR				
0-6-0ST	J24	472	CB&SCR		M	KT	
0-6-0	J25	222	GS&WR	222	M	L	
0-6-0T	J26	551	MGWR	E	Q	PT	
0-6-0ST	J27	Erin	GS&WR	Erin	S		
0-6-0ST	J28	299	GS&WR	299	T	ST	
0-6-0ST	J29	91	GS&WR	91	U		
0-6-0T	J30	90, 99	GS&WR	90, 99	U	TT	
2-6-0	K1	372			B	A	
2-6-0	K1A	393				B	
2-6-0	K2	461	D&SER		E	C	
2-6-0	K3	355	GS&WR	355	C	C	

Wheel Arrangement	Inchicore Class	GSR Class	Former Railway	Former Class	GSR Load Class 1925	1931	Remarks
2-6-0	K4	368	GS&WR	368	C	C	
2-6-0T	K5	Argadeen	T&CLR		T	ST	
0-4-2T	L1	486	W&TR		R	RT	
0-4-2ST	L2	Sambo	GS&WR	Sambo			Later 'RT'.
0-4-2T	L3	485	W&TR		T		
0-4-2T	L4	Sprite	GS&WR	Sprite			Not classified for loads.
0-4-2T	L5	Fairy	GS&WR	Fairy			Not classified for loads. Reclassified L4
0-4-2T	L6	St. Molaga	T&CLR		U	TT	
0-4-0T	M1	Elf	D&SER				Not classified for loads. Reclassified M2 (1926).
		Imp	GS&WR	Imp			
0-4-0T	M1	280					Later 'TT'.
0-4-0ST	M3	495				TT	
2-2-2WT	N1	483	W&TR		U	TT	
2-6-2T	P1	850			H	HT	

0-4-0ST No. 228 (ex GS&WR) was not included in this system as it was withdrawn in early 1925.
(1925 Load Class refers to the system in use until revised in 1931).

3-0 Gauge Locomotives (Load Class letters were not allotted to these locomotives).

Wheel Arrangement	Inchicore Class	GSR Class	Former Railway	Wheel Arrangement	Inchicore Class	GSR Class	Former Railway
4-6-0T	BN1	10C	WCR	4-4-0T	DN7	8K	C&MLR
4-6-0T	BN2	11C	WCR	0-4-4T	EN1	5K	C&MLR later 6S Class.
4-6-0T	BN3	3C	WCR	2-4-2T	FN1	4P	CB&PR later 10L Class.
4-6-0T	BN4	1C	WCR	0-6-4T	HN1	9L	C&LR
4-4-0T	DN1	4K	C&MLR	0-6-2T	IN1	5C	WCR
4-4-0T	DN2	1L	C&LR	2-6-0T	KN1	4T	T&DLR
4-4-0T	DN3	7K	C&MLR	2-6-0T	KN2	1T	T&DLR
4-4-0T	DN4	1S	S&SLR	0-4-0T	MN1	2S	S&SLR
4-4-0T	DN5	4S	S&SLR	2-6-2T	PN1	2C	WCR
4-4-0T	DN6	1K	C&MLR	2-6-2T	PN2	5T	T&DLR

GSR Steam Railcars

4-wheeled chain drive power bogie (Cyl. 6¾ x 9, driving wheels 2-6) - vertical boiler and cylinders.

No.	Date	Builder	Withdrawn	Seating	Remarks
354	1927	Sen	1941	55 3rd	Numbered in coaching stock series.
355	1927	Sen	1942	55 3rd	Numbered in coaching stock series.
356	1927	Sen	1942	55 3rd	Numbered in coaching stock series.
357	1927	Sen	1941	55 3rd	Numbered in coaching stock series.

4-coupled power bogie (Cyl. 7 x 10, driving wheels 3-6) - vertical boiler.

No.	Date	Builder	Withdrawn	Seating	Remarks
358	1928	CWL	1931	9 1st; 55 3rd	Numbered in coaching stock series.
359	1928	CWL	1931	9 1st; 55 3rd	Numbered in coaching stock series.
360	1928	CWL	1931	9 1st; 55 3rd	Numbered in coaching stock series.
361	1928	CWL	1931	9 1st; 55 3rd	Numbered in coaching stock series.
362	1928	CWL	1931	9 1st; 55 3rd	Numbered in coaching stock series.
363	1928	CWL	1931	9 1st; 55 3rd	Numbered in coaching stock series.

After withdrawal as steam powered coaches these vehicles were articulated in pairs as locomotive hauled stock and used on the Waterford & Tramore section).

CORAS IOMPAIR EIREANN

Stock: 475 5-3 and 28 3-0 gauge locomotives taken into stock from GSR (4 were named only) 1945.
1 new locomotive built 1957 (never taken into stock).
83 5-3 gauge locomotives taken into stock from GNRB 1958.
1 5-3 gauge locomotive acquired from Dundalk Engineering Ltd. 1960 (counted as service stock).

No.	Type	Class	Rebuilt by CIE	Withdrawn	Remarks	No.	Type	Class	Rebuilt by CIE	Withdrawn	Remarks
1	4-4-0	52		1955		15	4-4-0	2		1951	
2	4-4-0	2		1953		16	4-4-0	52		1959	
3	4-4-0	52	1952 B.Sh	1957		18	4-4-0	52		1959	
4	4-4-0	52		1957		20	4-4-0	52		1959	
5	4-4-0	2		1949		27	4-4-2T	27		1953	
6	4-4-0	2		1952		30	4-4-2T	27		1950	
7	4-4-0	2		1953		31	4-4-2T	27		1953	
8	4-4-0	2		1945		32	4-4-2T	27		1951	
9	4-4-0	52	1951 B.Sh	1955		33	2-4-2T	33		1957	
10	4-4-0	2		1951		34	2-4-2T	33		1957	
11	4-4-0	52		1949		35	2-4-2T	33		1959	
12	4-4-0	52		1949		36	2-4-2T	33		1957	
13	4-4-0	2		1953		37	4-4-2T	37		1954	
14	4-4-0	52		1957		38	4-4-2T	37		1950	

▲ GSR 4-6-0 800 Class No. 800 - the ultimate in Irish express classes (1939 GSR Inchicore) *(Real Photos)*
▼ CIE Turf burning Experiment - GS&WR 2-6-0 No. 356 in the early days of experimentation
(the late B. Haresnape)

▲ Oil burning days in 1947 - CIE 2-6-0 No. 397 passing Inchicore cabin (1930 GSR Inchicore) *(R.N. Clements)*
▼ CIE 2-6-0 393 Class No. 393 with large smokebox numberplate (1930 GSR Inchicore) *(T.J. Edgington)*

No:	Type	Class	Rebuilt by CIE	Withdrawn	Remarks	No.	Type	Class	Rebuilt by CIE	Withdrawn	Remarks
41	2-4-2T	33		1957		146	0-6-0	101		1955	
42	2-4-2T	33		1963		147	0-6-0	101		1956	
43	4-4-0	2		1945		148	0-6-0	101		1953	Oil
44	4-4-0	2		1950		149	0-6-0	101		1962	Oil
45	4-4-0	2		1945		150	0-6-0	101		1957	
47	0-4-4T	47		1945		151	0-6-0	101	1950 B.Sh	1965	
49	0-4-4T	47		1945		152	0-6-0	101		1959	
52	4-4-0	52		1949		153	0-6-0	101		1954	Oil
54	4-4-0	52		1959		154	0-6-0	101		1962	
55	4-4-0	52		1955		156	0-6-0	101		1961	
56	4-4-0	52		1951		157	0-6-0	101		1963	
57	4-4-0	52	1950 B.Sh	1957		158	0-6-0	101		1957	
58	4-4-0	52	1950 B.Sh	1953		159	0-6-0	101		1949	
59	4-4-0	52		1955		160	0-6-0	101		1955	Oil
60	4-4-0	60		1957		161	0-6-0	101		1963	
61	4-4-0	60		1955		162	0-6-0	101		1963	
62	4-4-0	60		1959		163	0-6-0	101		1955	
63	4-4-0	60		1955		164	0-6-0	101		1963	
64	4-4-0	60		1959		165	0-6-0	101		1945	
65	4-4-0	60		1959		166	0-6-0	101		1963	Oil
78	0-4-4T	47		1945		167	0-6-0	101		1960	
85	4-4-0	60	1952 B.Sh	1959		168	0-6-0	101		1962	
86	4-4-0	60		1957		170	0-6-0	101		1962	Oil
87	4-4-0	60	1949 B.Sh	1957		171	0-6-0	101		1961	
88	4-4-0	60		1957		172	0-6-0	101	1949 B.Sh	1963	
89	4-4-0	60		1960		174	0-6-0	101		1953	
90	0-6-0T	90		1959		175	0-6-0	101		1956	
92	0-6-4T	92		1945		176	0-6-0	101		1959	
93	4-4-0	60		1959		179	0-6-0	101		1965	
94	4-4-0	60		1959		181	0-6-0	101		1959	
95	4-4-0	60		1955		182	0-6-0	101		1962	Oil
96	4-4-0	60		1959		183	0-6-0	101		1965	
98	4-4-0	52		1954		184	0-6-0	101		1962	
100	0-6-0	90		1959		185	0-6-0	101		1959	Oil
101	0-6-0	101		1963		186	0-6-0	101		1965	
102	0-6-0	101	1947 B.Sh	1962	Oil	187	0-6-0	101		1963	
103	0-6-0	101		1957		188	0-6-0	101		1959	
104	0-6-0	101		1965		190	0-6-0	101		1963	
105	0-6-0	101	1949 B.Sh	1963		191	0-6-0	101		1962	
106	0-6-0	101		1965	Oil	192	0-6-0	101		1956	
107	0-6-0	101		1957	Oil	193	0-6-0	101	1948 B.Sh	1963	
108	0-6-0	101		1959		194	0-6-0	101		1959	
109	0-6-0	101		1964		195	0-6-0	101		1965	
110	0-6-0	101		1963	Oil	196	0-6-0	101	1953 B.Sh	1961	
111	0-6-0	101		1962		197	0-6-0	101		1965	See note.
114	0-6-0	101	1948 B.Sh	1961		198	0-6-0	101		1965	Oil
116	0-6-0	101		1964		199	0-6-0	101		1954	
118	0-6-0	101		1966		200	0-6-0	101		1960	
119	0-6-0	101		1962		201	0-6-0T	201		1963	
120	0-6-0	101		1955		202	0-6-0T	201		1955	
121	0-6-0	101		1963		204	0-6-0T	204		1952	
122	0-6-0	101		1963		207	0-6-0T	201		1959	
123	0-6-0	101		1963		208	0-6-0T	201		1959	
124	0-6-0	101	1948 B.Sh	1965		209	0-6-0T	201		1949	
125	0-6-0	101	1949 B.Sh	1965		210	0-6-0T	201		1959	
126	0-6-0	101		1959		211	0-6-0	211		1949	
127	0-6-0	101		1962		212	0-6-0	211		1951	
128	0-6-0	101		1963		213	0-6-2T	213		1952	
130	0-6-0	101	1947 B.Sh	1965		214	0-6-2T	213		1949	
131	0-6-0	101		1963		217	0-6-0T	201		1961	
132	0-6-0	101		1965		218	0-6-0T	201		1959	
133	0-6-0	101		1963		219	0-6-0T	201		1955	
134	0-6-0	101		1962		220	0-6-0T	201		1959	
135	0-6-0	101		1957		222	0-6-0	222		1949	
136	0-6-0	101		1962		223	0-6-0	101		1960	
137	0-6-0	101		1960		229	0-6-0	101		1962	
138	0-6-0	101	1947 B.Sh	1962	Oil	232	0-6-0	101		1963	
139	0-6-0	101		1961		234	0-6-0	234		1950	
140	0-6-0	101		1961	Oil	236	0-6-0	222		1951	
141	0-6-0	101		1959		237	0-6-0	222		1951	
						239	0-6-0	222		1949	
						240	0-6-0	101		1957	

No.	Type	Class	Rebuilt by CIE	Withdrawn	Remarks
241	0-6-0	101		1957	
242	0-6-0	101		1957	
243	0-6-0	101		1955	
249	0-6-0	351		1963	Oil
250	0-6-0	351		1963	
251	0-6-0	351		1963	
252	0-6-0	351		1962	Oil
253	0-6-0	101		1963	
254	0-6-0	101		1961	
255	0-6-0	101		1963	Oil
256	0-6-0	101		1959	Oil
257	0-6-0	257		1960	Oil
258	0-6-0	257		1963	Oil
259	0-6-0	257		1959	Oil
260	0-6-0	257		1962	Oil
261	0-6-0	257	1948 B.Sh	1965	Oil
262	0-6-0	257		1965	Oil
263	0-6-0	257		1962	Oil
264	0-6-0	257		1960	Oil
269	4-4-2T	269		1957	
270	4-4-2T	269		1949	
270	4-4-2T	269		1949	
271	4-4-2T	269		1949	
274	4-4-2T	269		1949	
276	2-4-0	276		1949	
279	0-4-4T	279		1953	
280	Sentinel	280		1948	
281	Sentinel	280		1948	
290	2-4-0	276		1951	
291	2-4-0	276		1959	
293	2-4-0	276		1954	
295	0-4-4T	295		1954	
296	4-4-0	296		1949	
298	4-4-0	296		1949	
299	0-6-0ST	299		1957	
301	4-4-0	301		1960	
302	4-4-0	301		1957	
303	4-4-0	301		1959	
304	4-4-0	301		1959	
305	4-4-0	305		1957	
306	4-4-0	305		1959	
307	4-4-0	305		1959	
309	4-4-0	310		1959	
310	4-4-0	310		1957	
311	4-4-0	310		1959	
312	4-4-0	310		1959	
313	4-4-0	310		1957	
314	4-4-0	310		1957	
317	4-4-2T	37		1955	
318	4-4-2T	37		1953	
319	4-4-2T	37		1950	
320	4-4-2T	37		1954	
321	4-4-0	321		1957	
322	4-4-0	321		1960	
323	4-4-0	321		1955	
327	4-4-0	321		1959	
328	4-4-0	321		1959	
329	4-4-0	321		1960	
330	4-4-0	321		1957	Oil
331	4-4-0	321		1959	
332	4-4-0	321		1959	
333	4-4-0	333		1955	
334	4-4-0	333		1955	Oil
335	4-4-0	333		1955	Oil
336	4-4-0	333		1957	
337	4-4-0	333		1955	
338	4-4-0	333		1959	Oil
339	4-4-0	333		1959	
340	4-4-0	333		1955	Oil
342	4-4-0	342		1959	
343	4-4-0	342		1959	
344	4-4-0	342		1959	Oil
345	4-4-0	342		1959	
346	4-4-0	342		1960	Oil
351	0-6-0	351		1963	Oil
352	0-6-0	351	1951 B.Sh	1955	Oil
354	0-6-0	351		1962	Oil
356	2-6-0	355		1957	Oil. See note.
357	2-6-0	355		1960	Oil
358	2-6-0	355		1957	
359	2-6-0	355		1959	
360	2-6-0	355		1955	Oil
361	2-6-0	355		1959	Oil
369	2-6-0	368		1957	
370	2-6-0	368		1957	
372	2-6-0	372		1960	Oil
373	2-6-0	372		1959	
374	2-6-0	372		1959	Oil
375	2-6-0	372		1957	Oil
376	2-6-0	372		1961	Oil
377	2-6-0	372		1960	Oil
378	2-6-0	372		1959	Oil
379	2-6-0	372		1959	Oil
380	2-6-0	372		1959	
381	2-6-0	372		1959	Oil
382	2-6-0	372		1955	Oil
383	2-6-0	372		1959	
384	2-6-0	372		1960	
385	2-6-0	372		1960	Oil
386	2-6-0	372		1959	Oil
387	2-6-0	372		1959	Oil
388	2-6-0	372		1962	Oil
389	2-6-0	372		1955	Oil
390	2-6-0	372		1955	Oil
391	2-6-0	372		1957	Oil
393	2-6-0	393		1954	Oil
394	2-6-0	393		1959	Oil
395	2-6-0	393		1957	Oil
396	2-6-0	393		1959	Oil
397	2-6-0	393		1957	Oil
398	2-6-0	393		1955	Oil
401	4-6-0	402	1952 B.Sh 1953 B.Sh	1961	Oil. See note.
402	4-6-0	402	1946 B.Sh 1953 B.Sh	1961	See note.
403	4-6-0	400		1957	Oil. See note.
405	4-6-0	400		1955	
406	4-6-0	400		1957	
407	4-6-0	402	1949 B.Sh	1955	Oil. See note.
409	4-6-0	400	1952 B.Sh	1958	Oil. See note.
423	2-4-0T	423		1955	
424	2-4-0T	423		1952	
425	2-4-0T	423		1953	
428	2-4-2T	428		1953	
430	2-4-2T	428	1948 B.Sat	1952	
431	2-4-2T	428		1950	
432	2-4-2T	428		1957	
433	2-4-2T	428	1948 RT.Sat	1957	
434	2-4-2T	434		1950	
435	2-4-2T	434		1950	
436	2-4-2T	434		1953	
437	2-4-2T	434		1951	
438	2-4-2T	434		1952	
439	2-4-2T	434		1952	
443	0-6-0	442		1955	
444	0-6-0	442	1947 RT.Sat	1957	
445	0-6-0	442		1957	
446	0-6-0	442	1951 RT.Sat	1957	
448	0-6-0	448		1950	
454	4-4-0	454		1949	
455	4-4-2T	455		1959	
456	4-4-2T	455		1955	
457	4-4-2T	455		1959	
458	4-4-2T	458		1955	
459	4-4-2T	458		1953	
460	4-4-2T	458		1960	

No.	Type	Class	Rebuilt by CIE	Withdrawn	Remarks	No.	Type	Class	Rebuilt by CIE	Withdrawn	Remarks
461	2-6-0	461		1965		604	0-6-0	594		1961	
462	2-6-0	461		1963		605	0-6-0	594		1957	
463	4-6-0T	463	1950 RT.Sat	1963		606	0-6-0	594		1963	Oil
464	4-6-0T	463	1946 B.Sh	1963		607	0-6-0	594		1962	Oil
465	4-6-0T	463		1945		608	0-6-0	594		1959	
466	4-6-0T	463	1947 B.Sh	1961		609	0-6-0	594		1954	
467	4-6-0T	463		1959		610	0-6-0	594		1963	
468	4-6-0T	463	1948 RT.Sat	1961		612	0-6-0	594		1961	
			1950 B.Sh			613	0-6-0	594		1963	
469	4-6-0T	463		1945		614	0-6-0T	614		1955	
470	4-6-0T	463		1961		615	0-6-0T	614		1951	
495	0-4-0ST	495		1949		616	0-6-0T	614		1950	
500	4-6-0	500		1955	Oil	617	0-6-0T	614		1959	
501	4-6-0	500		1955	Oil	618	0-6-0T	614		1949	
502	4-6-0	500		1957	Oil	619	0-6-0	619		1949	
530	4-4-0	530		1949		620	0-6-0	619		1949	
531	4-4-0	530		1945		621	0-6-0	619		1949	
532	4-4-0	530		1949		622	0-6-0	619		1945	
533	4-4-0	530		1953		623	0-6-0	623		1957	
534	4-4-0	530		1949		624	0-6-0	623		1962	Oil
535	4-4-0	530		1949		625	0-6-0	623		1961	Oil
536	4-4-0	536		1951		626	0-6-0	623		1961	Oil
537	4-4-0	536		1953		627	0-6-0	623		1961	
538	4-4-0	536		1950		628	0-6-0	623		1954	Oil
539	4-4-0	536		1952		629	0-6-0	623		1954	Oil
540	4-4-0	540		1953		630	0-6-0	623		1959	Oil
541	4-4-0	540		1959		631	0-6-0	623		1954	Oil
542	4-4-0	540		1959		632	0-6-0	623		1959	Oil
543	4-4-0	540		1959		633	0-6-0	623		1957	Oil
544	4-4-0	540		1955		634	0-6-0	623		1959	
545	4-4-0	545		1955		635	0-6-0	623		1957	
546	4-4-0	545		1959		636	0-6-0	623		1959	Oil
547	4-4-0	545		1954		637	0-6-0	623		1963	Oil
548	4-4-0	545		1955		638	0-6-0	623		1963	Oil
550	4-4-0	545		1957		639	0-6-0	623		1963	Oil
551	0-6-0T	551		1954		640	0-6-0	623		1960	Oil
552	0-6-0T	551		1963		641	0-6-0	623		1959	Oil. See note.
553	0-6-0T	551		1955		642	0-6-0	623		1961	Oil
554	0-6-0T	551		1960		643	0-6-0	623		1955	Oil
555	0-6-0T	551		1955		644	0-6-0	623		1957	
556	0-6-0T	551		1956		645	0-6-0	623		1955	
557	0-6-0T	551		1959		650	2-4-0	650	1947 B.Sh	1959	
558	0-6-0T	551		1960		651	2-4-0	650	1951 RT.Sat	1959	
559	0-6-0T	551		1960		652	2-4-0	650		1954	
560	0-6-0T	551		1963		653	2-4-0	650		1962	
561	0-6-0T	551		1959		654	2-4-0	650	1946 B.Sh	1962	
562	0-6-0T	551		1963					1950 RT.Sh		
567	0-6-0	567		1950		655	2-4-0	650	1954 RT.Sh	1961	
574	0-6-0	573		1963		656	2-4-0	650	1945 RT.Sh	1957	
575	0-6-0	573		1957					1951 B.Sh		
576	0-6-0	573		1957	Oil	657	2-4-0	650	1953 B.Sh	1961	
582	0-6-0	573		1959		658	2-4-0	650	1948 RT.Sat	1954	
583	0-6-0	573		1963	Oil	659	2-4-0	650	1950 RT.Sh	1961	
584	0-6-0	573		1955					1953 B.Sh		
585	0-6-0	573		1960		660	2-4-0	650		1959	
586	0-6-0	573		1957		661	2-4-0	650	1950 RT.Sat	1959	
587	0-6-0	573		1961	Oil	662	2-4-0	650	1949 B.Sh	1955	
588	0-6-0	573		1963		663	2-4-0	650	1949 RT.Sh	1959	
589	0-6-0	573		1962		664	2-4-0	650	1950 B.Sh	1961	
590	0-6-0	573		1961		665	2-4-0	650	1949 B.Sh	1959	
591	0-6-0	573		1959		666	2-4-0	650	1949 B.Sh	1957	
592	0-6-0	573		1962		667	2-4-0	650		1957	
593	0-6-0	573	1951 B.Sh	1965		668	2-4-0	650		1959	
594	0-6-0	594		1961		670	0-6-2T	670		1959	
595	0-6-0	594		1957	Oil	671	0-6-2T	670		1959	
596	0-6-0	594		1959		672	0-6-2T	670		1959	
597	0-6-0	594		1959	Oil	673	0-6-2T	670		1962	
598	0-6-0	594		1963	Oil	674	0-6-2T	670		1959	
599	0-6-0	594		1963		700	0-6-0	700		1963	
600	0-6-0	594	1950 B.Sh	1957		701	0-6-0	700		1959	
601	0-6-0	594		1959	Oil	702	0-6-0	700		1955	
602	0-6-0	594		1959		703	0-6-0	700		1960	
603	0-6-0	594		1965		704	0-6-0	700		1960	

No.	Type	Class	Rebuilt by CIE	Withdrawn	Remarks	No.	Type	Class	Rebuilt by CIE	Withdrawn	Remarks
710	0-6-0	710		1959		717	0-6-0	710		1959	
711	0-6-0	710		1962		718	0-6-0	710		1959	
712	0-6-0	710		1959		719	0-6-0	710		1962	
713	0-6-0	710		1959		800	4-6-0	800		1962	
714	0-6-0	710		1959		801	4-6-0	800		1962	
715	0-6-0	710		1959		802	4-6-0	800		1957	
716	0-6-0	710		1961		850	2-6-2T	850		1955	

Name	Type	Class	Rebuilt by CIE	Withdrawn	Remarks
Jumbo	0-6-0T	Jumbo		1957	See note
Sambo	0-4-2ST	Sambo		1962	See note
St. Molaga	0-4-2T	St. Molaga		1949	See note
Argadeen	2-6-0T	Argadeen		1957	See note

Notes

Accountancy numbers were used by CIE to identify the unnumbered locomotives in coal records as follows:

841 *Jumbo*; 842 *Sambo*; 844 *Argadeen*; 845 *St. Molaga*.

Dates of conversion to oil burning were as follows:

1945: 264.

1947: 102/6/7/10/40/53/60/6/82/5/98, 249/52/5-63, 330/4/8/40/4/6/51/2/4/6/7/61/72/4-9/82/6-91/3-6/8, 401/3/7/9, 500/1/76/83/7/95/7/8, 601/6/7/24-6/8-33/6-9/41-3.

1948: 138/48/9/70, 360/97, 640.

335/81/5, 502 were converted to oil burning but never ran in this condition.

All the above reverted to coal in 1948, except Nos. 372/97 & 401 which reverted in 1949.

356 was converted to an experimental turf burning locomotive in 1952.

197 was converted to oil burning in 1956 and reverted to coal burning in 1957.

401 Reverted to Walschaerts valve gear 1949. Original size Belpaire boiler 1952. Larger Belpaire boiler 1953.

402 Larger Belpaire boiler 1946. Original size Belpaire boiler 1953.

407 Larger Belpaire boiler 1949.

409 Larger Belpaire boiler 1952.

641 Scrapped as No. 633 (a purely nominal renumbering as this locomotive never ran as No. 633).

800-2 retained their names on CIE.

28 3-0 Gauge Locomotives ex-GSR

No.	Type	Class	Withdrawn	Remarks
1c	4-6-0T	1C	1953	
2c	2-6-2T	2C	1955	
3c	4-6-0T	3C	1953	
5c	0-6-2T	5C	1959	
6c	0-6-2T	5C	1956	
7c	4-6-0T	3C	1956	
9c	4-6-0T	2C	1954	
10c	4-6-0T	10C	1952	
11c	4-6-0T	11C	1953	
1	4-4-0T	1L	1949	Still named *Isabel*. Suffix never added.
2L	4-4-0T	1L	1960	
3L	4-4-0T	1L	1959	
4L	4-4-0T	1L	1960	
7	4-4-0T	1L	1945	Suffix never added
8L	4-4-0T	1L	1959	
10L	2-4-2T	10L	1959	
12L	2-4-2T	10L	1959	
13L	2-4-2T	10L	1954	
3s	4-4-0T	3S	1954	Still named *Kent*
4s	4-4-0T	4S	1954	
6s	0-4-4T	6S	1954	
1T	2-6-0T	1T	1954	
2T	2-6-0T	1T	1954	
3T	2-6-0T	1T	1959	
4T	2-6-0T	4T	1959	
5T	2-6-2T	5T	1959	
6T	2-6-0T	1T	1960	
8T	2-6-0T	1T	1955	

New Locomotive (5-3 gauge)

In 1957 an experimental turf burning locomotive was completed by CIE, 0-6-6-0 No. CC1, and although it ran trials in 1957-8 it was never taken into stock, being scrapped in 1963 (4 cylinders 12 x 14, driving wheels 3-7). Each bogie contained a 2-cylinder engine. The boiler had two square barrels attached to a central firebox with a superheater in each 'smokebox'.

83 locomotives taken into stock from GNRB 1958 (not renumbered but 'N' suffix added where shown. GNR classification and names were retained)

No.	Type	Class	Withdrawn	Remarks	No.	Type	Class	Withdrawn	Remarks
1	4-4-2T	T2	1959		15N	0-6-0	SG2	1963	
3N	4-4-2T	T2	1963		19	0-6-0	SG2	1959	
8N	0-6-0	SG3	1963		27	4-4-0	Ps	1959	
12	4-4-0	PPs	1959		29	0-6-0	AL	1959	
14N	0-6-0	SG3	1963		33	0-6-0	A	1959	

No.	Type	Class	Withdrawn	Remarks	No.	Type	Class	Withdrawn	Remarks
35	0-6-0	AL	1959		136	4-4-0	Qs	1959	
38N	0-6-0	NQGs	1960		139	4-4-2T	T2	1959	
44N	4-4-0	PPs	1960		143N	4-4-2T	T2	1963	
47N	0-6-0	SG3	1961		144	4-4-2T	T2	1959	
48N	0-6-0	SG3	1962		145N	0-6-0	UG	1961	
55N	0-6-0	AL	1961		147N	0-6-0	UG	1960	
57	0-6-0	AL	1959		148N	0-6-0	UG	1963	
58	0-6-0	AL	1959		150N	0-6-0	A	1961	
59	0-6-0	AL	1959		152N	0-6-0	QGs	1963	
60	0-6-0	AL	1959		153N	0-6-0	QGs	1962	
62N	4-4-2T	T2	1960		154N	0-6-0	QGs	1963	
63	4-4-2T	T2	1959		155N	0-6-0	QGs	1963	
65N	4-4-2T	T2	1960		158N	0-6-0	LQGs	1963	
67N	4-4-2T	T2	1960		159N	0-6-0	LQGs	1963	
71	4-4-0	PPs	1959		161N	0-6-0	LQGs	1963	
72	4-4-0	Ps	1959		163N	0-6-0	LQGs	1963	
73	4-4-0	Ps	1959		164N	0-6-0	LQGs	1963	
75	4-4-0	PPs	1959		170N	4-4-0	S	1963	Sold *Errigal*.
80N	0-6-0	UG	1963		171N	4-4-0	S	1963	Sold *Slieve Gullion*.
81N	0-6-0	UG	1960		174N	4-4-0	S	1963	Sold *Carrantuohill*.
84	4-4-0	V	1959	*Falcon*	177N	0-6-0	SG	1963	
85N	4-4-0	V	1963	*Merlin*	178N	0-6-0	SG	1961	
91N	2-4-2T	JT	1963		179N	0-6-0	SG	1963	
96N	0-6-0	SG3	1963		180N	0-6-0	SG2	1961	
99N	0-6-2T	QGTs	1960		181N	0-6-0	SG2	1963	
105N	4-4-0	Ps	1960		184N	0-6-0	SG2	1963	
106N	4-4-0	PP9	1960		188	4-4-2T	T1	1959	
110	0-6-0	LQGs	1959		191N	4-4-0	S2	1960	*Croagh Patrick*
112N	0-6-0	NQGs	1963		197N	4-4-0	U	1962	*Lough Neagh*
115	4-4-2T	T2	1959		198	4-4-0	U	1959	*Lough Swilly*
116N	4-4-2T	T2	1961		199N	4-4-0	U	1963	*Lough Derg*
117N	0-6-0	SG3	1963		203N	4-4-0	U	1962	*Armagh*
118	0-6-0	SG3	1959		204N	4-4-0	U	1963	*Antrim*
123	4-4-0	Qs	1959		206N	4-4-0	VS	1960	*Liffey*
130	4-4-0	Qs	1959		207N	4-4-0	VS	1963	Sold *Boyne*.
131N	4-4-0	Qs	1963		209N	4-4-0	VS	1960	*Foyle*
132N	4-4-0	Qs	1963						

Notes
Sold to UTA

1 locomotive taken into service stock from Dundalk Engineering Works in 1960

No.	Type	Withdrawn	Remarks
365A	0-6-0CT	1963	Formerly GNR No. 31. Numbered by CIE in the list of service stock.

Cork Coal Gantry Locomotive
Pat withdrawn 1963.

Departmental Locomotives
CIE recorded 3 such locomotives on takeover from GSR (see 0-6-4T No. 92, 0-6-0T *Jumbo* and 0-4-2ST *Sambo*). Later they were recorded as service stock.

Steam working on CIE finished on 31st March 1963 (with the exception of UTA penetrating duties to Dublin, which ceased on 29th October 1966). However, the following locomotives were kept in reserve, some until 1965:
ex-GSR: 104/6/9/16/8/24/5/30/2/51/64/72/9/83/6/95/7/8, 249/51/61/2, 351, 461/3, 560/2/74/93/9, 603/37 .
ex-GNRB: 3N, 8N,15N, 80N, 85N, 91N, 117N, 131N, 132N, 143N, 148N, 152N, 158N, 159N, 170N, 171N, 174N, 179N, 181N, 204N, 207N.
(Nos. 170N, 171N, 174N, 207N subsequently sold to UTA as noted above).

Cover Photographs by Jonathan Allen

Front: GNR V Class compound no. 85 *Merlin* approaches Belfast (York Road) on 16.05.88 at the end of a RPSI three day raitour from Galway and Limerick.

Back Upper: Now sited at Cork station, Bury 2-2-2 no. 36 was built for the GS&WR in 1848 and is the oldest preserved Irish Locomotive.

Back Lower: Built for Comhluct Suicre Eireann in 1933, two Orenstein & Koppel 0-4-0Ts are now undergoing restoration by the Downpatrick & Ardglass Railway at its Downpatrick base.

LONDONDERRY & LOUGH SWILLY RAILWAY
LETTERKENNY & BURTONPORT EXTENSION RAILWAY

Stock: 6 new 5-3 gauge locomotives built 1862-79.
20 new 3-0 gauge locomotives built 1882-1912.
2 secondhand 3-0 gauge locomotives acquired 1885.

3-0 Gauge Locomotives

Type	Years built	No. in class	Cylinders	Driving wheels	Locomotive Nos. (+ subsequently renumbered)
0-6-0T	1862	2	13 x 24	4-0	1, 2+
0-6-0ST	1864	2	13 x 18	3-6	3, 4+
0-6-0T	1876-9	2	15 x 22	4-6	4, 5
0-6-2WT	1882	1	13 x 19	3-6	1
0-6-2T	1883	2	13 x 19	3-6	2, 3
0-6-0T	1885	1	14 x 20	3-6	4
4-6-2T	1899	2	15 x 22	3-9	5+, 6+
4-6-2T	1901	2	15 x 22	3-9	7, 8
4-6-0T	1902	4	14 x 20	3-6	1-4
4-6-2T	1904	2	14 x 20	3-6	9,10
4-8-0	1905	2	15½ x 22	3-9	11,12
4-6-2T	1910	2	14½ x 22	3-9	13,14
4-8-4T	1912	2	16 x 20	3-9	5, 6
Outside cylinders: 0-6-0T 1, 2 (GW); all 3-0 gauge locomotives.					
Belpaire boiler: 4-8-0 11,12; 4-6-2T 13,14; 4-8-4T 5, 6.					

5-3 Gauge Locomotives

No.	Name	Type	Date	Builder	Renumbered	Withdrawn	Remarks
1	John Cooke	0-6-0T	1862	GW		1885	Probably not named until 1869. Sold to LPHC (see Contractors List).
2		0-6-0T	1862	GW	3 (1874)	1883	Hired out by L&LSR 1868-74. Sold to unknown purchaser 1883.
3	John Cooke	0-6-0ST	1864	RS		1869	Name later removed. Sold to LPHC (see Contractors List).
4	St. Columb	0-6-0ST	1864	RS	2 (1868)	1882	Name later removed. Sold to LPHC (see Contractors List).
4	St. Patrick	0-6-0T	1876	SS		1885	Sold to C&BR (No. 14).
5	St. Columb	0-6-0T	1879	SS		1885	Sold to C&BR (No. 15).

Line converted to 3-0 gauge 1885.

3-0 Gauge Locomotives
Note: The seperate numbering of L&BER stock was abolished in 1913.

No.	Name	Type	Date	Builder	Renumbered	Withdrawn	Remarks
1	J.T. Macky	0-6-2WT	1882	BH		1911	Sold to McCrea & McFarland (see Contractors List).
2	Londonderry	0-6-2T	1883	BH		1912	
3	Donegal	0-6-2T	1883	BH		1913	
4	Innishowen	0-6-0T	1885	BH	17 (1913)	1940	Name removed 1920-8*.
5		2-4-0T	(GIOHC)		5A (1899)	1899	Purchased 1885 (RS 2088).
6		2-4-0T	(GIOHC)		6A (1899)	1899	Purchased 1885 (RS 2089).
5		4-6-2T	1899	HC	15 (1913)	1954	Belpiare boiler fitted 1943*.
6		4-6-2T	1899	HC	16 (1913)	1953	
7	Edward VII	4-6-2T	1901	HC		1940	Name removed 1920-8*.
8		4-6-2T	1901	HC		1954	
1		4-6-0T	1902	AB		1940	L&BER stock.
2		4-6-0T	1902	AB		1954	L&BER stock.
3		4-6-0T	1902	AB		1954	L&BER stock.
4		4-6-0T	1902	AB		1953	L&BER stock.
9	Aberfoyle	4-6-2T	1904	KS		1928	Name removed, date unknown.
10	Richmond	4-6-2T	1904	KS		1954	Name removed, date unknown.
11		4-8-0	1905	HC		1933	
12		4-8-0	1905	HC		1954	
13		4-6-2T	1910	HL		1940	Later L&BER stock.
14		4-6-2T	1910	HL		1943	Later L&BER stock.
5		4-8-4T	1912	HC		1954	L&BER stock but exchanged with Nos. 13/4.
6		4-8-4T	1912	HC		1954	L&BER stock but exchanged with Nos. 13/4.

Note
GIOHC denotes Glenariff Iron Ore & Harbour Co. (Co. Antrim).

Line closed 1953.

WEST DONEGAL RAILWAY

Stock: 3 new 3-0 gauge locomotives built 1881.

Type	Years built	No. in class	Cylinders	Driving wheels	Locomotive Nos.
2-4-0T	1881	3	13 x 20	3-6	1-3

No.	Name	Type	Date	Builder	Withdrawn
1	Alice	2-4-0T	1881	SS	DR
2	Blanche	2-4-0T	1881	SS	DR
3	Lydia	2-4-0T	1881	SS	DR

3 locomotives taken into DR stock 1892 (numbers not altered).

DONEGAL RAILWAY

3-0 gauge.
Stock: 3 locomotives taken into stock from West Donegal Railway 1892.
12 new locomotives built 1893-1904.

Type	Years built	No. in class	Cylinders	Driving wheels	Locomotive Nos.
4-6-0T	1893	6	14 x 20	3-6	4-9
4-4-4T	1902	2	14 x 20	3-6	10, 11
4-6-4T	1904	4	15 x 21	3-9	12-15
Belpaire boiler: 4-6-4T Nos. 12-5.					

No.	Name	Type	Date	Builder	Withdrawn
1	Alice	2-4-0T	(WDR1)		CDRJC
2	Blanche	2-4-0T	(WDR 2)		CDRJC
3	Lydia	2-4-0T	(WDR 3)		CDRJC
4	Meenglas	4-6-0T	1893	N	CDRJC
5	Drunboe	4-6-0T	1893	N	CDRJC
6	Inver	4-6-0T	1893	N	CDRJC
7	Finn	4-6-0T	1893	N	CDRJC
8	Foyle	4-6-0T	1893	N	CDRJC
9	Columbkille	4-6-0T	1893	N	CDRJC
10	Sir James	4-4-4T	1902	NR	CDRJC
11	Hercules	4-4-4T	1902	NR	CDRJC
12	Eske	4-6-4T	1904	NW	CDRJC
13	Owenea	4-6-4T	1904	NW	CDRJC
14	Erne	4-6-4T	1904	NW	CDRJC
15	Mourne	4-6-4T	1904	NW	CDRJC

15 locomotives taken into CDRJC stock 1906, numbers were not altered.

COUNTY DONEGAL RAILWAYS JOINT COMMITTEE

3-0 gauge.
Stock: 15 locomotives taken into stock 1906 from Donegel Railway.
8 new locomotives built 1907-12.

Class	Type	Years built	No. in class	Cylinders	Driving wheels	Locomotive Nos. (+ subsequently renumbered)
5	2-6-4T	1907	5	14 x 21	4-0	16-20+
5A	2-6-4T	1912	3	15½ x 21	4-0	21+, 2A+, 3A+
Superheater: 2-6-4T Class 5A.						

No.	Name	Type	Class	Date	Builder	Renumbered & Renamed (1937)	Withdrawn	Remarks
1	Alice	2-4-0T	1	(DR 1)			1926	
2	Blanche	2-4-0T	1	(DR 2)			1909	
3	Lydia	2-4-0T	1	(DR 3)			1910	
4	Meenglas	4-6-0T	2	(DR 4)			1935	
5	Dumboe	4-6-0T	2	(DR 5)			1931	
6	Inver	4-6-0T	2	(DR 6)			1931	
7	Finn	4-6-0T	2	(DR 7)			1931	
8	Foyle	4-6-0T	2	(DR 8)			1937	
9	Columbkille	4-6-0T	2	(DR 9)			1937	
10	Sir James	4-4-4T	3	(DR 10)			1933	
11	Hercules	4-4-4T	3	(DR 11)			1933	
12	Eske	4-6-4T	4	(DR 12)		9	1954	Superheated 1921.
13	Owenea	4-6-4T	4	(DR 13)		10	1953	Superheated 1922.
14	Erne	4-6-4T	4	(DR 14)		11	1959	Superheated 1922.
15	Mourne	4-6-4T	4	(DR 15)		12	1953	Superheated 1933.
16	Donegal	2-6-4T	5	1907		4 Meenglas	1959	Superheated 1926. Saturated* Superheated 1954.

▲ CIE CC1 - "The Turf Burner" (1957 CIE Inchicore) (Deegan Photo Ltd.)

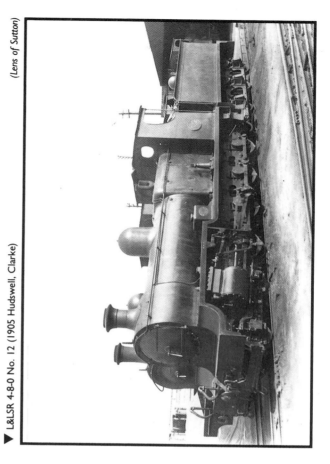

▲ L&LSR 0-6-2WT No. 1 (1882 Black, Hawthorn) (Real Photos)

▼ L&LSR 4-6-2T No. 8 (1901 Hudswell, Clarke) (R.G. Jarvis)

▼ L&LSR 4-8-0 No. 12 (1905 Hudswell, Clarke) (Lens of Sutton)

117

No. Name	Type	Class	Date	Builder	Renumbered & Renamed (1937)	Withdrawn	Remarks
17 *Glenties*	2-6-4T	5	1907	NW	5 *Drumboe*	1959	Superheated 1929.
18 *Killybegs*	2-6-4T	5	1907	NW	6 *Columbkille*	1959	Superheated 1925.
19 *Letterkenny*	2-6-4T	5	1907	NW	(7 *Finn*)	1940	Superheated 1924. Not renumbered.
20 *Raphoe*	2-6-4T	5	1907	NW	8 *Foyle*	1954	Superheated 1924.
21 *Ballyshannon*	2-6-4T	5A	1912	NW	1 *Alice*	1959	
2A *Strabane*	2-6-4T	5A	1912	NW	2 *Blanche*	1959	
3A *Stranolar*	2-6-4T	5A	1912	NW	3 *Lydia*	1959	

CVR No. 8, purchased by CDRJC in 1932, was converted to a diesel tractor by the new owner (No. 11).

Line Closed 1959.

SLIGO, LEITRIM & NORTHERN COUNTIES RAILWAY

Stock: 13 new locomotives built 1877-1951.
7 secondhand locomotives acquired 1897-1941.

Type	Years built	No. in class	Cylinders	Driving wheels	Locomotive Names
0-6-2T	1877	2	16 x 22	3-9½	*Pioneer, Sligo*
0-6-4T	1882-99	5	16½ x 20	4-9	*Fermanagh, Leitrim, Lurganboy, Lissadell, Hazelwood*
4-4-0T	1883	1	16 x 24	5-0	*Erne*
0-6-4T	1904-17	3	17 x 24	4-8	*Sir Henry, Enniskillen, Lough Gill*
0-6-4T	1949	2	18 x 24	4-8	*Lough Melvin, Lough Erne*
Belpaire boiler: 0-6-4T Sir Henry, Lough classes.					
Outside cylinders: 0-6-2T *Pioneer, Sligo*; 4-4-0T *Erne*.					

Name	Type	Date	Builder	Rebuilt	Withdrawn	Remarks
Pioneer	0-6-2T	1877	AE		1921	
Sligo	0-6-2T	1877	AE		1921	
Fermanagh	0-6-4T	1882	BP		1952	
Leitrim	0-6-4T	1882	BP		1947	
Erne	4-4-0T	1883	HC	1885 4-4-2T	1910	
Lurganboy	0-6-4T	1895	BP		1953	
Faugh-a-Ballagh	0-4-0ST	(F&L)			1905	Purchased from Fisher & LeFanu 1897. Sold to Rbt. Worthington (see Contractors List).
Waterford	0-6-0T	(F&L)			1928	Purchased from Fisher & LeFanu 1897 (see Contractors List).
Lissadell	0-6-4T	1899	BP		1954	
Hazlewood	0-6-4T	1899	BP		1957	
Sir Henry	0-6-4T	1904	BP		1957	
Enniskillen	0-6-4T	1905	BP		1957	
Lough Gill	0-6-4T	1917	BP		1957	
Blacklion	4-4-0	(GNR 118)			1931	Purchased 1921.
Glencar	4-4-0	(GNR 119)			1928	Purchased 1921.
Glencar 'A'	0-6-0	(GNR 31)			1949	Purchased 1928.
Sligo	0-6-0	(GNR 149)			1940	Purchased 1931. Sold to GNR (became No. 69).
Sligo	0-6-0	(GNR 69)			1949	Purchased 1940.
Lough Melvin	0-6-4T	1951	BP		1957	Ready in 1949. Sold to UTA (No. 26).
Lough Erne	0-6-4T	1951	BP		1957	Ready in 1949. Sold to UTA (No. 27).

Line closed 1957.

DUNDALK & GREENORE RAILWAY
DUNDALK, NEWRY & GREENORE RAILWAY

Stock: 6 new locomotives built 1873-98.

Type	Years built	No. in class	Cylinders	Driving wheels	Locomotive Nos.
0-6-0ST	1873-98	6	17 x 24	5-2½	1-6

No. Name	Type	Date	Builder	Withdrawn	Remarks
1 *Macrory*	0-6-0ST	1873	L&NWR	1951	
2 *Greenore*	0-6-0ST	1873	L&NWR	1951	
3 *Dundalk*	0-6-0ST	1873	L&NWR	1951	
4 *Newry*	0-6-0ST	1876	L&NWR	1951	
5 *Carlingford*	0-6-0ST	1876	L&NWR	1928	
6 *Holyhead*	0-6-0ST	1899	L&NWR	1951	See note

Note
Components from L&NWR 0-6-0 DX Class No. 900 (new 1867, built at Crewe) used in construction.

Line closed 1951.

(R.G. Jarvis)

▲ CDRJC 4-6-0T No. 8 at the end of its days (1893 Neilson)

(Real Photos)

▼ SL&NCR 4-4-0T *Erne*, later 4-4-2T (1883 Hudswell, Clarke)

(Lens of Sutton)

▲ L&LSR 4-8-4T No. 6 (1912 Hudswell, Clarke)

(R.G. Jarvis)

▼ CDRJC 2-6-4 No. 19 (1907 Nasmyth, Wilson)

WATERFORD, NEW ROSS & WEXFORD JUNCTION RAILWAY

The company purchased 1 locomotive from Edgworth & Stanford in 1870. It was originally MGWR No. 11 *Juno* and was disposed of in 1873.

LISTOWEL & BALLYBUNION RAILWAY

Monorail.
Stock: 3 new locomotives built 1887.

Type	Years built	No. in class	Cylinders	Driving wheels	Locomotive Nos.
3-cpld	1887	3	7 x 12	2-0	1-3

The L&BR locomotives were unconventional in many respects, having two boilers, outside cylinders and cylinders on the tenders (cylinders 5 x 7).

No.	Type	Date	Builder	Withdrawn
1	3-cpld	1887	HE	1924
2	3-cpld	1887	HE	1924
3	3-cpld	1887	HE	1924

Line closed 1924.

GIANTS CAUSEWAY, PORTRUSH & BUSH VALLEY TRAMWAY

3-0 gauge.
Stock: 4 new tram locomotives built 1883-6.

Type	Years built	No. in class	Cylinders	Driving wheels	Locomotive Nos.
0-4-0VB	1883	2	8 x 12	*	1, 2
0-4-0VB	1887-96	2	9 x 12	*	3, 4

No.	Name	Type	Date	Builder	Withdrawn	Remarks
1		0-4-0VB	1883	W	1908	
2		0-4-0VB	1883	W	1898	
3	*Dunluce Castle*	0-4-0VB	1887	W	1930	Sold to R. Faris (see Contractors List).
4	*Brian Boroimhe*	0-4-0VB	1896	W	1930	Sold to R. Faris (see Contractors List).

Steam workings ceased in 1916.

BELFAST STREET TRAMWAYS

5-3 guage.
Stock: 1 tram locomotive on trial 1877.

A Hughes (Loughborough) 0-4-0T named *Pioneer* (new 1876) worked on a trial basis during 1877.

CAVEHILL & WHITEWELL TRAMWAY

4-8½ gauge.
Stock: 2 new tram locomotives built 1882.
1 secondhand tram locomotive acquired 1886.

Type	Years built	No. in class	Cylinders	Driving wheels	Locomotive Nos.
0-4-0T	1882	2	7¼ x 12	2-4½	1, 2
0-4-0T	1881	1	7 x 12	2-3	3

No.	Type	Date	Builder	Withdrawn	Remarks
1	0-4-0T	1882	R	1895	
2	0-4-0T	1882	R	1891	Sold to Vale of Clyde Tramways (No. 10).
3	0-4-0T	1881	R	1895	Purchased 1886 (New to Leeds Tramways, No. 1)

Steam working ceased 1895.

CASTLEDERG & VICTORIA BRIDGE TRAMWAY

3-0 gauge.
Stock: 5 new locomotives built 1884-1912.
1 secondhand locomotive acquired 1928.

Type	Years built	No. in class	Cylinders	Driving wheels	Locomotive Nos.
0-4-0T	1884-91	3	12 x 15	2-9	1-3
2-6-0T	1904	1	13 x 18	3-1	4
0-4-4T	1912	1	12½ x 18	3-1	5

Lens of Sutton

▲ SL&NCR 0-6-0 *Glencar A* ex GNR A Class No. 31 (1890 Beyer, Peacock)

(R.G. Jarvis)

▼ CVR 2-6-2T No. 4 formerly C&VBT 2-6-0T No. 4 (1904 Hudswell, Clarke)

(J.M. Jarvis)

▲ SL&NCR 0-6-4T *Lurganboy* (1895 Beyer, Peacock)

(Lens of Sutton)

▼ DN&GR 0-6-0ST No. 4 (1876 L&NWR Crewe)

121

No.	Name	Type	Date	Builder	Withdrawn	Remarks
1	*Mourne*	0-4-0T	1884	K	1907	
2	*Derg*	0-4-0T	1884	K	1912	
3		0-4-0T	1891	K	1928	
4		2-6-0T	1904	HC	1933	Sold 1934 (by dismantling contractors) to CVR (No. 4).
5		0-4-4T	1912	HC	1933	
		2-4-0T			1933	Purchased 1928 from LMS(NCC) (No. 105). Nominally No. 3.

Line closed 1933.

CLOGHER VALLEY TRAMWAY
CLOGHER VALLEY RAILWAY

3-0 gauge.
Stock: 8 new locomotives built 1886-1928.
1 secondhand locomotive acquired 1934.

Type	Years built	No. in class	Cylinders	Driving wheels	Locomotive Nos.
0-4-2T	1886-7	6	13½ x 18	3-0	1-6
0-4-4T	1910	1	14 x 20	3-4	7
0-4-0VB	1928	1	7 x 10	2-6	8

No.	Name	Type	Date	Builder	Rebuilt	Withdrawn	Remarks
1	*Caledon*	0-4-2T	1886	SS		1934	
2	*Errigal*	0-4-2T	1886	SS		1942	
3	*Blackwater*	0-4-2T	1887	SS		1942	
4	*Fury*	0-4-2T	1887	SS		1929	
5	*Colebrook*	0-4-2T	1887	SS		1936	
6	*Erne*	0-4-2T	1887	SS		1942	
7	*Blessingbourne*	0-4-4T	1910	HC		1934	
8		0-4-0VB	1928	Wal		1932	Sold to CDRJC.
4		2-6-0T	(C&VBT 4)		1936 2-6-2T	1942	Purchased 1934 from contractor lifting C&VBT.

Line closed 1941.

DUBLIN TRAMWAYS COMPANY

5-3 Gauge.
Stock: 1 tram locomotive on trial 1877.

The Hughes locomotive *Pioneer* was given trial runs on this tramway's tracks during 1877 after tests on the Belfast Street Tramways. It was soon returned to Britain.

DUBLIN SOUTHERN DISTRICTS TRAMWAYS

5-3 Gauge.
Stock: 4 new tram locomotives built 1881-3.

Type	Years built	No. in class	Cylinders	Driving wheels	Locomotive Nos.
0-4-0T	1881	2	7¼ x 12	2-4½	1, 2
0-4-0VB	1883	2	*	*	3, 4

No.	Type	Date	Builder	Withdrawn
1	0-4-0T	1881	K	1884
2	0-4-0T	1881	K	1884
3	0-4-0VB	1883	W	1884
4	0-4-0VB	1883	W	1884

Steam working ceased in 1884.

DUBLIN & BLESSINGTON STEAM TRAMWAY

Stock: 10 new locomotives built 1887-1906.
2 secondhand locomotives acquired 1918-21*.

Type	Years built	No. in class	Cylinders	Driving wheels	Locomotive Nos. (+ subsequently renumbered.)
0-4-0WT	1887	6	9 x 18	2-3	1-6
2-4-2T	1892-9	2	13 x 20	3-6	7, 9
0-4-2T	1896	1	13 x 18	3-3	8
2-4-2T	1906	1	12 x 18	3-0¼	2+

No.	Type	Date	Builder	Renumbered	Rebuilt	Withdrawn	Remarks
1	0-4-0WT	1887	FE			1912	
2	0-4-0WT	1887	FE			1906	
3	0-4-0WT	1887	FE			1927	
4	0-4-0WT	1887	FE			1894	
5	0-4-0WT	1887	FE			1911	
6	0-4-0WT	1887	FE			1932	
7	2-4-2T	1892	TG			1915	
8	0-4-2T	1896	TG		1903 2-4-2T	1932	
9	2-4-2T	1899	BE			1932	
2	2-4-2T	1906	TG	10 (1914)		1932	
	0-4-0WT					1921*	Purchased 1918 from D&SER (No. 70). Sold to GS&WR (named *Imp*) in exchange for No. 5
5	0-4-0ST					1928	Purchased 1921* from GS&WR (*Cambria*). Name retained on D&BST.

Line closed 1932.

DUBLIN & LUCAN STEAM TRAMWAY
DUBLIN & LUCAN ELECTRIC RAILWAY
LUCAN, LEIXLIP & CELBRIDGE STEAM TRAMWAY

3-0 Gauge (later 3-6).
7 new tram locomotives 1882-92.

Type	Years built	No. in class	Cylinders	Driving wheels	Locomotive Nos.
0-4-0T	1882-4	5	8 x 12	2-4¼	1-5
0-4-0T	1887	1	10 x 12	2-4¼	6
0-4-0T	1892	1	9/14 x 14	2-6	7*
Compound (Worsdell von Borries): 7*.					

No.	Type	Date	Builder	Withdrawn	Note
1	0-4-0T	1883	K	*	See note
2	0-4-0T	1883	K	*	See note
3	0-4-0T	1883	K	*	See note
4	0-4-0T	1884	K	*	See note
5	0-4-0T	1884	K	1900	
6	0-4-0T	1887	K	1900	
7*	0-4-0T	1892	TG	1897	See note

Notes
3 locomotives (No. 4 and two of Nos. 1-3) were altered to 3-6 gauge in 1900. From 1903 to 1912 only one remained, retained for coal haulage to the power station after electric services started in 1900.
No. 7 was the property of the LL&CST and may not have had a number. It was used indiscriminately with the D&LST tram locomotives. In 1896-7 the Leixlip extension was worked by a contractor instead of the D&LST using this locomotive. Sold 1897* to Topham, Railton & Jones (see Contractors List).

A steam powered double deck tramcar was tried on the line in 1882-4. It was probably never owned by the tramway. It was built by Manlove, Alliot & Fryer (Nottingham) in 1881.

MISCELLANEOUS LOCOMOTIVES

The following locomotives were not supplied directly to railways, nor apparently to contractors for any railway projects in Ireland. Some passed into company ownership, but others remain very obscure and elusive. All listed were 5-3 gauge.

Builder	Date	Type	Cylinders	Driving Wheels	Remarks
*	*	2-2-2WT	13 x 18	5-7	Dargan obtained three locomotives from Fairbairn and put them to work on the
*	*	2-2-2WT	13 x 18	5-7	W&TR in 1853-4. They were originally built for the London & Birmingham Railway in
*	*	2-2-2WT	13 x 18	5-7	1837-8, being of Bury type by various builders and were taken by Fairbairn in part exchange for new locomotives built for the L&NWR (Southern Division). One had been No. 191 on the L&NWR and remained on the W&TR as No. 4 when the others were taken away in 1855-6* (disposal unknown). Counted as "Railway companies ex Britain - builders Not Known" in the builders table.
Fbn	*	0-4-2	16 x 22	5-0	Sold by Dargan to Lim&ER in 1859. Recorded as new in 1856, but any previous use is not known.
G	1848	2-2-2	14 x 18	5-7	Used by Dargan (possibly on loan) on W&LR 1848*-52. Sold to W&LR (No. 7) in 1853.
G	*	2-2-2T	10 x 12	4-0	No details, but was advertised for sale in a Liverpool newspaper in 1853.
G*	(tank)	*	*		Grendon offered D&BJR "New tank engine now in our possession" in 1858, which suggests that it may not be a Grendon locomotive.

Two Grendon 2-2-2 were advertised for sale in a Liverpool newspaper in 1853. They were probably the locomotives which became MGWR No. 33 in 1854 and W&LR No. 7 in 1853.

Two 0-4-2 were advertised for sale at Belfast in 1880. Only exceedingly slight evidence implicates Watson & Overend as having possibly owned this pair, but nothing reliable is known of their origin. (Some sources claim that they were Fairburn locomotives completed by Sharp, Stewart in 1864).

LOANS OF LOCOMOTIVES

Known borrowings of locomotives by the undermentioned railways:

Borrowing Railway	Lender	Loco No./Name	Period of use.
A&EJR	GS&WR	26	1872
	MGWR	30	1870
	MGWR	Two unidentified 1869-70* (but one may have been MGWR No. 13 *Condor*).	
	Edgworth & Stanford	1869 (ex-MGWR No. 11)	
A&TR	GS&WR	100	1872
B&CDR	GSR	428	1941-5
CB&PR	GS&WR	2	1850
	CDRJC	1	1918-21 (by order of Irish Railway Executive Committee)
C&LR	MR(NCC)	101A, 102A	1920-1 (by order of Irish Railway Executive Committee)
D&BST	GS&WR	*Cambria*	1919*-21*
GNR/GNRB	UTA	4	1954-5
		7	1954-5
		57	1952-4
		72	1954
		81	1952-4
LMS(NCC)	DN&GR	1	1942-3
		4	1942-6 (returned to Dundalk for repairs 1943-4)
		6	1942-4
L&LSR	McCrea & McFarland	*Barnesmore*	1883
MGWR	GNR	37	1921
		40	1921
		137	1921
		138	1921
		193	1921
	GS&WR	*	1921 (unstated number of locomotives borrowed)
SL&NCR	GNR	28	1950-1
		79	1935 and 1937 (as No. 69)
		193	1928 and 1947
T&CLR	CB&SCR	7	1893
WD&LR	DW&WR	20	1878
		22	1878
	GS&WR	*	1878 (unstated number of locomotives borrowed)
W&LR	GS&WR	100	1872-3 (continuation of loan to A&TR)

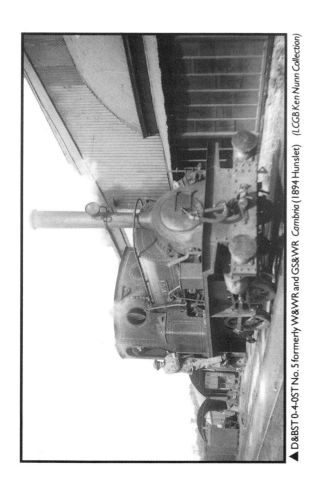

▲ D&BST 0-4-0ST No. 5 formerly W&VVR and GS&WR *Cambria* (1894 Hunslet) (LCGB Ken Nunn Collection)

▼ Comlucht Suicre Eireann 0-4-0T Thurles No. I (1934 Orenstein & Koppel) (R.N. Clements)

(Real Photos)

▲ D&BST 2-4-2T No. 9 (1899 Brush)

(F. Jones)

▼ Guinness 0-4-0T I-10 gauge No. 18 (1902 Spence)

125

The list is divided into seven parts. Unlike the lists of locomotives used on the public railways of Ireland, it is necessary to list locomotives by builder, stating known owners and numbers/names for each one. Owners outside Ireland are ignored in this list. An index of users is included, but no attempt has been made to show places of use by contractors, information outside the scope of this publication.

Dimensions where known are summarised at the end of the list.

1. LOCOMOTIVES SUPPLIED TO INDUSTRIAL RAILWAYS OR CONTRACTORS

Builder	Prog. No.	Type	Date new	Gauge	Arrived in Ireland	Irish user/s & No./Name	Withdrawn	Left Ireland
AP	1105	2-2-0TG	1875	3-6	New	Haulbowline Dockyard, Co. Cork	*	
AP	1432	2-2-0TG	1878	3-6	New	Haulbowline Dockyard, Co. Cork	*	
AE	1337	0-4-0T	1882	1-10	New	Arthur Guinness 6	1936	
AE	1552	0-6-0ST	1907	4-8½	*	S. Pearson Scott		c.1932
						E. Moir		
AE	1618	0-6-0ST	1912	4-8½	*	S. Pearson Courtney		c.1932
						E. Moir		
AE	1833	0-6-0ST	1919	4-8½	c.1928	S. Pearson 146 Littleton		c.1932
						E. Moir		
AE	1872	0-6-0ST	1920	4-8½	*	S. Pearson 152 Ashford		c.1932
						E. Moir		
AE	2021	0-6-0ST	1928	5-3	New	Londonderry PHC 3 R.H. Smythe	1962*	
WGB	1116	0-4-0ST	1889	3-0	1891	Braddock Brancher		*
						Faulkner Brancher		
						Pauling Brancher		
WGB	1416	0-4-0ST	1893	2-0	1893*	Fergus Reclamation Syndicate F R S No 2	*	*
WGB	1480	0-4-0ST	1897	3-0	New	John Best Crosshaven		c.1904
WGB	1551	0-4-0ST	1898	3-0	1899*	Fisher & LeFanu Mourne		1906*
WGB	1631	0-4-0ST	1900	2-6	c.1914	Portrush Columnar Bassalt Co.	1933	
WGB	1844	0-4-0ST	1907	3-0	c.1920	H.& J. Martin	1925*	
WGB	1945	0-6-0T	1911	2-0	New	Irish Industrial Minerals King George		1920
WGB	2081	0-4-0ST	1919	3-0	1920	H.& J. Martin		1924
WGB	2086	0-4-0ST	1919	3-0	1920	H.& J. Martin		1924
AB	297	0-4-0ST	1887	3-0	c.1898	John Best Tullibardine		c.1904
AB	703	0-4-0ST	1892*	2-0	1893	Fergus Reclamation Syndicate		c.1897
AB	770	0-4-0T	1896	3-6	New	Carnlough Lime Co. Otter	1946*	
AB	1408	0-6-0ST	1915	4-8½	c.1925	S. Pearson Adams		c.1932
						E. Moir		
AB	2263	0-4-0WT	1949	3-0	New	Bord na Mona 1 (later 43)	1953*	c.1978
AB	2264	0-4-0WT	1949	3-0	New	Bord na Mona 2 (later 44)	1953*	
AB	2265	0-4-0WT	1949	3-0	New	Bord na Mona 3 (later 45)	1953*	
BM	*	0-4-0ST	1882	3-0	New	T.S. Dixon Barnesmore	*	
						McCrea & McFarland Barnesmore		
BH	513	0-6-0ST	1879	3-0	New	Butler & Fry Lady Boyd	(see Ballycastle Railway)	
BH	514	0-4-0ST	1879	3-0	New	Belfast Harbour Commissioners 2	*	
Butt		2-2-2	1839*	4-6	1841*	Jeffs	(see D&DR)	
Ch	370	0-4-0VB	1863	5-3	New	Edwards Bros.		*
						Connor & Olley		
						Connor & Manisty		
Ch	1505	0-4-0VB	1872	5-3*	New	Belfast Harbour Commissioners 1	*	
Ch	*	0-4-0VB	1874*	4-8½*	1874*	T.W. Chester	1877*	*
Ch	*	0-4-0VB	*	5-3*	1878*	C.M. Holland	*	*
Ch	1939	0-4-0VB	1878	4-8½	1882	Sir J. Jackson (on hire from a dealer)		1882-3
Ch	2090	0-4-0VB	1879	4-8½*	*	E.J. Jackson	*	
Ch	2416	0-4-0VB	1887	3-6*	New	Board of Works, Dublin	*	
JC	3092	0-4-0VB	1926	5-3	New	CSE Carlow 2; Mallow 2	1955	
JC	3093	0-4-0VB	1926	5-3	New	CSE Carlow 1	1956	
JC	3096	0-4-0VB	1926	5-3	New	CSE Carlow 3	1956	
DK	*	0-4-0ST	1905	2-0	New	Marconi's Telegraph & Wireless Co.		c.1923
JF	4027	0-4-0T	1880	2-0	New*	H.C. Drinkwater - not 100% certain used in Ireland.		
FW	369	0-4-0ST	1878	3-0	New	*(not identified)	*	
						Belfast Harbour Commissioners 3		
GI*		2-4-0	1846	4-8½	New	Bromhead & Hemming Victoria	*	
						McCormick Victoria		
GI*		2-4-0	1846	4-8½	New	Bromhead & Hemming Albert	*	
						McCormick Albert		
G		4-cpld	1862*	5-3	New	Greene & King*	(see NW&RR)	
GR	164	0-6-0ST	1886	3-0	New	Collen Bros. Express		c.1889
HC	397	0-4-0ST	1892	3-0	1900*	John Best Whittledene		c.1904
HC	672	0-6-0ST	1903	4-8½	1913*	Naylor Bros. 1		1916*
HC	759	0-4-0ST	1906	3-0	New	Sir Robert MacAlpine 13 Donegal		c.1908

Builder	Prog. No.	Type	Date new	Gauge	Arrived in Ireland	Irish user/s & No./Name	Withdrawn	Left Ireland
HC	794	0-6-0T	1907	3-0	New	Sir Robert MacAlpine 14 *Strabane*		c.1909
HC	1079	0-4-0ST	1914	5-3	New	Arthur Guinness 2	1965	
HC	1094	0-4-0F	1915	5-3	New	British Portland Cement Manufacturers	1935	
HC	1152	0-4-0ST	1915	5-3	New	Arthur Guinness 3	1965	
HC	1166	0-4-0WT	1918	2-0	New	War Department	*	
						Lees & Nixon		
HC	1298	0-6-0WT	1917	2-0	1934	Sutton Sands	*	
HC	1310	0-6-0WT	1918	2-0	New	War Department 3200	*	
						Lees & Nixon		
HC	1311	0-6-0WT	1918	2-0	New	War Department 3201	*	1920
HC	1313	0-6-0WT	1918	2-0	New	War Department 3203	*	1920
HC	1497	0-6-0ST	1923	4-8½	c.1927	S. Pearson *Charlton*		c.1932
						E. Moir		
HC	1505	0-6-0ST	1923	4-8½	New	S. Pearson 158 *Ulster*		c.1932
						E. Moir		
HC	1508	0-6-0ST	1924	4-8½	New	S. Pearson 159 *Mourne*		c. 1932
						E. Moir		
HE	71	0-4-0ST	1871	3-0	c.1887	Lowry *Deer Hill*	*	*
HE	74	0-4-0ST	1872	3-0	c.1903	S. Pearson *Huddersfield*		c.1906
HE	156	0-4-0ST	1876	5-3	New	Smith & Finlayson *Waterford*		*
						Ashwell		
HE	178	0-4-0ST	1878	5-3	New	A.L. Tottenham *Faugh-A-Ballagh*	(see SL&NCR)	
						Fisher & LeFanu *Faugh-A-Ballagh*		
						R. Worthington *Faugh-A-Ballagh*		
HE	202	0-6-0ST	1878	5-3	New	C.M. Holland *Maghera*		c.1886
						McCrea & McFarland *Maghera*		
						W. Scott*		
HE	203	0-6-0ST	1878	5-3	New	C.M. Holland *Pioneer*	*	*
						J.W. Stanford *Pioneer*		
						Braddock* *Pioneer*		
						Falkiner* *Pioneer*		
HE	208	0-4-0ST	1878	3-0	1891	W.M. Murphy *Spondon*		1898
HE	268	0-4-0ST	1881	2-6	New	River Fergus Reclamation Syndicate *Fergus*		post 1883
HE	315	0-4-0ST	1883	5-3	New	R. Worthington *Flirt* renamed *Drogheda*	c. 1910	
HE	319	0-4-0ST	1883	5-3	New	R. Worthington *Liffey* renamed *Molly*	c. 1910	
HE	352	0-4-0ST	1884	5-3	New	R. Worthington *Beauty* renamed *Armagh*	c. 1910	
HE	382	0-6-0ST	1885	5-3	New	R. Worthington *Slaney*	(see T&CLR)	
HE	404	0-4-0ST	1886	3-0	1904	T.S. Dixon (Exs) *Isabella*	*	*
						Sir Robert MacAlpine *Isabella*		
HE	457	0-6-0ST	1888	5-3	1894	Fisher & LeFanu *Limerick*		*
						S. Pearson *Limerick*		
						Sir Robert MacAlpine *Limerick*		*
HE	482	0-6-0T	1889	5-3	New	R. Worthington *Newmarket* renamed *Mullingar* (see CK&AR)		
HE	557	0-6-0T	1892	5-3	New	Falkiner *Shamrock*	(see GS&WR 299)	
						Tralee & Fenit Pier & Harbour Commissioners *Shamrock*		
HE	558	0-6-0ST	1892	5-3	New	Falkiner *Rose*		*
						S. Pearson *Rose*		
HE	564	0-4-0ST	1892	3-0	New	T.S. Dixon *Bruckless*		1894
					1914	J. Mackay	*	
						H.& J. Martin		
HE	591	0-6-0T	1893	5-3	New	R. Worthington *Lady Mary*	(see SL&NCR)	
						Fisher & LeFanu *Waterford*		
HE	832	0-4-0ST	1903	3-0	New	T.S. Dixon *Coolmore*		1905-6*
						Sir Robert MacAlpine *Coolmore*		
HE	859	0-4-0ST	1904	5-3	New	R. Worthington *Kells*	(see CK&AR)	
HE	*	0-4-0ST	*	3-0	*	Collen Bros. *Victor*	c.1902	
K	796	0-6-0T	1860	5-3	*	J. Watson	*	*
KS	659	0-4-2ST	1899	3-0	New	G. Pauling		c.1903
KS	660	0-4-2ST	1899	3-0	New	G. Pauling		c.1903
KS	741	0-4-2T	1900	3-0	1930	R. Faris	1952	
KS	766	0-4-0ST	1903	4-8½	New	G.O. Watson *Doonagore*		1908
KS	889	0-4-0ST	1905	3-0	New	Dublin Port & Docks *Brian Boru*	1914*	
KS	1100	0-4-0WT	1910	2-0	New	Sulphate of Ammonia Co. *Moorhen*		1912
KS	2464	0-4-0ST	1915	2-0	1918*	Kynoch Ltd.	1936*	
KS	4252	0-4-0ST	1922	2-0	c.1929	Thompson & Sons		*
KS	4265	0-4-0ST	1922	2-0	*	J. Howard	*	
Lewin		0-6-0WT	1875	2-6	*	*		*
Lewin		0-4-0WT	1877	1-10	New	Arthur Guinness 2 *Hops*	1914	
Lewin		0-4-0WT	1877	1-10	New	Arthur Guinness 3 *Malt*	1927	
MW	4	0-6-0ST	1859	5-3	1864	Brassey & Field *Rutland*	(see INWR)	
MW	18	0-6-0ST	1860	5-3	1864	Brassey & Field *Malvern*	(see INWR)	
MW	237	0-6-0ST	1867	5-3	1891-2	Braddock *Glenloe*		c. 1895
						Falkiner *Glenloe*		

Builder	Prog. No.	Type	Date new	Gauge	Arrived in Ireland	Irish user/s & No./Name	Withdrawn	Left Ireland
MW	287	0-4-0ST	1870	3-6	1912	Haulbowline Dockyard, Co. Cork	1926	
MW	614	0-4-0ST	1876	3-0	1884	W. Scott *Lancashire Witch*		*
MW	773	0-4-0ST	1880	5-3	New	T. Dowling *Bantry*	1920	
						W.M. Murphy *Bantry*		
						J.W. Dorman *Bantry*		
						Allman & Co. *Bantry*		
MW	1038	0-4-0ST	1887	3-0	1893	Falkiner *Lizzie*		*
MW	1099	0-6-0ST	1889	5-3	1894	Fisher & LeFanu *Blackburn*	(see D&SER)	
						Naylor Bros. *Blackburn*		
MW	1220	0-6-0ST	1891	5-3	New	Braddock *Corrib*		*
						Falkiner *Corrib*		
MW	1357	0-4-0ST	1897	3-6	New	Haulbowline Dockyard, Co. Cork	1933	
MW	1399	0-4-0ST	1898	5-3	New	Fisher & LeFanu*		1917
						Scott & Middleton*		
						Naylor Bros. 1		
MW	*	0-4-0ST	*	5-3	1904*	Fisher & LeFanu	1906*	1906*
N	602	0-4-0T	1860	4-8½	1874*	T.W. Chester		1877*
OK	1240	0-4-0WT	1904	2-0	New	R. Worthington *Armagh*	c.1915	
OK	*	*	*	2-0	*	Whyte	*	*
OK	*	*	*	2-0	*	Whyte	*	*
OK	2488	1908	1908	2-0	1911	Irish Industrial Minerals *Derwent*	*	*
OK	12473	0-4-0T	1934	5-3	New	CSE Mallow 1	1945	
OK	12474	0-4-0T	1934	5-3	New	CSE Mallow 2	1969*	
OK	12475	0-4-0T	1934	5-3	New	CSE Thurles 1	*	
OK	12476	0-4-0T	1934	5-3	New	CSE Thurles 2	1974*	
OK	12477	0-4-0T	1934	5-3	New	CSE Tuam 2	1965	
OK	12478	0-4-0T	1934	5-3	New	CSE Tuam 1	1971	
OK	12662	0-4-0T	1935	5-3	New	CSE Mallow 3	*	
OK	12663	0-4-0T	1935	5-3	New	CSE Thurles 3	1960*	
OK	12664	0-4-0T	1935	5-3	New	CSE Tuam 3	1971	
P	679	0-6-0ST	1898	4-8½	*	S. Pearson 75 *Admiralty*		c.1932
						E. Moir		
P	680	0-6-0ST	1898	4-8½	*	S. Pearson 76 *Dover*		c.1932
						E. Moir		
P	806	0-6-0ST	1899	4-8½	*	S.Pearson 99 *Londonderry*		c.1932
						E. Moir		
P	1003	0-4-0ST	1903	3-0	New	Fisher & LeFanu *Cashel*		*
P	1026	0-4-0T	1904	3-0	New	British Aluminium 1	1960	
P	1097	0-4-0T	1906	3-0	New	British Aluminium 2	1956*	
						G. Cohen 2		
P	1189	0-4-0ST	1908	3-0	New	P.J. Kinlen	1925	
						McKee & McNally		
						Dublin Corporation		
						J. Mackay		
						H.& J. Martin		
P	1357	0-4-0T	1914	3-0	New	British Aluminium 3	1950	
P	1412	0-6-0ST	1915	2-0	1934	Sutton Sands	*	
P	1556	0-4-0ST	1920	5-3	New	Allman & Co.	(see GSR 495)	
P	2088	0-4-0ST	1948	5-3	New	Courtaulds *Patricia*	1968	
P	2113	0-4-0ST	1950	5-3	New	Courtaulds *Wilfred*	1968	
Robey		10hp	*	5-3	*	Derrylea Peat Co.	*	
Sen	6463	Sentinel	1926	2-0	1937	Cementation Co. 3	*	
Sen	6870	Sentinel	1927	2-0	1937	Cementation Co. 4	*	
Sen	9149	Sentinel	1946	2-6	1946	Bord Solathair an Lectreachais (ESB)		1947
SB	279	0-4-2	1845	5-3	New	W. Dargan *Lady Macneill* renamed *Pioneer*	(see Lim&ER 3)	
SS	2477	0-4-0T	1875	1-10	New	Arthur Guinness 1	1913	
SS	2764	0-4-0T	1878	1-10	New	Arthur Guinness 4	1925	
SS	2765	0-4-0T	1878	1-10	New	Arthur Guinness 5	1925	
Spence		0-4-0T	1887	1-10	New	Arthur Guinness 7	1948	
Spence		0-4-0T	1887	1-10	New	Arthur Guinness 8	1948	
Spence		0-4-0T	1887	1-10	New	Arthur Guinness 9	1948	
Spence		0-4-0T	1891	1-10	New	Arthur Guinness 10	1949	
Spence		0-4-0T	1891	1-10	New	Arthur Guinness 11	1948	
Spence		0-4-0T	1891	1-10	New	Arthur Guinness 12	1954	
Spence		0-4-0T	1895	1-10	New	Arthur Guinness 13	1956	1956
Spence		0-4-0T	1895	1-10	New	Arthur Guinness 14	1952	
Spence		0-4-0T	1895	1-10	New	Arthur Guinness 15	1957	
Spence		0-4-0T	1902	1-10	New	Arthur Guinness 16	1951	
Spence		0-4-0T	1902	1-10	New	Arthur Guinness 17	1959*	
Spence		0-4-0T	1902	1-10	New	Arthur Guinness 18	1951	
Spence		0-4-0T	1902	1-10	New	Arthur Guinness 19	1951	
Spence		0-4-0T	1905	1-10	New	Arthur Guinness 20	1956	

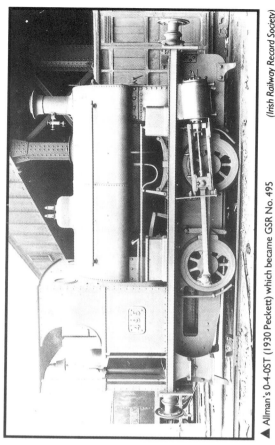

▲ Allman's 0-4-0ST (1930 Peckett) which became GSR No. 495

(Irish Railway Record Society)

▼ Faris' 0-4-2T (1900 Kerr Stuart) which arrived in Ireland in 1930, was put aside in 1939 and scrapped in 1952

(F. Jones)

▲ MacAlpine 3-0 gauge 0-4-0ST No. 13 *Donegal* (1906 Hudswell, Clarke)

(B.D. Stoyel)

▼ Falkiner's 0-6-0ST *Shamrock* (1892 Hunslet) later GS&WR No. 299

(M.P. Rowledge)

129

Builder	Prog. No.	Type	Date new	Gauge	Arrived in Ireland	Irish user/s & No./Name	Withdrawn	Left Ireland
Spence		0-4-0T	1905	1-10	New	Arthur Guinness 21	1959*	
Spence		0-4-0T	1912	1-10	New	Arthur Guinness 22	1957	
Spence		0-4-0T	1921	1-10	New	Arthur Guinness 23	1966	1966
Spence		0-4-0T	1921	1-10	New	Arthur Guinness 24	1967	
RS	1190	0-6-0	1859	5-3	New	Smith & Knight	(see N&AR 1)	
						Watson & Overend		
RS	1280	0-6-0	1860	5-3	New	Smith & Knight	(see N&AR 4)	
						Watson & Overend		
RS	2088	2-4-0T	1874	3-0	New	Glenariff Iron Ore & Harbour Co.	(see L&LSR 5)	
RS	2089	2-4-0T	1874	3-0	New	Glenariff Iron Ore & Harbour Co.	(see L&LSR 6)	
RS	2738	0-6-0ST	1891	5-3	New	Londonderry PHC 1	1962*	
RS	2836	0-6-0ST	1896	5-3	New	Londonderry PHC 2	1928	
T(B)	*	VB	1885	Mono	1887	Lartigue Construction Co. No. 1	1900*	
*	*	0-4-2T	*	3-0	*	Carnanee Quarry	1909*	
*	*	0-6-0T	*	4-8½	1874*	T.W. Chester	*	*
						Edwards		
*	*	2-4-0T	*	5-3	*	Watson & Overend	(see N&AR 5)	
*	*	*	1861*	3-6	New	Wicklow Copper Mine Co.	(see DW&WR)	
*	*	*	1861*	3-6	New	Wicklow Copper Mine Co.	(see DW&WR)	
*	*	6hp	*	5-3	*	Derrylea Peat Co.	*	

2. LOCOMOTIVES OBTAINED FROM IRISH RAILWAY COMPANIES

Former Railway	No./Name	Type	Gauge	Sold	User/s and No./Name	Withdrawn	Note
B&CDR	4	2-2-2	5-3	1858	Moore		A
B&NCR	1	2-4-0T	5-3	1863	J. Killeen	1872*	
					French & Cheyne		
D&DR	12	2-2-2	5-3	1853*	Moore	*	
D&ER	*	0-4-2	5-3	1849	W. Dargan	*	B
D&KR	Britannia	2-2-2	4-8½	1843	McCormick	1845*	
D&KR	Kingstown	2-2-2WT	4-8½	1846	McCormick & Dargan	*	C
			5-3		W. Dargan		
D&KR	Manchester	2-2-0	4-8½	1846	McCormick	*	
D&KR	Victoria	2-2-2WT	4-8½	1846	McCormick & Dargan	*	C
			5-3		W. Dargan		
D&MR	2 or 3	2-2-2	5-3	1872*	Edwards	1892*	
DW&WR	6A	2-2-2T	5-3	1903	Sir Robert MacAlpine	1903-5*	
DW&WR	Banshee	2-2-2WT	5-3	1894	Fisher & Le Fanu	1894*	
DW&WR	Elfin	2-2-2WT	5-3	1891	W.M. Murphy	1892*	
DW&WR	Kelpie	2-2-2WT	5-3	1889	R. Worthington	*	
DW&WR	Oberon	2-2-2WT	5-3	1891	W.M. Murphy	1892*	
DW&WR	Titania	2-2-2WT	5-3	1889	R. Worthington	*	
GCP&BVT	3	0-4-0VB	3-0	1931	R. Faris	1933	
GCP&BVT	4	0-4-0VB	3-0	1931	R. Faris	1934	
GNR	31	0-6-0CT	5-3	1958	Dundalk Engineering Works		D
GNR	86A	0-4-2T	5-3	1884	Collen Brothers	1885*	
GS&WR	10*	2-2-2	5-3	1877	J.J. Bagnall*	*	
GS&WR	13	2-2-2	5-3	1876	J.W. Stanford	*	
GS&WR	124	0-4-2	5-3	1882	J. Cunningham	*	
GS&WR	*	2-2-2	5-3	1870	W.J. Dougherty	*	E
L&LSR	1	0-6-0T	5-3	1886	Londonderry PHC 1 John Cooke	1891*	
L&LSR	2	0-6-0T	5-3	1882	Londonderry PHC 2	*	
L&LSR	3 (RS)	0-6-0T	5-3	1869	Londonderry PHC 1 John Cooke	*	
					McCrea & McFarland		
L&LSR	3 (GW)	0-6-0T	5-3	1883	* (purchaser unidentified)	*	
LL&CST	7*	0-4-0VB	3-0	1898	Topham, Jones & Railton	*	
MGWR	3	2-4-0	5-3	1880	S. Bolton	*	
MGWR	11	2-2-2	5-3	1867	Edgworth & Stanford		F
MR(NCC)	103	0-4-2ST	3-0	1911	an Antrim iron mine*	*	G
N&AR	1	4-cpld	5-3	1864	Watson & Overend	*	
N&AR	3	2-2-0WT	5-3	1874	Connor & Manisty Greenore	1876*	
NW&RR	4 Drogheda	*	5-3	1885	McCrea & McFarland	*	
SL&NCR	Faugh-a-Ballagh	0-4-0ST	5-3	1905	R. Worthington Faugh-a-Ballagh	1913	H
W&KR	8	4-2-2T	5-3	1859	Carlisle & Hutchings	*	
					Moore*		
					Ronayne*		

Notes

A Probably the locomotive purchased by C&BR in 1867 (No. 2).

B One out of four locomotives used by Dargan on his D&ER haulage contract and kept when the others were returned to the D&ER in 1850.

C Gauge apparently altered after purchase by Dargan.

D Retained at Dundalk Works on dissolution of GNRB. Sold to CIE in 1960 and taken into service stock (No. 365A).

E May have been GS&WR No. 17.

F   Sold to Waterford, New Ross & Wexford Junction Railway in 1870.
G   Sale not verified.
H   HE 178 (see earlier and SL&NCR).

3. LOCOMOTIVES OBTAINED FROM BRITISH RAILWAY COMPANIES

Former Railway	No./Name	Type	Date	Builder	Sold	User/s and No./Name	Withdrawn	Remarks
Brampton	*Gilsland*	0-4-0	1835	RS	1836*	4-8½ gauge - said to have been shipped to Ireland but no factual information is available.	*	
L&NWR	125 *Soho*	0-4-2	1838	Hick	1850	McCormick	*	See note
Slamannan	*Glenelrig*	0-4-0	1841	MA	1841	Jeffs - 4-6 gauge	*	

Note
125 was taken to Ireland 1851-2 and gauge later altered to 5-3 (McCormick was in partnership with Daglish in England when he purchased *Soho*).

4. LOCOMOTIVE OWNING CONTRACTORS & INDUSTRIAL RAILWAYS

The users of steam locomotives are listed in alphabetical order. Locomotives are identified by builders progressive numbers, by previous owner when obtained from a railway company, or by wheel arrangement or number/name if necessary.

User	Locomotive/s	Period of use	Remarks
Allman & Co., Bandon	MW 773	1885/6-1920	
	P 1556	1920-30	Sold to GSR (No. 495)
An Antrim iron ore mine*	MRNCC 103	1911*-*	Purchase from NCC not confirmed.
Ashwell	HE 156	1876-8	
J.J. Bagnall	GS&WR 10*	1877	
Belfast Harbour Commissioners	BH 514	1879-*	
	Ch 1505	1872-*	
	FW 369	1882-*	
John Best	WGB 1480	1897-1904*	
	AB 297	1899*-1903	
	HC 397	1900-3	
Board of Works, Dublin	Ch 2416	1887-*	Place/s of use not located.
S. Bolton	MGWR 3	1880-*	
Bord na Mona	AB 2263-5	1949-52	
Bord Solathair an Lectrachais (ESB)	Sen 9149	1946-7	
C. Braddock	WGB 1116	1892	
	HE 203	1892	Not confirmed.
	MW 237	1892	
	MW 1220	1891-2	
Brassey & Field	MW 4, 18	1864-6	Sold to INWR (Nos. 30 and 31).
British Aluminium, Larne	P 1026	1904-60	
	P 1097	1906-55	
	P 1357	1914-50	Stationary boiler 1950-3
British Portland Cement, Magheramorne	HC 1094	1915-35	
Bromhead & Hemming	Gryll* (two)	1846-7	*Victoria, Albert.*
Butler & Fry	BH 513	1879-80	Sold to Ballycastle Railway.
Carlisle & Hutchings	WKR 8	1859-60	
Carnanee Quarry Co., Londonderry	0-4-2T (one)	*-1909	
Carnlough Lime Co., Co. Antrim	AB 770	1896-1946*	
Cementation Co., Poulaphouca, Co. Wicklow	Sen 6463	1937-42	
	Sen 6870	1937-42	
T.W. Chester	Ch *	1877	
	N 602	1877	
	0-6-0T (one)	1874*-1877	12 in. cylinders.
G. Cohen	P 1097	1955	
Collen Bros.	GR 164	1884-8	
	HE *	1886-8	*Victor*
	GNR 86A	1884-5	
Comlucht Suicre Eireann	JC 3092/3/6	1926-65	
	OK 12473-8	1934-74	
	OK 12662-4	1935-71	
Connor & Manisty	Ch 370	1874-6	
	N&AR 3	1874-6	
Connor & Olley	Ch 370	1868*-70	
Courtaulds, Carrickfergus	P 2088	1948-68	
	P 2113	1950-68	
J. Cunningham	GS&WR 124	1882-*	Stationary use only?
W. Dargan	SB 279	1845-54	
	D&ER 0-4-2	*	Either D&ER No. 3 or No. 4
	D&KR (two)	1847	*Kingstown, Victoria.*
Derrylea Peat Co., Co. Kildare	Robey (one)	*	For sale 1870
	(one)	*	

User	Locomotive/s	Period of use	Remarks
T.S. Dixon (and Executors)	BM (one)	1882	
	HE 404	1904-5	
	HE 564	1892-3	
	HE 832	1903-5	
W.J. Doherty	GS&WR (one)	1870-*	
J.W. Dorman	MW 773	1884-5	
T. Dowling	MW 773	1880-3	
H.C. Drinkwater	JF 4027	1880-*	Not absolutely certain that this locomotive was used in Ireland.
Dublin Corporation (Roundwood reservoir construction, Co. Wicklow)	P 1189	1912-3	
Dublin Port & Dock Board	KS 889	1905-1914*	
Dundalk Engineering Works	GNR 31	1958-60	Sold to CIE (No. 365A).
Edgworth & Stanford	MGWR 11	1867-70	Sold to Waterford New Ross & Wexford Junction Railway.
J. Edwards	D&MR (one)	1871-5	Either D&MR No. 2 or No. 3.
Edwards	0-6-0T (one)	*	Purchased from T.W. Chester.
Edwards Bros.	Ch 370	1863-*	
T.H. Falkiner	WGB 1116	1892-5	Actually owned by MGWR.
	HE 203*	1892-5	Not confirmed. May have been owned by MGWR - ex Braddock.
	HE 557	1893	
	HE 558	1893-1901	
	MW 237	1892-5	Actually owned by MGWR.
	MW 1038	1893-5	
	MW 1220	1893-5	Actually owned by MGWR.
R. Faris, Carnanee Quarry, Co. Londonderry	RS 741	1930-9	
	GCP&BVT 3	1931-3	Stationary use only?
	GCP&BVT 4	1931-4	Stationary use only?
Fergus Reclamation Syndicate, Co. Clare	WGB 1416	1893-*	Use in Ireland not certain.
	AB 703	1893-7*	
Fisher & LeFanu	WGB 1551	1899-1906*	
	HE 178	1893-5	Sold to SL&NCR 1897.
	HE 457	1893-5	
	HE 591	1893-5	
	MW 1099	1893-1906	
	MW 1399	*-1906*	Requires confirmation.
	MW *	*-1906	0-4-0ST
	P 1003	1903-6	
	DW&WR (one)	1894	*Banshee*
French & Cheyne	B&NCR 1	1864	
Glenariff Iron Ore & Harbour Co.	RS 2088/9	1874-5	Sold to L&LSR 1885 (Nos. 5 and 6).
Greene & King	G	1862*	Later NW&RR *Drogheda*
Arthur Guinness, Dublin	AE 1337	1882-1947	
	Lewin (two)	1877-1927	
	SS 2477	1875-1913	
	SS 2764/5	1878-1925	
	Spence (18)	1887-1967	See earlier for numbers and dates.
	HC 1079	1914-65	5-3 gauge
	HC 1152	1915-65	5-3 gauge
Haulbowline Dockyard, Co. Cork (Admiralty until 1921)	AP 1105	1875-*	
	AP 1432	1878-*	
	MW 287	1912-26	Passed to Irish government 1921.
	MW 1357	1897-33	Passed to Irish government 1921.
C.M. Holland	Ch *	1878-80	
	HE 202/3	1878-80	
J. Howard, Cluntoe, Co. Tyrone	KS 4265	*	Period of use not known.
Irish Industrial Minerals, Achill, Co. Mayo	WGB 1945	1911-6	
	OK 2488	1911-6	
E.J. Jackson	Ch 2090	*	
Sir J. Jackson	Ch 1939	1882	On hire only - returned to Britain.
Jeffs	Butt (one)	1841-4	*Firefly*
	MA *	1841-*	
Kynock Ltd., Arklow	RS 2464	1918*-1936*	
J. Killeen	B&NCR 1	1863-4	
P.J. Kinlen	P 1189	1908-9	
Lartigue Construction Co., Listowel	Tubize VB	1887-8	
Lees & Nixon, Glenfarne, Co. Leitrim	HC 1166	1919-20*	
	HC 1310	1919-20*	
Londonderry Port & Harbour Commissioners	AE 2021	1928-62	
	RS 2738	1891-*	
	RS 2836	1896-1928	
	L&LSR 1	1886-91	
	L&LSR 2	1882-*	
	L&LSR 3	1869-82	

User	Locomotive/s	Period of use	Remarks
Lowry	HE 71	1887	
McCormick	D&KR (one)	1843-4	*Britannia*
	D&KR (one)	1846	*Manchester*
	Gryll* (two)	1847*-*	*Victoria, Albert*
	Hick (one)	1851*-*	*Soho*
McCormick & Dargan	D&KR (two)	1846	*Kingstown, Victoria*
McCrea & McFarland	BM (one)	1882-95	
	HE 202	1880	
	L&LSR 3	1882-*	
	NW&RR 4	1885-*	
McKee & McNally	P 1189	1909-12	
Sir Robert MacAlpine	HC 759	1906-8	
	HC 794	1907-8	
	HE 404	1906-8	
	HE 457	1904-6	
	HE 832	1906-8	
	DW&WR 6A	1903-5*	
J. Mackay	HE 564	1914	
	P 1189	1914	
Marconi's Wireless & Telegraph Co., Clifden, Co. Galway	DK (one)	1906-1927*	
H. & J. Martin	WGB 1844	1920-5	
	WGB 2081/6	1920-4	
	HE 564	1919-23	
	P 1189	1919-23	
E. Moir (successor to Pearson)	AE 1552	1930-2	
	AE 1618	1930-2	
	AE 1833	1930-2	
	AE 1872	1930-2	
	AB 1408	1930-2	
	HC 1497	1930-2	
	HC 1505	1930-2	
	HC 1508	1930-2	
	P 679/80	1930-2	
	P 806	1930-2	
Moore	B&CDR 4	1858-62*	
	D&DR 12	1853*-1855*	*Firefly*
W.M. Murphy	HE 208	1892	
	MW 773	1884	
	DW&WR (two)	1891-92*	*Elfin, Oberon*
Naylor Bros.	HC 672	1913-6	
	MW 1099	1914-6	Taken over by D&SER.
	MW 1399	1913-6	On loan from Scott & Middleton?
G. Pauling	WGB 1116	1899-1903	
	KS 659/60	1899-1903	
S. Pearson	AE 1552	*-1930	
	AE 1618	*-1930	
	AE 1833	1928*-30	
	AE 1872	*-1930	
	AB 1408	1925*-30	
	HC 1497	1927*-30	
	HC 1505	1923-30	
	HC 1508	1924-30	
	HE 74	1903-6	
	HE 457	1903-6	
	HE 558	1903-6	
	P 679/80	*-1930	
	P 806	*-1930	
Portrush Columnar Bassalt, Craigahulliar Quarry, Co. Antrim	WGB 1631	1914*-33	
River Fergus Reclamation Syndicate, Co. Clare	HE 268	1881-3*	Also known as H.C. Drinkwater.
Ronayne	W&KR 8	*	Use by Ronayne not certain.
W. Scott	HE 202	1886	Use by Scott uncertain.
	MW 614	1886	
W. Scott & Middleton	MW 1399	1903-11	Verification required.
Smith & Finlayson	HE 156	1876-8	
Smith & Knight	RS 1190	1859-62	
	RS 1280	1860-2	
J.W. Stanford	HE 203	1880-3	
	GS&WR 13*	1876-8	
Sulphate of Ammonia, Larne	KS 1100	1910-2	
Sutton Sands, Newbridge, Co. Kildare	HC 1298	1934-*	
	P 1412	1934-*	

User	Locomotive/s	Period of use	Remarks
D. Thompson & Sons, Balbriggan, Co. Dublin	KS 4252	1929*-*	
Topham, Jones & Railton	LL&CST 7*	1898-*	
A.L. Tottenham	HE 178	1878-82	
Tralee & Fenit Harbour Commissioners	HE 557	1899-1900	Became GS&WR No. 299.
War Department (British Government)	HC 1166	1918-20	Gormanston Aerodrome, Co. Meath.
	HC 1310	1918-20	Tallaght Aerodrome, Co. Dublin.
	HC 1311/3	1918-20	Baldonnel Aerodrome, Co. Dublin.
G.O. Watson, Doonagore, Co. Clare	KS 766	1903-8	
Watson & Overend	K 796	1860-4	
	RS 1190	1863-4	Sold to N&AR No. 1.
	RS 1280	1863-4	Sold to N&AR No. 4.
	N&AR 1	1864	4-cpld. Requires verification.
Whyte	OK (two)	*	For sale 1906.
Wicklow Copper Mining Co.	(two)	*-1861	Hodgson's Tramway (see DW&WR)
R. Worthington	HE 178	1905-10	See SL&NCR *Faugh-a-Ballagh*
	HE 315/9/52	1883-1910	
	HE 382	1885-90	See T&CLR *Slaney*
	HE 482	1889-1910	Purchased for independent working of the Kanturk & Newmarket Railway in 1890-1.
	HE 591	1893-4	
	HE 859	1904-10	
	OK 1240	1904-10	
*	FW 369	1878-*	Unkown user in Co. Antrim
*	L&LSR 3 (GW)	1883-*	Unidentified user.
*(Watson & Overend?)	2-4-0T (one)	*-1864	Sold to N&AR No. 5.
*	Gilsland (RS)	1836*	Unidentified user on Lough Foyle reclamation works.

5. LOCOMOTIVES NOT IDENTIFIED

The following list gives brief details of unidentied locomotives which have worked in Ireland. It should be kept in mind that some may well be unrecorded use of locomotives listed beforehand, or in some cases more than one entry for a locomotive since this section can list only by owner or location.

User	Gauge	Remarks
Antrim Iron Ore Co.	3-0	Seems to have had a locomotive for sale in 1886.
J.J. Bagnell	5-3	*Lady de Burgh* (1862 - most likely special naming of a locomotive, possibly W&LR, for opening of Killaloe line).
Bolton	5-3	Used a locomotive in 1847-9 on building of C&BR.
C. Brand	*	Two (or more) in 1905-6 at Rosslare Harbour.
Bromhead & Hemming	4-8½ & 5-3	Two (or maybe four) in addition to Gryll* 2-4-0 in 1846/7. Three locomotives passed to McCormick later.
Camden Fort, Cork Harbour	1-6	May have had locomotive/s.
H.J. Cooper, Drinagh, Co. Wexford	5-3	Four-wheeled chain drive machine c.1885-6.
J.D. Cooper	*	Had a locomotive in 1866 (possibly ex-GS&WR).
J.B. Crawley	5-3	Used a locomotive in 1877 (Ilen Valley Railway contract).
Cromelin Mining Co., Co. Antrim	3-0	Had a locomotive overhauled by Barclay in 1901.
W. Dargan	5-3	Bury type (one) in 1848-50.
	5-3	*Duchess of Leinster* used in 1847-9.
	5-3	*William Dargan* (Bury type) used in 1848-54.
J. & R. Edwards	5-3	Used two in 1863 and two in 1864 (possibly the same pair) - might have been obtained from Dargan.
T. Edwards	5-3	One used in 1852 (possibly one of Dargan's).
	5-3	One Bury type ex-Dargan used in 1867-72.
Eglinton Lime Co.	2-6	One tank locomotive used in 1916*-25.
Greene & King	*	Used a locomotive in 1858-9 (possibly McCormick's *Soho*)
Jeffs	4-6	Most likely owner of two 4-6 gauge locomotives up for sale in 1849 - one perhaps *Glenelrig*
J.W. Kelly	5-3	Had a locomotive in 1868 (possibly Watson & Overend's Kitson 0-6-0T).
	5-3	Had a locomotive in 1875-6 (possibly the same as above).
Kent & Smith	5-3	Wanted a locomotive in 1864 - refused one offered by B&CDR.
J. Killeen	5-3	Used a locomotive in 1862-4.
Killeen & Moore	5-3	Used a locomotive in 1854.
Koch	*	Sold a locomotive in 1861.
Lewis, Larne	*	Had a locomotive named *Mona* (possibly not in Ireland).
McCrea & McFarland	3-8*	One or two in 1883.
	5-3	One in addition to HE 202 in 1880.
	3-0	One used on a contract finished in 1889.
H. & J.Martin	*	Two narrow gauge locomotives purchased from GS&WR in 1888.
Sir Robert MacAlpine	*	Reputed to have used 0-4-0ST HE 536 1904-6 on Waterford - Rosslare Strand contract.
Murphy	*	Had a vertical boiler locomotive (Possibly Chaplin) 1881-2*.
Naylor Bros.	*	Used two narrow gauge locomotives in 1913-6 (possibly German) on D&SER deviation contracts.

User	Gauge	Remarks
Ravenhill Brick & Tile Co., Belfast	2-0	Alleged to have had a locomotive (claimed to be WGB 210, but it is extremely unlikely that it ever worked in Ireland).
Scott & Best	*	Alleged to have had a locomotive at Haulbowline c.1898.
Smith & Knight	*	Had two locomotives in 1862 other than RS 1190 and 1280 on Athlone-Castlebar job and two on Longford-Sligo contract.
T. Tyrell	5-3	Had a locomotive which was stored on (and perhaps used by) L&ER c.1854-9 (stated to be very old).
Tuck & Co., Dublin	2-6	Had a six-coupled saddle tank for sale in 1900-3 (may not have actually been in Ireland).
R. Worthington	*	One named *Shannon* mentioned c.1886 (but may in fact be in error for HE 382 *Slaney*).
*	5-3	One 0-6-0ST (possibly MW) known only from a photograph of 1888 (on Queenstown branch) - perhaps 5-3 locomotive offered for sale by Philips, Newport, Mon. in 1892.
*	5-3*	One six-wheeled tank for sale at Waterford in 1879 (possibly B&CDR No. 4, previously No. 1 Tank, sold in 1878).

6. DIMENSIONS OF CONTRACTORS AND INDUSTRIAL LOCOMOTIVES
(For locomotives not listed dimensions are not known).

Builder & Prog. Nos.	Gauge	Cylinders	Driving wheels	Builder & Prog. Nos.	Gauge	Cylinders	Driving wheels
AP 1105, 1432	3-6	*	3-0	HE 315, 319	5-3	9 x 14	2-8½
AE 1337	1-10	7 x 8½	1-10	HE 352/82, 557/8	5-3	12 x 18	3-1
AE 1552, 1618, 1872	4-8½	14 x 20	3-3	HE 404, 564, 832	3-0	9½ x 14	2-6
AE 1833	4-8½	14½ x 20	3-3	HE 457	5-3	13 x 18	3-1
AE 2021	5-3	14 x 22	3-3	HE 482	5-3	15 x 20	3-4
WGB 1116	3-0	9½ x 13	2-3	HE 859	5-3	10 x 15	2-10
WGB 1416	2-0	6 x 9	1-6	K 796	5-3	11 x 17	3-6
WGB 1480	3-0	8 x 12	2-0½	KS 659, 660	3-0	9½ x 15	2-3½
WGB 1551, 2081/6	3-0	7 x 12	1-9½	KS 741	3-0	7½ x 12	2-0
WGB 1631	2-6	6 x 9	1-7	KS 766	4-8½	9½ x 15	2-9
WGB 1844	3-0	5 x 7½	1-3¼	KS 889	3-0	6 x 9	1-8
WGB 1945	2-0	7 x 12	2-3½	KS 1100, 2464,4252, 4265	2-0	6 x 9	1-8
AB 297	3-0	9 x 17	2-6	Lewin 0-6-0WT	2-6	9 x 12	3-0
AB 703	2-0	5 x 10	1-10	Lewin 0-4-0WT	1-10	6¼ x 8	*
AB 770	3-6	7½ x 14	2-0	MW 4, 18	5-3	11 x 17	3-3
AB 1408	4-8½	14 x 22	3-5	MW 237	5-3	12 x 17	3-1⅜
AB 2263-5	3-0	8½ x 12	2-0	MW 287	3-6	8 x 14	2-8
BH 513	3-0	12 x 19	3-3	MW 614	3-0	7 x 12	2-6
BH 514	3-0	7 x 12	2-3	MW 773	5-3	9 x 14	2-9
Ch 370, 1505, 2090, 2416 (12hp type)	various	6 x 13	*	MW 1038	3-0	9 x 14	2-9
Ch T.W.Chester (15hp type)	*	7 x 14	*	MW 1099	5-3	14 x 20	3-6
Ch C.M.Holland, 1939 (9hp type)	*	5¼ x 11	*	MW 1220	5-3	12 x 17	3-1⅜
JC 3092/3/6	5-3	11⁷⁄₁₆ x 12½	2-3¼	MW 1357	3-6	8 x 14	2-6
Dick Kerr 0-4-0ST	2-0	4 x 8	*	MW 1399	4-8½	12¼ x 17	3-1
Fbn 2-2-2WT (ex-LNWR)	5-3	13 x 18	5-7	OK 1240	2-0	6½ x 11¹³⁄₁₆	1-10²⁷⁄₃₂
JF 4027	2-0	4½ x *	*	OK 2488	2-0	6½ x 11¹³⁄₁₆	2-1¹⁹⁄₃₂
FW 369	3-0	9 x 14	2-6	OK 12473-8, 12662-4	5-3	11⁵⁄₁₆ x 15¾	2-7
Hick 0-4-2 *Soho*	5-3	13 x 18	5-8	P 679, 680	4-8½	16 x 22	3-10
HC 397	3-0	10 x 16	2-9	P 806	4-8½	14 x 20	3-7
HC 672	4-8½	12 x 18	3-1	P 1003	3-0	8 x 12	2-3
HC 759	3-0	9 x 15	2-6	P 1026/97, 1357	3-0	7 x 10	1-8
HC 794	3-0	12 x 18	3-1	P 1189	3-0	10 x 15	2-6½
HC 1079, 1152	5-3	15 x 22	3-4	P 1412	2-0	7 x 10	1-8
HC1094	5-3	14 x 20	2-3½	P 1556	5-3	10 x 15	2-9
HC 1166	2-0	5 x 8	1-8	P 2088, 2113	5-3	14 x 22	3-2½
HC 1298, 1310/1/3	2-0	6½ x 12	1-11	Sen 6463, 6870	2-0	6¾ x 9	1-8
HC 1497,1505	4-8½	14 x 20	3-7	Sen 9149	2-6	6¾ x 9	1-8
HC 1508	4-8½	14 x 20	3-3½	SB 279	5-3	13½ x 20	4-6
HE 71, 74	3-0	8 x 14	2-9	SS 2477	1-10	4½ x 6	1-3¼
HE 156	5-3	10 x 15	2-9	SS 2764/5	1-10	6½ x 8	1-6
HE 178	5-3	12 x 18	3-2	Spence	1-10	7 x 8½	1-10
HE 202/3	5-3	10 x 15	2-6	RS 1190, 1280	5-3	16 x 24	4-7½
HE 208	3-0	9 x 14	2-4	RS 2088/9	3-0	15 x 20	3-9
HE 268	2-6	6 x 10	1-8	RS 2738	5-3	13 x 18	3-6
				RS 2836	5-3	14 x 22	3-6
				2-4-0T (later N&AR 1)	5-3	15 x 22	5-0

The majority, irrespective of gauge, had outside cylinders. None were superheated and only the Bord na Mona 0-4-0WT had Belpaire boilers. The known inside cylinder locomotives were:

HC	672.		MW	237, 1099, 1220, 1399.
HE	352/82, 457/82, 557/8.		SB	279.
KS	766.		RS	1190, 1280.

Vertical boiler locomotives: Chaplin, Cockerill and Sentinel.

7. LOCOMOTIVES USED ON SHANNON HYDRO-ELECTRIC SCHEME.

The undermentioned were imported from Germany by the contractors (Siemens Bauunion) in 1925-30 and were taken back to Germany when the work was completed in 1930. They were moved to and from Ireland as necessary. All these locomotives were 0-4-0T.

No.	Maker	Date	gauge	Known Nos.	Known Progressive Nos.
(2)	Henschel	1919	1-11½	38,1018	
(3)	Krauss	1920	2-11½	6-8	7608-10
(1)	Jung	1920	1-11½		
(10)	Linke Hofmann	1923	1-11½	1030/1	
(11)	Henschel	1924	2-11½		20246-9, 20304-10
(15)	Henschel	1925	2-11½		20616-30
(21)	Rhine Metal Works	1925	2-11½	9, 12/3/5, 25/7/8	921-9,1003-7 (plus 5 others)
(5)	Borsig	1925	2-11½		11725-9 or 11760-4
(5)	Hanomag	1925	2-11½	5031-5	9416-20
(13)	Borsig	1926	2-11½		11618-21/57-65
(6)	Henschel	1927	2-11½	4004/6/16	
(14)	Hanomag	1928	2-11½	34/6/7	9421-6, 9428 (plus 7 others)

Most of the locomotive numbers quoted were observed by a visitor to Killaloe during construction. Other known numbers were 5003-5/7/9.

Four locomotives ordered by the contractors were lost at sea in 1926. It is not clear whether they were additional to those listed above or were part of one of the batches listed (possibly the Borsig 1926 batch).

Dimensions of Shannon Hydro-electric contract locomotives

Builder & Type	Gauge	Cylinders	Driving wheels
Borsig	2-11½	12⅜ x 12⅜	2-7½
Hanomag	2-11½	13 x 17	2-8⁹⁄₃₂
Henschel	2-11½	12³⁄₁₆ x 17	2-7½
Henschel	2-11½	12⅜ x 17	2-7½
Henschel	1-11½	7⁵⁄₁₆ x 9⅝	1-9²¹⁄₃₂
Jung	1-11½	7½ x 11¹³⁄₁₆	1-11⅝
Krauss	2-11½	12 x 15⅝	2-8¹¹⁄₁₆
Linke Hofmann	1-11½	8½ x 11¹³⁄₁₆	1-11⅝
Rhine Metal Works	2-11½	13¾ x 13¾	2-3¹⁹⁄₃₂

PLEASURE RAILWAYS

BELFAST CORPORATION (BELLEVUE PARK)

1-3 gauge.
Stock: 1 secondhand locomotive 1934.

Name	Type	Former Identity	Remarks
Jean	0-4-0	Romney Hythe & Dymchurch Railway No. 4 (known as *"The Bug!"*)	Purchased 1934. New in 1926 (Krauss 8378). Put aside for scrap in 1950, but later rescued and returned to the Romney Hythe & Dymchurch Railway. Cylinders 4⁹⁄₁₆ x 6⁵⁄₁₆; driving wheels 1-3¾ (Named *Sir Crawford* at one time).

CORK INDUSTRIES FAIR AND EXHIBITION

1-1 gauge.
Stock: 2 locomotives 1932.

Two Krauss 4-6-2 miniature railway locomotives were used at the exhibition in 1932, being Prog. Nos. 8351 (1925-6) and one of 8352/3 (1925-6) or 8445/6 (1928).

IRISH STEAM PRESERVATION SOCIETY

3-0 gauge
Stock: 1 secondhand locomotive.

Former Bord na Mona 0-4-0WT No. 44 (previously No. 2) is used by this railway, running as No. 2.

SHANE'S CASTLE (LORD O'NEILL)

3-0 gauge
Stock: 3 secondhand locomotives 1971-2.

No.	Name	Type	Former Identity	Remarks
1	*Tyrone*	0-4-0T	British Aluminium No. 1	
3	*Shane*	0-4-0WT	Bord na Mona No. 45	Previously Bord na Mona No. 3
5	*Nancy*	0-6-0T	Staveley Minerals Ltd.	Never previously used in Ireland. Purchased by Lord O'Neill in 1972 (cylinders 10 x 16; driving wheels 2-6½). New in 1908, builder AE.

LOCOMOTIVE PRESERVATION

PRESERVED IN IRELAND

(i) Locomotives of main line companies (5-3) in working order
D&SER 15; GNR 85; GNR 171; GS&WR 90; GS&WR 184; GS&WR 186; NCC 4; SL&NCR *Lough Erne*.

(ii) Locomotives of main line companies (5-3) as static exhibits
B&CDR 30; GNR 93; GNR 131; GSR 800; GS&WK 36 (Bury); NCC 74.

(iii) Locomotives of narrow gauge companies (3-0) in working order
T&DLR 5;

(iv) Locomotives of narrow gauge companies (3-0) as static exhibits
CDRJC 2; CDRJC 4; CDRJC 5; CDRJC 6; C&LR 2; WCR 5.
(CVR/CDRJC 0-4-0T is preserved as a diesel).

(v) Tram locomotive (3-0) as static exhibit
Portstewart No. 2.

(vi) Locomotives from industrial sources in working order
Londonderry PHC 3 (AE 2021); Guinness 3 (HC 1152).

(vii) Locomotives from industrial sources as static exhibits
CSE 1 (OK 12475); CSE 3 (OK 12662); Londonderry PHC 1 (RS 2738); Guinness 15, 17, 20, 21; British Aluminium 2 (P 1097).

PRESERVED OUTSIDE IRELAND

(i) Locomotives of narrow gauge companies (3-0) in working order
C&LR 3 (in USA).

(ii) Locomotives from industrial sources in working order
Bord na Mona 43 (AB 2263) - Talyllyn Railway, Towyn, Wales (heavily rebuilt as 2-3 gauge 0-4-2WT in 1992. Now No. 7 *Tom Rolt*).

(iii) Locomotives from industrial sources as static exhibits
Guinness 13, 23.

(iv) Tram locomotive (3-0) as static exhibit
Portstewart No. 1.

LOCOMOTIVE NAMES INDEX

This index is intended to enable users to locate a locomotive by means of its name in the locomotive lists. However only the owner at the time of naming is given, no indication of subsequent owners (or renumberings) being given. A date in parentheses indicates that the name was not affixed when the locomotive was new but at a later date.

1. RAILWAY COMPANIES

Name	Railway	No.	Date	Name	Railway	No.	Date
Aberfoyle	L&LSR	9	1904	*Apollo*	D&DR	17	1847
Achill	MGWR	115	1893		GNR	133	1899
Achilles	D&DR	12	1871	*Arabian*	MGWR	20	1851
	GNR	77	1898	*Ardee*	GNR	7	(1885)
	UR		1841	*Argadeen*	T&CLR		1894
Active	MGWR	30	1876	*Ariel*	DW&WR		1865
	MGWR	30	1898		MGWR	29	1851
Adavoyle	GNR	161	1908		MGWR	32	1876
Adonis	GNR	134	1899		MGWR	32	1898
Africa	MGWR	146	1904	*Arklow*	DW&WR	50	(1891)
Airedale	MGWR	35	1886	*Armagh*	GNR	26	1880
Ajax	D&DR	10-11 *	(1862)		GNR	203	1948
	MGWR	130	1895	*Arnott*	C&YR	10	1862
	UR		1841	*Arran Isles*	MGWR	135	1895
Albert	D&DR	4	1844	*Arrow*	MGWR	33	1876
	D&KR		1844		MGWR	33	1898
	GNR	89	1885	*Aster*	GNR	90	1898
	GNR	89	1904	*Athenry*	MGWR	142	1901
Alert	MGWR	31	1876	*Athlone*	MGWR	69	(1867)
	MGWR	31	1897		MGWR	69	1889
Alfred	D&DR	9	1844		MGWR	126	1903
Alice	CDRJC	21	(1912)	*Atlantic*	MGWR	131	1895
	D&DR	8	1844	*Atlas*	MGWR	131	1895
	WDR	3	1881	*Aurora*	D&DR	15 *	(1859)
Ant	W&LR	6	1890		MGWR	34	1876
Antelope	GS&WR				MGWR	34	1898
Antrim	GNR	80	1886	*Australia*	MGWR	144	1904
	GNR	204	1948	*Avalanche*	GNR	43	1879
Antrim Castle	LMS(NCC)	75	(1924)	*Avonside*	MGWR	96	1880
				Badger	MGWR	94	1876

Name	Railway	No.	Date	Name	Railway	No.	Date
Ballinasloe	MGWR	70	(1867)	Carlow	GNR	145	1888
	MGWR	70	1889	Carntual	UR	35	1866
Ballybay	GNR	158	1906	Carra Castle	LMS(NCC)	83	(1925)
Ballybrack	DW&WR	42	(1883)	Carrantuohill	GNR	174	1913
Ballynahinch	MGWR	4	1910	Carrick Castle	W&LR	47	1894
Ballyroney	GNR	162	1908	Carrickfergus Castle	LMS(NCC)	81	(1925)
Ballyshannon	CDRJC	21	1912	Carrickmines	DW&WR	49	(1891)
Balmoral	GNR	101	1901	Castle Hackett	W&LR	51	1895
Banbridge	GNR	163	1908	Cavan	GNR	79	1882
Bann	UR	16	(1857)		MGWR	136	1895
Banshee	DW&WR		1865	Celtic	MGWR	129	1902
Baron	MGWR	46	(1860)	Cerberus	GNR	124	1902
	MGWR	51	(1880)		UR	11	1847
	MGWR	52	1880	Chambers	C&YR	4	1860
Barrow	DW&WR	15	(1860)	Chichester Castle	LMS(NCC)	78	(1924)
Bat	MGWR	110	1890	Childers	MGWR	19	1851
Bear	MGWR	91	1876		MGWR	22	(1852)
Beaver	MGWR	90	1876	City of Cork	C&AMLR	1	1887
Bee	MGWR	27	(1851)	Clanaboy	UR	25	1862
	W&LR	5	1893	Clancarty	MGWR	81	1872
Belfast	GNR	33	1891		MGWR	81	1893
Belleek	GNR	102	1901	Clara	MGWR	28	1897
Belleisle	D&KR		1841	Clare	GNR	153	1903
Ben Madigan	LMS(NCC)	66	(1905)	Clifden	MGWR	27	1897
Beragh	GNR	39	1911		WCR	3	1887
Bernard	WL&WR	55	1897	Clonbrock	MGWR	82	1872
Besborough	WCR	4	1887		MGWR	82	1892
Bessborough	W&LR	2 *	1847	Clones	GNR	100	1900
Bessbrook	GNR	10	1904	Clonmel	DW&WR	5	(1897)
Binevenagh	LMS(NCC)	3	(1902)	Clonsilla	MGWR	29	1897
Birdcatcher	MGWR	23	1852	Coachford	C&MLR	2	1887
	MGWR	38	(1856)	Colebrook	CVT	5	1887
Bison	MGWR	89	1876	Colleen Bawn	W&LR	45	1893
Bittern	MGWR	92	1876	Columbkille	CDRJC	18	(1907)
Blackburn	D&SER		1889		DR	9	1893
Blacklion	SL&NCR		(1885)	Comet	D&KR		1836
Blackrock	DW&WR	26	(1864)		D&KR		1851
Blackwater	CVT	3	1886		MGWR	7	1871
	GNR	2	1881		MGWR	73	1892
	UR	2	1859	Conciliation	S&SLR	3	(1914)
Blanche	CDRJC	2 A	(1912)	Condor	MGWR	13	1848
	WDR	2	1881	Cong	MGWR	116	1893
Blarney	C&MLR	4	1888	Connaught	GNR	129	1911
	C&MLR	4	1919		MGWR	54	(1862)
Blarney Castle	WL&WR	21	1897		MGWR	48	1887
Blessingbourne	CVR	7	1910		UR	29	1863
Boyne	GNR	207	1948	Connemara	MGWR	73	1869
Breffney	UR	24	1862		MGWR	7	1889
Brian Boroimhe	GCP&BVT	4	1896		MGWR	7	1909
Brian Boru	W&LR	52	1895	Cootehill	GNR	159	1906
Britannia	D&KR		1834	Cork	DW&WR	65	1905
	MGWR	26	1880		GNR	57	1895
	MGWR	26	1900	Countess of Antrim	Ballycastle	2	1880
Britannic	MGWR	125	1905	County Antrim	LMS(NCC)	61	(1897)
Buffalo	GS&WR			County Donegal	LMS(NCC)	60	(1897)
	MGWR	88	1876	County Down	LMS(NCC)	51	(1890)
Bulldog	MGWR	95	1876	County Londonderry	LMS(NCC)	24	(1898)
Bullfinch	MGWR	86	1876	County Tyrone	LMS(NCC)	58	(1890)
Bundoran	GNR	71	1896	Croagh Patrick	GNR	191	(1915)
Burgoyne	D&KR		1845		MGWR	5	1910
Butterfly	MGWR	93	1876	Crocus	GNR	95	1898
Buzzard	MGWR	87	1876	Culloville	GNR	160	1906
Cahir	W&LR	*	1881-2	Cyclone	GNR	107	1906
Caledon	CVT	1	1886		UR	7	1871
Caledonia	MGWR	98	1880	Cyclops	D&KR		1847
Callan	UR	14	(1853)		GNR	135	1899
Cambria	MGWR	99	1880		MGWR	25	1852
	W&WR		1894		MGWR	25	1880
Camel	GS&WR				MGWR	25	1901
Camellia	W&LR	37	(1881)		UR	7	1846
Canada	MGWR	143	1904		WL&WR	57	1897
Carlingford	DN&GR	5	1876	Cygnet	MGWR	16	1848
Carlisle	C&YR	3	1859		MGWR	23	(1852)

Name	Railway	No.	Date
Daffodil	GNR	72	(1895)
Dahlia	W&LR	32	(1874)
Daisy	GNR	82	(1892)
Dalkey	DW&WR	9	(1890)
Dalriada	Ballycastle	1	1880
	UR	21	1861
Daphne	GNR	125	1902
Delgany	DW&WR	41	(1882)
Derg	C&VBT	2	1884
Derry	GNR	65	1877
Derry Castle	W&LR	13	1891
Diana	D&DR	18 *	(1854)
	GNR	126	1907
Donard	GNR	50	1911
	UR	36	1866
Donegal	CDRJC	16	1907
	GNR	63	1877
	L&LSR	3	1883
Donoughmore	C&MLR	5	1892
Down	GNR	64	1883
	GNR	205	1948
Dreadnought	W&LR	49	1895
Dripsey	C&MLR	8	1904
Drogheda	D&DR	17	1847
	D&DR	4	(1856)
	GNR	32	1894
	NW&RR	4	(1862*)
Dromedary	GS&WR		
Dromore	GNR	11	1903
Drumboe	CDRJC	17	(1907)
	DR	5	1893
Drumconora	A&EJR	1	(1847)
Dublin	D&DR	6	1844
	D&KR		1834
	DW&WR	66	1905
	GNR	27	1879
	MGWR	67	(1867)
	MGWR	67	1888
Duke	MGWR	44	(1860)
	MGWR	53	1880
Duke of Abercorn	DW&WR	53	(1893)
	LMS(NCC)	90	(1933)
Duke of Connaught	DW&WR	52	(1893)
Duke of Leinster	DW&WR	54	(1893)
Dunananie Castle	LMS(NCC)	82	(1925)
Duncannon	W&LR	35	1881
Dundalk	D&GR	3	1873
	GNR	60	1890
Dunkellan	MGWR	84	1872
	MGWR	84	1891
Dunleary	DW&WR	44	(1883)
Dunleer	GNR	103	1901
Dunluce Castle	GCP&BVT	3	1896
	LMS(NCC)	74	(1924)
Dunsandle	MGWR	7	1847
	MGWR	86	1872
	MGWR	80	1891
Dunseverick Castle	LMS(NCC)	80	(1925)
Eagle	B&BR	11	1847
	GNR	83	1932
	MGWR	38	1886
Earl	MGWR	48	(1861)
	MGWR	54	1880
Earl of Bessborough	DW&WR	64	(1896)
	W&LR	12	(1886)
Earl of Carysfort	DW&WR	63	(1884)
Earl of Courtown	DW&WR	60	(1883)
Earl of Fitzwilliam	DW&WR	59	(1885)
Earl of Meath	DW&WR	62	(1896)
Earl of Ulster	LMS(NCC)	97	1935
Earl of Wicklow	DW&WR	61	(1883)
Eclipse	MGWR	18	1851
	MGWR	21	(1851)

Name	Railway	No.	Date
Edward VII	L&LSR	7	1901
Elephant	MGWR	66	(1864)
	MGWR	66	1889
Elf	GSR		(1906)
	MGWR	28	(1851)
Elfin	DW&WR		1865
Emerald Isle	MGWR	9	1869
	MGWR	9	1890
	MGWR	9	1912
Emperor	MGWR	40	(1856)
Empress of Austria	MGWR	36	1881
	MGWR	36	1900
Ennis	WCR	10	1900
	W&LR	31	1874
Enniscorthy	D&SER	18	1910
Enniskillen	GNR	29	1895
	N&ER	3*	1853
	SL&NCR		1905
Ennistymon	WCR	3	1922
Era	W&LR	22	1890
Erebus	GNR	127	1907
Erin	D&KR		1843
	S&SLR	4	1888
	W&WR		1894
Erin go Bragh	MGWR	74	1869
	MGWR	11	1890
	MGWR	11	1915
	W&LR	46	1893
Erne	CVT	6	1887
	DR	14	1904
	GNR	210	1948
	SL&NCR		1883
	UR	3	1860
Errigal	CVT	2	1886
	GNR	170	1913
Eske	DR	12	1904
Etna	GNR	3	1877
	UR		1841
Express	UR		1839
Fag-an-Bealach	D&DR	3	1844
Fairy	GS&WR		1894
	MGWR	27	1851
	MGWR	29	(1851)
Falcon	B&BR	9	1847
	GNR	84	1932
	MGWR	33	(1854)
Faug an Ballagh	C&BR	3	1849
Faugh-a-Ballagh	MGWR	10	1869
	MGWR	10	1889
	MGWR	10	1909
	SL&NCR		1878
	WL&WR	17	1896
Fergus	WCR	9	1898
Fermangah	GNR	67	1879
	SL&NCR		1882
Fermoy	C&YR	6	1861
Finn	CDRJC	19	(1907)
	DR	7	1893
Fintona	GNR	164	1908
Firefly	D&DR	12	1841*
	UR		1841
Fly	MGWR	109	1890
Foyle	CDRJC	20	(1907)
	DR	8	1893
	GNR	105	1906
	GNR	209	1948
	UR	32	(1866)
Fury	CVT	4	1887
	UR		1839
Gabriel	S&SLR	1	1906
Galgorm Castle	B&NCR	33	1890
	LMS(NCC)	57	(1895)
	LMS(NCC)	3	1926

139

Name	Railway	No.	Date	Name	Railway	No.	Date
Galtee More	GNR	173	1913	John Cooke	L&LSR	1	1862
	W&LR	20	1892		L&LSR	3	(1864)
Galway	GNR	31	1890	Jubilee	B&NCR	50	1895
	MGWR	71	(1867)		WL&WR	53	1896
	MGWR	71	1887	Jumbo	GS&WR	(201)	(1876)
Garryowen	W&LR	9	1886	Juno	GNR	24	1910
Geraldine	WL&WR	18	1897		MGWR	11	1847
Gertrude	C&LR	5	1887		MGWR	3	(1857)
Giant	MGWR	101	1880		MGWR	3	1880
Giantess	MGWR	100	1880		MGWR	3	1901
Gladiator	B&BR	3	1847	Jupiter	D&DR	14 *	(1859)
Glenaan	LMC(NCC)	3	(1926)		D&DR	16 *	(1861)
Glenageary	DW&WR	2	(1885)		D&KR		1848
Glenariff	LMS(NCC)	4	1931		GNR	75	1898
Glenarm Castle	LMS(NCC)	69	(1914)		MGWR	5	1847
Glenart	DW&WR	25	(1864)		MGWR	2	(1857)
Glencar	SL&NCR		(1887)		MGWR	2	1880
Glencar 'A'	SL&NCR		(1890)		MGWR	2	1900
Glendalough	DW&WR	33	(1873)		UR	10	1846
Glendun	LMS(NCC)	2	(1924)		UR	10	1869
Glengall	W&LR	1 *	1847	J.T. Macky	L&LSR	1	1882
Glenhesk	LMS(NCC)	1	(1924)	Kate Kearney	DW&WR		1865
Glenmalure	DW&WR	32	(1873)	Kathleen	C&LR	2	1887
Glenmore	DW&WR	24	(1864)	Keady	GNR	112	1911
Glen of the Downs	DW&WR	14	(1860)	Kells	CK&AR		(1904)
Glenties	CDRJC	17	1907		GNR	9	1911
Gnat	MGWR	113	1891	Kelpie	DW&WR		1865
Goliath	WL&WR	58	1897	Kenbaan Castle	LMS(NCC)	7	(1925)
Gort	A&EJR	3	(1862)	Kent	S&SLR	3	(1914)
Granston	W&LR	48	1894	Kerry	GNR	58	1896
Greenore	D&GR	2	1873	Kesh	GNR	38	1911
Grouse	GS&WR			Kestrel	GNR	87	(1932)
Harkaway	MGWR	22	1852	Kilcoole	DW&WR	21	(1864)
	MGWR	39	(1856)	Kildare	GNR	82	1886
Hartington	C&YR	9	1862	Kilkee	WCR	11	1908
Hawk	B&BR	1	(1839)	Kilkenny	GNR	59	1894
	B&BR		1847	Killemnee	WL&WR	54	1896
	MGWR	39	1886	Killiney	DW&WR	16	(1860)
Hawthorn	MGWR	24	1852	Killybegs	CDRJC	18	1907
Hazlewood	SL&NCR		1899	Kilrush	WCR	1	1912
Hecla	GNR	15	1876	Kincora	W&LR	19	(1876)
Hector	MGWR	80	1871	Kingstown	D&KR		1834
	MGWR	75	1891	King Edward	C&LR	9	1904
Hercules	B&BR	4	1847	King Edward VII	B&NCR	3	1902
	DR	11	1902	King Edward VIII	LMS(NCC)	98	1937
	D&DR	5	1872	King George	D&SER	20	1911
	GNR	76	1898	King George VI	LMS(NCC)	99	1938
	GNR	127	(1907)	Kite	B&BR	8	1847
	MGWR	105	1890	Knockagh	LMS(NCC)	65	(1905)
	UR		1842	Knocklayd	LMS(NCC)	34	(1901)
	W&LR	50	1895	Knockma	W&LR	43	1893
Heron	MGWR	12	1848	Kylemore	MGWR	6	1911
	MGWR	14 *	(1848)	Lady Boyd	Ballycastle	3	1879
Hibernia	D&DR	15	1845	Lady Edith	C&LR	3	1887
	D&KR		1834	Lady Inchiquin	WCR	7	1892
	MGWR	97	1880	Lagan	GNR	1	1876
Holyhead	DN&GR	6	1898		GNR	43	1911
Hornet	MGWR	112	1891		GNR	208	1948
Howth	GNR	94	1896		UR	1	1859
Hyacinth	GNR	51	1892	Lahinch	WCR	10	1903
	W&LR	38	(1882)	Lambeg	GNR	154	1904
Ida	S&SLR	2	1886	Lark	MGWR	106	1891
Ilen	S&SLR	3	1886	Laytown	GNR	110	1908
Imp	GS&WR		(1906)	Leinster	GNR	44	1911
Inchicore	GS&WR	320	1901		MGWR	51	(1862)
India	MGWR	145	1904		MGWR	43	1887
Innishowen	L&LSR	4	1885		UR	28	1863
Inny	MGWR	55	(1863)	Leitrim	GNR	81	1886
	MGWR	55	1885		SL&NCR		1882
Inver	DR	6	1893	Leopard	GS&WR		
Isabel	C&LR	1	1887		MGWR	64	(1864)
Iveagh	UR	22	1861		MGWR	64	1888

Name	Railway	No.	Date
Letterkenny	CDRJC	19	1907
Lewis	C&YR	1	1859
Liffey	GNR	25	1911
	GNR	206	1948
	MGWR	56	(1863)
	MGWR	56	1885
	UR	34	1866
Lightning	MGWR	76	1871
	MGWR	76	1892
Lily	GNR	115	1889
	MGWR	40	1886
	W&LR	30	(1874)
Limerick	DW&WR	14	1905
	GNR	152	1903
	MGWR	141	1901
	W&LR	4 *	1847
	W&LR	25	1874
Lion	GS&WR		
	MGWR	63	(1864)
	MGWR	63	1888
Lisanoure Castle	LMS(NCC)	84	(1929)
Lisburn	GNR	97	1885
Liscannor	WCR	4	1901
Lisdoonvarna	WCR	8	1904
Lismore	DW&WR	4	(1897)
Lissadel	SL&NCR		1899
Londonderry	L&LSR	2	1883
Longford	GNR	150	1890
Lord Masserene	UTA	101	(1939)
Lord Roberts	GS&WR	302	1900
Lough Corrib	MGWR	57	(1863)
	MGWR	57	1885
Lough Cutra	A&EJR	2	(1847)
Lough Derg	GNR	199	(1915)
	W&LR	14	1891
Lough Erne	SL&NCR		1949
Lough Gill	GNR	196	(1915)
	MGWR	58	(1863)
	MGWR	58	1885
	SL&NCR		1917
Lough Melvin	GNR	200	(1915)
	SL&NCR		1949
Lough Neagh	GNR	197	(1915)
Lough Owel	MGWR	60	(1863)
	MGWR	60	1885
Lough Swilly	GNR	198	(1915)
Louth	GNR	34	1880
	GNR	202	1948
Lucan	MGWR	83	1872
	MGWR	83	1892
Lucifer	GNR	123	1903
	UR	8	1846
	UR	8	1867
Lugnaquilla	GNR	190	(1913)
Luna	MGWR	10	1847
	MGWR	79	1871
	MGWR	74	1891
Lurgan	GNR	152	1903
Lurganboy	SL&NCR		1895
Lydia	CDRJC	3 A	(1912)
	WDR	3	1881
Lynx	MGWR	61	(1864)
	MGWR	61	1887
Macha	GSR	801	1939
Macrory	D&GR	1	1873
Maedhbh	GSR	800	(1939)
Maeve	GSR	800	1939
Majestic	MGWR	128	1902
Malahide	GNR	111	1908
Malbay	WCR	7	1922
Manchester	D&KR		1834
Marion	S&SLR	1	1886

Name	Railway	No.	Date
Marquis	MGWR	45	(1860)
	MGWR	49	1879
Mars	D&DR	2	(1864)
	GNR	128	1907
	MGWR	2	1847
	MGWR	5	(1857)
	MGWR	5	1884
May	C&LR	6	1887
Maynooth	MGWR	137	1895
Mayo	MGWR	85	1872
	MGWR	79	1892
McNeill	D&DR	13	1845
Meath	GNR	25	1911
	GNR	201	1948
	MGWR	11	(1864)
	MGWR	85	1886
Meenglas	CDRJC	16	(1907)
	DR	4	1893
Mercuric	MGWR	124	1905
Mercury	D&DR	10 *	(1862)
	GNR	132	1901
	MGWR	4	1847
Merlin	GNR	85	1932
Minerva	GNR	136	1899
Moira	GNR	109	1911
Monaghan	GNR	66	1879
Mourne	C&VBT	1	1884
	DR	15	1904
	NW&RR	2 *	1851
Moy	MGWR	117	1893
Mullingar	CK&AR		(1889)
	MGWR	68	(1867)
	MGWR	68	1887
Munster	GNR	42	1911
	MGWR	52	(1862)
	MGWR	46	1887
	UR	27	1863
Muskerry	C&MLR	6	(1893)
Myrtle	W&LR	31	(1874)
Narcissus	GNR	83	(1892)
Navan	GNR	155	1904
Neagh	UR	15	(1853)
Negro	GS&WR	(202)	(1876)
Nephin	MGWR	138	1895
	W&LR	44	1893
Neptune	D&DR	21/22 *	(1863)
	GNR	113	1904
Nestor	D&DR	1	1843
New Ross	DW&WR	51	(1891)
Newbliss	GNR	165	1911
Newry	DN&GR	4	1876
	GNR	83	1882
	N&AR	2	(1854)
	NW&RR	3 *	(1850)
Nora Creina	D&DR	1	1843
Nore	DW&WR	38	(1876)
	UR	30	(1866)
North Star	GNR	11	1884
	W&LR	39	1882
Oberon	DW&WR		1865
Olderfleet Castle	LMS(NCC)	76	(1924)
Olive	C&LR	7	1887
Omagh	GNR	56	1896
Orion	MGWR	1	1847
	MGWR	1	(1860)
	MGWR	1	1883
Orpheus	GNR	157	1904
Ostrich	B&BR	7	1851
Ousel	MGWR	17	1848
	MGWR	42	(1856)
	MGWR	42	1883
Ovoca	GNR	104	1906
	UR	31	(1866)

Name	Railway	No.	Date	Name	Railway	No.	Date
Owenea	DR	13	1904	Rob Roy	MGWR	16	1873
Owenreagh	GNR	4	1880		MGWR	16	1895
	UR	4	1861	Rocklands	WL&WR	16	1896
Pallas	MGWR	30	1851	Roney	C&YR	2	1859
Pandora	GNR	156	1904	Roscommon	GNR	149	1890
Pansy	GNR	45	(1885)	Rose	GNR	118	1885
Parkmount	B&NCR	55	1895		UR	18	(1857)
Pat	GS&WR		1883	Rostrevor	GNR	74	1896
Patience	West Cork	1	1865		NW&RR	1	(1851)
Peake	C&MLR	7	1898	Rover	MGWR	15	1873
Pelican	MGWR	15	1848		MGWR	15	1895
Peregrine	GNR	86	1932	Roxborough	W&LR	15	1894
Perseverence	West Cork	2	1865	Saint Patrick	GS&WR	303	1900
Petrel	MGWR	14	1848	Saint Senan	WCR	6	1892
Pettigo	GNR	78	1908	Sambo	GS&WR	(75)	(1856)
Pheasant	GS&WR				GS&WR		1914
Pike	C&YR	5	1860	Samson	D&DR	6 *	(1844)
Pilot	MGWR	102	1880		MGWR	22	1873
Pioneer	LM&ER	3	(1845)		MGWR	22	1896
	MGWR	103	1880		UR		1842
	SL&NCR		1877	Sarsfield	W&LR	24	1886
Planet	MGWR	78	1871	Saturn	D&DR	9	(1844)
	MGWR	78	1893		GNR	130	1901
Pluto	D&DR	19	(1855)		MGWR	3	1847
	GNR	9	1882	Scarva	GNR	153	1903
	GNR	121	1904	Shamrock	D&KR		1842
	MGWR	132	1895		GNR	117	1885
	UR	9	1846		MGWR	75	1870
Pomeroy	GNR	108	1908		MGWR	12	1890
Portadown	GNR	55	1895		MGWR	12	1913
Precursor	GNR	70	1896		UR	17	(1857)
Primrose	GNR	73	1895		W&LR	39	(1882)
	W&LR	8	(1881)	Shanganagh	DW&WR	43	(1883)
Prince	B&BR	6	1847	Shannon	MGWR	59	(1863)
	D&DR	11	1844		MGWR	59	1885
Princess	D&DR	7	1844		UR	33	1866
	D&KR		1841		W&LR	6 *	1847
Princess Ena	GS&WR	304	1900		WL&WR	2	1900
Princess Mary	DW&WR	46	(1888)	Sighe Gaoithe	C&BR	2	1849
Progress	W&LR	7	1888	Silver Jubilee	LMS(NCC)	96	1935
Queen	B&BR	5	1847	Simoom	UR	41	1876
	D&DR	10	1844	Sir Henry	SL&NCR		1904
	MGWR	49	(1862)	Sir James	DR	10	1902
	MGWR	45	1886		W&LR	10	1889
Queen Alexandra	B&NCR	34	1901	Sir William Goulding	GS&WR	341	1913
	LMS(NCC)	63	(1905)	Sirius	MGWR	6	1847
	LMS(NCC)	87	1936	Siroco	GNR	45	1909
Queen Elizabeth	LMS(NCC)	100	1939		UR	40	1876
Queen Victoria	C&LR	8	1887	Slaney	DW&WR	37	(1876)
Racer	MGWR	14	1873		T&CLR		1885
	MGWR	14	1893	Slemish	LMS(NCC)	4	(1903)
Ranger	MGWR	18	1873	Slieve Callan	WCR	5	1892
	MGWR	18	1893	Slieve Donard	GNR	172	1913
Raphoe	CDRJC	20	1907	Slieve Gallion	LMS(NCC)	68	(1908)
Rapid	MGWR	13	1873	Slieve Gullion	GNR	171	1913
	MGWR	13	1893	Slievebane	LMS(NCC)	9	(1904)
Rathcoole	DW&WR	68	1905	Slievenamon	GNR	192	(1915)
Rathdown	DW&WR	55	(1895)		W&LR	23	1892
Rathdrum	DW&WR	58	(1896)	Sligo	GNR	61	1883
Rathmines	DW&WR	56	(1895)		MGWR	72	(1867)
Rathmore	DW&WR	67	1905		MGWR	72	1888
Rathnew	DW&WR	57	(1896)		SL&NCR		1877
Regal	MGWR	41	(1856)		SL&NCR		(1882)
	MGWR	41	1883		SL&NCR		(1890)
Regent	MGWR	43	(1860)	Snipe	MGWR	17	(1848)
	MGWR	51	1880	Snowdrop	GNR	52	(1892)
	MGWR	52	(1880)	South of Ireland	W&LR	28	(1864)
Reindeer	MGWR	17	1873	Speedy	MGWR	20	1873
	MGWR	17	1894		MGWR	20	1894
Richmond	L&LSR	10	1904	Spencer	MGWR	19	1873
Rith Teineadh	C&BR	1	1849		MGWR	19	1894
Robin	MGWR	107	1891				

Name	Railway	No.	Date
Spitfire	UR		1839
	UR	13	(1847)
	UR	13	1869
Sprite	GS&WR		1857
	GS&WR		1873
	MGWR	24	1873
	MGWR	24	1897
St. Aidan	D&SER	27	1907
St. Annes	C&MLR	3	1887
St. Brendan	DW&WR	8	1903
St. Brigid	DW&WR	12	1901
St. Columb	L&LSR	4	1864
	L&LSR	5	1879
St. Iberius	D&SER	30	1909
St. Kevin	DW&WR	11	(1896)
St. Kieran	DW&WR	45	(1886)
St. Lawrence	DW&WR	28	(1887)
St. Mantan	DW&WR	29	1906
St. Molaga	T&CLR		1890
St. Patrick	D&DR	2	1843
	DW&WR	3	1898
	L&LSR	4	1876
	MGWR	8	1870
	MGWR	8	1890
	MGWR	8	1913
St. Selskar	DW&WR	40	1902
St. Senans	DW&WR	10	(1896)
Stag	GS&WR		
Star	D&KR		1833
	MGWR	77	1871
	MGWR	77	1892
Stillorgan	DW&WR	47	(1889)
Stockwell	MGWR	36	(1855)
Stork	MGWR	114	1891
Stuart de Decies	C&YR	7	1861
Strabane	CDRJC	2A	1912
	GNR	78	1908
Stranorlar	CDRJC	3 A	1912
Stromboli	UR	37	1872
Suir	DW&WR	39	(1876)
	W&LR	5 *	1847
Sutton	GNR	93	(1895)
Swallow	B&BR	10	1847
	MGWR	108	1891
Swift	MGWR	21	1873
	MGWR	21	1896
Sylph	MGWR	23	1873
	MGWR	23	1896
Tailte	GSR	802	1940
Tara	MGWR	139	1895
Tempest	UR	39	1874
Tenerife	GNR	16	1878
The Bann	LMS(NCC)	92	(1933)
The Braid	LMS(NCC)	95	(1934)
The Bush	LMS(NCC)	91	(1933)
The Foyle	LMS(NCC)	93	(1933)
The Maine	LMS(NCC)	94	(1934)
The Muskerry	C&MLR	6	1893
Theseus	GNR	114	1904
Thistle	GNR	119	1887
	UR	19	(1857)
Thomas Somerset	LMS(NCC)	103	1942
Thomond	WL&WR	27	1899
Thunderer	WL&WR	56	1897
Tiger	MGWR	62	(1864)
	MGWR	62	1888
Titan	MGWR	133	1895
	W&LR	40	1883
Titania	DW&WR		1865
	MGWR	28	1851
Titanic	MGWR	127	1903
Tornado	GNR	106	1906
	UR	6	1872

Name	Railway	No.	Date
Torrent	GNR	42	1879
Trostran	LMS(NCC)	64	(1905)
Tuam	W&LR	32	1874
Tulip	GNR	13	1902
Typhoon	GNR	46	1909
	UR	5	1874
Tyrone	GNR	62	1877
	UR	23	1861
	UR	23	1874
Ulidia	UR	20	1861
Ulster	GNR	12	1911
	MGWR	53	(1862)
	MGWR	44	1887
	MGWR	6	(1884)
	UR	26	1863
Ulysses	D&DR	13	(1860)
Uranus	GNR	131	1901
Urus	GS&WR	-	
Vauxhall	D&KR		1834
Venus	D&DR	7	(1847)
	GNR	120	1904
	MGWR	9	1847
	MGWR	4	(1857)
	MGWR	4	1884
Verbina	W&LR	25	(1874)
Vesta	MGWR	8	1847
	MGWR	6	(1857)
	MGWR	6	1884
Vesuvius	GNR	14	1876
Viceroy	MGWR	50	(1862)
	MGWR	47	1886
Victoria	D&DR	5	1844
	D&KR		1836
	GNR	88	1885
	GNR	88	1904
	GS&WR	301	1900
	NW&RR	3	1850
Viola	GNR	14	1902
Violet	C&LR	4	1887
	GNR	116	1889
	W&LR	36	(1881)
Viscount	MGWR	47	(1860)
	MGWR	50	1879
Volcano	UR	38	1873
Voltiguer	MGWR	21	1851
	MGWR	37	(1855)
Vulcan	B&BR	2	1847
	D&DR	20 *	(1858)
	D&KR		1848
	GNR	122	1903
	MGWR	18 *	(1851)
	MGWR	26	1852
	MGWR	134	1895
	UR	12	1847
	UR	12	1867
	W&LR	40	1883
Warrenpoint	NW&RR	5	1882
Wasp	MGWR	111	1890
	W&LR	7	(1888)
Waterford	DW&WR	13	1905
	GNR	36	1893
	SL&NCR		1893
	W&LR	3 *	1847
	W&LR	30	1874
Westmeath	GNR	151	1894
Wexford	DW&WR	36	(1900)
	GNR	28	1888
Wicklow	DW&WR	17	(1899)
	GNR	146	1888
Windsor	BCR	4	1880
	GNR	99	(1885)
Wolf	MGWR	65	(1864)
	MGWR	65	1888

Name	Railway	No.	Date		Name	Railway	No.	Date
Wolfdog	MGWR	37	1881		Zetland	W&LR	3	1892
	MGWR	37	1900					
Wren	MGWR	35	(1854)					
	MGWR	104	1886					

The following names were allotted to the locomotives numbered but never applied

Name	Railway	No.		Name	Railway	No.
Ballygally Castle	LMS(NCC)	77		Mount Hamilton	GNR	192
Ben Bradagh	LMS(NCC)	63		Portmuck Castle	LMS(NCC)	70
Carlingford	GNR	191		Richard de Burgh	LMS(NCC)	92
Carra Castle	LMS(NCC)	73		Samson	(WL&WR)	(11)
Craiggor	LMS(NCC)	59		Shamrock	GS&WR	304
Earl of Ulster	LMS(NCC)	90			(WL&WR)	(4)
John de Courcy	LMS(NCC)	93		Shane's Castle	LMS(NCC)	72
King Edward VII	LMS(NCC)	86		Slieveannorra	LMS(NCC)	67
Lurigethan	LMS(NCC)	58		Sorley Boy	LMS(NCC)	91

2. CONTRACTORS AND INDUSTRIAL USERS LOCOMOTIVES

Names are listed against the Builder's progressive number or the former owning railway's number.

Name	Builder's No.		Name	Builder's No.
Adams	AB 1408		Kingstown	ex D&KR
Admiralty	P 679		Lady Boyd	BH 513
Albert	Gryll*		Lady de Burgh	*
Armagh	HE 352		Lady McNeill	SB 279
	OK 1240		Lady Mary	HE 591
Ashford	AE 1872		Lancashire Witch	MW 614
Banshee	ex DW&WR		Liffey	HE 319
Bantry	MW 773		Limerick	HE 457
Barnesmore	BM		Littleton	AE 1833
Beauty	HE 352		Lizzie	MW 1038
Blackburn	MW 1099		Londonderry	P 806
Brancher	WGB 1116		Maghera	HE 202
Brian Boru	KS 889		Malt	Lewin
Britannia	ex D&7R		Malvern	MW 18
Bruckless	HE 564		Manchester	ex D&KR
Cashel	P 1003		Molly	HE 319
Charlton	HC 1497		Moorhen	RS 1100
Coolmore	HE 832		Mourne	WGB 1551
Corrib	MW 1220			HC 1508
Courtney	AE 1618		Mullingar	HE 482
Crosshaven	WGB 1480		Newmarket	HE 482
Deer Hill	HE 71		Oberon	ex DW&WR
Derwent	OK 2488		Otter	AB 770
Donegal	HE 759		Patricia	P 2088
Doonagore	KS 766		Pioneer	HE 203
Dover	P 680			SB 279
Drogheda	HE 315		R.H. Smythe	AE 2021
Duchess of Leinster	*		Rose	HE 558
Elfin	ex DW&WR		Rutland	MW 4
Express	GR 164		Scott	AE 1552
Faugh-a-Ballagh	HE 178		Shamrock	HE 557
Fergus	HE 268		Slaney	HE 382
Firefly	Butterley		Soho	ex L&NWR 125
Flirt	HE 315		Spondon	HE 208
Gilsland	RS		Strabane	HC 794
Glenelrig	Ex Slamamman Railway		Tullibardine	AB 297
Glenloe	MW 237		Ulster	HC 1505
Greenore	ex N&AR 3		Victor	HE
Hops	Lewin		Victoria	Gryll
Huddersfield	HE 74			ex D&KR
Isabella	HE 404		Waterford	HE 156
John Cooke	ex L&LSR 1			HE 591
	ex L&LSR 3		Whittledene	HC 397
Kells	HE 859		Wilfred	P 2113
King George	WGB 1945		William Dargan	*

3. PLEASURE RAILWAY LOCOMOTIVES

Name	Builder's No.	Remarks		Name	Builder's No.	Remarks
Jean	Kr 8378	Named Sir Crawford at some time.		Shane	AB 2265	
Nancy	AE 1547			Tyrone	P 1026	